Sheila Rabb Weidenfeld

# First Lady's Lady

*With the Fords at the White House*

# First Lady's Lady

*With the Fords at the White House*

by
Sheila Rabb Weidenfeld

G.P. PUTNAM'S SONS NEW YORK

Copyright © 1979 by Sheila Rabb Weidenfeld

All rights reserved. This book, or parts thereof, must
not be reproduced in any form without permission. Published simultaneously in
Canada by Longman Canada Limited, Toronto.

SBN: 399–12292–3

**Library of Congress Cataloging in Publication Data**

Weidenfeld, Sheila Rabb.
  First Lady's lady.

   1. Ford family.    2. Ford, Betty, 1918–
3. Weidenfeld, Sheila Rabb.    4. Social secretaries—Washington, D.C.—
Biography.
I. Title.
E867.W43    973.925    78-10662

PRINTED IN THE UNITED STATES OF AMERICA

To Edward

## ACKNOWLEDGMENT

I want to express my deep appreciation to Linda Cashdan for her invaluable assistance.

"Why is this thus? What is the
reason of this thusness?"
                    Artemus Ward
                    Artemus Ward's Lecture

# TABLE OF CONTENTS

*Introduction:*

# TOUCHING HISTORY

For two years, one month, and three weeks, I served as First Lady Betty Ford's Press Secretary. The job offered unprecedented satisfactions, unbearable frustrations, and a first-hand look at the world's most prestigious office building: The White House, Washington, D.C.

My first responsibility was to project Betty Ford and her four children to the public as effectively as possible. And in the process, I learned a lot about the White House—both the place and the state of mind that goes with it.

That's what this book is about.

It's about the fallout of political success, about what happens when a family suddenly becomes the First Family and the glare of the unrelenting public spotlight falls on the President's wife and children. It's about the magnet the First Family is to all types of opportunity seekers and political groupies. It's about the luxury and the grandeur of the White House.

It's about White House journalism and White House journalists—the media and the message, how what you do may be less important than how you translate it.

It's about male chauvinism, White House style.

15

It's about the White House caste system, and those little tell-tale status indicators: where you are seated at State Dinners, which car you are assigned in a motorcade, and how many perquisites (special favors called "perks" that are doled out by the White House Military Affairs Office to the Important) you have.

It's about power—not only the awesome power of the President of the United States, but also the scrambling for power among his staff which spreads workaholism, crushes marriages, and creates bureaucrats as frequently as it moves mountains.

It's about the Presidency in general, but it's also about the Ford Presidency, a two-year recuperation period for a nation that weathered almost a decade of internal and external turmoil, culminating in upheaval at the very top—the Watergate Scandal and Richard Nixon's removal from office.

But most of all, of course, it's about the Fords, the people who soothed the wounds, who added a human dimension to high-level politics at a time when the country desperately needed to know that there were decent, compassionate people living in the big white mansion at 1600 Pennsylvania Avenue.

Gerald Ford was sworn in as President of the United States on August 9, 1974, only minutes after his predecessor, Richard Nixon, was exiled to the West Coast, in the midst of a national furor over Watergate. In less than one year, Ford had progressed from House Minority Leader to Vice President to President—the first President in American history who had never even been elected Vice President. Like millions of other Americans, I watched him being sworn in on television. And like millions of others I was charmed by his inaugural speech—charmed and calmed.

"I am acutely aware that you have not elected me as your President . . ." he began, simply, almost humbly. "If you have not chosen me by secret ballot, neither have I gained office by any secret promises. I have not campaigned either for the Presidency or the Vice Presidency. I have not subscribed to any partisan platform. I am indebted to no man, and only to one woman, my dear wife."

This was a man of value, a man to end the trauma. I felt relieved and surprisingly moved. I turned to my husband, Edward, and said, "I have the strangest feeling I'm going to end up working for that man." I don't know why I said it. I do know we shrugged it off. I was, after all, a television producer, not a politician.

One week later, I got a call from a woman who identified herself as Nancy Howe, Mrs. Ford's personal assistant. She said that Mrs. Ford had asked members of the White House Press Corps for suggestions for the job of Press Secretary and my name had been submitted. Could I come for an interview?

Why not?

I was not interested in the job. I liked the job I had. But I was interested in the interview. How often do you get a chance to meet the President's wife? To touch history? I was also apprehensive. Rumors that she had a drinking problem were circulating at the NBC station where I worked. She had recently taped a spot for the Heart Association and given an awful performance. People who worked on the spot said she "slurred her words" and seemed "spaced out." The finished product was so bad NBC did not want to run it.

I wondered if it were just stage fright or if she did have a drinking problem. In either case, I did not know what I would find in a face-to-face interview.

The Fords had not yet moved into the White House and I got lost trying to find their house in Virginia. I was late but no one seemed to notice. Things were informal, to say the least. I was greeted at the door by Nancy Howe, an attractive, stylishly dressed woman in her forties with blond streaked hair, who then disappeared to get Mrs. Ford as I waited in the living room. It was an unpretentious suburban home filled with packing boxes ready to be shipped to the White House. In the den, off the living room, a man was talking on the telephone. In the kitchen, the Fords' teenage daughter, Susan, was sipping coffee in her bathrobe, reading the society page stories about the State Dinner at the White House the night before.

"We just inherited that State Dinner," Mrs. Ford explained to me as she came downstairs in a hostess robe. "You can imagine how chaotic it is to find out one day that your husband is President and the next day that you are scheduled to entertain King Hussein!"

It was as though she were saying, "Jerry showed up with a business associate last night and all I had was meatloaf." This was more housewife than White House wife.

The interview was less than auspicious. She talked too slowly; I talked too fast. And the more we talked, the more we seemed to exacerbate the natural condition. We were also handicapped by a lack of subject matter, since neither of us had any idea *what* the job of Press Secretary entailed.

"Well, what would you do?"

"Well, what would you want me to do?"

Happily, we had to go on to other topics, small talk, but relaxed small talk. We gradually warmed up to each other. I liked her, although I must admit I was a little disappointed. I had come to "touch history," after all, and here I was touching a normal person.

In the car driving home, I tried to figure out Betty Ford. On one hand, there were the newspaper stories of the conservative, perfect politician's wife: smiling countenance, mother of four all-American types, Mrs. 50's Housewife. On the other hand, there were the stories about Betty Ford, the former model and dancer whose brief first marriage had ended in divorce, who sought psychiatric help . . . and there was talk of a drinking problem.

I wondered if the White House would change her. Being genuine and open were hardly typical qualities for First Ladies. But then after spending an hour or so with her, I found it hard to picture a stuffy, uptight Betty Ford.

But could she take the spotlight?

I remembered the spot for the Heart Association. Was that the lady? Or was that a combination of the wrong material and the tension of being on camera?

My gut reaction was the latter.

She could use a producer, someone who could create the atmosphere necessary to bring out her real personality.

I was a producer. But what would this show entail? An open, honest, real, live First Lady pouring tea? What else did First Ladies do? Plant trees? Encourage volunteerism? Give White House tours? Not my bag. But maybe because it was not done right. If Pat Nixon had had a better producer, she might have had a more interesting public image, and a resulting rapport that could have helped her husband. Julie and Tricia were used too late; and badly produced, at that. Of course, nothing could or should have changed the course of things for Nixon in the end. But the Fords were not the Nixons. And now more than ever the country needed to feel a sense of humanity in the White House. Betty Ford was a natural but that was not enough. Someone had to help convey that image.

Of course, a First Lady could do more than give teas. I had fantasies of Mrs. Ford as Eleanor Roosevelt. I saw her championing the causes of the day such as women's rights. She could go down in history as the First Lady who helped pass the Equal Rights Amendment to the United States Constitution! By the time I got home, there were headlines and fireworks and a grand finale salute to the most outstanding First Lady in American History—Betty Ford! (A Sheila Rabb Weidenfeld Production.)

I told Edward I wanted the job. Unfortunately I had not told Mrs. Ford.

Time passed; the idea dimmed. President Ford pardoned Nixon and I lost some of my enthusiasm. I became preoccupied with the fact that there was network talk about syndicating my local television program.

It was almost a month before I was called back for a second interview, this time at the White House. It was easier to "touch history" in these environs. Realizing that this could very well prove my last as well as my first visit to the Ford White House, I was determined to enjoy myself. I had iced tea served by a butler and a wonderful two-hour conversation with Mrs. Ford. She spoke faster this time. I, more slowly. We had each done some research on the responsibilities of the First Lady's Press Secretary.

Nancy Howe was again present, as was the man I had seen in the den making the phone call. He introduced himself as Ric Sardo, a Marine who was a Military Aide to the President.

After the interview, Sardo walked me downstairs. He told me that he had been assigned to Gerald Ford when he was Vice President and had become very close to the whole family, that he had the greatest respect for them, and would do anything to help them out. He was excited about the possibilities of my job, and explained that he saw Mrs. Ford's Press Secretary as someone who could "orchestrate" everything and I knew what he meant immediately. We had a good talk, reinforcing each other's enthusiasm.

I found out I had the job unofficially—*very* unofficially—the next day. "She wants you," announced David Kennerly, the White House Photographer, when he took me out to lunch at a restaurant nearby. "Believe me, I know. You've got the job." Kennerly, who won a Pulitzer Prize in 1972 for feature pictures he took on assignment with UPI in Vietnam, was assigned by *Time* magazine to cover Ford as a Vice Presidential prospect. In the process, he became very close to the whole Ford family. The day after Gerald Ford took the Presidential oath, he appointed David White House Photographer. David is a rogue—a bearded, blue-jean-clad twenty-seven-year-old wise guy, with a youthful irreverence that I am told appeals to the Fords. He's supposed to know everything happening in the residential quarters of the White House, a fact he reiterated himself over lunch. (Personal modesty is *not* David Kennerly's strong suit.) As though to prove his point, he told me it might be a while before I would be offered the job because Mrs. Ford was going into the hospital that night. He wouldn't tell me why.

Sure enough, the next day the newspapers carried stories of Mrs. Ford's mastectomy. Along with everyone else, I read the stories and stared at the picture of the teary-eyed President. Along with everyone else, I felt the emotional tug—with added sympathy for those who must suffer personally on the front page. Later in the week, there was more from Betty Ford herself. The expressed desire to make this public so other women would profit. Stiff upper lip. Courageous smile. Inner strength. It confirmed a lot of my first impression. Underneath the conventions was a gutsy lady.

On October 6, 1974, I was offered the job; I accepted. The night before the White House officially announced my appointment, I became my *own* press secretary.

Isabelle Shelton of the *Washington Star* called me at home to say that she had heard a rumor that I was to be Mrs. Ford's Press Secretary. Was it true? I said that well, I believed so, but I was not sure, really, and I could not be sure, actually, until it was definite and I never believed anything until it was definite.

I had blown my first news release. I turned to Edward for husbandly support and he pointed out that if I were this nervous about making such an insignificant statement, the future would be a difficult one. And so I relaxed, with appalling results.

In an interview the next day, I talked and talked and talked as Judy Bachrach of the *Washington Post* wrote and wrote and wrote. When I read the story I was devastated. It was me all right, my words (so *many* of my words!). She thought it was great because she had captured me in all my excitement, and I thought it was awful because she had done precisely that.

For eight years I had earned my living on the other side of the camera, getting other people to talk, and the change in the direction of the spotlight made me uncomfortable. I found myself at times handling the interview. When *Women's Wear Daily* asked me what I thought was "fun," the producer in me exploded. It was a stupid question, and stupid questions tend to elicit stupid answers. I turned the question around. "Well, what do *you* think is fun?" I asked sweetly. She was not sure. It was one of my shorter interviews.

While publicly relating myself, I tried to find out more about the job. I talked to all my predecessors: I tracked down Tish Baldrige, Jackie Kennedy's social secretary, in New York. I interviewed Helen Smith, who handled the press for Mrs. Nixon. I spent hours and hours with Lady Bird Johnson's Press Secretary, Liz Carpenter. Truthfully, I considered Liz my only real predecessor. Jackie Kennedy, after all, had hated publicity. Pat Nixon had expected her Press Secretary to shield her rather than publicly relate her, especially at the end. But Lady Bird Johnson was a doer, and Liz Carpenter had masterfully publicized her doings. I knew Liz had had many things going for her I would not have. She was a shrewd politician herself, and an intimate personal friend of both Lyndon and Lady Bird Johnson. That gave her access to the top and the ability to make what I had been told was the ultimate White House threat: "*Do I have to bother the President with this?*" (In contrast, I could picture President Ford saying, "Sheila *WHO?*")

Although my situation was different, I learned much from Liz. I went through all her scrapbooks, and took notes as she told me the daily details of the job. And the nightly details. And the round-the-clock marital side effects. Above all, she urged me to warn Edward about how difficult it would be to be married to the Press Secretary. She had other pearls of wisdom: "Get to know Bill Gulley," she said. "He is the man in charge of all White House perquisites. To know him is to have them! And if you can't tell the press what they want to know, tell them something that will make it fun and distract them." I left with a copy of her book *Ruffles and Flourishes* ("To Sheila, with best wishes for a great production. . . . That set deserves all you can give it!") which I read, re-read, and later underlined.

I sought advice from the other side, too, my cohorts in the press. Common categories included: "Be accessible." "Return all phone calls." "Never lie." "Keep a diary." My friend Clare Crawford, a correspondent for *People* magazine, added a new dimension: "No matter how good a friend a reporter is, remember that she is a reporter first."

I was in and out of the White House during the three weeks before I was officially scheduled to begin. I met some new faces. Mrs. Ford was still recuperating from the mastectomy and she had good days and bad days. On all days, she was accompanied by Nancy Howe, who seemed to function as a protective lady-in-waiting, anticipating Mrs. Ford's needs: An ashtray? Some tea? A hair dresser's appointment? Certainly a very dedicated person. Nancy had been a volunteer White House book seller one summer with Susan Ford. Through Susan she had met Mrs. Ford. Nancy was married and had a daughter a few years older than Susan. It was at Nancy's insistence that Mrs. Ford went for the routine medical examination that had revealed the breast tumor. For that reason alone, she will be eternally grateful to Nancy Howe. When the Fords moved to the White House, Nancy was put on the White House payroll as Personal Assistant to the First Lady.

Ric Sardo was usually close by too. An attractive, clean-cut man in his early forties, he looked perfect for the part of Military Aide, although I had no idea what a Military Aide did. I was told his functions were largely ceremonial. But Ric was too smart to be just ceremonial. A Wesleyan graduate, with two MAs from Princeton, he had his own ideas. (Too many, according to the reporters who complained that he had once arbitrarily ended a news conference because he felt things were getting too chaotic for Mrs. Ford.) I found Ric a big help and a good sounding board. He knew the White House; I didn't.

Also circling Mrs. Ford was Dr. William Lukash, the White House physician, a very serious, methodical man, gifted with the perfect bedside manner. He seemed extremely cautious and conscientious, interested in the emotional stresses as well as the physical stresses at work in the patient. He could explain complicated medical matters simply, without sounding condescending. Lukash had worked at the White House on a part-time basis under Johnson and Nixon, while continuing in his specialty, digestive diseases. Now he had, temporarily at least, given that up for a kind of "family practice," albeit with an exclusive family. Aided by two physician assistants, he had overall responsibility for the health of the President, Vice President, their families and the working staff of the White House. He told me when it was good to talk to Mrs. Ford, and when she was not up to talking. I respected his advice.

Most of my introductions were informal, brought about by happenstance—with one exception. One day I got a call at NBC from the White House. An official voice told me that Donald Rumsfeld wanted to see me in his office that afternoon at 1:00. Rumsfeld, I knew, was the President's Chief of Staff, and although I had no idea what that title meant, my general interpretation was "top banana." I speedily switched my schedule around and arrived at his office at the appointed hour.

He looked the part, I thought to myself. The conservative suit, the aviator glasses, the soft, neat brown hair, the perfect teeth clutching the proper pipe. Put them together and add the Princeton degree and the enormous green-carpeted office with the large desk and the conference table and you have Mr. Big undoubtedly on his way to becoming Mr. Bigger.

I had a lot of time to think about it, because Rumsfeld spent practically our entire session on the phone. He talked and talked as I watched and watched, trying not to appear as uncomfortable as I felt. Each time he began a sentence the phone would ring and he would take the calls. All calls. Finally, in between rings, I blurted out: "Was there something you wanted to talk to me about?"

"No," he said, smiling a Truly Winning Smile, and standing to formally signify the end of our meeting. "I just wanted to welcome you aboard."

*Chapter One*
## NOVEMBER, 1974:

# FIRST LADY'S LADY

*NOVEMBER 1, 1974*

President Ford is in California today on a campaign trip for Republican Congressional candidates. The United Nations is urging foreign troops to pull out of Cyprus. South Vietnam's President Thieu is firing more top army officials in hopes of satisfying his critics. The World Food Conference is about to get underway in Rome. Former President Richard Nixon is still on the critical list in California following surgery for a blood clot.

And I am celebrating my first day on the White House payroll.

I've had to make many important decisions. Such as whether to tell Mr. Kim of the *Joong Ang News* that it was all right to write that neither Susan nor Mrs. Ford will be accompanying the President to the Far East later this month. And how to answer Bonnie Angelo of *Time* magazine who called to ask, "Did the Fords pay for the thank-you notes they sent out in response to the get-well wishes Mrs. Ford received after her surgery out of their own money or White House funds?" And the *National Enquirer* was anxious to know—as soon as possible—whether the Fords' golden retriever, Liberty, would pose for pictures with the newspaper's

25

mascot, Lucky. Henry Kissinger has his issues. These are mine.

I spent my day trying to find the answers to this national White House trivia game while at the same time trying to find my way around the White House.

I did manage to locate the Mess, a special dining room for senior staff. But they said I was too late; I arrived at one. They told me I was on the twelve o'clock list (the what?). I took out a tray instead, but I have to see if I can change my shift. I can't eat lunch that early, and it is a long journey with a tray full of food from the Mess back to my office.

There are two sides to the White House: his and hers. The West Wing houses the Mess, the President's executive staff offices, the press room. The East Wing is for the First Lady's Staff: my office, the social secretary's office, and so on. The difference in decor between East and West is striking: masculine for the boys, feminine for the girls. My office is positively dainty. Small, beautifully upholstered Victorian couches, delicate tea tables, muted gold carpeting, long draperies—all done in a kind of "Conservative Chic" style. At first I was delighted by its elegance and intrigued by the idea of becoming the type of person who occupied this kind of office. I'm now changing my mind; I am not serving tea, after all, I am serving news. I'm not a lady; I'm a working woman. How on earth does one work in such splendid Victorian isolation?

Isolation is the right word, too. There are no AP or UPI wire machines, necessities in my line of work. I immediately set about ordering some. There is also no easy contact with "His" side. How will I know what my West Wing counterpart, the President's Press Secretary, Ron Nessen, is telling the press? My second act was to order a briefing box, a special electrical (3 by 2 inches in size) receiver that is hooked up to the West Wing press room, so that every time Nessen says something on the record, I can monitor it in my office. It is just a white plastic box, a fairly common White House device. Certainly it is a time-saving one, since the only alternative is to have one of my staff spend the day standing outside the briefing room just in case Ron decides to hold a news briefing.

Given the size of my "staff," that would be impractical. There are exactly three of us here in the First Lady's press office. Me; my secretary, Nancy Chirdon, a short, dark-haired woman in her twenties who comes highly recommended; and my assistant, Patti

Matson, who also comes highly recommended. But Patti is a Nixon holdover and this is a period of self-consciousness about the Administration that just left power. There is a pervasive feeling that to get rid of "them" is to be able to forget "him." I share it, I must confess. I have told Patti that I am giving her a month to prove herself to me. It is harsh, I know, but if she is as good as she is supposed to be, she'll have no trouble.

I made two unsolicited press announcements today. One was that Susan will take her college board examinations tomorrow. The other was that Steven, the Fords' nineteen-year-old son who is taking this year off between high school and college to work on a ranch in Montana, will be coming home tonight to visit his folks. In Susan's case, I just wanted to stress that Presidents' daughters, like other high school students, have to go through the grueling experience of college boards. I think it is important to stress non-events, especially in Susan's case. The Ford sons all live outside Washington. Michael is a divinity student living with his wife, Gayle, in Massachusetts. Jack is at college in Utah. But Susan is in the goldfish bowl here, front and center, with all the criteria necessary for instant exploitation: she is blond, beautiful, and seventeen and—by her own frequent admission—her daddy's darling. She's so potentially sensational that I'd like to emphasize the non-sensational aspects of her life.

In Steve's case, the announcement was a preventive measure: I wanted to avoid having to explain it after the fact defensively to a press that would have fumed because they weren't told. ("He just came home to see his parents and did not want any publicity.") Besides, when Mrs. Ford told me he was coming, she laughed and said "Every good boy comes home to his mother!" I liked that, and the announcement gave me an excuse to share it with reporters.

In both cases, I suppose I made the announcements because they made me feel more like a bona fide Press Secretary.

It was a long day. After all, I had to return all calls. I told Mr. Kim that yes, he could say neither Mrs. Ford nor Susan would be accompanying the President to the Far East. I told Bonnie Angelo that Wilbur Jenkins, who is in charge of such things, said that the money for the thank-you notes came out of appropriated funds for Mrs. Ford's correspondence. And when I called to tell the *Nation-*

*al Enquirer* that, sorry, Liberty was not up to posing with Lucky, I found myself talking to the office janitor. The inquisitive reporter apparently had long since gone home.

## NOVEMBER 4, 1974

In the group of nearly thirty people, there was only one man, and only one reporter under the age of thirty. I had invited all those who cover the First Lady to an informal press conference so we could get to know each other. I looked out at my guests; these are the veterans, I thought, the tough ladies. Most had become career women decades before the Women's Liberation movement made it a fashionable thing to do, in times when journalism was literally a man's profession and male stereotypes—aggression, strength, competition—were the tools of the trade. They bear battle scars from the years spent in such a tense occupation; many smoke too much, exercise too little, drink too much and all of them live their work. Some have made it. They are covering the White House for major news organizations. Some have made it in a female sort of way, as top society reporters. They are every bit as aggressive as their political-writing counterparts, but instead of barking, they meow.

I had a few winners in the audience today, some society reporters, and many losers. It was a typical First Lady coverage turnout, and it intensified my desire to change the image of First Lady, to get Mrs. Ford into substantive issues and off the society pages, if only to attract a more legitimate press corps.

I spent a lot of time talking about myself. My father, Maxwell Rabb, was Secretary of the Cabinet under Eisenhower from 1952 to 1958. It was my father's job to draw up the agenda for the weekly Cabinet meetings, to brief both the President and the members of the Cabinet on issues to be discussed, and then to see that those decisions made at the meetings were implemented. The reporters wanted to know what my recollections were of my "previous White House years." I tried to think of some, but they were, I'm afraid, the recollections of a child. I remembered swimming in the pool. I remembered meeting Eisenhower—head on. My mother had brought me in to see the White House physician for some reason and as I raced out of his office, I rammed into the President. I have no physical image of Eisenhower that day, but a vivid recollection of the expression on my mother's face. I also remember my father taking all of us—I have one brother and two sisters—to the Cabinet room just before we left Washington and telling us to sit in the President's chair and make a wish. I wished that I would come back.

After indulging in my reminiscences, it was business as usual.

"Do you feel you have complete access to Mrs. Ford?" one asked me.

"Certainly."

"What about Nancy Howe?" several shouted out in unison.

"What *about* Nancy Howe? I asked.

"She doesn't get in your way?"

"I have no problems with Nancy Howe," I assured them.

"That makes you very unusual!" (Laughter.)

Then came the barrage of follow-up questions:

"What do you mean by access?" When do you see Mrs. Ford?"

"How many times a day?" "Where is Nancy Howe then?" "Every afternoon?"

This is an habitual technique. Keep the questions coming—faster, faster, more demanding of specifics. That way you either uncover the *Truth* or you at least trip up the Press Secretary and get a news story on a non-news event. Today I think it was more than technique. Nancy Howe is one of a breed of people who follow those in power, whose status is dependent upon being a best friend to the best and such people are very protective of their closeness. I know the reporters have had problems with her because she keeps them away from Mrs. Ford. But I was sincere; I really don't feel she and I have any problems. Perhaps because I have no desire to take her place: I think it is essential in my job that I have a friendly but professional relationship with Mrs. Ford. That's why I call her Mrs. Ford.

The rest of my day was spent with the other side of my job: White House people. I attended Press Secretary Ron Nessen's daily staff briefing, thus setting a record as the first member of the East Wing staff to attend. (Why is there so little coordination?) But if today was any indication, no one has missed anything. I hope future meetings are more interesting. I hope Ron is more interesting. A "Former NBC Correspondent-Turned-Top-White-House Official," Ron Nessen seems to me to lack both the affectation and the glamor usually associated with each title. He is no smoothey.

But I may be unduly hostile, because I was told today that I can't just ask for a briefing box. I must submit the request in writing to Ron Nessen. I did, but it seems such a waste of time. That means that for at least one more day I will have to detail Patti over to wait for briefings in the West Wing.

I also met with Dr. Lukash, who wanted to explain to me that Mrs. Ford was starting chemotherapy treatments today. The treatment involves nothing more than taking a series of pills, but, he said, there may be side effects. Some people feel nauseous or lose hair. The chemotherapy is just a precautionary measure; nothing new has been detected. I was grateful for the details he gave me, because the reporters are, quite naturally, preoccupied with her health. They are constantly sizing up her appearance. One amusing sidelight is that lately they have been saying she looks thin. She does, but because she has been conscientiously dieting. She told me that a few years ago she decided to stop worrying about gaining weight, and just grow old gracefully. When she tipped the scales at 139 pounds, she decided such growth is not graceful and vowed she would *never* reach 140. She never did; she lost ten pounds in two months, and has now lost a total of thirty pounds. She is no longer actively dieting, but she is very careful about what she eats.

I also "met" the President today. Mrs. Ford was having a staff meeting in the West Hall living room about 3:00 P.M. and he walked by wearing an orange sweat suit, completely distracted because he had a tennis date and he couldn't find his racket. As meetings go, it was about as intense as my encounter with Dwight Eisenhower— although less physical.

## NOVEMBER 7, 1974

When you're at the top, you want to be the top of the top. At the White House level, the scrambling is exhausting. And I am definitely not in the penthouse.

I found out that in the Mess, the more important you are, the later you are assigned to eat. (Hence, my brunch shift.) All right. That is unimportant. (I must admit, however, that since I found out, I have been quietly sitting in later and later.) I discovered that unlike my predecessors, I will not have a car at my disposal. Let them have their pecking order! As long as it isn't counterproductive.

This is a very status-conscious place.

I could not believe that I had to write Ron Nessen a formal memo requesting a briefing box. Imagine my disbelief when I got an official memo back saying "no."

His explanation was long, kind, and apologetic. "There aren't many. Why, the President's top advisors, Bob Hartmann and Donald Rumsfeld, don't even have one," he said, completely missing the point. They don't *need* briefing boxes. I do. What he was really saying is, Sheila, this is a case of supply and demand. If you get one, others will demand one also. They are status symbols.

"It's a shame," sighed the man in "administration" when I told him my problems.

I sighed, too. I waited.

"Of *course* I'll get you a briefing box, Sheila!" the man in "administration" went on, "just send me a memo saying: 'This is to confirm our conversation of November 7th . . .'"


## NOVEMBER 10, 1974

I finally solved one mystery. Ever since I got here, I have noticed people running around with WIN buttons on. I assumed the buttons were for the election, although this year's election was not for any national office. Also, they did not even say *who* should win. Some campaign.

Today I discovered that WIN stands for "Whip Inflation Now." It's a program designed to encourage Americans to economize. I think. I decided to find out more about it since I'm looking for areas where Mrs. Ford can lend her support. Thus far, the only fact I have uncovered is that the White House is spending about $17,000 to mail pledge cards and WIN buttons to urge people to spend less. Some program.

That is not to say that it is ineffective. At least one American family is economizing to the hilt. The Fords have been serving only domestic wines ("Buy American"), religiously turning off lights not in use in the family quarters ("Conserve Energy"), and economizing on food as well. As a really close friend who visited the Fords recently put it: "Who would have thought that my first meal at the White House would be stuffed green peppers!" I don't know whether she did it for the man or for the economy, but Mrs. Ford has also put the President on a diet.

"Does he eat everything on his plate, without wasting food?" I asked jokingly.

"He'd eat the plate if they didn't take it away,"she said.

## NOVEMBER 14, 1974

*People* Magazine says Gayle Ford is pregnant. Gayle is married to Michael, the Fords' oldest son, who is a divinity student in Massachusetts. It is news to Gayle. Mrs. Ford called to check and Michael and Gayle assured her there would be no Presidential grandchildren in the foreseeable future.

I called Clare Crawford, my friend who works for *People* Magazine.

"Is she pregnant?"

"No, she isn't," I said. "Why didn't you ask me that *before* you ran the story?"

"I didn't know about it. It wasn't my story," Clare said. "It came out of Boston. As I understand it, a reliable source there has seen Gayle make several trips to the obstetrical unit of a hospital there."

The Presidential spotlight extends to Boston.

"I understand it is a *very* reliable source," Clare continued. "Are you *sure* she's not pregnant?"

Mrs. Ford called again. ("Are you *sure* you're not pregnant, dear?") By this time, Gayle's parents had called, too, hurt that their daughter had told *People* Magazine before she told them.

"I'm not pregnant," Gayle said.

"She's not pregnant," Mrs. Ford told me. "In fact," she whispered, "she's on the pill. But don't tell the press."

"She's not pregnant," I told Clare, this time with conviction. It is possible, I thought, that *People* Magazine's reliable source saw Gayle visiting the hospital to replenish her supply of pills, or to have the regular check-ups you are supposed to have when you are on the pill. Possible. I couldn't throw the idea out to Clare for speculation, however, since I was forbidden from revealing the fact that a married woman was taking birth control pills.

## NOVEMBER 15, 1974

President Ford has announced formally that he plans to run for President in 1976.

I said, "Mrs. Ford, Fran Lewine of the Associated Press wants to know what your reaction was when the President told you he would run."

She said, "Oh God, what *else* is new?"

We said, "Mrs. Ford has always been happy with whatever decision he's made. Whatever makes him happy makes her happy."

## NOVEMBER 16, 1974

I find myself repeatedly shocked by the exploitive people who take advantage of the White House and the instant publicity that the mention of the name creates. And I am shocked that the press helps them.

Today's case in point: the new chef who wasn't.

Late yesterday afternoon I got a call from the managing editor of a radio station in Oklahoma. Haven McClaren, the chef of the Skirven Plaza Hotel in Oklahoma City, it seems, had just held a news conference to announce that he had been offered the job as executive chef at the White House.

"Nonsense," I said. "Chef Haller is excellent and has been here at the White House for almost a decade. There is no talk of replacing him." I double-checked, just to be sure; I was right.

The Washington correspondent for the *Daily Oklahoman* called. He understood McClaren had until Monday to make up his mind about accepting the offer. "Nonsense," I said.

Two phones rang simultaneously. It was AP and UPI. It seems there was this chef in Oklahoma City. . . .

I called. I called Mrs. Ford and I called Social Secretary Nancy Lammerding. I called Donald Rumsfeld, the President's special assistant. I called Rex Scouten, who is head usher and in charge of all household staff. Each time I got the same response: "Who?"

Finally I called Haven McClaren. He told me the President had stopped off in Oklahoma while on the campaign trail and had had breakfast at the hotel. I checked; that was true. McClaren said the President had really liked his English muffins. I checked; that was possible. McClaren said that a man named John Anderson had called from the White House to offer him the job of chef.

While we talked, I had my secretary, Nancy Chirdon, track down anyone by the name of John Anderson. At last she found a John Anderson—totally removed from staff operations, but a John Anderson nevertheless. I called this John Anderson. Had he offered a job as chef to a man in Oklahoma named Haven McClaren? He said, "Who?"

"Mr. McClaren," I said in my most sympathetic voice, "I don't know what is going on, but you have not been offered the job of executive chef. To save face and social embarrassment, why don't you just say that there was a misunderstanding or say that you were the victim of a practical joke. People will understand."

"Fine," he said. "I'll do that."

The next day McClaren held a news conference to announce that the White House had withdrawn the offer because "the President is cheap."

UPI carried the story.


## NOVEMBER 19, 1974

President Ford went to Japan two days ago for the first part of a trip that should end in a meeting with Leonid Brezhnev in Vladivostok. I got a call this morning from Maxine Cheshire, a reporter for the *Washington Post*. A society reporter, Maxine is really a caricature of the breed: the soft lilting voice waits patiently for the scoop, all the time sweetly trying to squeeze it out of you and then suddenly—*pounce*! Whatever morsel has been her target is slurped up and—victorious—she is on her way to meet her deadline. Today she was all a-flutter. The President had arrived in Japan in a morning suit, she told me, and his pants were too short.

"Yes?" I waited for the punchline. That was it. I thought she was joking. This was, after all, an historic occasion, the first incumbent American President ever to visit Japan; surely she couldn't care. . . .

She cared.

Now I must pause here to explain that I am terrible at clothes. And to my horror, I have discovered that clothes are a very important part of my job. I am the intermediary between a First Lady with impeccable taste and a press corps dying to know every detail. I am convinced that if I were to announce: "Last night Mrs. Ford burned down the White House," the reporters' response would be, "What was she wearing?" And they want details. A "light-blue, long dress" is not only incomplete, it is probably inaccurate. Colors, I have discovered, don't come in the basic shades I used in coloring books as a child. They come in poetic abstractions like dusty rose, coffee cream. I am embarrassed to admit that if Mrs. Ford did not tell *me* what she was wearing, I could not tell *them*. And it is really terrible to approach someone all dressed up and say, "What *is* that?" I've tried to be a little subtle. "Hello," I say cheerily, simultaneously fingering Mrs. Ford's outfit. "Wool, isn't it? No? . . . Jersey?"

She is good about it. As good as a former model and fashion designer and present clothes horse can be. She tries to teach me, and occasionally suggests—subtly—that a "scarf tied like this would look lovely with what you're wearing, Sheila."

All this is to explain that I am, at best, an apprentice in describing women's clothes to women. I could not even begin to condone the formal attire of a President half a world away. Or rather, I would have *thought* I could not, had I been asked yesterday. Today, I worked very hard at perfecting my expertise. I had trouble keeping a straight face as I called fancy men's stores all over Washington to find out, among other things, whether it was appropriate for the President of the United States to arrive in Japan in a morning suit. I understood little of what I was asking, let alone what the answers I was busily writing down meant. I was just an intermediary.

"The theory that's running around," Maxine Cheshire hissed into the phone when I gave her my research returns, "is that the President is wearing Ron Nessen's pants!"

"Really," I said, trying to suppress my amusement. "Whatever is Ron Nessen wearing?"

It all seems so silly. But I wish we were both laughing. Maxine is disturbingly serious. There have been too many phone calls; I have a feeling she is about to make a big splash.

## NOVEMBER 20, 1974

(SPLASH!) "It isn't the Emperor's new clothes but the President's that everyone at the White House is pretending not to notice," the Cheshire column purred in this morning's *Washington Post*. She quoted me as suggesting that perhaps the President had hitched his suspenders up too high. People think it's a clever line; so do I. But I never said it. Until I read her article, I had no idea a man wore suspenders with a morning suit.

Maxine Cheshire started my day, but the real event was my White House tour. I've never been awed by the White House, probably because I visited the place as a child. But I've always been very curious about the "other" White House, the upstairs family quarters. When you can have the very best, what do you choose? How does the First Family really live? (the *National Enquirer* is not alone in wanting to know.)

This morning, Mrs. Ford gave me a private tour. In all, the family quarters are composed of two floors, twenty-five rooms, twelve and a half bathrooms, and about sixty closets. What first caught my eye were the butlers and the maids scurrying around, the fresh flowers in almost every room . . . little touches of elegance. The beauty parlor was not bad either—fully equipped with basin, mirrors, chairs and hair dryers. Apparently this is where the First Lady's beautician works when he makes "house calls." I never realized that there was a beauty parlor.

"You know, there wasn't a kitchen up here before the Kennedys," Mrs. Ford explained as we surveyed a room that looked like any other kitchen. "The First Family ate downstairs in the family dining room on the State Floor. But Jackie Kennedy decided that the setting was too stiff for family eating and installed the kitchen and," Mrs. Ford continued moving to the room next door, "she made *this* into a family dining room."

The walls of the "casual, family" dining room were covered with battle scenes, men in revolutionary war attire fighting each other all over the wall.

"I'm sure it's very valuable, and historically significant, but it's *so* depressing! I can't wait to paint this room a bright sunny yellow!"

The Fords use the West Hall as a living room. "This is my favorite window, especially in the afternoon when the sun pours in,"

Mrs. Ford said, kneeling down on the sofa positioned in front of the big, round, arch-shaped West Hall window, and looking out. "I like it because I can see the Oval Office. It reminds me that my husband is close by. And I can see the press room, or at least the reporters coming and going. And I can see the street a little with people walking by—*real* people. You can't imagine how isolated the White House feels at times," she said. "It is a luxury to be able to see people, to see without being seen. I love to walk out on the Truman Balcony, for example, and take in that beautiful view of the south lawn of the White House and the Ellipse. But there is no privacy out there. There are always people at the fence with binoculars trying to catch a glimpse. That's what is so confining."

We walked all the way down the hall to the last room on the right, the Lincoln Sitting Room. Masculine, conservative, majestic.

"That smokey smell," Mrs. Ford said, "is coming from the fireplace. This is where Nixon would come for seclusion. They say he spent hours and hours in here, especially at the end, sitting by the fire with the music turned way up and all the doors closed. Alone."

We both searched the walls in silence for clues. White House ghosts.

"The smell lingers, but the music is gone," Mrs. Ford laughed, completely changing the tone. "One of the first things my son Jack did when we moved in was to take the stereo upstairs to his bedroom!"

We peered briefly into the pinkest room I have ever seen. Pink rug, pink bedspread, pink draperies, pink everything. "This was Tricia Nixon's room," Mrs. Ford said, moving on. "Susan didn't want it. And this," she stopped dramatically, "this is the Treaty Room. I love to come in here," she said moving slowly, almost reverently, into a large room with an enormous crystal chandelier at its center, hanging over an impressive table. "If I have a lot of mail and pictures to sign, I bring it all in here. It's just so *authentic*."

Next was the yellow Oval Room, elaborately decorated in the period of Louis XVI. "I call it the standing room," Mrs. Ford said drily, "because no one who comes here feels like sitting down. It's so formal. The Nixons re-did it this way, and unfortunately it was finished shortly before they left. I loved the room when the Johnsons were here. They used it as a family room. I'm not sure I even want to entertain formally in it. How can you get to know a head of state in these surroundings?"

Walking out, I noticed a vase of flowers. At its base were the figures of two delicate angels, back to back, one kneeling in supplication, her hands almost touching. *Almost* touching. There was a tiny gap between the hands, and I was startled to see that one of the angels was clutching a cigarette. Mrs. Ford saw me staring and burst into laughter. "Oh, *that*," she said, "I put it there. That's just my way of testing whether the maids have cleaned the room!" She was still chuckling as we walked out.

"You know, this whole thing took us by surprise," Mrs. Ford said, as we walked slowly down the corridor. "He never sought the Presidency. Jerry's one great political desire was to be Speaker of the House of Representatives. But that majority of Republican Congressmen never came about, and I think both of us were at the point where we were looking forward to the period where he would serve his last term. And then everything caved in. I remember when Nixon called to ask him to be his Vice President, I was shocked—largely because I thought Jerry was too valuable to Nixon where he was, in Congress. Anyway, I lost a $5.00 bet to Susan. I don't know where she got her information, but she was right.

"And then the Presidency. I had a very heavy heart when I met with the Nixons just before they left, to say good-bye. I remember that day we came to the White House as one of the saddest days of my life. But I said when we moved in here that it couldn't change my way of life—not deep down. I've spent too many years as me; I can't suddenly turn into a princess. I think the staff was taken aback by our friendliness at first. I'd say a cheerful 'good morning,' for example, and the help was stunned. At first I thought no one liked me because no one was talking to me. Later I discovered it was just a matter of getting used to our style after the Nixons.

"Something else no one seems to expect," Mrs. Ford said, opening another door, "is for a First Lady to sleep with the President! This," she said, gesturing around her, "is *our* bedroom, and that is *our* bed. We are the first President and First Lady to share a bedroom in an awfully long time. To my great surprise, though, people have written to me objecting to the idea of a President of the United States sleeping with his wife."

The room, which had been Pat Nixon's bedroom, was spacious and airy, even with the comfortable sitting area and the desk for working. Off the bedroom was extraordinary closet space which houses Mrs. Ford's well-organized wardrobe. "The President has a valet," she explained to me as she showed me the clothes, "Nancy Howe helps me."

It must be an incredible undertaking. Each hanger in Mrs. Ford's closet has a tag that tells when and where the garment on it was last worn. She has four closets for clothes, one for her formal gowns, one for long dresses, one for shoes and pocketbooks, and one for her day clothes. One entire bureau is devoted to her scarves which are arranged according to color.

They may share a bed, but they do not share bathrooms. The Presidential bathroom includes a Jacuzzi, a magazine rack, and several photos, including one I really liked of a relaxed and pensive President Ford walking with his dog. "That," Mrs. Ford said, pointing to the telephone next to the toilet, "was installed at President Johnson's insistence, and so were these," she said, showing me a line of about ten different electrical outlets just over the sink. "I understand he ordered these one day in a moment of frenzy when the one existing outlet did not work."

Next to the Fords' bedroom, in what used to be President Nixon's bedroom, is a room Mrs. Ford has made into a den for the President. "I wanted to create a room he could really relax in. A room with *our* furniture, as opposed to White House furniture."

The room is warm and cozy. Personal. Football trophies and mementoes on the mantel, family pictures everywhere. Pictures of four little children, turning into four bigger children—three boys, one girl, all blond and beautiful—round with baby fat in one photograph, leaner and more serious in another, hair darkening, features becoming more defined. "Those are all old Christmas cards," Mrs. Ford said. "Jerry is so proud of his kids. We've always sent out a family Christmas picture. This year will probably be the first year we don't. People talk about the generation gap; I don't think we've ever had it in our family. We've always had a very open and free feeling with the children. I was thirty-two when we had Michael, our first; Jerry was thirty-five. With Susan, I was thirty-nine. I think maturity might help.

"We also always stressed that the family was a unit, no matter what. Michael and Jack, for example, who are so different from each other, are very supportive of each other as a result. Michael, who is devoting his life to religion, is both the least political and the most like his father (if that is possible!). He is very serious, very organized, and thorough. Jack on the other hand is my rebel, as the second child often is. He and I argue all the time, but my husband says that is because we are so much alike."

She looked at one of the earlier cards. "That was when it was difficult," she said. "Jerry traveled a lot, giving speeches for fellow Republicans all over the country, and when he was gone, I had to serve as the heavy hand of discipline—and the ambulance driver, too. There was a period there when it seemed that someone was always getting hurt and it always seemed to happen at dinner time."

Another picture, more recent. "You know, the boys grew up in very difficult times. Drugs were prevalent, and I was very concerned about keeping them close, about knowing what they were doing. One way I tried to work it out was to encourage them to come home with their friends. And the house was always filled, as a result. A few teenagers practically lived at the house with us. In fact, there was one who had an electric guitar and left it over at our house because his parents didn't like it. I miss it," she said. "I'd like to fill up the whole White House with my friends and the children's friends."

Just off the President's study there was a picture of the Fords with the Nixons and Tricia Nixon Cox. I stopped dead, cringing inside. I did not like having Richard Nixon portrayed so prominently here in the Family quarters. Mrs. Ford saw me pause and looked at the picture sadly. "I feel so sorry for Pat," she said, completely ignoring the smiling countenance of the former chief executive. "She is a wonderful woman, a good friend of mine. I have never met anyone who did not like Pat Nixon, actually. A strong woman. Luckily. She's certainly had her share of problems." We stared at the picture some more. "It's a funny thing," Mrs. Ford said. "When that picture was taken, we were all at San Clemente together. Tricia's engagement to Ed Cox was not official but it was about to become official. We all *knew* it was; she even had the ring on. She was sort of sitting on it in this picture, so it would not show. There we were, all close friends, old friends, but instead of sharing the happy personal news with us, Pat kept chatting about how Tricia was still dating 'many boys', giving Jerry and me the official line. That's the way Pat is. She is warm and kind and considerate, but closed. A very private person."

The Fords live on the second floor. The Ford children, when in town, all stay up on the third floor. These days, Susan dominates as the child in residence. I went up to see her after my tour today, with a *Life* Magazine photographer who is taking pictures for a story on Susan. We found the President's daughter in her favorite hideout, the solarium. It's an open, airy, window-filled room with a television set, a small refrigerator, and a lot of space. Susan likes to entertain friends there. Today she was there with Gardner Britt, her boyfriend. Her present boyfriend. Gardner is a tall, good-looking freshman at V.P.I. who seems to me to belong more to the 50's than the 70's. This is no deep-and-murky loose-living philosopher. Far from it. This is a clean-shaven, white-teethed intellectual lightweight—a "jock." But then Susan is certainly a 50's old-fashioned-girl type, in the sense that she is thoroughly non-rebelling, quite willing to live within parental guidelines, "preppy," as opposed to "protesting." Maybe it is all coming back.

Since Mrs. Ford and I had discussed the fact that Susan's at an age where "boyfriends come and go" and that they should come and go as quietly as possible, I tried to keep Gardner out of the pictures today. Actually, I was trying to do two things: keep him out of camera range and do funny things to make Susan relax and look good on camera. It worked, but I think everyone thought I was a little peculiar.

We then moved to Susan's room for more pictures. The room used to belong to Julie and David Eisenhower, but unlike the other places in the White House Family quarters, all past history had been erased. The new occupant had completely taken over. She loves plants and she loves to needlepoint. The room is filled with plants and needlepoint pillows. The decor is strictly teenager: school papers spread all over the floor, the telephone in the midst of everything, obviously the most frequently used object in the room, and, underneath the debris, Susan's new prize possession—a splendid brass bed. No White House ghosts here. Just Susan Ford.

## NOVEMBER 21, 1974

"You have to have a sense of humor about these things," I told the silent men from the West Wing sitting around me at the Mess table. It was after 1 P.M. and I had not turned into a pumpkin. Perhaps that explained my good mood. Or perhaps it was just the Mess itself. It's a very nice place to eat, offering excellent food at low prices, served by Navy stewards in an atmosphere that not only *is* exclusive, but *feels* exclusive. The blue menus with the gold Presidential seal list everything from sandwiches to a complete meal of soup and appetizer and main course and dessert. Today was Thursday, the only day the Mess serves liquor, or what it calls "Thursday refreshers." A choice of piña colada, Bloody Mary, margarita, or ice-cold beer. Staff members who eat in the Mess are billed at the end of the month for their meals. There are no prices on the menu, but a complete meal comes to about $2.50—an incredible buy. There are goodies everywhere: cigarettes, White House matches, nuts, mints and chocolate on the small table next to the maitre d'.

Close to the Mess entrance is a large round table for staff who are dining alone. In the middle of the table is a large lazy Susan overflowing with bread and butter, peanut butter, relishes, and delicious, unusual crackers that taste very fattening. This was where I was sitting. I had joined other loners: Bob Orben, talented comic writer who had provided material for Dick Gregory, Red Skelton, Bob Hope and now, Gerald Ford. Jim Cavanaugh, who works on the President's Domestic Council, and Gerry Warren, who had been Ron Zeigler's Deputy Press Secretary and is one of the few Nixon people still around. I had been going on at length, telling the men about Maxine Cheshire, McClaren, and the other anecdotes that made up my week. No one was laughing. I tried a new tactic: business. I asked Jim Cavanaugh if there were any cancer hearings coming up on the Hill in the near future.

"Mrs. Ford has been getting requests left and right to appear at cancer benefits," I explained, "but I don't want her to get exhausted by traveling so much. I thought solid testimony delivered in front of a nationally publicized Senate hearing would be a more effective use of her energies."

"You're right," he said. "I'll check it out and let you know."

Another conversation stops dead. What is the matter with these men?

"Did you see *New York* Magazine?" Bob Orben asked me, finally.

I had. The cover story by Richard Reeves was on Gerald Ford's campaigning for Republican Congressmen, and both the cover and the story portrayed the President as Bozo the Clown, a sort of stumbling, bumbling halfwit.

"Yes," I said, "it was dreadful."

"Dreadful?" Bob Orben replied, coming alive for the first time. "Dreadful? I'd call it devastating. And I would also call it inaccurate—inaccurate, unfair, and distorted. How do you handle something like that?" he asked me. "How do you fight back?"

"You don't fight back," I said. "I think you look at the article, laugh, and rectify it immediately, either by pointing out the inaccuracies or by making sure Ford does things in the future that create a very different image of the President."

Pause. No comments. I went on.

"I think his traveling, his overexposure is increasing his vulnerability to articles like this and decreasing the impact of what he has to say," I said.

"What do you mean 'laugh' at it?" Gerry Warren chimed in. "It isn't funny. You can get into a lot of trouble with a sense of humor like that."

"I don't mean think it is humorous. I just mean toss it off, be elastic about it, take it in stride, don't over-react in a brittle way," I told the Nixon holdover.

"Inaccurate," Bob Orben was saying, "incredibly inaccurate."

The President is still off on his Far East trip, and Mrs. Ford has been waiting anxiously for a postcard. She really misses him. When he called her last week, he told her he had just sent her some postcards. She couldn't figure out why they were so long in coming, but apparently they went through traditional channels by mistake, and the whole correspondence section got to read them before she did.

Mrs. Ford is decorating the Oval Office while the President is gone. Janet Ford and Nancy Howe are helping. Removing Nixon's *office* from office is apparently the final step in the Ford transition. "The blue and gold colors," Mrs. Ford told me, "seemed to reflect a kind of 'Imperial Presidency'!" She is changing them to earth tones, with plants and personal mementoes and family pictures on the walls. She's quite pleased with the way it's turning out.

Susan has been accepted at Mount Vernon College. She was accepted even before she went in to have the required interview;

such is the "luck" of a Presidential daughter. The result was—as she so aptly put it—"a bummer." It really depressed her to know so definitely that she was accepted because her father was President. She told me she felt terrible because she had friends who had *had* the interview and had not yet heard from the college. She was embarrassed and a little hurt by the special treatment and I don't blame her at all.

## NOVEMBER 25, 1974

When the President got back from his trip, Mrs. Ford told him that if he did not like the way she had fixed up his office, he shouldn't call her; she did not want to know. She sat by the phone and waited. She got anxious. Finally, he called; he loved the office. He would have called sooner, but he was a little busy.

## NOVEMBER 27, 1974

Ambassador Walter Annenberg just called me from England. He had heard about the changes in the Oval Office and was furious that the oil painting of Benjamin Franklin which he had donated in the 60's had been moved out and replaced by a different portrait of Franklin. He said his, painted by David Martin, was historically important because it was the only one for which Franklin had posed. He was especially displeased that the portrait had been re-hung in the Thomas Jefferson Room, which Mrs. Nixon had made into a French room, and which Ambassador Annenberg described as "like filet of sole with chocolate."

## NOVEMBER 28, 1974 (Thanksgiving Day)

The 30-30 Club came to the White House today for brunch. The 30-30 Club is President Ford's high school football team, so named because in 1930 the team won city and state championships for South High School.

More incredible than that is the fact that for the last forty-four years the club has gotten together every year on Thanksgiving Day. It is a stag affair, except for every five years when the members can bring their wives and families. Usually they meet in Grand Rapids, but this year was special: one of their teammates is President of the United States.

At their brunch, everyone stands up and talks about what he has been doing, how his children are, whether or not he's retired yet. It was off-limits to the press, but I sat outside munching the leftover eggs Benedict and wine that were brought me, and took copious notes. Not for the press, really. I was just fascinated. This was raw material for a novel, each man sharing a personal kind of introspection with those who have been his friends for forty-four years.

I found myself becoming very involved in what was happening. The result was my first "defensive" press briefing. I described the beautiful scene to the cynical reporters.

"Why didn't Bob Orben write a joke for the President?" they asked.

"Everyone was having such a good time. He didn't need a joke. He was just reminiscing."

"What did he say?"

"He said something about . . . 'Our star is rising—' "

"Was he referring to inflation?" UPI reporter Helen Thomas wanted to know. That was when I got defensive. It had just been so nice that I didn't want anyone to misunderstand it.

"You're getting defensive," said Helen Thomas.

After the brunch, I thought it might be nice for the men, but more important, for the photographers, if they tossed a ball around. Nancy Howe ran up and got the football the Washington Redskins had given Mrs. Ford when she had surgery.

"Hi, Sheila," the President said. "What do you want us to do?"

"Scrimmage," I said, unsure whether it was a noun or a verb, unsure of what it meant either way, but thrilled that he knew my first name.

They passed the football around and the photographers snapped and everyone had a good time.

Except for Edward, my husband, who spent Thanksgiving alone.


*NOVEMBER 29, 1974*

"Gulley," I said, "Liz Carpenter told me that you are the one man who can get anything around here." He reared back and

guffawed, warmed by both the reference to Liz and the reference
to his power. A big balding man in his fifties, Bill Gulley is the jocu-
lar type who howls when he laughs and roars when he is angry—a
real character to those who love him, a boor to those who don't.
He was not smoking a cigar, but somehow I felt he should have
been.

Bill Gulley began his White House career many, many years ago
as the Marine sergeant in charge of handing out gas masks during
civil defense drills. He is now head of the Military Affairs Office.
That's quite a jump.

As Commander-in-Chief of the Armed Forces, the President has
at his disposal the Army, Navy, Air Force, and Marines. That
means military protection for the nation, and military perquisites
for the White House. The Navy runs the White House Mess, for
example, and the Presidential yacht, *Sequoia*. The Air Force provides a fleet of Presidential planes, ranging from Jet Stars to large
transports, to Air Force One to jumbo jet commando planes. The
Army offers a fleet of chauffeured limousines, and the ability to
construct anything anytime to help out. The Marines offer a fleet of
choppers. The Military Affairs Office has technical support, too.
The Military controls the videotape room, for example, the place
where network programs are videotaped for Presidential viewing at
a later date. The Military Affairs Office therefore determines which
White House staff can order a program taped and which cannot,
which staff are to be helped out by the Military Affairs Office's
messenger service (which can hand-deliver something to the Ambassador in Afghanistan by this afternoon, if need be), which
White House offices can get extra staff people "loaned" to them,
and which cannot.

I don't know how Bill Gulley got into this powerful position, or
how he stays there. But the Military Affairs Office is also the liaison with former Presidents, the office that authorizes all the little
privileges not specifically authorized by Congress. And, since
President is not the most secure of professions, Presidents must
look at Gulley and see their future vulnerabilities. Within the White
House, Gulley seems to have discovered that if you do not question which perquisites the very top advisors seize, they will not
care how you treat subordinates.

Despite the fact that Liz Carpenter had told me to go to Gulley,
and despite the fact that his office is directly across the hall from

mine, I waited until today to actively seek his aid. I was a little put off by his sense of humor, which consists of posting enlarged pictures of women with enlarged breasts on the walls outside his door, with "clever" captions that don't make me laugh.

But today was the last straw. I got my second briefing box rejection, in response to my second formal briefing box memo, looked around in exhausted depression at my understaffed office and, shutting my eyes to avoid the silicone murals in the hall, I made my way to Bill Gulley.

"You've come to the right place," he assured me, as I reported my briefing box setbacks and my staff needs. "Just sit back; I just might be able to help you."

I assured him I would. But I left feeling less than comfortable. Had he noticed the way I cringed a little each time he mentioned a possible "*broad*" who could join my staff?

## NOVEMBER 30, 1974

Weeks ago, when I decided to change my office around to make it less like a Victorian tea room, I told the woman from the General Services Administration what kind of furniture I like. She told me that I would have to take whatever was available from the warehouse. Fine. Well, today they delivered a Navy-blue sofa and two gold chairs. The gold chairs looked familiar. The Imperial Presidency! These were the two chairs that had been on either side of Richard Nixon's desk in the Oval Office. I looked at the chairs and laughed to myself. If Nixon only knew where his chairs ended up.

*Chapter Two*
DECEMBER, 1974:

# LET'S BE FRIENDS

*DECEMBER 4, 1974*

East is East and West is West. Granted. But it is counterproductive to have a cold war going on within the White House.

When I first came here, I saw myself as a liaison between the press and the First Lady. I did not think that was a terribly unusual interpretation of First Lady's Press Secretary. For that reason, it seemed odd that the very basic tools of the trade were missing—such as UPI and AP wire machines, a briefing box, a large enough staff to be a creative and efficient office organization. When I requested these basic tools, I found myself fighting with the West Wing every step of the way. That seemed even more peculiar. Aren't we all in this together? Isn't the East Wing married to the West Wing?

Quietly, I have been accumulating data (that would not stand up in a court of law)—a sentence here, a look there, a chat about how it was—and this data seems to add up to the fact that no, quite frankly, we are not in this together. It tells me that West Wing sentiment goes along these lines: President Nixon may not have been a terrific President, but Pat Nixon was the best First Lady possible. She was seen and not heard.

It is a rather negative attitude. I mean, is it not possible for a wife to be an attribute—an intelligent, credible, mind-of-her-own attribute? As I see it, a spouse is a reflection of a spouse. Each chose the other. Together, they are a marital unit, but separately they have two very distinct sets of characteristics. Can't hers give him extra dimensions, the ability to be something he isn't? This is an unusually compassionate, warm woman, a real mother figure, and if ever the country needed to know there was such a presence in the White House, it needs to know that now.

The country needs more than that. It needs to know that there is a whole family of human beings in the White House, a real family who cares, understands, faces similar problems, and wants to help. I see my job as providing the public with a window on the White House by projecting the human side of the President, the First Lady, and their children, and, in the process, demonstrating the human side of political programs.

That does not in any way conflict with the West Wing, which is the source of Presidential policy. Nor does it conflict with Ron Nessen's job, which is to translate those policies so the public understands what the administration is doing and why. The West Wing is the mind . . . the "head" of the administration. The East Wing is the heart. For the administration to work it needs both.

Let's be friends!

Well, at least the theory should bring about a truce. I have written it all up in a five-page memo (the ultimate White House weapon) which "summarizes the responsibilities of the East Wing Press Office, and sets forth a proposed re-organization of the office." (It also requests a briefing box.) I am scheduled to present the memo in person to Donald Rumsfeld tomorrow morning at 11 A.M.

I hope I am more successful in presenting the memo to Rumsfeld than I was giving it to Mrs. Ford this afternoon. She was scheduled to attend a Christmas party for the children of men missing or killed in action in Vietnam. It took about forty minutes to get to the party and I thought I would ride out with her and tell her about my memo, but she was preoccupied with the MIA wives. "I feel so awfully sorry for those women," she said, "trying to raise their children alone, especially those with boys. It must be so hard."

We talked. About child-rearing, from her perspective as a mother, but also from her perspective as a daughter. Mrs. Ford's parents are both dead. Her father died when she was only sixteen, and her mother died about fifteen years later, soon after she married Gerald Ford. But her recollections of her parents, especially her mother, are vivid and warm. She admires her mother because she was a strong woman, capable of raising three children singlehandedly during the Depression, and because she was both a source of comfort, and a source of inspiration. "I remember when I was very, very young," Mrs. Ford said. "There was an enormous storm and my mother took me in her arms on the front porch and told me how beautiful storms were, how exciting the sound of rain could be. Well, it worked. To this day, I love to watch storms. I'll go out of my way to watch them, and I love the sound of rain falling on the roof." She laughed. "My mother confessed to me much later that storms scared her to death."

I put the memo away for the trip back. Instead we talked about an experience she had as a volunteer when she was only about fourteen and she taught dance therapy to four-year-old children with physical handicaps. "It is so important to train these children early," she explained, "because early training can make a tremendous difference in their later capabilities."

The experience had meant a lot to her, and the recollection excited her. She showed me what the steps were and how to coordinate the hand and foot motions. There was a song that went with it, a song about a bear. She began to sing it for me.

There we were, in the bullet-proof car with two expressionless Secret Service men in the front seat staring straight ahead, the memo burning a hole in my pocket, as the First Lady of the United States did a song-and-dance routine designed for handicapped four-year-olds.

It was not exactly the show I had in mind, but it was a nice production anyway. I gave her the memo when we got back. She said she'd read it.


## DECEMBER 5, 1974

I practically knew it by heart, but I re-read it and smiled all the way over to Rumsfeld's office. I knew he'd like it; it made so much sense. It delineated turf; it was a good starting point for a discussion of the tasks of my office. I welcomed his ideas.

We never had time to talk. He began to read, and suddenly howled. What bothered him was the sentence that explained that the East Wing Press Office could provide the nation a window on the First Family.

"First *family?*" Rumsfeld roared, his even features taking on a reddish hue. "You are *not* responsible for the President. Remember that. You are just responsible for the First Lady!"

I stared at him, confused.

"Do you understand?" the steel-blue eyes were piercing. "You will write in here '*with the exception of the President.*'"

I was shocked to hear my own voice repeating sheepishly, "With the exception of the President."

The meeting came to an abrupt halt; he had other things to do. Unfortunately the window phrase came in the sixth line, so he did not get much of my five-page memo read before the eruption. But he said he would read the rest. After I asked him to. After he appeared on the verge of heaving it into the wastebasket.

Well, at least one person liked it. "I think it's great!" Mrs. Ford told me over the phone tonight. "I started to tell the President about it but tonight wasn't a good time. He was exhausted. Don't worry, I'll do it soon."

## DECEMBER 6, 1974

A White Christmas is a dream. A White House Christmas has nightmarish dimensions. Especially when there is no time to prepare. Even the newly inaugurated administration has ten months. Those who enter the White House suddenly, at summer's end, miss the luxury of planning time.

The first time the topic of Christmas came up was a few weeks ago, when Mrs. Ford was having her hair done. We were in high spirits, because we had been looking at a picture of singer Vicki Carr who had entertained at a recent State Dinner posing with Nancy Howe, Janet Ford, and Mrs. Ford. Vicki Carr's dress was extremely low cut, and the photographer had managed to capture that moment of truth: all three women were staring point blank at Miss Carr's cleavage, with totally shocked expressions on their faces. Mrs. Ford thought the picture was hilarious and somehow our merriment spread to talk of Christmas.

"Wouldn't it be wonderful if we could do something that would get millions of people involved?" Mrs. Ford said in between her wash and her set. I whipped out my pencil and paper. "Maybe we could ask anyone who wanted to to make ornaments for the Christmas tree."

Even in the euphoria of the moment, reality hit. We had visions of millions of ornaments stilling the Christmas mails, and completely overwhelming the men in charge of White House security.

Besides, the tree only holds about three thousand ornaments. Who would judge which ones made the grade? And on what basis?

The Johnsons and the Kennedys had taken their tree ornaments with them. The Nixons had left theirs behind, but they were the golden creations of Saks Fifth Avenue's top designer. Not Mrs. Ford's style. She has always used either handcrafted ornaments or ones with sentimental value. She thinks a Christmas tree should be warm and personal and familial, even if it is 19½ feet tall and stands in the middle of the White House.

We compromised. We commissioned several crafts groups—a quilters workshop, a handicapped training center, a farm women's cooperative and so on—to make decorations for this year's tree. Then, to share a little of the White House to encourage families to save money and spend more time together making their own ornaments, I had instructions prepared for making several of the ornaments.

I keep trying to add meaning to the rituals, and I sometimes wonder if it is worth the effort. Last week, for example, the traditional pageantry began with Mrs. Ford officially receiving the tree. It was a concolor fir tree from Michigan. Since I am sick and tired of the fact that everything around here comes from Michigan (the President will *not* be running for Congress in the near future) and since "concolor fir" tells me nothing, I tried to find human interest for the story. I ended up tracking down the lady from whose front yard the tree was cut: Mrs. Ouina Gardner of Mayville, Michigan. There. I liked that. It made it a real tree for me. (Did anyone else care?)

Then I decided that Mrs. Ford should make something too, something she could hang on the tree at the press briefing. I asked her to go through her things and find some sentimental fabric, and make an ornament out of it. She found a perfect fabric: a piece of lace that had belonged to her mother. But she was less than enthusiastic about creating an ornament. ("Susan's the seamstress in the family.") I had someone else make the ornament, but Mrs. Ford decorated it. Quickly. The reporters were waiting expectantly inside the Blue Room on the State Floor as she stood outside the door, madly embroidering "B.F." on a "small patchwork pentagon ball."

A bit corny?

Maybe. But the fact is so much of the commercial ugliness of Christmas filters up and into the White House that I think it is important to stress family feelings and sentimentality. Most White House Christmas telephone calls fall into the "gimme" category. "Gimme" a White House Christmas card. "Gimme" an invitation to the party. "Gimme" an invitation for my Aunt Miranda. "Gimme" a VIP tour of the White House for my cousin who is visiting. Apparently, the more people you include, the more there are who feel excluded. The Fords are sending out 40,000 Christmas cards which they personally pay for. There are many, many people who have called recently blatantly suggesting the number be increased to 40,001. The Fords are inviting about 1,000 people to a press party on the 19th. They are serving liquor and they are footing the bill themselves. It is strictly for the working press. Yet every public relations man in town who ever was a member of the working press has called to proclaim his offense at not being invited. And all invitees want to bring their children.

In the meantime, the real working press are driving me crazy with Christmas stories. The White House chef, the White House caligrapher, the White House florist, all are being hotly pursued for the "ultimate" slant.

I'm being unfair. There *are* pleasant aspects of a White House Christmas. There are the parties—for children, for Congress, for the press—that create a festive feeling. There is, for the Fords, the happy anticipation of the trip to Vail, Colorado, at the end of the month. They've been going there for years. This year, however, they won't be staying at their condominium because it isn't large enough to accommodate the Secret Service detail. But Dick Bass, the owner of another ski resort, is lending them the use of his home. I warned Mrs. Ford that NBC has rented the house next door, but she just laughed. "I'll keep the drapes pulled," she said.

For me, the nicest part of the White House Christmas festivities came at the very beginning. Last Sunday, Edward and I stopped in at the White House late in the afternoon because I knew the Christmas decorations were going up, and I was curious to see what the decorating process was like, and how the finished product looked.

The work was still being done when we arrived, and there were about fifty different volunteers on ladders hanging the ornaments, mounting window wreaths, placing poinsettia plants. These "Christmas elves" consist of professional florists and amateurs who belong to garden clubs, who come to the White House from all over the country each year, at their own expense, just to help with the Christmas decorations.

We were—I thought—the only spectators, until I noticed another group of fascinated bystanders also in casual attire: the President, Susan, and Mrs. Ford. Edward had never met the President before, and it was one of history's less formal introductions. "Hi," said the smiling man, casually extending his hand, "I'm Jerry Ford."

## DECEMBER 7, 1974

"Petunia and the President had some fun in bed last night!" Nancy Howe gushed raucously as I tried to sink unobtrusively into the floor of the passport office. We were getting our passports for a trip with the Fords to Martinique next week, and Nancy was treating the man doing the processing to an earful. "She told me when he came back from the Oval Office, she was wearing her adorable blue robe, and she said. . . ."

Would it make the man more or less interested, I wondered, to find out that "Petunia" was Nancy Howe's nickname for the President's wife. I shuddered at both alternatives and walked over to the other side of the room. If I were not standing near her, whom would she have to tell? She followed. "We had such fun talking about it all this morning," Nancy giggled. "Petunia and I had our tea and we. . . ."

Everything is "we" with Nancy Howe and her Petunia, and most "we" anecdotes are adolescent. ("We put a skeleton in the upstairs window of the White House on Halloween, and we had such fun.") She does not understand the difference between funny and silly. Nor does she realize that confidantes do not use public address systems.

If she is telling the passport office about the Fords' sex life, what on earth is she telling the cocktail party circuit?

## DECEMBER 11, 1974

I have no idea how it happened. I have imagined several different possibilities.

I see them munching a Whip Inflation Now tunafish casserole (noodles are in season) by candlelight in the family dining room. "Darling," the First Lady whispers in the President's ear, "now can I tell you about Sheila's memo?"

Maybe.

"Give it to her!" Bill Gulley bellows into the telephone.

Perhaps.

I see Donald Rumsfeld, standing in the middle of his wastebasket, completely immersed in the paper he has just plucked from the trash. "Now this," he says out loud, "this is what I call a memo!"

I like that one best.

I have no idea what really happened. All I know is that at this very moment I have a memo in my hand which reads: "Ron Nessen has agreed to make a rare exception in policy and authorize a press briefing box to be installed in Sheila Weidenfeld's office in the East Wing."

## DECEMBER 13, 1974

Mrs. Ford is *not* going to Martinique with the President today to meet with French President Giscard d'Estaing. I had a feeling she wouldn't be going. Her old back condition flared up a few days ago and I told Edward yesterday that I thought she might want to cancel.

She's had the back problem for ten years now, ever since August, 1964, when she was supposed to spend a week at the beach in Rehobeth with the children and she ended up spending the week in the hospital. It is called osteoarthritis, which is, primarily, a fancy way of saying back ailment, and, like most back ailments, it creates a great deal of discomfort, and like most back ailments, it comes and goes, and no one understands why it comes, and why it goes.

When you're in the White House, however, you don't have something "like most back ailments." You have osteoarthritis and the press becomes very suspicious. I think White House reporters have always been very skeptical about health. They felt Eisenhower's doctors were not honest with them. They point to recent evidence that Kennedy had Addison's disease as yet another example of hidden facts. Many of them have told me they are certain that Nixon was on pills, although the charge was repeatedly denied. And two reporters who cover Mrs. Ford have already announced that—in view of Mrs. Ford's cancer surgery—they will not believe a thing I tell them about her health. They don't believe that if Mrs. Ford does have a recurrence of cancer I will tell them honestly.

So my credibility gap preceded my news item.

For obvious reasons, I was very careful today. First I became a veritable expert on osteoarthritis and then I issued a simple statement that Mrs. Ford was suffering from a recurrence of a long-standing back ailment, and could not go to Martinique. Instead of just saying she was not going, I thought it was important to stress that her doctor wanted her to stay home and continue therapy for the back. I also stressed that this had nothing whatsoever to do with her chemotherapy treatments which were going very well, in fact, without even the expected side effects.

I was the only one who believed me.

It didn't matter much. No one was listening. Maxine Cheshire wanted to know whether "the handcrafted items on this year's Christmas tree cost more than the donated items on last year's tree," undoubtedly for some new scoop. Everyone else was completely absorbed by the *real* news of the day. The Fords' son Jack has come home from college for a visit. ("I never know what he's going to look like when he arrives," Mrs. Ford said. "He likes to experiment. There was a moustache three years ago, a long full beard the year before last. He usually shaves whatever it is right off, providing we don't tell him we don't like it.")

Today he "wore" a new friend instead: former Beatle, George Harrison. Presidents' children, I suspect, attract many "new friends" among the famous, as such friendships are mutually beneficial. Jack, who made it clear the first time we met (by both his words and his silence) that he disliked publicity in general and

Press Secretaries in specific, wasted no time jumping into the spotlight with his Beatle. I gather public recognition is dreadful, but recognition by rock stars is another thing.

The White House press corps was hysterical. "It's just such a welcomed change of pace," one reporter told me by way of explanation. "Can you imagine Tricia bringing a rock star home to meet Dad?"

Attired in a brown plaid jacket, an Indian shirt, bright orange pants, and red boots, George Harrison dined in the solarium, chatted with "Dad" in the Oval Office, and finally proclaimed, "I feel good vibes about the White House," as camera crews, wire services, and an unusually large assortment of national and international news organizations trampled each other to get the details.

Obviously osteoarthritis does not hold a candle to Beatlemania.


## DECEMBER 17, 1974

I can't remember what my thoughts were when I was seventeen, but I'll bet they would not have looked good in print. I'm certain that few of the teenage boys I dated would have proved appropriately articulate for the national news media.

It is not his fault. But it is a problem.

Here is Mrs. Ford, slowly espousing the cause of women's rights, and there is Gardner Britt, "steady boyfriend of Susan Ford" loudly espousing the cause of male chauvinism in the *Ladies Home Journal* on the newsstands today. Mrs. Ford says there should be a woman in the Cabinet. Gardner says only the kitchen cabinet. And *he* gets greater publicity!

*"He said he's against women's liberation and said of Susan: 'She's not like some of those Miss Teenage Americas who always have some fancy career in mind like nursing!' "*

Cringe.

*"Of Gardner's male chauvinism, Susan says: 'I give in to him too often. Mother's the same way. We tease each other about it twenty-four hours a day. We're like two little girls.' "*

Double cringe.

That's Susan. But that's not Susan. All she is saying is that she hasn't thought about it much, but she would like to be like her mother. Had she had a different kind of childhood, she might have "deplored women's place in this sexist society." And she would have done it just as inarticulately and just as thoughtlessly. Because Susan is seventeen years old.

Her brothers say she is spoiled rotten, silly, and self-centered. She calls herself "Daddy's little girl" and supports it with anecdotes that substantiate both her statement and her brothers'. Yes, she has been sheltered and yes, she has—as the youngest child, the only girl—been smothered with love and attention, and yes, both the sheltering and the smothering show now. But so does the solid emotional base that has been created.

The *Ladies Home Journal* interview was done before I "took office," but when AP reporter Ann Blackman interviewed Susan a few weeks ago, I sat in on it. The results, I suspect, won't be much better. I tried to be detached, but when I heard her tell the reporter matter-of-factly that she hates to read, something in me snapped and I went rushing in like a stage prompter. "But what about your interest in photography and fashion design, Susan. . . ."

I was displeased by both our performances.

I turned down hundreds of requests before permitting the AP interview. And I suppose I should protect Susan more. I want to keep the press happy, but I also want to keep Susan unspoiled. She has a lot of growing up to do, and it is easier to grow off-camera. Now all I have to do is convince the camera crews of that fact.

I do not have to convince Gardner Britt, however. His own words in print did it for me. He came to see me today, and we agreed that in the future, before he talks to any reporter, he'll talk to me.


## DECEMBER 22, 1974

There's something special about climbing aboard a plane that carries the blue-and-gold seal of the President at its center with the words UNITED STATES OF AMERICA emblazoned across the top. The special feeling of Air Force One is by no means limited to its exterior. If my maiden voyage was any indication, it is a truly elegant way to travel.

I entered through the rear entrance (there is one up front for the President) and was greeted by large photos of the Ford family, and a cup of hot coffee handed to me by a steward.

All seats are assigned, and on each chair there is a small blue-and-white card that says "Air Force One" with the name of the seat's occupant typed on top. The far back of the plane is reserved for the press pool: two wire service reporters (Fran Lewine of AP and Helen Thomas of UPI rode today), one network correspondent, and one member of the writing press—a newspaper or magazine reporter. (The rest of the press travels in a press plane that precedes Air Force One.) There are a few rows of passenger seats for the television crew and wire photographers and then a table for the pool, with bowls on top filled with the goodies available on all the tables of Air Force One: fresh fruit, all varieties of candies, and cigarettes that say "Air Force One" on the package, matches similarly branded.

In front of the press area there are tables—one on either side of the plane, for the Secret Service agents. The next area is reserved for the plane's crew. Then there is another compartment for the secretaries, wives and guests of the President's staff. Next is a special staff compartment, and in front of that is an office—a real office with typewriters, a photocopying machine, the works. In front of the office sits the President's top staff (which today included me nestled in between Ron Nessen and Donald Rumsfeld). In front of us there is a lounge, with a small video cassette television set, comfortable chairs, a sofa, fresh flowers. There are family pictures on the wall. Just ahead of this lounge is the President's suite, two rooms, one a living room and the other an office, both with couches for sleeping. The President and Mrs. Ford have their own private steward. Directly across from the President's compartment is the communications center, staffed by radio operators whose sole function is to keep the President in constant communication with the White House.

Communications is one of the plane's specialties. There are teletype machines and at every seat there is either a telephone or a jack where a phone can be plugged in.

Communications and comfort. Attentive stewards, a general ambience of elegance. Good food served at low military PX prices. Little amenities. The bathroom counters are invitations to petty theft, filled as they are with samples of hair spray, colognes, razors, tooth paste, and miniature sewing kits.

Then there is the special luxury of knowing your trip will be crash-free. I mean, the President's plane? The plane that gets more mechanical attention than any vehicle in the world? In more than twenty-seven years of operation, there has never been a single accident or fatality aboard a Presidential plane. They're careful, that's why. Every time the President makes a trip, all air control people take note, and before the President takes a trip, the pilot (or co-pilot) of Air Force One flies the proposed route just to test it out. If such rationalizing does not work, the overall mood aboard Air Force One wipes out all fears. One is practically unaware of take-off and landing. There is no real sense of being up in the air. For the first time in my airborne experiences, I skipped the little silent prayer, good luck charms, and neurotic thoughts that have always been a part of take-off for me.

It felt good, surrounded by a Presidential party attired in slacks and sweaters and accompanied by wives and children. Ron Nessen's Korean-born wife Cindy was aboard, along with their toddler son, Edward. All the Rumsfelds were present: wife Joyce, daughters Marcy and Valerie, son Nicholas. Each one is good-looking and together they are an unusually beautiful family. Dr. Lukash was aboard with his wife—an attractive woman with the same trim physically fit look the long, lean doctor has—and their sixteen-year-old son. There was the Ford family, and some extra young people as well. Susan had brought along her friend Barbara Manfuso, Michael was with his wife, Gayle. David Kennerly brought a girl friend. There was a festive feeling.

And for some reason (mistake?) I had been seated with the "big boys" up front: Ron Nessen and Donald Rumsfeld, who were talking in hushed tones about how to handle the big news story of the day. A *New York Times* exposé on the CIA, which reported that the CIA had mounted a massive intelligence operation against American dissidents during the Nixon years in direct violation of the CIA charter, which forbids the Agency from engaging in espionage activities within the United States. Rumsfeld was lecturing, Ron was listening. I believe they knew the *Times* report was coming, but I think the details of the story itself caught them off guard. A few times Rumsfeld got up to check something with the President, and then returned to his seat. It was not a Ford Administration crisis, the violations had occurred under Nixon. But basically Rumsfeld was insisting that it had to be handled in the right way. I missed a lot because I had to go back and forth periodically to tell the press pool what was happening up front (a champagne

birthday party for Barbara Manfuso) but even though my eaves-
dropping was fragmented and uninvited, I managed to put in an
opinion. When I heard Rumsfeld suggest a statement on how "national security" was at stake, I said, "No way. That means nothing. National security is a catchall word for 'cover-up.'"

There was no response, not even a pause in their conversation.
("Ron, why don't we put off a statement and have a meeting when
we get to Vail?") I decided it was time to see if there were any
questions back in the press compartment.

"Who is paying for the guests' trips to Vail?" Fran Lewine
wanted to know. "Who pays for Barbara Manfuso? Mrs. Nessen?
Mrs. Rumsfeld?"

Most of the press questions I had to check out, but I knew the
answer to this one because I had researched guest fares already. I
had asked about Edward, and had been told he would have to pay
his own way if he traveled on Air Force One. I told the reporters
that the families were paying their own way.

On my next trip to my seat, I relayed the question and answer casually to my traveling companions. Unlike my last offering, this
one drew an instantaneous response. Both Rumsfeld and Nessen
became furious.

"Why didn't you coordinate a question like that with our
offices?"

"Because I knew the answer; I had checked on Edward." Anger. "Wasn't that the correct answer? Was I wrong?"

No response.

The anger intensified with each question.

My spirits came down along with Air Force One's landing gear.
Welcome to Colorado.

I stepped from Air Force One to a chopper, there to take me and
the press pool to Vail. From safety to suicide. Almost literally.
There was a blizzard, and visibility was non-existent and whereas
Air Force One does not crash, choppers do.

"One crashed just recently."

"The Secret Service chopper."

"When Nixon was President."

Such were the reassuring mumbles of my terrified companions.
When I saw Helen Thomas, who has flown on many an unsafe vehicle actually cross herself, I said all the little silent prayers I had
not used on Air Force One. It worked.

Welcome to Vail.

Vail is a winter wonderland—for those who sell thermal underwear. My New England background is showing. On the basis of about two hours experience, however, it appears that Colorado cold is more than a dip in temperature. It is winter in an active state of assault—an aggressive, piercing frigidity. It hurts! And it appears that the weather and I will be spending a lot of time together, since I have been assigned to the Hilton Hotel, far away from both the Fords and the press room, and since no transportation has been provided for me to get around town.

Welcome to Vail.

## JANUARY 1, 1975

It has been a nice respite for the Fords. This is their sixth family Christmas in Vail, and although it is impossible for the President of the United States to spend a quiet family vacation any place, the Fords have come as close to that goal here as is possible. A snowy holiday surrounded by good friends means relaxation for the vacationers. But it spells exhaustion for those whose job it is to feed the details to the ravenous press corps.

The fact is, when nothing sensational happens, nothing becomes sensational. ("The Ford's Vail Christmas tree, in the living room, right in front of the fireplace, was provided by the Vail Associates and decorated by the wives of the Rotary Club. The ornaments include a little tree made out of dough, a hand-carved chimney sweep, a round disc made by children. . . .") I have become the Sherlock Holmes of trivia. Under my magnifying glass, for example, a "casual dinner with friends" is rapidly transformed into breath-taking details like: "Steaks, french potato balls, stuffed tomatoes and Grand Marnier Soufflé."

The investigation begins with appropriate subtlety.

"Hello, this is Sheila Weidenfeld, Mrs. Ford's Press Secretary. I understand you are having a little party tonight for the Fords and I hate to bother you, but, well, you know the press is curious . . ."

Charm, friendly persuasion, gradually intensifying pressure—these are my weapons. My goal is to compel the women of Vail to reveal their deepest secrets. ("Oxtail consommé with sherry, lamb

à la palewi, endive salad, strawberries Moscow.") You must understand, madame, if you are entertaining the President of the
United States, there can be no surprises. No detail is too private.
No detail is too boring. Before the party begins, the working press
must know not only who is coming, but how they spell it, and
where they went to school, and how they know the Fords, and
what they do for a living. And no abstractions! What exactly does
the manufacturer make? What has the architect designed? How
*many* oil wells?

"Is it *your* son who is a member of the Colorado State Legisla-
ture? When will the guests arrive? What are you serving? What
does 'Colorado-grass-fed tenderloin of beef steer' taste like? Could
you translate the French for me please? Is that a white wine?"

Every day, endless phone calls produce scribbles on thousands
of pieces of paper, which are then organized into one long information sheet for press distribution: "The Fords tonight will be guests
of Fitzhugh and Eileen Scott. . . ."

When I am not supersleuthing, I am choreographing. My biggest
production number to date was "Mrs. Ford goes shopping." The
press grouped at the specified street corner at the appointed hour,
and then, marching several paces behind, they followed Mrs. Ford
to the Gondola Ski shop. Mrs. Ford entered and began looking at
the clothes on display. I brought in the writing press, who watched
Mrs. Ford looking at the clothes on display. I brought in the still
photographers who took pictures of Mrs. Ford looking at the
clothes on display. And then I brought in the camera crews who
took moving pictures of Mrs. Ford looking at the clothes on display.

Christmas morning was a bigger challenge, because of the sheer
potential for details (who gave whom what?) and because Michael
and Gayle Ford insisted there be no pictures. Christmas morning
was a private family affair, they said. This naturally heightened
both curiosity and suspicion. Without pictures, how can you be
*sure* they're sitting down to "eggs, sausage, toast, muffins and
juice?" To add to the confusion, the Fords have a family tradition
where they each choose straws to see who fills whose stocking, and
then they buy little presents and prank gifts as fillers. The interest
potential of this tradition alone is mind-boggling.

So my assignment was formidable: who chose whose stocking

and what clever things did who put in whose stocking? To say nothing of who gave whom what and who got what from whom? What a day.

I began the research ahead of time by securing Mrs. Ford's gift list and promising not to let the reporters know, for example, that the President was getting brass book ends from Williamsburg, Virginia, before he found out himself. On Christmas morning, I decided I would begin with my closest family ally other than Mrs. Ford.

"Hello, this is Sheila. Can I speak to Susan?"

Susan proved a valuable source ("I gave mother three pairs of bedroom slippers, one beige, one red, and one black, and I gave Dad a turtleneck sweater"). Susan then passed the phone to Jack ("a blouse and a skirt mother can wear when friends come over") who passed the phone to Steve ("it's a piece of wood, whittled into a scene by Henry Larum in Montana") who handed the receiver to Michael ("a bracelet from Massachusetts made out of a whale's tooth") and gradually, the mysteries of this private family Christmas began to unfold into one gigantic news release. ("Susan filled Jack's stocking, Gayle filled Steve's stocking, Jack filled Mrs. Ford's stocking, Mrs. Ford filled the President's stocking . . . .") Some of the more obscure details were harder to come by ("Who was it who gave the President the sugarless chocolate candy for his diet?") but by the end of Christmas day, I had the satisfaction of knowing that no gift had been left unturned . . . and of being able to report that the Fords had roast turkey with ham stuffing, mashed potatoes with gravy, buttered fresh green peas, cranberry salad, hot dinner rolls, and pecan pie à la mode.

My prime research tool has been the telephone, the one in the corner of the very crowded, very noisy press room. Ron Nessen has a nice private office, but who's complaining? Having no desk heightens the challenge. Besides, working under stress is a perfect follow-up to traveling. I still have no transportation but I have acquired two things since my arrival: Edward, who flew out last week, and appropriately warm ski-wear. It helps.

Or so we told ourselves New Year's Eve. Edward and I had been invited to the Fords' for New Year's Eve, and although we had no car and there were no taxis, we thought we would have no trouble getting there because the Vail bus could drop us off within the equivalent of several city blocks of where they were staying. But the buses were not running. We waited in the freezing cold (it was below zero) for what seemed an interminable amount of time outside our hotel. No bus. We tried hitchhiking. Nobody wanted to pick us up. We decided to walk and flag a passing bus down en route. For forty minutes we walked, my long dress picking up patches of snow from the ground. We were two thirds of the way there when a bus came by. It was overflowing with people but we didn't care. We jumped on—never did get inside—and clung to each other and everyone else for dear life on the bus steps. Everyone was in a holiday mood, singing, joking, screaming, making noise—except for these two frozen waifs on the bus steps, who were en route to being wined and dined by the President of the United States.

*Chapter Three*
JANUARY, 1975:

# UPSTAIRS, DOWNSTAIRS

*JANUARY 3, 1975*

"Actually, the East Wing is *outside* the White House," sneer the President's advisors.

"Mrs. Ford can't see you today, can't see you today, can't see you today," chirps Nancy Howe.

"I have complete access," my voice pleads as the press choruses in the background, "Credibility, credibility, credibility."

It's a nightmare with daytime validity. After losing sleep in Vail contemplating the realities of the scenario, I've made a New Year's resolution: there will be some changes made.

I have assured the press, time and again, that Nancy Howe is no problem. Well, she is. And if I lied about it to the reporters, it was only because I was lying about it to myself.

I have been weak. I called it "being professional" and "being sensible." (After all, Mrs. Ford can have a best friend and a best Press Secretary without conflict.) I called it "respecting privacy" (I don't think a Press Secretary should just barge in unannounced). I called it "being practical" (there's no reason Mrs. Ford has to be disturbed for every question I need answered). But the fact is, I have been weak. And a combination of events has helped me see the light.

First of all, there is Nancy Howe herself, and the girlish giggles of her "travels with Petunia" anecdotes.

Then there was the Maxine Cheshire flap just before we left Washington. Maxine had a question. I called Mrs. Ford for the answer. Nancy answered the question instead ("Mrs. Ford is resting."). The answer was wrong. Maxine yelled "credibility!" Ron Nessen announced that "from now on the West Wing will handle all Maxine Cheshire inquiries." And I made a mental note: No more Nancy Howe answers.

Then there was happenstance. Nancy was not invited to Vail, and I got my first taste of how wonderful it was to *really* have "complete access to Mrs. Ford." Questions were handled quickly and efficiently. There was no emotional red tape. Press coverage was simplified. And Mrs. Ford, frankly, seemed a good deal happier. We got closer, and I realized the closeness was very helpful in my job.

And then, the last straw. On the trip home on Air Force One, David Kennerly showed me an article by Betty Beale, a *Washington Star* society reporter, on the portrait of Mrs. Ford painted by John Ulbricht, which will be unveiled in a few weeks. Nancy is a close friend of Betty Beale and had given her the story. I went directly to Mrs. Ford's cabin and we talked about it. This was not the first time Betty Beale had gotten a special handout and I had told both Mrs. Ford and Nancy before that it had to stop. It is not fair to other reporters who cover the First Lady to give special scoops to friends. It hurts my relationship with the White House press corps. It cuts into my job, which is Press Secretary. Most important, it is counterproductive; Betty Beale is a society reporter with limited circulation. Even a small story, like the portrait, could be handled in a way that makes the story meaningful and the coverage national. Mrs. Ford agreed. I returned to Washington feeling good about the New Year and my New Year's resolution.

Today I decided to proceed, literally and figuratively. I forced myself to go upstairs to talk to Mrs. Ford. (A casual gesture. Everybody else does it all the time. No more weakness. Happy New Year.)

I found Mrs. Ford in her bedroom with Nancy, finishing the process of unpacking Mrs. Ford's clothes from Vail.

"Good morning!" I said cheerfully.

"Sheila!" said Mrs. Ford with a warm smile. "Come on in."

I did and there was an explosion. A human explosion.

"What is this business of accusing me of talking to Betty Beale? Betty is my friend. I can talk to whomever I want!" Nancy was hysterical.

I'm not sure what it was that shocked me so. The tone? The anger? Screaming has never been my style, and for a person who believes in suppression, the decibel level alone was devastating. The audience and the setting added to my discomfort. A cat fight in the Presidential bedroom in front of Mrs. Ford!

My voice was in control, but my words were sharp.

"Most of my friends are reporters, Nancy, but it is important to draw the line—"

"Yes, and I'll tell you, I don't think you're doing a very good job," she shouted. "That Associated Press story on Susan was terrible."

I can't remember all the words. I was keenly aware of just wanting them to stop. I felt the kind of helpless humiliation that accompanies adolescence. She was completely out of control. But I was by no means in control. At last I got my wish. It stopped.

"I'm leaving," she said. "I'm going and I may even be gone for the rest of the day."

Exit.

Silence.

Mrs. Ford and I stared at each other. She began talking about the Betty Beale story. I didn't want to. Either we should say out loud that something very peculiar had just happened, or we should completely change the subject.

I changed the subject and pulled out my planned agenda. "The President is signing the executive order making this International Women's Year this Thursday, and I really think this is an excellent time to get involved in the women's rights issue."

Empty words. I could get up no enthusiasm. When Nancy walked back into the room ten minutes later, I was relieved to have an excuse to leave.

What does Nancy want? Why does Mrs. Ford keep her around? Sympathy? Gratitude for her devotion? Is Mrs. Ford just too weak to get rid of her? Does Mrs. Ford realize that I'm right?

I went back to my office to mull it over, but I never got around to it. I was greeted by a visitor: Susan had come to talk. Apparently she found having Gardner visit her in Vail was a social hindrance. (Mrs. Ford says thus far Michael's wife Gayle is the only one of her children's dates to survive a vacation in Vail.) Susan wants to date other people, but she finds it difficult to meet new people in the White House. We didn't get to talk about it much because Gardner suddenly arrived in my office. I have no idea what *he* came to talk about.

Between the morning histrionics in the Presidential bedroom and my "Dear Abby" youth counseling session, it's been a peculiar day. I had no idea "providing the nation a window on the First Family" would mean producing my first soap opera.


## JANUARY 6, 1975

"Would anyone like coffee or tea or something else to drink?" Mrs. Ford asked. The butler took orders and quietly served us as we talked. I was sitting on the West Hall sofa, next to Susan Porter, Mrs. Ford's Appointments Secretary, who had her schedules spread out over her lap. Nancy Howe sat in a chair next to me. The others sat in chairs that had been placed in a semi-circle—Mrs. Ford to the right of the sofa, Social Secretary Nancy Lammerding, Marba Perrott, the Correspondence Secretary. Besides Mike Farrell, the director of the Visitors Office, the only other male in attendance at the staff meeting was Head Usher Rex Scouten, a handsome man with strong, firm features, thick salt-and-pepper hair, and an all-consuming dedication to his job, which is the management of the Executive Mansion.

It was announced that John Ulbricht, who had painted Mrs. Ford's portrait, would be in Washington for about a week and would sketch the President.

I said I had a slightly different subject I wanted to bring up: Mrs. Ford's direction. "Mrs. Ford is doing too much and too little. We have to either skip the ceremonial gestures or make them meaningful. I think we should plan for the months ahead, defining Mrs. Ford's areas of interest and then thinking about how to direct those interests.

Yes. Someone said that Clem Conger, the White House Curator, felt Ulbricht's portrait of Mrs. Ford was too large. He hoped the President's portrait would not be that large.

"Wouldn't it be wonderful," I asked, "if Mrs. Ford could be known as the woman who was First Lady when the Equal Rights Amendment was passed?"

Yes. Clem Conger has a whole theory about portrait sizes, they said. He thinks that the least significant Presidents have the largest official White House portraits. Case in point: President Fillmore's portrait is eight feet high.

## JANUARY 9, 1975

The *National Enquirer* called today. That is not unusual. At least one *National Enquirer* reporter calls every day, and usually the number is closer to three or four. Since I frequently tell them to put their requests in writing, they send me lots of letters, too.

The *Enquirer* is part of a whole group of commercial ventures that seems to understand mass mentality well enough to overcome whatever inadequacies they have as news gatherers. I have been surprised at how often the *National Enquirer* people call, as I thought many of their stories were sourceless, complete fabrications.

Now it appears that my original assumption was not far off base. Today's call from the *Enquirer* office announced that they had a picture of Betty Ford holding the winning caricature from their President-Ford caricature contest. Would I like to see the picture before they publish it?

Definitely. Most definitely.

My curiosity was intensified by the fact that I knew Betty Ford had never held the winning caricature in their contest.

A slight young man with a British accent (practically all the *National Enquirer* people who call me are British) arrived at my office with what was obviously a doctored photograph. It was an old shot of Mrs. Ford (she looked dumpy, so it must have been taken before her diet) with the winning caricature inserted in her hand.

"Ridiculous," I told the man. "This is a phony."

Finally he admitted it, but gave me an ultimatum. "It's up to you," he said in his clipped accent. "Do you want us to run this or take another picture?"

My answer of course was, "Neither." But I did not give him that answer until after I had Karl Schumacher, Mrs. Ford's photographer, take a picture of the doctored *Enquirer* photo. He was trying to bully me; why not return the bluff?

I doubt that they will run the photo, but the whole thing infuriates me every time I think of it. What nerve!

I'm getting more and more skeptical about what I read in the papers these days. And more and more amazed at how difficult it is to erase erroneous reporting.

*McCalls* called me this morning. They want to do a story on Mike and Gayle, a story they plan to have come out "about the time Gayle's baby is due."

## JANUARY 10, 1975

"Anything you want to tell us today, Sheila? Any *important* thing?" Ron Nessen laughed and leaned back in the chair behind his desk, his feet up. We all laughed. Many of Ron's staff meetings ended with his taking a kidding jab at me, or my taking a kidding jab at him. Today there were about ten or twelve people present at the staff meeting. Some sat on the sofa, others around a round table. A fire sparkled from his office fireplace. It was the regular morning meeting, set up to go over news items that might come up at the press briefing and discuss ways to handle it.

"Mrs. Ford is getting ready to become actively involved in International Women's Year, specifically the passage of the Equal Rights Amendment," I said casually, scanning the faces for reaction. "She may even be doing some traveling to different states to prod the legislators to pass the resolution."

I was a little surprised to hear that, as I had not really said that to myself before telling the group, but most of the people at the table yawned.

"Is that meddling in states' rights?" asked one staff member. He was more curious than concerned. "I mean to have the President's wife pressing state government leaders?"

I'll check.

## JANUARY 11, 1975

"How did he get to be head of the Military Affairs Office?" I asked Ric Sardo. We had just inspected the latest Gulley "girlie" poster on display.

"I don't know. I think his first White House job was sergeant in charge of the bomb shelter."

"The what?"

"The bomb shelter. In the basement."

I'd never heard of it. Nor had I heard the rumor that went with it—that several years ago someone in the East Wing press office was fired because she was caught having sex in the bomb shelter with a social aide.

My curiosity was definitely aroused.

Ric led the way. The bomb shelter, it turns out, is in the basement of the White House in the East Wing. It was put in after World War Two for Truman, and, although I don't think it could do much good in today's kind of warfare, it is still preserved in the protective security of the military. You don't just walk down the stairs and enter. You have to announce yourself to the guard.

You then enter what resembles a 50's motel: a few bedrooms, cramped space, a conference room. Everything is covered in plastic. But still guarded.

## JANUARY 13, 1975

"I know Mrs. Ford is on her way to Bethesda Naval Hospital," UPI reporter Helen Thomas announced to me over the telephone at 8 A.M. this morning. "My question is, 'why?' "

My question was "How?" How did she find out? Were there really Helen Thomas sources everywhere, as I had heard? Is it true that the FBI has fewer informants than Helen Thomas?

Actually her secret source was much more interesting to me than the secret story she had uncovered. Mrs. Ford was just going in for a regular check-up. I had tried to keep it quiet, not for medical reasons, but just so the press wouldn't bother Mrs. Ford at the hospital.

As it was, the tests went well and the results were excellent. The doctors said there was no evidence of a recurrence of the malignancy, and said she could take on more activities. Mrs. Ford said that the results were so positive they made her feel physically better.

She celebrated with a portrait unveiling of the picture John Ulbricht had painted of her which (Clem Conger is right) is big, about six feet high, but wonderfully sensitive, moody, I think, as opposed to glamorous. It captures an inner feeling, a sense of soul. The unveiling was followed by a dinner party for about thirty close friends and staff, and Edward and I were invited. I had never been entertained at a dinner party at the White House and the experience was special. Butlers scurry around providing service that is both smooth and subtle. You get your food without being quite sure how you got it, because as you walk through a buffet line, you are so mesmerized by other sensations, the exquisite look of the wallpaper, the glow of the chandelier, the feel of the delicate china between your fingers, contrasted with the balanced heaviness of the silver. Everything is perfect and everyone is beautiful and elegant because they are part of the most beautiful and elegant setting in the world.

Even the talk of Michigan's football season (this is, after all, the Ford White House!) seemed somewhat lofty.

The guest of honor was the portrait painter, Ulbricht, who was there with his wife and his sister. Originally from Chicago, Ulbricht now lives in Spanish Mallorca. He's in town not only for the unveiling of Mrs. Ford's portrait, but also to begin work on one of the President. He's doing one of Susan, too. He is appealing for artistic reasons but he is also a terribly practical portrait painter for those with busy schedules, because his technique does not involve long sittings. With Mrs. Ford's picture, for example, he says he spent two days (about four hours each day) taking photographs and sketching her as she moved around the garden and house in Alexandria, returned to Mallorca and painted the portrait.

The Rockefellers were there. Happy Rockefeller, who underwent two mastectomies less than two months ago, seemed to be completely recovered, bright and sparkling. She told me that, like Mrs. Ford, she has gotten an endless stream of requests from cancer groups across the United States to speak or appear before them, but that she had been turning them all down because she had no time. She said she was really busy with the Rockefellers' two sons and additions she was making in the Vice Presidential residence.

There were automobile people from Michigan who are old close friends, and there were old close friends who are also new Presidential staff members, like Counsel to the President Phil Buchen and his wife, Bunny. The President went to grammar school with Bunny Buchen and set up a law practice with Phil before he ran for Congress. They are an interesting contrast, the Buchens. Phil, white-haired and distinguished, looks more like a judge than a lawyer. He had polio as a child and walks slowly, methodically, with two canes, which somehow intensifies his serious, judicial appearance. Bunny, on the other hand, is a live wire: fast talking, vivacious, thoroughly enjoying every minute in the limelight.

There were reminders of Ford's old status and indications of the new. On one side of the room Robert Hartmann, *Los Angeles Times* reporter turned Congressional assistant, turned Presidential assistant, leaned against the wall, drink in hand, talking politics with those around him. His many years with Gerald Ford have earned him an important White House position and Mrs. Ford's deep resentment, which is only normal considering the years he controlled her husband's comings and goings.

On the other side of the room, surrounded by a group of "new guard," stood Donald Rumsfeld, younger than Hartmann, trimmer, and shinier. Rumsfeld has known Ford a long time, too (as a "Young Turk" member of Congress he helped make Ford Minority Leader) but he is in the White House for his professional credentials, not for his personal affiliation. A Congressman at twenty-nine, he showed enough promise to become a Nixon Cabinet member at thirty-seven, and then showed enough foresight to leave for a NATO post in Brussels before the Nixon Cabinet crumbled. He was one of the first people Ford called when he became President, and he is the first person Ford calls every day. He and Bob Hartmann are usually on opposite sides of the room.

Ron Nessen was there with his wife as were Ford's old friends and political cronies from Michigan, Senator Griffin and Representative Cederberg and their wives. Nancy Howe was everywhere, moving from one guest to the next, talking and laughing non-stop, glancing every so often in Mrs. Ford's direction to see whom the First Lady was with.

Nancy was impeccably dressed, as she always is, her hair meticulously in place, her make-up ingeniously applied, just right—

immaculate in appearance, manic in manner. Overpowering.Her husband, Jimmy Howe, by contrast, was underpowering. He looked like the former military man he was, somewhat stiff, conservatively dressed, slender with a soft southern drawl. Edward tried commiserating with him about how "our wives are spending more time here than at home," but Edward said he got the feeling Jimmy Howe felt the investment was worth it. He liked being in the White House. He preferred discussing other things such as the fact that it was his theory that a warm climate made for a weaker people than a cold climate, and that the history of the world was the history of colder climates conquering warmer climates. (A strange theory for a southerner—an ominous outlook for the war in Vietnam.) Aside from this conversation, he spent much of the evening alone, quietly taking it all in, absorbing his surroundings, and seeming very comfortable in his self-inflicted solitude. He and Nancy arrived together but spent the rest of the time apart. It was as though each was delighted to have made it—to be guests in the White House—but each was savoring the moment a different way.

Mrs. Ford's Social Secretary, Nancy Lammerding, was there with her fiancé, Nick Ruwe. A tall blond woman in her late thirties, Nancy worked in the White House press office under Nixon, and then at the State Department before coming back to the White House now under the Fords, this time as chief official party giver. State Dinners are her prime concern, and she is a social strategist of formidable skill. She has a flair for giving good parties, and, obviously pleased to attend one that she had not had to plan, she mingled well in the group, an amusing, extroverted raconteuse.

It was an elegant evening. But it was also a very comfortable evening with much laughter and people sitting on the floor as well as the beautifully upholstered finery—a tribute to the mood set by our host and hostess. Only the Fords could entertain about thirty people in the White House and have it feel like a cozy family gathering.

## JANUARY 16, 1975

The first telephone call I ever received at the White House came from NBC's Barbara Walters. She wanted to put in an early bid for an interview with Mrs. Ford.

It was a fluke that I received the call at all, since it came about two weeks before I was to begin work. The body of my predecessor was not yet cold. Quite the contrary. I took the phone call in what was still Helen Smith's office as Helen listened. She had been in the midst of explaining to me what the duties of a Press Secretary were.

No one beats Barbara Walters to the punch.

I was a little embarrassed and a little amused. But I was also impressed. I was impressed by her drive. I was impressed that she had dialed the number herself, rather than have a secretary do it. It was the gesture of an ambitious, hard-working woman rather than a television star.

In the weeks since, I have been impressed by her persistence. She has called often. But Mrs. Ford, I feel, has to develop some strong feelings about people issues before she is ready for a Barbara Walters interview. And so I have put Barbara Walters off. Or tried to.

"If not an interview, Sheila, then perhaps some kind of televised White House tour?"

The ghosts of former White House tours loomed before me— Jackie Kennedy, Tricia Nixon. Too stale. Then I thought about the tour Mrs. Ford had given me.

"Barbara, how about a tour of the family quarters, a light, personal tour as opposed to an historical one?"

Barbara was ecstatic. I was a little hesitant. I knew if the idea were to work, Mrs. Ford had to be completely at ease. I suggested Barbara come and meet Mrs. Ford and see how they hit it off. The meeting was scheduled for lunch today.

Barbara arrived right on time, and we sat in my office for quite a while. We talked shop. We gossiped about mutual acquaintances at NBC and about the rigors of a job in network television. She finds that in addition to the normal demands of her job on the "Today" show, the incredible hours, she is under the constant pressure of having to prove herself. I asked if she could see herself doing something else, something more than the "Today" show. She doesn't know. She said that frankly she thinks her career may be over soon. She's getting older, and, she said, people don't like to watch women age on camera.

The talk was interesting. It was also an excellent delaying tactic. Nancy Howe had called me just before Barbara arrived to tell me that Mrs. Ford was not feeling good and that she was not sure she could meet with us, and if the meeting did take place, it would have to be a short one and not for lunch.

I finally got the call to come upstairs. Mrs. Ford looked wonderful. We sat in the West Hall—the Fords' living room—and talked. I don't know if Barbara was consciously attempting to make Mrs. Ford relax, or if she herself was just responding to the warmth between them, but Barbara was extremely open and personal. There was serious talk about the anxieties of child rearing. Mrs. Ford mentioned how she was trying to maintain a sense of normalcy for Susan in the White House. Barbara talked about her daughter, Jacqueline, and how she misses her terribly when she travels, but still doesn't like to take Jacqueline with her on assignment because she does not think the disruption is good for her. She wants Jacqueline to have as routine and normal a life as possible. No matter how bad her schedule is, Barbara said, she sets aside a certain time to spend with Jacqueline every day, and she allows no interruptions during that time. Her daughter is very important to her.

There was also lots of laughter, and some serious talk about their own childhood experiences. Mrs. Ford brought up her interest in doing something about mental retardation and Barbara talked about her own retarded sister, and how difficult it had been, for herself and for her whole family.

The women just clicked. Mrs. Ford looked radiant; she was enjoying herself. I suddenly realized how dull it has been for her to be isolated upstairs. She was hungry for mental stimulation. I decided that whether or not the tour came off, I was going to do this more often—bring interesting people upstairs.

After about an hour, Mrs. Ford took us on the tour. Barbara was really excited by the whole thing, from Lyndon's bathroom telephone to the Fords' double bed. Mrs. Ford also thoroughly enjoyed herself. And I would have enjoyed myself, had I not felt so frustrated about being cameraless. It was just too good to lose, so easygoing and unrehearsed.

Nancy Howe came back and was visibly surprised we had not left. ("Mrs. Ford has a doctor's appointment, you know.") Mrs. Ford suggested we eat lunch instead.

Nancy Howe returned during lunch, and Barbara, ever the talk show hostess, tried to bring her into the conversation. "Sheila and I were thinking this would be the perfect set for a television show," Barbara said merrily. Nancy snapped back that she thought it was much too private a place.

"Who exactly *is* Nancy Howe?" Barbara asked as we were leaving.

"Don't worry about her." I was surprised at my tone of assurance.


## JANUARY 22, 1975

Maxine Cheshire reports that in the middle of a meeting between President Ford and Henry Kissinger in the Oval Office, Susan barged in to ask for some money.

It is news to me. But my real question, when I saw the story in The *Washington Post,* was: Who made it news for Maxine? Her good friend Nancy Howe, who perhaps overheard the incident being discussed in the family quarters?

"Absolutely *not!*" insisted Nancy Howe. "As a matter of fact, I corrected Maxine's version, which was that Susan sprang out from under the President's desk!"

(Shades of Caroline Kennedy?)

"It had to be David Kennerly," she said. "He was no doubt in there snapping pictures. No one else other than the President and Kissinger would have witnessed it."

I found Kennerly in Dr. Lukash's office and pounced. "Absolutely *not!*" he fumed and then rushed out in a state of fury, apparently to challenge Nancy Howe to a duel.

They are frequent adversaries. It is all part of the "Upstairs-Downstairs" set-up around here. "Downstairs" in the White House is the office. "Upstairs" is the Family quarters. Downstairs people are sometimes invited upstairs for a drink at the end of the day, to continue a Presidential conversation after hours.

But there are also "Upstairs" people: Nancy Howe who "works" out of the Family quarters; Dr. Lukash, whose work frequently entails visiting the Family quarters; Ric Sardo who often stops in to chat, and David Kennerly, whose candid picture-taking enables him to bridge the gap between Downstairs and Upstairs on a regular basis. Among Upstairs people, the favorite game is musical chairs: Who gets the seat closest to the First Family?

Dr. Lukash's closeness is based on his profession. He is incredibly dedicated to his work. (He even goes over to George Washington University Hospital from time to time to practice in their emergency room, just to stay on top of his skills and "be prepared in the event of an emergency.") The man is at the White House when the President arises just about every morning, and usually does not leave until the President goes to bed every night. (He has a staff of doctors who could take over some of that.) That means that in the event of a State Dinner, he's around until the early hours of the morning. I don't see how he has any other life left.

During the day, he is usually in his office, sitting, reading, or treating other patients, but always close to the electronic box that lists the First Family "principals" by their code names and tells where each is at all times during the day. His office is right across from the elevator to the Family residence, and whenever his box shows that the President is on his way home, Lukash stands outside just to check out his patient as he bounds by for the elevator and give the President a chance to say "I have a headache. . . ." When Mrs. Ford is sick, he is at her bedside. The President is rarely ill at all, but Lukash takes pains to insure that he stays healthy. He has carefully worked out a diet and exercise program for the President, for example, which includes special knee exercises (to undo some of the damage done by football injuries in the past) where weights are strapped to each of the President's legs and raised twenty-five times each, followed by twenty-five push-ups, twenty-five sit-ups, and fifteen minutes on the exercycle each day. He monitors the President's activities, too, suggesting a swim or a game of golf or some other exercise when he feels he needs it. (And he *still* finds time to take care of Susan's cramps!) In short, Dr. Lukash is devoted (fanatic?). He is part Marcus Welby, M.D., part servant, part savant, and part something I can't yet figure out. At any rate, he is a frequent Upstairs person on house call.

Ric Sardo is often there because he is a sort of Presidential chaperone. He is also close to Mrs. Ford. I still don't know what military aides do (they act as liaison between the President and the military but what does that mean?). I just know that there are four of them and they rotate so one is always assigned to the President. I also have been told they carry the "football," an object so called because it looks like a football that is placed in a black attaché case and contains highly sensitive defense material to be used in the event of war. And I also know that ceremonial football carrying is not enough for Ric Sardo, who enjoyed being a part of the Ford inner circle during the Vice Presidency, and who now finds the limitations of his job frustrating, especially the limitations imposed by Rumsfeld who feels Sardo is trying to get "too close to the Fords." Ric is frequently upstairs trying to get closer.

Nancy and David go there partly for work and partly to be familial. Both linger and each is very protective of his or her closeness to the family. This creates both competition and friction. When David tried to enhance his parents' trip to Washington by getting them on the invitation list for a State Dinner, Nancy Howe hit the ceiling and took pains to point out to Mrs. Ford that it was an outrageous request. David, on the other hand, often complains that Nancy is not good for Mrs. Ford, that she is overprotective of the First Lady and cuts Mrs. Ford off from her family and friends. He is supported by Susan, who complains bitterly that the giddy references to "Petunia" make her sick and Nancy's presence makes it difficult for her to have private conversations with her mother.

In terms of family acceptance, David wins the Upstairs competition. The Fords all like him and indulge his excesses with fond amusement. In the case of today's Nancy-David duel, he won hands down. As I was getting ready to leave the office, Mrs. Ford called. I could hear David in the background, talking and laughing. Obviously his mood had changed.

"I'm sorry," Mrs. Ford said. "I know how difficult it is for you when other people leak to the press, and I know Nancy is a constant problem. Everyone tells me she is. My kids don't like her; they complain that she regulates my time so much she even keeps them from seeing me. There are a lot of people over here who don't like her. And I know it's been difficult."

I was tempted to rush in and blurt out everything—how Nancy denied everyone access and then delighted in showing how close she was by telling the personal details of Mrs. Ford's life to everyone she came in contact with outside the White House.

I resisted the temptation.

"It has been hard," I said.

Mrs. Ford talked more. She felt grateful to Nancy for her devotion. She needed someone who could serve as a personal assistant, handling some of the little chores that are so time consuming. But she did not need a shield who blocked her from human contact. Nor did she need a substitute, someone who tried to be best friends with Mrs. Ford's best friends. She had purposely prevented Nancy from accompanying her to Vail. Nancy had told her repeatedly she was ready, willing, and able to leave at any time.

I was supportive of the point of view, and fought off the overwhelming urge to contribute to the data.

I still wonder who Maxine Cheshire's source was. Maxine would be delighted.

*JANUARY 31, 1975*

Lo and behold: the Equal Rights Angel has been listening!

A few days ago, I received a phone call from Doug Bailey and John Deardourff, who identified themselves as two political consultants who have been hired by the National Organization of Business and Professional Women to help get the Equal Rights Amendment ratified. Could they come and see me?

Could they!

They came today and brought with them a slide presentation to illustrate the progress of the Equal Rights Amendment. They said that the general impression seems to be that the Republican Party is against passage. Would Mrs. Ford be interested in trying to correct that image?

Would she!

It was one of the most effective presentations I have ever seen. Detail for detail, state by state, they explained to me what had been done, what was needed. If she were interested, there was something Mrs. Ford could do immediately. North Dakota was scheduled to vote on the issue Monday (just three days away). They had brought with them the draft of a letter Mrs. Ford could send to William Kretschmar, the major proponent of ratification in the North Dakota House of Representatives, expressing Mrs. Ford's support for ratification.

"Would Mrs. Ford's lobbying in any way create a national versus states' rights conflict?" I asked.

"No," they said. "After all, we're lobbying for state passage of a national amendment to the Constitution. There's no conflict."

They left. I had the letter typed up for Mrs. Ford's signature. I told Mrs. Ford that the letter was coming and how excited I was, that this was the perfect time for her to get into the Equal Rights Amendment issue.

Then I thought. This was a beginning; I could feel it. But there could be more. The letter was a gesture—an important gesture—but a gesture nonetheless. Someone else's words. Why use someone else's words?

I picked up the phone and called Max Friedersdorf, the assistant to the President for legislative affairs. I told him that Mrs. Ford might be calling legislators around the country to urge them to vote in favor of the Equal Rights Amendment. I told him he needn't worry about any states' rights conflict, because it is a national amendment she is lobbying for.

*Chapter Four*
FEBRUARY, 1975:

# Peaks to Pits

*FEBRUARY 3, 1975*

Doug Bailey called me yesterday. The Illinois Senate had the ERA locked up in committee, and was scheduled to vote on February fourth as to whether or not the measure should be released. Senator William Harris, the ranking Republican minority member of the committee was against releasing it. Would Mrs. Ford. . . .

Yes, but how? No more form letters. They are cold and distant. Washington, D.C., is just a postmark, Mrs. Ford is just a signature. If she's going to really convince anyone, she's got to have more of a personal impact.

All of which leads to phone calls, What do you do when you want action? When you want to get your point across immediately? You pick up the phone. Well, why should the President's wife be any different? When we find a situation like this one in Illinois where lobbying might help, we lobby verbally. We call the legislator directly, person to person. Mrs. Ford is good at persuasion because she has that quality rare in debate—she knows how to listen, and compassion often makes converts. Even if she doesn't convince the specific legislator, the phone call itself will be a subtle announcement of her stand on the issue.

No press announcements prior to the calls. If the White House reporters knew, it would look too much like a publicity stunt. Let the news travel back from the hinterlands.

The more I thought about it, the more excited I was about the whole idea. Surely one phone call was worth a hundred ERA receptions.

I called Mrs. Ford first thing this morning; Nancy Howe answered. "Mrs. Ford will call you back."

I red-tagged a memo with all the details to Mrs. Ford. (If one attaches a red tag, a White House memo is delivered to the person immediately.)

I called Mrs. Ford at 11:30. Again Nancy Howe. "Mrs. Ford will call you back after lunch."

It was 2:30 when we made contact. Mrs. Ford told me to come on up. I did, dragging Nancy Howe's secretary, Carolyn Porembka, with me so someone there could take notes on the call. I briefed Mrs. Ford, and I had the White House operator place the call. My nerves calmed down as I listened:

*Hello . . . yes, well, it is good to talk to you. . . . Oh, yes, he's an old pal of ours. I'm sorry to see him retire. I guess he wants to play golf! . . . Well, I'm calling because I know that you have the ERA in your committee and I am, of course, very interested in the enactment of ERA. I know you have feelings other than mine. . . . I'm just doing a little lobbying and I tell you, I checked it out very carefully to make sure that I'm not doing anything that is illegal. . . . Well, you know, sometimes you can vote something out of committee and perhaps you vote your convictions on the floor. I do think the Senate should have a chance to consider it as a whole, don't you. . . .*

Casual, smooth, warm—a nice tone for the first attempt. We have begun.

## FEBRUARY 5, 1975

Yesterday started normally enough. I called Mrs. Ford as I always do. She was not around. I said I'd call later. The press called to find out what was on the schedule. I said "Nothing official. Mrs. Ford is upstairs relaxing in the residence and she has no appointments."

At 12:15 the phone call I had been waiting for came through, Senator Harris from Illinois with good news: the ERA had cleared the committee 9–8. The Senate will vote on it next month. He said he had not voted for it because he had a deep, longstanding conviction that there was no need for a Constitutional amendment. But he told me he had been singularly impressed with what Mrs. Ford had to say on the subject, and that he had announced on the floor of the Senate that she had called him.

I called Mrs. Ford to tell her the good news. No answer. I was about to run upstairs and find her myself when I got a phone call from a reporter in New York City. "What is Mrs. Ford doing in New York City?"

"Where?"

"She has been spotted just now on Seventh Avenue in the heart of the fashion district."

Impossible, I thought to myself. I double talked, hung up, and called Rex Scouten, the head usher.

"Is Mrs. Ford in New York City?"

"Yes."

And my walls came tumbling down.

Why? For fun. She love clothes; Nancy loves clothes. They wanted a lark, a buying spree. (So much for WIN.) I could see them excitedly planning, talking about it all yesterday morning while I was red-tagging memos about a State Senator in Illinois. But why not tell me? An act of vengeance? Of defiance? Of thoughtlessness? Did she realize what an awful spot she's put me in? (Nancy did. I'll bet on that.)

Here I was, her Press Secretary, telling reporters she was here when she was there—off by about two hundred fifty miles. I was furious. I was hurt. I was humiliated. I was also in hot water. My mistress had fed me to the hungry wolves. Credibility credibility credibility. Any minute now, the news would hit the White House press.

Bam. It hit.

"Is Mrs. Ford in New York?"

"Yes."

"Why didn't you tell us?"

"I didn't know."

"Why did she go without telling you?"

"She wanted to see if she could go to New York and not be recognized, and she found out she couldn't."

The television producer writes fiction. Not a bad explanation under the circumstances. But I felt bad—really bad. I took it personally, because, frankly, there was no other way to take it. I spent a sleepless night, agonizing, raging, and contemplating resignation. And I bounced upstairs to the Family quarters this morning determined not to let any of it show.

"Gee. I tried to call you yesterday to tell you the great news, and I discovered you'd sneaked out on me!" (Laugh, clown, laugh.) "Seriously though," (fade smile somewhat, eye to eye contact imperative) "you really can't do that again. I have to know these things. It is impossible for you to go someplace and not attract attention. It completely destroys my credibility. And if that happens, I'll be no use to you."

She promised she would never do it again. And I believe her.

But once was too often.


## FEBRUARY 6, 1975

News from the war zone: chartered busloads of fundamentalist protestants and Roman Catholics have been arriving in Jefferson City, Missouri, for the past two days to tell legislators the Equal Rights Amendment would mean unrestricted abortions, homosexual marriages, "desexigrated" hospital and dormitory rooms, and a complete breakdown of the family. The Missouri House of Representatives is drowning in WWWW (Women Who Want to be Women) leaflets proclaiming, "Militant women are determined to liberate you—whether you want it or not!"

The Missouri House was to vote on the ERA today.

It looked shaky. There was Peg Miller, for example, a responsible Republican, one of the original sponsors of the bill, who was wavering because of the tremendous last-minute pressures from the anti-forces. The pro-ERA people felt she just needed a little bolstering.

She got some at 10:00 A.M.:

*Hello. . . . How are you, Mrs. Miller? . . . Now, don't be bowled over, we have to keep you on your feet! . . . Well, it's a pleasure talking to you. . . . I realize you're under a lot of pressure with the voters today, but I'm just calling to let you know that the President*

*and I are considerably interested. . . . Yes, we are both interested
in the outcome. . . . I think the ERA is so important. As a matter
of fact, the wife of the Prime Minister of Pakistan and I were discussing it at the State Dinner last night. She's very much for an ERA in
Pakistan. We had a really delightful time chatting about
it. . . . Yes, well, I know the agitators. . . . Oh, I am not a wild-
eyed Liberal on this. I enjoy being a wife and a mother and all those
things. That's not the point. . . . But women should have equal opportunities. I was very pleased to read in the paper this morning that
the Senate has confirmed Betty Southard Murphy as a member of the
National Labor Relations Board, and that she will become the first
woman chairman in the board's history . . . yes . . . yes
. . . Well, I know it's very difficult to have the pressure on both
sides, and, as you say, coming from a rural area, it is especially difficult. . . . But you know there are lots of women there too that want
to have equal rights. Oh yes, of course. Well, I think you have to vote
your conscience.*

*As I told my husband early in his career, if it were a case of voting
in a situation where, in fact, he felt the Democrats were right, he
should vote according to his conscience. . . .*

She made one more call, to Republican Bill Stoner, a bright
young man who had become, we were told, a little shaky at the arrival of busloads of constituents hostile to the amendment. Mrs.
Ford should be gentle. Mrs. Ford was very gentle.

A few hours later, we got the news: the House had approved the
measure. Representatives Miller and Stoner had both voted
"aye."

The excitement created new energy levels. I went over the details for tomorrow with Mrs. Ford. It will be a big day. First of all,
she has invited all White House staff to see the Deardourff/Bailey
slide presentation on the Equal Rights Amendment at 11:00 A.M. in
the Family Theater. We talked about the remarks she'll make as introduction. After that, I've set up an interview with her for Fran
Lewine and Helen Thomas. They've been after me for weeks, but
before Mrs. Ford got involved in the ERA, I frankly thought the interview would lack substance. We talked about that. Nancy Howe
even sounded enthusiastic when she called me to report that Mrs.
Ford's two follow-up telegrams had been sent to Representatives
Miller and Stoner. ("Thank you so much for helping make the
dream of equal rights for women a closer reality.")

And—at last—the news was coming back from the hinterlands. There is delight in accomplishment. There is also delight in having the answer to a question ready before the question comes up. I was ready. ("She just wanted them to know she was very much interested in the ERA.") It would be low key. Very low key. The phone calls began. Tom Chase of AP had heard from some people in Kansas that Mrs. Ford had called two Congressmen in Missouri. True? The UPI needed confirmation. Fran Lewine needed an aspirin. Why hadn't I *told* her that Mrs. Ford would be calling legislators?

What fun. Mrs. Ford felt good. I felt good. The office was buzzing. Little by little the news was traveling and everyone wanted to know the details. Well, nearly everyone.

A reporter from the *National Enquirer* called to ask, "Does Mrs. Ford believe in UFOs?"

## *FEBRUARY 7, 1975*

From the peaks to the pits.

Nancy Howe called at 10:00 A.M. Mrs. Ford was not feeling good. She probably would not make the slide briefing.

No. Impossible, Not today. Not the one time I had felt sure enough about her health and her convictions to tell the press she would be (not "might" be, but "would" be) at the slide presentation. Not the day of her very first scheduled interview. People were already lining up outside the East Wing Family Theater. I imagined Fran and Helen, their pens turning into daggers.

But most of all I pictured Nancy Howe, sitting upstairs persuading Mrs. Ford not to go. Nancy Howe, the barrier, the human blockade. What had *she* planned for today? Another trip to New York? I became even more furious. This was it. The last straw. I ran upstairs, ready for a fight.

But the villain turned out to be osteoarthritis.

The room was dark and Mrs. Ford was lying in bed, trying to rest, apparently, in hopes of making the slide presentation. She was obviously in great pain, for the first time I realized how great that pain was. She looked so pale, so weak, so different from the healthy woman of yesterday. She mumbled something about getting dressed and attending, but that was out of the question. Even if it had been physically possible, her appearance would have done her greater disservice than no appearance. My anger became self-directed. I guess, for the first time I realized what a tremendous obstacle her health was, and how courageous she was to be able to go through bouts like this, never knowing when they would come and for how long.

I came downstairs, and went right to the Family Theater.

"I'm Sheila Weidenfeld, Mrs. Ford's Press Secretary. Mrs. Ford is not able to be here herself. She has arthritis, and from time to time it flares up. . . ."

Next I spoke to Fran and Helen, who took the news surprisingly well. At 12:30, my phone rang. It was Mrs. Ford, who wanted to know how the slide presentation had gone. She still sounded terrible and I was touched by her concern.

Then it was time for the daily mood-breaker: a call from the *National Enquirer*. The paper's mascot, Lucky, had not been invited to Liberty's birthday party tomorrow. Could the *Enquirer* photograph Lucky and Liberty together sometime after the party?


## FEBRUARY 15, 1975

What is osteoarthritis anyway? Is it caused by muscular tension? Emotional tension? Both? Am I, in my tug of war with Nancy Howe, adding to the pressure that is creating it? Would Mrs. Ford prefer to relax and be Petunia?

No. Petunia is not a healthy mental state. Neither is passive political wife. This is a woman who has been living in someone else's spotlight too long. She is now in a position to do something and be someone in her own right, and if I have anything to say about it, she is going to do it and be it.

She is a little scared. That's why she steps back before stepping forward. That's why she hesitated the day Barbara Walters came for a visit. That's why she flew to New York last week. But little by little she is becoming more self-assured, and more excited by the accomplishment. And little by little, I keep pushing. In this situation, it just so happens, what is good for the Equal Rights Amendment is good for Mrs. Ford, too.

The State Legislatures of Georgia, Nevada, and Arizona all voted on ERA measures this week, and Mrs. Ford, neck brace and all, was at the phone:

*I know you come from a pioneering family and perhaps in that spirit, you can look at ERA as giving women at least a choice. . . .*

*I know you don't feel the way I do on this, but I admire the fairness with which you have approached it. . . .*

*Frankly, I enjoy being a mother and I am not about to burn my bra—I need it!*

*In a divorce case, why should a man pay alimony when his wife is perfectly able to go out and earn her own living? Why should he be stuck with it? In that area, you know, the ERA frees men.*

*We like to think of the Republican Party as being a leader in supporting the cause of basic human rights.*

Flattery, friendly persuasion, charm, all were used. To say nothing of that old political asset, the ability to chew the fat. Farmers learned about Steve's work taking care of cows on the ranch in Utah. For legislators with daughters, there was conversation on the cost of raising a girl: "It just isn't right that we pay so much to educate them, only to find that they don't have the same chance to use their education!" For the liberals, there was talk of her career before marriage, for those who thought the ERA would destroy families she waxed poetic on the joys of motherhood, occasionally throwing in: "Phyllis Schlafly only has two more kids than I have, you know."

The only one who outdid her at her own game was Senator Barry Goldwater:

*I'd love to come out to Phoenix, Barry, but you people wouldn't let me work there. . . . Yes, but I'm afraid my work would be against your religion. . . . I'm trying to get enough states to ratify the ERA. . . . I know what your position is, Mr. Goldwater! Yes . . . Yes. Well, you have a couple of daughters working. You wouldn't want them underpaid, would you? One of them is overpaid?. . . . Well, she is one of the few!*

The weekly totals were two to one against us: Only the Nevada House passed the ERA, but in terms of general victories, it's been a winning week. We have evoked response. The League of Women Voters has offered its services for source material requests for help from pro-ERA groups which have come in from all over the country, especially from local organizations in the states that will take up the measure this year. And the anti-ERA folk are coming in loud and clear. Anti-champion Phyllis Schlafly (head of Stop-ERA) has already telegrammed, and letters are pouring in from lesser antis.

And I love it. Because I believe controversy helps clear the air and clarify the issues. Because I think we're helping to activate ERA supporters at a time when the proponents had begun to lose steam. Because issues excite me more than hemlines.

And because Mrs. Ford seems to love it too.

## FEBRUARY 17, 1975

My phone began ringing tonight at about 9:30 with call after call from London. They were calling about the new romance. Is it true that rock star Rod Stewart had rented a private plane to fly to Washington from his New York City singing engagement to have dinner alone with Susan at the White House? That was, I told them, entirely possible. I knew nothing about Mr. Stewart's activities. But if he had gone to all that trouble, it was for naught, because he had never dined with Susan at the White House or any place else, for that matter.

Right after the first call, I checked my notes. Susan went to a Rod Stewart concert last Saturday night. I knew because Garvin Walsh of the Cellar Door (a Washington night spot) called to tell me where she and her friends would pick up their tickets. I knew nothing major happened because I had checked with the Secret Service detail. I knew she went with a group of friends. I knew we did not publicize her going. I knew she had had a good time.

Was that enough to know?

My phone rang again. "London, England, calling. . . ."

I called Susan.

No, she laughed, she was most certainly not in love with Rod Stewart. No, she had neither dined with him at the White House nor invited him to the White House. She had called to thank him for the free tickets he sent. That doesn't spell romance, does it?

Well, not in the American dictionary.

The calls were getting more and more hysterical. Knowing I was right and then carefully erasing all rumors was not enough. I called Pierre Lehu, who is with Stewart's public relations firm in New York City, and told him I didn't know who was responsible for putting out this ridiculous story, but he had better set the record straight.

Susan is less concerned about it than I am. She's absorbed in

something else these days—photography (which I find a more de-
sirable career aspiration than her other recent choice, marriage).
David Kennerly has been giving her lessons, and everywhere you
go around the White House you find the two of them giggling and
snapping pictures. He says, "She has a good eye." She says,
"He's a terrific teacher." And the reporters say "romance?" But
it's hard to fall in love with your little sister, and Susan is only seventeen, a good ten years younger than he.

It might be easier to fall for your "big brother" though. A few
weeks ago, David, ever the celebrity-seeker, was escorting movie
star Candice Bergen around the White House. She, too, apparently
has taken on photography as a new career aspiration and the Ken-
nerly-Bergen liaison was mutually beneficial. He was her ticket inside the White House to take pictures for a story she's doing for
*Ladies' Home Journal*, and she was his ticket to increased publicity. The liaison worked: for David there were stories like "Clicking
at the White House" and "Sweet on Candy . . ." in the newspapers and for Candice Bergen, there was unusually easy access to
the First Family.

Susan and I were talking one day in my office when Candice and
David bounced into the room, laughing merrily.

"Hi," Candice cheerfully called out to Susan.

"When are you leaving?" Susan asked bluntly, her face taut.

"Tomorrow."

Susan beamed with joy and walked away.


## FEBRUARY 18, 1975

*Good Housekeeping* wants to know if Mrs. Ford would like to
write a column for the magazine like Eleanor Roosevelt's diary.
One legislator who actively opposes ERA has issued a statement
saying "My goodness, I think it's marvelous for the First Lady to
be involved in the governmental process!" Everybody, but everybody has begged for a chance to talk to the First Lady about what
she thinks.

And Mrs. Ford is having second thoughts. A group of pickets
marched in front of the White House today, charging that "Betty
Ford is trying to press a second-rate manhood on American wom-
en!" There were only about seven of them dressed in mourning

clothes, and looking a bit silly. Both their costumes and their rhetoric were picked up on the eleven o'clock news. Edward and I watched it with glee and had a good laugh. But as soon as the spot ended, the phone rang.

It seems making headlines as the first First Lady who is picketed for her *own* views rather than those of her husband is not exactly the historical niche Mrs. Ford had in mind. The woman who told the press in the afternoon, "I'm going to stick to my guns on this. I expected criticism and I'm not bothered by it," needed reassurance after the eleven o'clock news.

Luckily I had some to give. The hours of this job are so "extensive" that I had been lying in bed thumbing through the ERA mail when the news went on. So I quickly picked up some positive mail and read it to her. It was pep talk time. It worked.

It made me think, though, that it might be a good idea for Mrs. Ford to read more of the mail she is getting. I think it's important for her to get closer to the human element. It also might be good for her to publicize her mail more. The hostile letters are outnumbering the favorable ones. If we admit that, the tide may turn.

## FEBRUARY 19, 1975

"Britain's rock superstar Rod Stewart has one very special fan," the *London Daily Express* screams, "a president's daughter. In fact, Rod is such a hit with President Ford's daughter Susan that he's been invited to dinner. At the White House, of course."

It must have been a bad trans-Atlantic connection.

## FEBRUARY 20, 1975

I told the White House reporters today that the mail count is running three to one against Mrs. Ford's stand on the ERA. Then Mrs. Ford said that those *against* are the people doing all the writing. "Those who are for it sit back and say good for her. Push on!"

Now we'll sit back and hope we've stimulated a little letter-writing from supporters.

Meanwhile, Rod Stewart's people called to tell me that Romantic Rod feels so awful about the incident that he wants to send Susan a dozen long-stemmed white roses.

## FEBRUARY 22, 1975

I got a call at home from Mrs. Ford this morning, because the *Washington Star* version of the Rod Stewart affair came out today. (Ah, the fall-out from just one rock concert!) The *Star* was factually more correct than the *London Express*, but more caustic, too. The *Star*'s reporter had been there and he described the activities of the President's daughter and her friends with sneering sarcasm. Mrs. Ford was furious because the story was so "inaccurate" and because it made Susan sound like a "groupie with a White House phone." I told her it wasn't really that serious, that Susan was like any other teenager who liked contemporary music and that (since one of the few attributable direct quotes was " 'S---!' she muttered") I thought I might remind Susan to be careful of what she says in public.

The long-stemmed white roses arrived. But only after the Rod Stewart people called to inquire about them.

"Have they come?" they asked.

"No."

"Oh. Well, you know it is difficult to get long-stemmed white roses at this time of the year."

"Oh."

I hope Susan lays off the rock concert circuit for a while.


## FEBRUARY 24, 1975

ERA update: 1,763 oppose Mrs. Ford's stand, 1,430 in favor.


## FEBRUARY 27, 1975

We returned yesterday from what really amounted to a two-day vacation in Florida. Mrs. Ford sported an enormous ERA pin which proved to be the perfect gesture. It enabled her to relax, but still make a political statement.

It sparked conversation among the staff as well. Mrs. Ford and I were standing with Donald Rumsfeld next to the pool in Fort Lauderdale when he started teasing her about her cause. "Are you going to equalize things at the White House, too?"

"Yes sir. You'd better watch out!"

Aha. A perfect opening. "Things really aren't equal, you know," I said and launched into my plea for an additional staff person. Ron Nessen came along and joined in the banter.

More teasing . . . laughter . . . joking.

"Ron, I'll race you for one of your forty-five staff people!" He and I were both in bathing suits. The pool was empty. Why not?

"Sure, sure."

"Really, let's race. Let's get it over with once and for all. I promise, if I lose, you will be free. I'll never mention the subject again."

A very tempting offer. He gave me a quick athletic evaluation: she's little and she's female and so she's probably a weak swimmer and she'll never mention it again if I beat her. The kind of offer you can't turn down.

"Okay."

"But if I win, Ron, you *promise* in front of all these people that I can have one of your staff people?"

(Win? That's a laugh.)

"Yes, I promise."

The crowd got excited. So did I. Luckily, I was too excited to think about the fact that I was about thirteen years old the last time I engaged in swimming competition.

Ready—GO!

I dived in. My body seemed to go on automatic pilot. I remember hearing Mrs. Ford cheering me on, yelling and clapping. I don't remember breathing. I reached the finish line before Ron had reached the halfway point. Victory!

Ron took it well enough. (Is that because he is a good loser or because he has not accepted the loss?)

"Remember Ron, you promised!" I gasped, out of breath, but anxious to cash in my chips. His eyes did not meet mine.


## FEBRUARY 28, 1975

We have turned the corner! Today's White House mail count: 3,246 in favor of Mrs. Ford's stand, 2,119 opposed.

*Well, Governor, it is something that I am interested in, and all I am asking is for it to have a chance on the floor of the Senate. . . . Well, I have not been in politics twenty-six years without having a little rub off. . . . Well, you know I just came back from Florida and, of course, they were coming up and they were waiting for me to say something, but I just went down there with my husband who was speaking there and I did nothing except relax in the sun and enjoy the sunshine. I never said a word about the ERA. I agree with you. . . . I'm certainly not trying to twist anybody's arm or anything.*

*Chapter Five*
MARCH, 1975:

# TIME ON MY HANDS

*SUNDAY, MARCH 2, 1975*

We were still in bed when the phone rang. A *Family Weekly* story on Nancy Howe had come out, it seems, and the reviews from Camp David were not good. The first call came from Nancy, who was very upset because Mrs. Ford was apparently very, very upset. What especially bothered the First Lady, Nancy said, was the title: "Mrs. Ford's Best Friend: Nancy Howe."

Oh my.

But Nancy had had no *idea* they were going to use that title and she was even more surprised and, well, frankly, hurt, by Mrs. Ford's reaction to the story.

Yes, well—

And Nancy had *explained* to Mrs. Ford that Sheila knew all about the story and had, in fact, sat in on the interview.

Hold on. It was time to review the bidding. "Now, Nancy, you know I told you I thought it was inappropriate to talk to the reporter. I never endorsed the idea. But you invited the reporter anyway, and never mentioned it to me until she arrived at the White

97

House." (I was willing to play appeaser; I was not willing to play scapegoat.)

I told Nancy I had not seen the article, but that I would go and get the paper and then try to smooth things over with Mrs. Ford. (Why is it that when the time comes to say "I told you so!" it is just not the right time?)

I had progressed from the bedroom to the study when the telephone attacked again. This time it was Mrs. Ford, and she was, indeed, hysterical. Her children had teased her about how awful the story in *Family Weekly* was and how awful Nancy was, calling Mrs. Ford "Petunia" all the time, and giggling. "She is *not* my best friend!" Mrs. Ford sobbed into the telephone. "I am so mad. I am so mad that right now, as I talk to you, I am rolling this article up into a ball and throwing it into the fire, where it belongs! I'm going to fire Nancy!"

I tried to smooth and soothe. "I haven't seen the article yet, but it's just one article. It isn't that important. You *need* someone like Nancy to take care of things like the checkbook, the hair appointments, clothes, odds and ends like that. You *need* a personal assistant."

We talked some more. Then she put David Kennerly on the phone. He and I talked for a while and he promised he would try to placate her. I hung up and just sat there for a while. I could picture the scene that preceded the outburst: everyone's sitting around the breakfast table, joking about "Petunia's Best Friend." With Susan and David Kennerly like two kids, only too happy to put down Nancy and contribute. And suddenly Mrs. Ford snapped. But why? Out of fatigue? Out of depression? Out of anger? Out of a whole array of emotions that have been building up? Is it a love/hate relationship she has with Nancy? She *is* grateful to her. She *does* find the silliness a welcome escape. But at the same time, she seems to resent the fact that Nancy tries to get too close (sometimes I think she is trying to *be* Mrs. Ford) and she also senses the disapproval of everyone close to her—both personally and professionally.

And today it all exploded.

I had longed for this day. Why did I feel so awful?

Because hysteria unnerves me.

Because I wanted to get rid of Nancy rationally, not irrationally. (It's one thing to fire her because she lacks the discretion and sensitivity necessary to perform her job. It's another thing to dismiss her arbitrarily in a state of emotional despair.)

And because Nancy's departure would indeed leave a gap. A frightening gap. There was no way I could do all the little odds and ends upstairs and still perform my job. No way.

I called Camp David and asked for Susan. She told me her mother was better, but suggested a call from Ric Sardo might help. I called Ric at home. He had not seen the article. He went out and bought a Sunday paper and then called Mrs. Ford. It helped.

## MARCH 3, 1975

All is quiet upstairs in the Family quarters. A calm after the storm.

But the really important news is that my AP and UPI wire machines arrived today. (Just four months and two days after I requested them!) They look a little tired. I suspect that they have sputtered in many, many other offices in their long careers. They told me the machines were used in the Oval Office by Johnson, but I think they meant Andrew Johnson. These are definitely antiques. But they are *my* machines and I welcome them!

And now, to recap my scorecard in the White House perk department: I have gotten extra telephones, a briefing box, and wire machines. I still have: no car, no extra staff person, and no permission to dine in the White House Mess after one o'clock. Three down. Three to go.

## MARCH 4, 1975

The wire machines broke down, but the repairman fixed them.

## MARCH 7, 1975

Bill Coleman was sworn in today as Secretary of Transportation, and since he is an old friend of my parents, my father came in for the ceremony. It was fun showing him around "my" White House. Actually, I was surprised at how many people on the household staff he remembered from back in the 50's. He said hello to Mr.

Bruce, a butler who has been here since even before the Eisenhower years, Rex Scouten, who was with the Secret Service when my father worked in the White House, Ray Hare, who works in the ushers' office. There was a surprisingly large number of familiar faces. He's been back other times since 1958, but he didn't know many of the Ford people.

The size and fanfare of the swearing-in ceremony itself impressed him because so many people had come in from all over the United States to witness it. He said in the Eisenhower days the President would walk across the hall to the Roosevelt Room for the few minutes the swearing-in took, and that was it.

The White House has changed, too. The alterations since the 50's, he said, have made the mansion much more palatial, much more elegant than it was before. He couldn't get over the new press quarters. The press in the Eisenhower era had a very simple, small room right off the West Wing reception room. It was incredibly crowded with telephones and people practically on top of each other. The new press quarters, built in April, 1970, by President Nixon at a cost of $574,000, are positively luxurious.

But he covered up the old White House swimming pool to do it and that absolutely devastated my father. "There were other places Nixon could have used," my father said. "He didn't have to cover over the pool where Franklin Roosevelt swam, where John F. Kennedy loved to swim. It was a White House tradition for the First Family and staff, that pool. I remembered all the excitement you children felt, that you could use this great pool."

I remembered, too. I remembered that we used to bring Tricia and Julie Nixon with us when we came because part of this White House tradition was that the Vice President didn't have pool privileges. My mother loves to tell the story about taking all of us—my sisters and brother and me and Julie and Tricia—swimming one day, and then, just for a special treat, taking us to the Willard Hotel nearby for lunch afterward. The maître d' recognized the Nixon girls. We were told it was a special lunch and we could have whatever we wanted. Tricia and Julie wanted hot dogs, my mother says. The Willard Hotel didn't sell hot dogs, but the maître d' sent out to the nearest delicatessen and brought in hot dogs just for the Nixon children.

"You know, that may answer the question," my father was saying. "I mean Nixon never had any special friendship for the press.

He was always at war with them, in fact. To give them quarters that were so splendid, he had to have some reason. I bet there was a psychological reason there—maybe the fact that he was excluded from the pool, with all its attendant implications. I bet that rankled him over the years. Maybe he built the lavish press quarters just to fill in the pool.''

Certain things, I was interested to hear, have not changed. "The East Wing and the West Wing of the White House have always been in sharp conflict," he told me. "What you have to do is show the West Wing that you can make Mrs. Ford an outstandingly popular First Lady with or with*out* their support. You can do it."

Well, he's my father.

## MARCH 8, 1975

Mrs. Ford's osteoarthritis is bad again and they've called in Dr. William Felts, the head of rheumatology at George Washington University's Medical School, who has treated Mrs. Ford in the past. Dr. Lukash just called to tell me that, and to tell me Ron Nessen will be releasing a statement to the press.

*Ron Nessen?*

Why Ron Nessen? After all, I'm the person who has been answering all press questions on her health. I know how to explain it to reporters in a way that is least likely to arouse false suspicions about a cancer relapse. I'm the one from whom they expect such information. *I am Mrs. Ford's Press Secretary.*

"Ron Nessen is going to make the statement." Dr. Lukash was firm and cold and almost surprised at my annoyance.

They feel this is an important announcement, and they feel important announcements must come from the West Wing. That's it. That's all there is to it. Stick to table cloths, they're telling me. Stick to dresses and Susan's love life. Leave the hard news to us.

I can think of no more appropriate way to celebrate today, which—irony of ironies—happens to be International Women's Day, than by having a bunch of men arbitrarily decide that descriptions of one woman's health are too important to be handled by another woman. Perhaps Mrs. Ford should stop calling state legislators and zero in on the West Wing.

What bothers me more than the obvious sexism is the questionable competence. I don't like their statement. It is too pompous, too complicated, and the heavy verbiage has an ominous sound. "Mrs. Ford has developed moderately severe pain and discomfort." (What on earth does *that* feel like?) "Such episodes have been related to excessive fatigue resulting from physical stress."

President Ford put it better at the Republican National Committee dinner last night when he said, "Betty has one of those uncomfortable pinched nerves in her neck and every once in a while it acts up."

## MARCH 11, 1975

Don Hewitt, the executive producer of "60 Minutes," wants to do an interview with Mrs. Ford. Not now. Sometime when she is feeling better. I told him others have asked first. There's the tour of the Family quarters Barbara Walters and I have been talking about. "Face the Nation" has also submitted a request.

Neither offer tempts me. Barbara wants to do the tour as part of the morning "Today" Show. I think it should be a special and it should be in the evening. (Mrs. Ford is a disaster before 10:00 A.M.) "Face the Nation" is much too formal a set-up for Mrs. Ford. She's not the type to face the nation. She *is* the type to chat with it, though.

Which brings me back to "60 Minutes." I would love her to do it, because it is the best produced show on the air, one of the only programs capable of portraying people as they really are. It is egoless in the sense that the interviewer makes himself inconsequential. It isn't show-biz. It's art. Television painting a multi-dimensional portrait of a human being. The result with Mrs. Ford would be fascinating.

When she is ready. Not yet.

I told Don I'd let him know.

And then I tuned in for the play by play from the combat zone, brought to me each day at this time by my trusty briefing box. The daily White House (vs?) press briefings are unbecoming for both sides.

First of all, the reporters haven't gotten over Watergate yet. After all, they blew it. The story was right here under the collective nose of the White House press corps and it was broken instead by two reporters on the *Washington Post* city desk. So now they over-compensate. They are unusually suspicious. They can be very ir-ritating.

And Ron plays right into their hands by being irritated. And testy. And hostile. Instead of understanding his former fellow jour-nalists, Ron considers himself now "on the other side." It's the "them" and "us" mentality at work all over again. "I find it harder and harder to believe that I was once one of those jerks," he says at morning staff meetings as the White House guys chuckle along with him.

And although he's left the nostalgia for his old news days be-hind, he's brought some of the old hostilities with him to the White House. He and Phil Jones covered Ford together (Phil for CBS, Ron for NBC) when Ford was Vice President. They were not close and the rivalry went beyond the normal network competition. It still flares up. Once when Phil got permission for a CBS camera crew to film something inside the White House, the permission was revoked by Ron arbitrarily at the last moment. In Vail, when Ron was having trouble answering one reporter's question, he saw Phil smiling and he snapped, "How would *you* answer that question if you were White House Press Secretary—*which you'd dearly love to be!*"

Ah, the lofty level of it all.

The fact is, the subjects brought up at the White House daily press briefings are rarely lofty, usually nit-picky and petty. As is the general exchange. Take today's offer via my briefing box:

Q:     Is the President leaving for a vacation?
RON:  We haven't announced any trip to Palm Springs, Jim.
Q:     He did say that he was going to California for Easter, as a matter of fact.
RON:  There is no trip to Palm Springs announced at the mo-ment.
Q:     He announced it *himself* in the Oval Office. He said that he was going to California for Easter.
RON:  There has been no trip announced, and you know those trips aren't official until they are announced.

Ah, the lofty level of it all.

## MARCH 17, 1975

Mrs. Ford is better, but not well enough to resume normal activities, and I have been spending time trying to catch up on my correspondence. Some of it is ERA-related. The letters and phone calls—on both sides—continue to pile up. I think it is essential that replies, especially to the negative mail from Conservative Republicans be handled carefully: ("Your letter on Mrs. Ford's involvement with the ERA thoughtfully raises some troubling questions"). With friendly persuasion: ("She realizes that the public is not used to First Ladies speaking out on controversial issues, but she hopes that her public identification with ERA will help make people realize that the ERA is not a symbol of radical feminism"). But with persuasion, nonetheless: ("As you know, ERA proponents include the League of Women Voters, the Business and Professional Women's Clubs, and many Republican women's organizations. I think it would be as unfair to lump all those who support the ERA with NOW as it would be to align all those who oppose it with the John Birch Society"). Occasionally, a little pre-campaign oratory does not hurt: ("If we Republicans are to build the national base we need, all of us must understand that there will be disagreement on some issues. Our basic values and priorities, however, are similar and I hope you will agree the President deserves the support of conservative people").

Unfortunately, most of the letters I've been answering are not ERA-related, and thus not terribly challenging in spite of the fact that they require detailed research:

Dear Mr. DeFries,

Your letter to the President regarding Steven Ford's interest in wrestling has been referred to me.

And enthusiasm:

Dear Mr. Carlinsky,

Thank you for your interest in the White House Easter Egg Roll . . .

And the ability to discreetly distribute White House secrets:

> Liberty, during warm weather loves to go for dips in the White
> House fountain, and in colder months can be found visiting staffers
> who keep fresh supplies of dog biscuits in their desks.

This month's award for the most fascinating request goes to the
Shrine for Democracy Museum located at the foot of Mt. Rush-
more in South Dakota. "President Ford is now the man of the hour
and needs to be added to the Parade of Presidents," the letter pro-
claims. It seems they just need a few facts, including, for example,
"the circumference of the head horizontally about one inch above
the ear tops," and the "distance from the inside corner of the eye
to the bottom of the chinbone." I kept picturing an enormous wax
President, and thousands of Lilliputians scampering around him
with tape measures. The fact that the letter was sent over from the
West Wing with a note: "Ron would like for you to reply to this on
his behalf . . . do what you can," only intensified my urge to
scrawl across the top, ONLY HIS HAIRDRESSER KNOWS FOR SURE."

The only thing worse than having time to catch up on my correspondence is having time to deal with Ford family friends. I se-
cured a lot of tickets and White House tie clasps today.

One of the non-official functions of the First Lady's Press Secretary appears to be catering to the desires of "old, close, family
friends" of the Fords, friends who "don't want to bother Betty or
Jerry with something as silly as" theater tickets for the Kennedy
Center, an autographed picture for a nephew, White House souvenirs, or a Ford endorsement for a pet project. "Could you fix it for
me, Sheila?" is the question, spoken or implied. When things are
busy, I am not easy to locate. This month I am a sitting duck.

It is a vicious circle, too. If you do them favors, they are grateful. If they are grateful, they stop by when visiting the family. If
they stop by, they often think of new favors. Some don't even ask.
One of the Fords' closest friends, a man of formidable finances
who spends the winter in Vail, came to my office recently, spotted
some pictures from Vail that I had hanging on the wall, and just removed them. He didn't ask. He didn't steal. He was last seen walking out, pictures under his arm, smiling.

Then there is the Reverend Billy Zeoli, one of the more fascinat-

ing members of the Ford circle of friends. A fast-talking fortyish
evangelical minister with long slicked-down hair, flashy clothes,
platform heels, and the overall appearance of a Forty-second-
Street hustler, Billy Zeoli comes to the White House not to take,
but rather to give the word of the Lord. (Sometimes his three-piece
suit matches the Bible he's carrying.) He spreads God's word in his
own words, however, often in sports jargon, as Billy (or "Z" as he
is known in the trade) ministers to professional athletes and has,
for example, delivered pre-game sermons to players in the last five
Super Bowl games. He did *not* write the country music song
"Drop-Kick Me, Jesus, Through the Goal Posts of Life," but he
could have and should have and would have, had someone inspired
him with the idea. That's a typical Zeoli concept—that life is a big
football game with Jesus quarterbacking you. ("I'm a total liberal
when it comes to methods, but very conservative in theology," he
explains.) He is also a Christian entrepreneur, the President of Gospel Films, one of the world's largest distributors of religious films.

He is something else, too. He must be, because athletes swear
by him (or at least pray by him) and the Fords adore him. He and
the President have known each other since 1960. I believe he was a
major influence in Michael's decision to turn to religion. Mrs. Ford
explains, adoringly, that "Billy carries his church with him. He
doesn't need a building to make you feel close to God." All the
Fords say he has been a tremendous help in times of family trauma. He was the first non-family member at Mrs. Ford's bedside
after her mastectomy. He gives the President a one-page prayer every week (which the President reads and which includes a recommended Bible verse, and a poem or essay to the Lord in Zeoli's
own words). At the top of the page it says "GOD'S GOT A BETTER
IDEA." At the bottom it says "COPYRIGHT WILLIAM J. ZEOLI.
ALL RIGHTS RESERVED."

And I set up a shopping trip for his wife at Loehmann's.
*Hallelujah!*


## MARCH 24, 1975

A "breather" is a blessing. Three weeks to "catch up on paper
work" is a curse. I am bored, depressed, and a trifle paranoid. I
think it's safer to stay in perpetual motion around here because

once there is time to pause and look around, the view is unnerving. We are all trying to claim a piece of the pie, and with Mrs. Ford still recuperating, the pie is small. But the vultures wait. Nancy Howe wants to use whatever time Mrs. Ford has for fun—to choose clothes and furs or talk cosmetics. Nancy Lammerding Ruwe (Nancy Lammerding, Mrs. Ford's Social Secretary, got married last month and is now Nancy Ruwe) wants Mrs. Ford to talk about White House decor with the *House Beautiful* people. And I stand poised with the latest ERA returns.

The only one who has had a lot to do lately is Dr. Lukash. And he guards his piece of the pie, too.

I went upstairs to see Mrs. Ford today. She looks better. She is up and around more. But she is still very uncomfortable. She described where her pain was. It started on her left side, she said, and went over her left shoulder and down the left side of her back. She said she was also having trouble hearing on her left side. That concerned me. I asked if it was because of the pinched nerve, sinus, or what. "I don't know. I'm going to the hospital tomorrow for tests. They're also going to check my eyes."

That surprised me. Back in my office, I called Dr. Lukash. "Is Mrs. Ford going to the hospital tomorrow?"

"Yes"

"Why?"

"Just for an eye check-up."

"Isn't she going to have her hearing problem checked out too?"

"How did you know about that?"

"She just told me."

"Keep that quiet!"

"I'm not going to tell anyone," I said, feeling a little hurt, a little confused, a little angry and more than a little paranoid.

"We're both on her side, remember?"

## MARCH 25, 1975

Dr. Lukash called to tell me that the X-ray of Mrs. Ford's spine was normal, and showed no progression in the arthritis. Her hearing tests revealed no abnormalities. The eye test revealed a slight change in prescription so she has selected new glasses.

I thanked him for keeping me posted.

## MARCH 26, 1975

A muskrat is a North American aquatic rodent yielding a valuable fur and secreting a substance with a musky odor, sometimes called musquash.

It's amazing the things I learn on this job. But in my position, I can go right to the experts. Dr. Ward Stone, associate chief pathologist of the New York State Department of Environmental Conservation says there are more muskrats than there are people, that if we did not capture them and kill them they would ruin the land, not only for people, but for water fowl and birds.

Marius Scopton, the public relations man for the American fur industry, says that muskrats are trapped by the Conibear trap and if you *have* to go it's the best way. Kills instantly, and he too insists, muskrats *have* to go. Otherwise, they will become pests. They will multiply like mad. Rodents do, you know.

I am impressed. I only hope Mark Hegedus of the Humane Society will be impressed. He called me today, very upset about muskrats, or rather the trapping and killing of muskrats.

Susan is getting a muskrat coat for graduation.


## MARCH 29, 1975 (PALM SPRINGS)

Just as Christmas means Vail to the Fords, Easter means Palm Springs. They have been coming here for years. They used to stay at the country club, but now with the Secret Service accommodations, there isn't room. Last year when Ford was Vice President they stayed at the Annenberg Estate, but they didn't enjoy it very much. Apparently, Walter Annenberg believes that a person has to have solitude, his own territory, a place that is off limits to others. And whereas he graciously offered his solitary castle to the Fords, the press was prohibited from entering the grounds, Jack Ford had an impossible time getting past the Annenberg security system himself, and Mrs. Ford said that she was afraid to touch anything in the house.

This year they're staying at the home of old friends, the Fred Wilsons. Mrs. Ford is happy for the first time in weeks. I'm happy, too. We left osteoarthritis and Nancy Howe and cold weather and general March depression behind. It is sunny, warm and beautiful and life is looking up.

*Chapter Six*
APRIL, 1975:

# SERPENT IN THE EAST WING GARDEN

*APRIL 3, 1975 (PALM SPRINGS)*

The weather has been glorious, the surroundings exquisite. I have been dividing my time between Mrs. Ford and the press room and enjoying both. I have also had my fair share of tennis and swimming and evenings socializing with either the Fords or their friends or members of the press.

There is, of course, a serpent in the Garden of Eden. The North Vietnamese are sweeping down the South Vietnamese coast capturing major South Vietnam cities. Da Nang . . . Chu Lai . . . Quang Ngai. . . . Qui Nhon. . . . Every day the list grows and every day the anxiety intensifies. The reporters write that the President golfs as Vietnam burns, but according to Mrs. Ford his golf provides him only temporary relief, a momentary lapse in the pre-occupation with Vietnam and the sense of hopelessness that accompanies that pre-occupation.

The political became personal last night as David Kennerly returned from a brief visit to Vietnam. I've never seen him look worse—pale, tired, obviously shaken. Vietnam is an important place to him, because of the friends he made while on assignment there and because his Vietnam photographs won him the Pulitzer

Prize. And he wanted to go back and see for himself. The President encouraged him. I think he even lent David money for the trip.

As it turned out, David narrowly escaped injury himself. He was photographing a ship at Cam Ranh Bay that had just brought some 9,000 Vietnamese soldiers in from Da Nang, he said, when the helicopter he was riding in was shot at from the ground. "When the pilot saw the rifles aimed at us and the muzzles flashing, he decided to stop circling the ship," David told us. He was evacuated with other Americans later in the day, and arrived here at about 11:00 P.M. Mrs. Ford told me this morning that she and the President sat up with him until 4:00 A.M. talking. He was terribly upset about what is happening. He told the Fords that many of his Vietnamese friends begged him to take their children with him when he left, so they could get them out of the country safely. She said David was furious about how people were being mistreated. Mrs. Ford was furious, too. And worried about getting people out.

We are existing on so many levels out here. On the surface, there is the sublime sense of vacation—needed vacation. Below the surface, there is the constant concern about Vietnam. And in the middle, the official bravado (to stall for time?) such as: "At the moment, we do not anticipate the fall of Vietnam."

Vietnam is not the only evil. There is a serpent lingering in the East Wing's garden, too (albeit a lesser one).

"Sheila—telephone!" someone shouted in the press room at about 5:00 P.M.

"Hello?"

"Hello, Sheila? This is Maxine Cheshire."

I deliberately put her on hold and took the call in the back of the office where I could hear but not be heard. It was instinct. I knew from experience Maxine Cheshire would talk softly, and I knew from experience that she would talk about something I would not be anxious to spread. That's Maxine.

"I'm so sorry I have to call you about this, Sheila, but I have some information that must be checked out." The voice was sweet. The tone was one of friendly concern.

At this very moment, she explained, Nancy Howe and her husband Jimmy and her daughter Lise Courtney were all in the Dominican Republic where they were staying as guests of Tongsun Park.

"Who?"

"Tongsun Park, a big South Korean influence peddler in Washington." Maxine went on. Tandy Dickinson, Park's girl friend, was down there with them. Park was not. But he had paid for the trip—both the airline ticket and the villa—and, Maxine said, Park had also arranged to take the Howes to Mexico during Christmas but at the last minute, Jimmy Howe had been ill and the trip was canceled. Lise Courtney had gone, however. And Nancy and Jimmy, Maxine whispered, had cashed in their plane tickets and kept the money.

"You can imagine how upset this makes me, Sheila. You know Nancy is a good friend of mine."

"Yes." If the story were true, Nancy was in direct violation of the Federal laws which prevent government employees from accepting gifts and favors. Ah, friendship.

"I know nothing about this, Maxine." (Incredible. Incredible story. And incredible that, in fact, I knew nothing. How little we know of people's non-White House existences!) "But I'll check it out and let you know."

"I also wondered if Mrs. Ford knew anything about this."

"I'll check it out and let you know."

Maxine suggested that I give Nancy a call at Casa de Campo, Golf Villa #11. She proceeded to give me the telephone number there, too.

I called the White House instead and asked the operator to track down Nancy Howe for me immediately. Fifteen minutes later, Nancy called; I have no idea from where. The private phone at the back of the room was taken, and the only available one was surrounded by reporters. I asked Nancy to call me back in one hour in my hotel room. She said she couldn't, she was leaving shortly. (Leaving where?) I told her I had something important to talk to her about, but privacy was important. She said she would call me at 8:00 A.M. tomorrow.

I got back to my hotel room and called Mrs. Ford. "I just got a call from Maxine Cheshire. She had some questions about Nancy's vacation plans. Do you know anything about them?"

"No, not really. Let me see. I think she said something about going to Florida, but the house was not ready," (What house?) "so those plans fell through. And then I remember she talked about going to some club, but it was going to run too much a day for the three of them. To tell the truth, I really don't know."

I went over the specifics of what Maxine had told me. It was all news to Mrs. Ford. Nancy had never said anything about that. I asked her if she knew Tongsun Park. She told me she'd met him once when they had attended a birthday party for Congressman Tip O'Neill that Park had thrown at the Georgetown Club. But that was a while ago, when Ford was Minority Leader. She said, "Park seems to entertain everyone."

I told her that I planned to talk to Nancy in the morning and that in the meantime I thought it was best if she not say anything about it to anyone. She said she wouldn't.

Maxine definitely thinks she's on to something big. I can tell.

Is she?


## APRIL 5, 1975

Nancy didn't call back at 8:00 A.M. yesterday. I waited almost an hour, and then called the White House operators again. They gave me a number in Florida. I called and she explained that she hadn't called me because she had just arrived there. (From where?) I told her about Maxine's call and went over the accusations one by one. She denied them. She said she had American Express receipts to prove she paid for everything. Stressing the need to be honest, I went over each point with her again, this time role-playing, trying to ask her questions the way I told her Maxine Cheshire would. She denied each one again in a very matter-of-fact manner. I asked her whether she wanted me to call Maxine back. She said she wanted to do it herself and I was relieved. That cleared me of the apologist's role. I had a nagging feeling Nancy was not being completely honest with me.

Maxine called back. I told her Mrs. Ford knew nothing of Nancy's vacation plans and that Nancy would call her directly.

Then we went on to more upsetting traumas. The first planeload of South Vietnamese orphans, bound for the United States and adoption by American families, crashed shortly after taking off from Saigon yesterday. More than 200 people were killed, the majority of them children, and Mrs. Ford, like everyone else, was horrified at the news. It seemed to be the ultimate disaster in a country of endless disasters—a cruel attack on the most innocent victims of war, and when they were so close to safety and comfort and familial love.

The airlift continued nonetheless and this evening, the President, Mrs. Ford and the rest of us flew to San Francisco on Air Force One to be there when the first planeload of orphans arrived. It was an incredible scene. There were more than 300 children on board, and most were unsettled and some had been sick. It had been an exhausting trip, and the arrival was emotionally draining for all, passengers and observers. Since they had not released the list of yesterday's crash victims, there were prospective parents at the airport who did not know whether their adoptive children were alive or dead. I'll never forget the look on the face of one woman who was waiting nervously to find out. She got good news, her child had arrived safely. She remained composed until she looked up and saw Mrs. Ford standing there and then something—a compassionate look from the First Lady?—made her crumble, and she began crying and crying.

Mrs. Ford was upset because she could not get close to the children. The chemotherapy has lowered her resistance to disease and the doctors would not let her mingle with the children. She had to stand in a separate viewing area, and she found it very frustrating. She loves children and she said she really wanted to adopt one of the orphans, but would settle for just holding one or two in her arms. And she couldn't even do that. The President did. The touching of the flesh was more than a symbolic gesture, I think, more than a pose for a picture. These children—sleepy, crying, scared, sick, confused—seemed to symbolize the suffering of a nation. And there was a feeling that by soothing the children, you could somehow help soothe away some of that suffering.

We flew back to Palm Springs tonight.

## APRIL 6, 1975

Chalk up one more loss for *Truth-in-Journalism.*

"President Ford's daughter, seventeen-year-old Susan, has struck up a relationship with British Rock Singing Star Rod Stewart. He has had dinner with Susan and First Lady Betty Ford at the White House," says the *National Tattler* (close relative of the *National Enquirer*, in caliber at least) in its lead story on page one, just under a declaration that "Sirhan didn't kill RFK" and a promise that the "truth about Julie Nixon and her troubled marriage" is on page three.

## APRIL 8, 1975

"I'm a real mountain freak," the President's second son said. "I don't think I could handle life at the White House."

"You'd love it!" David Kennerly, swinger-at-large, insisted. "I'll show you around; you'll see. Believe me, you're crazy if you go anyplace else."

Kennerly's White House extends from the big mansion on Pennsylvania Avenue all the way across town to the Georgetown discos and celebrity night life. I could see he was ready to give Jack the big tour. And he was also ready to share the public attention that would result.

We were on Air Force One returning to Washington from Palm Springs, and David, Jack, Mrs. Ford and I were discussing what Jack should do when he graduates from college next month. I was holding back a little. This was my longest encounter with Jack to date, and I didn't want to scare him off. I suspect he sees me as the press person anxious to feed him to the wolves of newspaperland. Back at the beginning, he expected me to get him involved in all sorts of events. I haven't. And that has made him a little less standoffish. But just a little.

This, his mother tells me, is the son most anxious to do it "my way," the very, very bright kid who had always been fascinated by current events and bored by scholastics. Of all the Fords, it is Jack who loves to discuss the issues with his father, and he is both his father's sharpest critic, and the Ford least tolerant of public criticism of his father.

I told him I thought he should spend a year in Washington and get involved in the Presidential campaign, that the chance to experience White House living was a once-in-a-lifetime thing.

"But it's so *restricting*," his soft dark-blond hair rustled as he shook his head. "Then you have to play 'President's son' and everyone has a preconceived idea of what you should be and they're disappointed if you don't live up to it."

I watched him protest, this jean-clad, ruggedly handsome twenty-three-year-old with the solid square jaw, the trim athletic build, the blue-gray eyes. He looks perfect for the part.

"I don't know," he was saying, shifting uncomfortably under my casting eye. "The mountains and forests, they're just good for my head."

And so I asked him about the forests. He spent last summer as a forest ranger. As the President's son, however, he is prevented by law from working for the United States Government, and that includes the National Park Service.

I kept asking him questions. The things I *don't* know about forestry could fill a book. As could the things he does know. His mother's right. He's very, very bright. Gradually, he seemed to warm up, to come alive, the eyes sparkling as he described the details of the planting of trees, how long it takes them to grow ("A whole lifetime!").

By the end of the trip, we were almost friends, thanks to forestry.

We arrived in Washington in time to celebrate Mrs. Ford's birthday. She is fifty-seven years old today, and perfectly willing to admit it. "It's public record," she told me. "Anyone who wants to, can find out, so I might as well be sporting and announce it myself! Besides, I love birthdays because all my children call me. They all call collect, but at least they call."

I was in the midst of answering reporters' birthday questions when I got a call from Rumsfeld. "Sheila, I want to tell you something in strictest confidence. I just heard from Ben Bradley at the *Washington Post* that there is apparently some Maxine Cheshire story on Nancy Howe—"

"I know." I told him about last week's phone calls and how I had handled them. He said Bradley had planned on running the story, but that Nancy had been so distraught about it that he was having second thoughts. He'd let me know when Bradley let him know.

He called back a few hours later. The story had been squelched. Apparently Nancy's psychiatrist had called Bradley several times, insisting that Nancy might do something drastic if the story appeared. Rumsfeld wanted to be sure I had still not told anyone. I resisted the temptation to remind him that I had kept it quiet for almost a week before he found out about it.

"Nancy's psychiatrist," "Nancy distraught." These were strange images, sharp contrasts to Nancy Howe, clothes-conscious, status-seeking, fun-lover. These were also different from the Nancy Howe who could whip out the American Express receipts. Again it hit me; how little we really know. For some reason, I was not anxious to know more. I realized when I hung up that I had not even asked Rumsfeld any of the details of the story.

Ric Sardo supplied some. He said that Nancy had called him yesterday and told him about Maxine's pressure. Then Jimmy Howe called him today and told him that Rumsfeld had contacted Nancy and she was not in good shape. She had been hysterical, and she was being heavily sedated.

Clare Crawford's warning came back to haunt. "No matter how good a friend a reporter is, remember that they're a reporter first."

Dr. Lukash called me this afternoon and said there was trouble brewing. How many people has Rumsfeld told "in strictest confidence?"

I mentioned none of the latest developments to Mrs. Ford. I didn't what to ruin her birthday celebration tonight. She went with close friends to see *Hello, Dolly!* at the Kennedy Center. After the show, there was a little party and Mrs. Ford invited Pearl Bailey who starred in the show to join her. She and Pearl Bailey left the Presidential Box arm in arm singing the Michigan fight song. I have no idea what prompted it, but it was quite a sight. Both women were enjoying themselves immensely. I told Mrs. Ford later that only *she* could make Pearl Bailey sing off key!

## APRIL 9, 1975

"Does either the President or Mrs. Ford snore?" the reporter from the *Wall Street Journal* wanted to know.

It had been a long day; I was tired. This was silly. "What?" I asked. (Perhaps I had misunderstood.)

"Yes," she said with a chipper laugh, "I know it sounds silly, but it is really historically fascinating. Thus far I have uncovered the fact that twenty out of thirty-two Presidents snored. Let me see now, Washington, yes, Washington snored. They think it was due to his denture problems. Both Adamses snored, as did Van Buren, Fillmore, Pierce, Buchanan, Lincoln, Grant, Hayes, Arthur, Harrison.

McKinley,
   Taft,
      Cleveland,
         Hoover,
            Both Roosevelts. . . . "
"zzzzzzzzzzzzzzzzzzzzzz"

## APRIL 10, 1975

There really was a calm before the storm. There was nothing on Mrs. Ford's schedule today, except for listening to the President give his State of the World Message to Congress tonight. And it was a quiet day. Unusually quiet. Almost eerie, Patti Matson said.

Then all hell broke loose.

At 7:00 P.M. Rumsfeld called. "I've just heard something. I'm not 100 percent sure, but I'm sure enough that I think you should know. Jimmy Howe just shot himself in the head with a gun."

"Oh God."

"I believe he is still alive; he is at a hospital. I'll let you know as soon as I find out the details. In the meantime, answer no questions."

I sat there alone, too stunned to begin to try to understand. It was very quiet; then the phone rang. "Hello, this is Robin in Maxine Cheshire's office. I called to find out Mrs. Ford's reaction to Jimmy Howe's death."

My shock turned to rage. I couldn't believe this phone call. "I don't know what you're talking about!" I hung up the phone, and decided I'd better get out of my office. Bill Lukash would know the details. I went to his office.

The President had already been told, Dr. Lukash said, but the decision was that Mrs. Ford would not be told anything until after the President gave his speech. By then, we both felt certain, there would be a definitive answer on what had happened. We mumbled confused generalizations, and, still without word on Jimmy Howe, left in the motorcade for the Capitol.

I wanted to make sure no reporters got to Mrs. Ford before the speech. As soon as we got to the Capitol, I jumped out of my car and raced over to the President, Susan, and Mrs. Ford and quickly ushered the First Lady upstairs in the elevator to her seat. Once in that box, she was safe.

I went to watch the speech on the television in the radio-TV correspondents' section. I was curious to see how he would come across on TV. He wasn't convincing reading a speech. I had talked to him in Palm Springs about his delivery, and suggested he try talking from notes instead of a written-out text because he would be more natural. I was curious to see if he would take my advice. But I watched the television set and saw nothing. The President was asking for 972 million dollars in aid to South Vietnam. I was lost in smaller thoughts. What on earth prompted him to do it? Nancy was the one, prone to hysteries, in need of tranquilizers. Jimmy Howe always seemed to exude calmness. I kept picturing him at the White House that night back in January, inhaling and exhaling the elite atmosphere.

*"The options before us are few and the time is short. . . ."*

Mrs. Ford thought of him as a "real southern gentleman." He was a college professor, a specialist in Spanish literature or something. A retired military man. Very well educated.

*"This moment of tragedy for Indochina is a time of trial for us. It's a time of national resolve. . . ."*

I knew him very superficially, of course. But he seemed so mild mannered. The type who never raised his voice. He seemed a little too passive, if anything. Was it all a front? A cover-up for internal suffering?

I knew him very superficially.

*Applause.*

I ran upstairs. I was outside her box when Mrs. Ford began to leave, escorted her downstairs ("a wonderful speech. . . .") and into the car. I breathed a sigh of relief.

Back at the White House, I sat waiting in Dr. Lukash's office. Then Edward called. Fran Lewine, he said, was going crazy trying to reach me. She called to say that Jimmy Howe had died. Just then the eleven o'clock news went on with the same story. Jimmy Howe was dead "of a self-inflicted gunshot wound to the head."

Lukash returned with additional news. The President had told Mrs. Ford. She took the news well, considering, and had called Nancy immediately.

I returned to my office. All the phones were ringing. I had been told by Rumsfeld not to say anything to the press, but that was before Jimmy Howe had died. Not to say anything now would have made Mrs. Ford seem callous and indifferent. The right words were important. "Condolences," for example, would be out of character for Mrs. Ford. It had to be simple words, conveying concern over the tragedy of a friend. What could be simpler than the truth?

"President Ford told Mrs. Ford what had happened after his speech tonight, when they were alone in the residence," I told reporters. "She was sad and concerned for Nancy. She called her shortly after learning about it and tried to be supportive."

Before I left the White House tonight, I called Ron Nessen to let him know what I had done. He told me he had avoided all calls and I should have done the same thing.

## APRIL 11, 1975

In the end, Maxine Cheshire had to share the byline. Today's *Washington Post* story combines the report on the Howes' accepting favors from Tongsun Park with news of the suicide. The suicide part is replete with details: when the police were called, when he died, how his body was discovered, etc. The Cheshire part includes an exotic cast of characters ("Tongsun Park, a forty-year-old Korean who lives lavishly here and in Seoul and has described himself as being in the shipping and import-export business") and a clear indication that either innocently or guiltily, the Howes probably did accept favors from Tongsun Park.

A White House connection to a lavish-living influence peddler culminates in death. It certainly has the trappings of a murder mystery with international implications. But just the trappings. One might indeed ask why this Tongsun Park spends so much money in Washington—and I bet more and more people *will* be asking that— but the Howes are not a very formidable White House connection. It is clearly a case of fame by association. And that is what is so sad. Nancy was so dazzled by the glitter of celebrity politics that she mistook parasites for friends. Park was her friend. Maxine was her friend. You don't make friends when you work in the White House. The only real friends are the ones you had before you took the job and the ones after you leave.

And you can't be weak. You don't necessarily have to be strong to play politics, but you cannot be so weak that you crumble under pressure. That's the final irony—Maxine Cheshire's big story on power in Washington is really the story of weakness.

And a tale of personal tragedy. A man doesn't kill himself for big fancy international political reasons, but for little tiny tragedies.

Only those could hurt enough to make you put a pistol to your head.

Mrs. Ford went over to visit Nancy first thing this morning and called me as soon as she got back.

"Nancy was in better shape when I talked to her last night. Today she is in such a state of shock. Each person she sees—the Argentine Ambassador, the neighbor, me, the maid—causes her to break down completely. They are not keeping her sedated. Dr. Lukash says it is better that way, that it had to come out. Really, I guess you've got to just get by one day at a time. Lise Courtney is holding up very well."

She told me that when she left, reporters outside asked her if Nancy Howe would continue working at the White House. She told them she expected her to continue as soon as she felt up to it.

"I expect her back," she said to me, with hesitation. She waited. For me to agree? To disagree? Then she added "She's my friend."

Meanwhile, the West Wing, I have a hunch, already considers Nancy Mrs. Ford's *former* personal assistant. Rumsfeld has ordered me to answer all inquiries by simply saying, "It is a personal matter." Period. Which is a perfect way to convince every reporter that it is much more than a personal matter. So I have been compromising somewhat. This afternoon, Mrs. Ford was scheduled to participate in an anniversary reception for the Visiting Nurses Association. I tried to warn her that the only interest reporters had in the ceremony was Nancy Howe, that she should be prepared for questions. The thought angered her.

"Maxine Cheshire killed Jimmy Howe! I don't think I'll say anything if they press me. No comment. They would find me too angry. My husband feels the same way. I have no comment to make about the whole thing. Frankly, at this point, I just want to be as helpful as possible to Nancy and her daughter Lise Courtney. Anything I can do to help them through this period, I will."

When people called, I gave them the last portion of the quote. It was more than Rumsfeld permitted, but it kept the press from asking Mrs. Ford more questions at the ceremony.


*APRIL 12, 1975*

Today's newspaper follow-up, "HOWE SEEN AS DISTURBED MAN" stimulated an early morning phone call from Mrs. Ford. The article documented a history of alcoholism, psychiatric treatment, and marital problems. It offended Mrs. Ford because she felt it was a terrible invasion of privacy. She was shocked by it, too, shocked at how very little she knew of the personal details of Nancy Howe's life. "I had no idea of the psychiatric problems," she murmured. "And I always thought their marriage was a happy, solid one."

She told me she is going to the funeral on April 14th. Then as though the knowledge learned from the *Washington Post* article made her feel insecure, she said, "I'm assuming there's nothing else there. What's in the paper, that is the only thing. Now I want to put this behind me. If there is something else, tell me." She felt the West side was not telling her everything. They weren't.

The President's Counsel, Phil Buchen, told the *Washington Post* yesterday that an investigation into the allegations against Nancy Howe had been underway prior to the suicide. "Investigation" seemed a strong word to use under the circumstances. And I knew that when the *Star* saw the *Post* I would be called. I decided to check with Buchen.

"I guess it is not that important," I said, "but 'investigation' has such heavy negative implications to me. Is it all right if I call it an 'inquiry' instead?"

"Sure," he said. "I see what you mean. 'Inquiry' may be a better word." So I told the *Star* "Yes, the White House Counsel had already been looking into the trip allegedly paid for by Tongsun Park, conducting an 'inquiry' rather than an 'investigation.'"

The *Star* hit the newsstands, and Rumsfeld hit the phone, furious.

"I thought I told you not to talk to anyone!" he yelled. "You don't *correct* a newspaper story. You *ignore* a newspaper story."

(*I* correct.)

I hung up. The phone rang again, bringing similar tidings from Ron Nessen, this week's recipient of the Don Rumsfeld Gold Star Award. Quoth the *Star*: "At the White House, Press Secretary Ron Nessen declined to comment."


## APRIL 15, 1975

North Carolina votes tomorrow on the Equal Rights Amendment. We've sent telegrams to four legislators. Dr. Lukash thought it would be too much for Mrs. Ford to make a bunch of phone calls right now, and he's probably right.

Nancy Howe hangs over us. The tragedy haunts. The indecision surrounding Nancy's status intensifies everything. I know that she will not be returning. Mrs. Ford knows, deep down, that Nancy will not be returning. Under the circumstances, she *should not* return. But Rumsfeld is still insisting that all inquiries be "no comment" ed. There must be a tactful, graceful, dignified way to have Nancy exit. I can think of several.

I called Rumsfeld, Nessen, and Dick Cheney, Rumsfeld's assistant, Buchen, and Jerry Jones today to suggest some. When they didn't return my calls, I called each one back. I waited. I finally left for home. When I got home, the phone was ringing. It was Ron Nessen.

"I thought you worked so late."

"Why should I, Ron? Nobody returns my phone calls. Only reporters call me—hundreds of reporters who want to know what Nancy Howe's status is."

"We've prepared a statement on Nancy. I can't give it to you now. I'm supposed to be at Carl Rowan's for dinner and I'm already late. But I'll give it to you first thing tomorrow."

Suspense.

"I'll be in at 7:45."

"OK, 7:45."

Unnecessary suspense.

"Is there anything you want to tell me now, Ron?"

"No. Tomorrow at 7:45."

During dinner, Sandy Rovner from the *Washington Post* called. I told the housekeeper to say I was not in, something I had never done before. I have such trouble saying "No comment," I was afraid to get on the phone.


*APRIL 16, 1975*

I should have taken the call from Sandy Rovner. I would have learned something. Apparently ten minutes after Ron Nessen called me last night, the *Washington Post* called him and he gave them the story. Today's headline reads: MRS. HOWE LEAVING HER WHITE HOUSE POST. "In response to a question as to whether she had been asked to leave or had resigned voluntarily, Ron Nessen, President Ford's Press Secretary, said, 'Mrs. Howe's circumstances were discussed with her and the conclusion was that this arrangement was appropriate in view of all of the factors involved.'"

"No comment" would have been more explanatory.

Why had he told the *Post*, but not me? I clenched my teeth but did not get angry. Edward had suggested a new approach—be nice.

Ron bestowed upon me the official line, the teachings of Rumsfeld. Rumsfeld had found an answer to "every possible question" on Nancy Howe, and, though they were not written on stone, they were at least written on memo paper:

FACT: Mrs. Howe is on a leave of absence through May 31, 1975.
QUESTION: Will she be returning to her position at the White House?
ANSWER: No.
QUESTION: What is the reason for the six weeks leave of absence?
ANSWER: Mrs. Howe has accumulated approximately that combination of sick leave and compensatory time.
QUESTION: Was Mrs. Howe fired?
ANSWER: Mrs. Howe's circumstances were discussed with her and the conclusion was that the above arrangement was appropriate in view of all the factors involved.
QUESTION: Was the Tongsun Park matter a factor in the White House decision?
ANSWER: No.
QUESTION: Then what was the reason that Mrs. Howe will not be continuing her position?
ANSWER: There has been a tragedy in the Howe family and I feel it would be insensitive to discuss the matter further.

No matter what question I was asked, Ron explained, I had to find the answer on the memo. And I had to follow the exact wording of the memo. (No substituting "inquiry" for "investigation" this time!)

Be nice.

"Helen Thomas called and she's furious," my secretary, Nancy Chirdon, said as I walked in.

"Ron Nessen told her that you knew about the Nancy Howe decision last night."

What is going on here?

I took Ron out of a Cabinet meeting. On the walk over I had vowed to be nice for Edward, but one conversation had already been misunderstood two times in twelve hours. This was ridiculous.

"Look, Ron, you know I did not know about this last night."

"I thought I told you."

"You were running out to Carl Rowan's and you did not have time."

"I was sure I told you."

"Nope. No way. I'm going to tell Helen there was a misunderstanding, that you've had a lot on your mind, very important things—"

He began yelling. "They're going to dump shit on you! What is this stupid need of yours to always give answers out?"

"This is unnecessary, this screaming at me—"

"I *know* who I work for. I work for the President. Where's your allegiance? To the press? Who do you work for?"

I knew where my allegiance was, but I didn't know where the conflict was. My allegiance was to Mrs. Ford. Did that mean I had to let Helen Thomas think I had deliberately withheld a story?

I cooled off for at least an hour before I called Helen back; I hoped she had cooled off, too. I can't stand it when she yells at me. I called. She yelled. Maybe I should have waited two hours.

"Ron's had a lot on his mind, Helen. He didn't tell me."

Mrs. Ford had a staff meeting this afternoon and told us that Nancy would not be coming back. "Since Nancy is under medical care, Dr. Lukash was the appropriate person to tell her," Mrs. Ford said. "I feel very sorry that it happened. I really consider it a great tragedy. I hope everyone understands that I plan to continue my friendship."

Life goes on. They're going to serve a tea-based punch at Susan's Senior Prom next month. Mrs. Ford said she, Susan, and Ellison and Reagan Golubin, friends of Susan who are twins, made up a batch the other night to experiment and it was delicious.

## APRIL 17, 1975

North Carolina voted the ERA down yesterday, which means it won't be passed this year. We need four more states and there are only three more votes scheduled to take place in 1975. They thought they would win in North Carolina, too. As it turned out, the vote was 62–57.

## APRIL 18, 1975

The Fords went to see *Give 'em Hell, Harry* (the play about Harry Truman) last night at Ford's Theater. It was the first time a U.S. President had attended a performance at Ford's Theater since Lincoln's assassination there in 1865. But it was the play, not the historic breakthrough, that captivated Mrs. Ford. She said she thought everyone should see it—especially everyone in government. She was so taken with it she couldn't stop talking about it this morning.

"You have to understand that timing is very, very important to me, and Truman was President when we first moved down here to Washington. So he was an important person at an important time in my life. And I thought he was a wonderful man—so down to earth. We both thought so."

President Ford was a Truman fan, too. That's why Mrs. Ford had been so excited about finding a bust of Truman in the warehouse while she was redecorating the Oval Office last fall. Ford was delighted at her find. The Truman bust occupies a very prominent position in his office today.

She said the play rekindled many memories for them, and that when they got back to the White House, they bumped into Ray Hare, who works in the ushers' office now, but was on Truman's Secret Service detail. He walked them to the residence elevator, reminiscing with them about Harry Truman.

## APRIL 20, 1975

According to Betty Beale's story today, Tongsun Park is a Perle Mesta type, not a lobbyist. She quotes many top-ranking defenders, such as House Majority leader Tip O'Neill ("He has never asked me for a single thing."). Representative John Brademas ("He has been gracious and kind to me and never asked me for a single thing."). President Ford's Congressional Assistant Max Friedersdorf ("I don't know anybody he's asked for anything.").

Frank Ikard, the President of the American Petroleum Institute ("I think he's very clean."). Park himself ("Some people just enjoy making other people happy.").

Maybe all the fuss about Nancy was unfair.

Maybe reporters *can* be friends.

## *APRIL 21, 1975*

It was our usual Monday morning conversation. We worked on scheduling the week ahead, and then relaxed and talked about the weekend.

"Susan went to the University of Virginia for the weekend," Mrs. Ford said, "and she says she had a wonderful time, but the first person she bumped into down there was Gardner Britt—with a date. Susan said she was jealous. And I told her that was ridiculous, that she was being too possessive. 'You just want to have them all,' I told her."

Mrs. Ford went on to tell me that she had spoken to Nancy Howe during the weekend. It was the second time she had talked to her since the funeral, and she felt Nancy was better each time.

"You know, you should start thinking about a replacement for Nancy. You need someone with really good secretarial skills, I think, someone like my secretary, Nancy Chirdon."

"You took the words right out of my mouth. I would like Nancy Chirdon! Actually, I've decided to have two secretaries who can share the responsibilities equally and be interchangeable. One would be Nancy Chirdon and Carolyn Porembka, Nancy Howe's former secretary, could be the other."

My three-person staff has been reduced to two.

## *APRIL 28, 1975*

For once it was quiet. Quiet enough, in fact, for me to be able to have dinner with Edward. We decided to go out, to celebrate this sudden tranquility and we went to The Palm, a very nice restaurant. Just the two of us. Or as close to "just the two of us" as you can be when you're wired. All senior staff in the White House wear "beepers" clipped to their belts, hidden in pockets, or in some way "connected." (I keep mine in my purse.) Wherever the President of the United States is, the whole area is wired for beepers, so that at any moment his staff can be contacted for some type of emergency or urgent need. It's easy to "beep." You just call the central number, the signal corps, and ask them to track down the person you want. The signal corps then activates the person's beeper, which tells the person to call the central number from wherever he is at the moment.

So there we were, sipping wine, talking in soft, low tones, enjoying the knowledge that a delicious meal was on its way, when my beeper went off. "*Beep Beep Beep,*" my purse said, "*Weidenfeld Weidenfeld beep beep beep.*" People at nearby tables shifted uncomfortably. A human voice. Inside a purse. With an inhuman sound. You can't ignore a beeper, because after a certain amount of time it begins all over again. "*Beep beep beep . . .*"

Tommy Jacomo, the maître d', took me to the restaurant's office, where I called the White House. My caller, it turned out, was Mrs. Ford.

She and the President had just had dinner, and he was back at work. "He has a lot on his mind," she told me. "There's been persistent bombing in Saigon airport all day and he's so worried about evacuating all the remaining Americans."

"Oh."

"Listen, I talked to the President about the trip to New York the day after tomorrow, and he doesn't want me to go commercial. He said I should use the Jet Star. He said that way the ride would be more comfortable and the departure and arrival would be much easier."

"I see." The maître d' was waiting around to find out what the White House emergency was. So was I. I wondered if my steak was cold by now, my french fries soggy . . .

"But I told him I wouldn't want to do it if the cost is out of line," Mrs. Ford was saying. "Now, we arrive in New York City at 11:35, right. . . ."

Suddenly I realized that she had no idea where I was. The President was working and she was lonely and anxious about Vietnam, and she wanted to talk. Just talk!

\* \* \*

*APRIL 30, 1975*

Mrs. Ford and I took off on the Air Force Jet Star plane this morning at ten bound for New York City. The Jet Star is really a lovely little plane. It seats eight people and has one steward. A very intimate way to travel. It was the only tranquil part of the trip.

We were going because Mrs. Ford was to be guest of honor at an American Cancer Society Benefit luncheon. The trip proved to be a learning experience. I learned that one should never underestimate the aggressiveness of the New York press. And I learned that Betty Ford is a very popular person. All three learning experiences occurred simultaneously when we walked into the press room and discovered four camera crews and seventy-five to one hundred reporters crammed into a tiny airless area . . . spectators lined up outside, closing in on Mrs. Ford as the stanchions holding them back went down and they rushed across the "off limits" line. I looked at Mrs. Ford's face and saw an expression of unadulterated horror. I ran in front of the press, hoping to block them. I spelled out a few ground rules. Then I held my breath and prayed the moment would pass uneventfully, and it did. But next time there will be a press advance person to make arrangements way ahead of time. There are better ways to cope.

I think we had both underestimated Mrs. Ford's crowd-drawing abilities. This is her first official trip to New York, and the people really came out. The reporters told me that that was the biggest press turnout they'd seen since Lord Snowden came to New York. I relayed that to Mrs. Ford, thinking she would be impressed. Instead she said, "Oh, I know! I really wanted to see Lord Snowden when he came to Washington!"

This evening, back in the White House, Mrs. Ford, Susan, Dave Kennerly, Bill Lukash, John Ulbricht and I were upstairs viewing Ulbricht's portrait of Susan (enthusiastically, it really captures her) when President Ford and Ric Sardo came in. They were talking about Vietnam. The end is now official. The South Vietnamese government surrendered to the Communists and Viet Cong, and North Vietnamese troops have taken over Saigon. I got up to leave, and the President said, "Sit down." So I sat down.

Someone asked me if I wanted a drink, and I said, "No, thanks," and Mrs. Ford said, "Have a drink, Sheila." So I had a drink. I never feel comfortable "settling in" up there, especially when the President is there. President Ford and Ric sat down and continued talking about the evacuation. The President said that, had it been an hour later, it might have been disastrous. "They were very lucky there were not more mishaps," he said. "This was not the best thing the military has done."

Still, he admitted, the results seemed good—many people had gotten out very, very quickly. He was concerned about the two Marine guards who were killed in the artillery attack at Ton Son Nhut yesterday.

"They were only nineteen and twenty-two. I read the files on them today, the papers on them. They had very good records." The reaction was more paternal than Presidential. He looked tired. Very tired.

"You should write notes to their parents," Mrs. Ford said.

"Can you get a confirmation?" he asked Ric. "Is it certain that they were killed in the act of duty—that they were still working?"

Ric nodded.

"You should write notes to their parents," Mrs. Ford said again. The President said he would.

## Chapter Seven
## MAY, 1975:

# C'EST LA PROTOCOL

*MAY 15, 1975*

Their Imperial Majesties, the Shahanshah of Iran and the Empress Farah, were wined and dined at the White House tonight surrounded by the Truman china, the Kennedy crystal, the Monroe vermeil, and some of America's most important people. The attire was white tie, and the repast was elegant, from the salmon en gelee with sauce verte to the praline mousse and demitasse. The occasion: that quintessential American diplomatic maneuver, the State Dinner.

The Fords have had eleven State Dinners since they moved into the White House last August, and each one has required advance precision planning for everything from the guest list to the menu to the after-dinner entertainment to the decorations in the dining room. The State Department, which foots the bill, initiates the idea—usually after several months of negotiations on military aid and trade agreements—when it decides the time has come to invite the other country's Head of State here to officially finalize the documents the bureaucrats on each side have drawn up. There is rarely any spontaneity involved. The arrival and the high level talks between the two national leaders are usually as pre-planned as the State Dinner at the White House that culminates the visit. C'est la Protocol.

The planning begins a few weeks before the visit. Consultations with the visiting dignitary's Washington Embassy supply details on food, such as likes, dislikes, allergic or dietary restrictions, and entertainment preferences.

Thus, for Israeli Prime Minister Rabin, who likes classical music, there was Eugene Fodor, a young violinist. Prime Minister Bhutto, a jazz enthusiast, watched Billy Taylor perform. And tonight, the Shah of Iran watched Ann-Margret sing and dance. ("The Shah likes attractive young ladies," Mrs. Ford explained with a twinkle in her eye. "He's supposed to be a swinger.")

The guest list is always a mixed bag. (Tonight's, for example, included Senator Alan Cranston and Glenn Beall, Bob Hope, Fred Astaire, Tom Wicker of the *New York Times,* Chief Justice of the Supreme Court Warren Burger, Henry Ford, and New York Knickerbocker basketball star Bill Bradley.) But the general guest list formula is: people suggested by the guest's Embassy, top government officials, in some way relevant to the guest, an appropriate sprinkling of celebrities for glitter, an appropriate sprinkling of politicians for debt-paying, leaders in sports, entertainment, media and the arts, and always—under the Ford administration—*some*one from Grand Rapids, Michigan. ("The White House is our home, after all. Family friends are welcome here!")

Mrs. Ford thinks State Dinners should be as informal and relaxed as possible, given the pre-existing conditions. She thinks people should have fun. To help, she has shied away from the formal style of her predecessors. Guests tonight, for example, sat at small round tables, which are better for conversation, she says, than the U-shaped head table arrangement. And the White House dance floor has never been busier. Unlike the Nixons who excused themselves from their guests after the entertainment, the Fords themselves set the pace, dancing often into the early hours of the morning after many of their guests have tired.

Both Fords work at seeing that their guests have fun, actively introducing people to each other. I think Mrs. Ford sees herself as a hostess, not a celebrity or a symbolic wife of the head of state. She frankly likes to throw a good party. And she worries beforehand the way all hostesses worry and she endures some of the typical before-the-company-arrives mishaps, too. (She planned on wearing a blue chiffon dress to the State Dinner for Prime Minister Harold Wilson in January, but as she was putting on a dab of perfume, a last touch, the bottle accidentally spilled all over the dress and she had to make a rapid change.)

Economy is on Mrs. Ford's mind these days, and under her instruction, the menu is carefully planned, and a new procedure for serving has been implemented, where guests help themselves to the portion size they desire. This, she feels, cuts waste. "Stress American" is another of her themes. ("If I were to visit Italy, I wouldn't expect them to show me a cowboy movie!") Thus the State Dinner is a showcase for the finest American entertainment (at the lowest possible cost; performing at the White House is a priceless honor. Literally) and the finest American art. Bronze sculptures loaned to the White House from the Corcoran Gallery of Art adorned the dinner tables tonight. ("They're conversation pieces. The first thing people notice when they sit down is the centerpiece. Why not stimulate a discussion on American arts?")

Mrs. Ford does the planning for State Dinners, with the aid of Chef Haller, and Social Secretary Nancy Lammerding Ruwe. Sometimes I have suggestions for the guest list, but my real participation does not begin until two or three days ahead of time, when my office releases the details of the dinner and I go over the logistics of press coverage with Rex Scouten and Nancy Ruwe. The day of the dinner, I make last-minute arrangements: see that the lights and cable equipment are set up to cover the toasts, go over the details for the lighting for the entertainment, see that phones are working in the little theater for the wire services, let the ushers' office know how many reporters there will be to make arrangements for the refreshments. And so on. And so on. Then, early this evening, as some of Washington's finest women were donning their finest finery, I donned mine: an apricot chiffon dress with matching shawl designed by Haehie Chang of Georgetown. ("White Tie" means white tie, for White House Staff and press, too.) As I dressed in my office in fifteen minutes time, I pictured elegant Washington ladies languishing in perfumed baths, happily contemplating the fact that "The President and Mrs. Ford" had requested the pleasure of their company "on the occasion of the visit of his Royal Highness the Shahanshah of Iran. . . . " It must be nice to be a guest.

At seven o'clock sharp, I pick up the photographers who wish to view and photograph the State Dining Room, all set up for the big occasion. Green and white was tonight's color scheme, a garden theme, with greenery all around the room, lilies of the valley surrounding the bronze centerpieces, and garlands attached to everything—the walls, the chandeliers, the mantelpieces, the back of the dining chairs.

It was very spring-like. And very beautiful. Especially in the splendid silence that fills the State Dining Room when it is all ready for the crowd, but still completely empty. At 7:00 P.M. the only occupant is a very pensive Abraham Lincoln, in portrait form over the mantel.

My next chore is the entrance shot. As the guests begin arriving via taxi cab, chauffeured limousine, or car and sweep through the entrance into the Diplomatic Room where they are greeted by music, social military aides in dress uniform and a place to check their wraps, I am positioning the press behind stanchions in the hallway outside. For after checking their things, the guests will move on through the camera crews, flash bulbs, and inquiring reporters, up the staircase to a table covered with white envelopes, which contain their seating assignments and name cards. The guests present their name cards to the announcer, and then enter the East Room as the syllables of their names ricochet off its walls. Mixed drinks are served.

I position the photographers for the staircase shot. As all this was happening at the Diplomatic entrance, the President and Mrs. Ford greeted the Shahanshah and Shabanou (it took several State Department phone calls to establish that that is indeed what she is called) of Iran at the North Portico Entrance (*click! click! flash! flash!*) and proceeded upstairs with their guests of honor and Henry Kissinger to the Yellow Oval Room, where they stay until the others are all happily drinking in the East Room. At that point (a little after eight) the Fords' entourage promenades down the North Portico staircase (hence the "staircase shot") and then proceeds to the East Room, where they, too, are announced: "LADIES AND GENTLEMEN, THE PRESIDENT OF THE UNITED STATES AND MRS. FORD, AND THE SHAHANSHAH OF IRAN AND THE EMPRESS FARAH."

Hail to the Chief.

Farewell to the press.

As the Heads of State and their wives form a receiving line, ushering their guests into the Cross Hall (where an honor guard of twenty-five social aides stands at attention) and into the State Dining Room for dinner, I bid adieu to the White House press corps for about an hour and a half, and proceed downstairs to the White House Mess. My job is about one-third done.

In the State Dining Room, two butlers serve every ten people. Tables are adorned with bowls of nuts, silver containers containing ten different brands of cigarettes, and place settings which contain four different wine glasses, three forks and three knives each.

In the White House Mess, it's steak, salad, and ice cream sundaes for my staff, Nancy Ruwe's staff, Dr. Lukash, who stays around the White House during all such official occasions, and the social aides (military aides whose job it is to mix, mingle, and dance with guests at State Dinners).

Upstairs, Downstairs.

There is a place to plug in phones at the table in the Mess, and during dinner, I periodically call the ushers' office upstairs for an update on the meal: ("We're just serving the saddle of veal and tomatoes Saint Germain."),

When they give me the go-ahead signal ("We're finishing the salad and going on to dessert") I go back to the press room and pick up the reporters to take them to the Little Theater where the toasts of the President and the Shah will be piped in. More easily said than done. The Little Theater is in the East Wing, a long walk from the press room. So there I go, the scout leader clearing the path for my pack of about forty "scouts" in formal attire as we hike through corridor after corridor. The arrival at the "campsite" is usually accompanied by a general lack of harmony, despite the fact that there are butlers on duty in the Little Theater serving drinks. I am usually the prime beneficiary of the ill will, as reporters yell because there is a lack of seating charts or because the after-dinner guest list is incomplete. (An additional eighty to 100 people are always invited to come for the entertainment and dancing that follow a State Dinner.) It is by no means a unified group, the bevy of journalists, and usually, if I am patient, they get bored with me and begin fighting each other. Tonight, for example, Betty Beale took on the others. There are two types of State Dinner reporters: those who are obviously reporters (you can tell by their notebooks and those tell-tale ball-point pen stains on their gowns) and those who deep down would like to "pass" for an invitee. Betty Beale is the latter. She parks her car where the guests park, enters where they enter, checks her mink where the guests check theirs, and portrays what her colleagues call the "hide-behind-a-potted-plant" approach to investigative reporting. Tonight she began lecturing others about how gauche she thought it was to carry around notebooks and pens at a State Dinner. The group counterattacked. To my great relief, at just about that moment, somewhere, many, many corridors away, Gerald Ford began his toast. The noise in the Little Theater came to an abrupt halt.

As soon as the toasts end, Fran Lewine and Helen Thomas run for the two telephones I made sure this afternoon were plugged in.

The guests are now finishing dinner and passing serenely from the State Dining Room, to the Red, Green, and Blue Rooms, where liqueurs, coffee and butlers wait, along with the President and his guest of honor.

The second Helen and Fran finish filing their stories, they all want to go upstairs to where the action is. I try to stall. People like to linger over dinner and when the press hit the guests, it always causes a terrible traffic jam, preventing people from leaving the Dining Room. "Please be careful tonight not to block the exit from the Dining Room; you know it causes a terrible traffic jam." Lots of luck.

The troop is ready to break camp. I try walking slowly. I am the leader, after all. It is my prerogative to set the pace. They barge ahead. As soon as we get upstairs, they attack. Within seconds, there is a terrible traffic jam. The Koffee Klatches begin. Either it is a group of reporters huddling around one guest, or a group of reporters huddling together, sharing tidbits.

By 10:15, I move the press into the East Room. "Writing press stands against the wall!" I tell them. "Remember, you're not a guest. The seats *must* be saved for guests!" My goodness, I *am* a scout master. I shudder at the demeaning tone of my own voice. I look around the room and shudder again. There are reporters sitting in guests' chairs.

The room fills and at 10:30 the entertainment begins. It is usually a good show. Many veteran entertainers say that they get an extra spurt of adrenalin in such esteemed surroundings. Some even confess a touch of stage fright is justified. When Edward Villela and Violette Verdy danced at the State Dinner for the Prime Minister of Singapore, the portable stage was positioned under an enormous chandelier which somewhat cramped the dancers' style. Villela later complained that they had to be unusually careful during their leaps and lifts.

If Ann-Margret had any fears tonight, she didn't show it. Instead, she brought a little Americana and a lot of Las Vegas into the East Room, with a rousing song-and-dance repertoire that began with "I Won't Last a Day Without You" and culminated in a crescendo-like "Salute to the Bicentennial" with Ann-Margret, clad in a rather skimpy red, white, and blue-spangled bathing suit that will probably be forever linked in the Shah's mind with the strains of "I'm a Yankee Doodle Dandy."

On to the Grand Ballroom, where the scene from now on consists of dancing, mingling in the Hall and State Rooms, and, in nice weather such as tonight's, standing and talking on the balcony. The weather is vitally important to my job, because this is the stage of the evening when reporters file their stories. That means they must traipse back and forth to the press room. And they must be escorted. In good weather, I escort them to the North Portico Entrance and they use the outdoor route (under the watchful eye of the Executive Protection Service) to the press lobby in the West Wing. But in the freezing cold of winter, this is not possible. We tread the interior route instead, all the way around to the press room. And back. On the average, that means I make fifteen different round-trips. I may be the only one whose feet hurt from walking, not dancing, at State Dinners.

After the entertainment in the East Room, things usually become very spontaneous and informal. It is not unusual to hear the question, "Mr. President, may I have this dance?" answered with an enthusiastic affirmative. I understand that at the Fords' very first State Dinner—one held for King Hussein last August—CBS commentator Eric Sevareid did a Mexican hat dance with Senator Mark Hatfield. Just last month, the President of Zambia stood up with his delegation and sang some songs. It is quite normal for performers who are also White House guests to just grab a microphone and entertain. Pearl Bailey did just that tonight.

It is now after two. I have returned to my office to drop off the extra press releases, change into more comfortable shoes, and pick up the clothes I wore to work about eighteen hours ago.

The State Dining Room has been undressed, scrubbed, and rendered immaculate once again. The guests have taken home menus, place cards, and matches for scrapbooks, and memories that will be conversation pieces for years to come. The Shah is nestled all snug in his bed as visions of "Bicentennial Salutes" dance through his head.

And I am about to depart, which means I am about to discover the answer to the most important question raised all evening: will my Volvo start? It didn't after the last State Dinner.

## Chapter Eight
## JUNE, 1975:

# A FRIED EGG UPSIDE DOWN

*MAY 28, 1975*

Today at 6:45 A.M., I reported to the distinguished visitors'
lounge at Andrews Air Force Base. So did about twelve other staff
people. At 7:15 we were joined by six more. At 7:20, Donald
Rumsfeld, Ron Nessen, Bob Hartmann and Dr. Lukash boarded
Army One on the South Lawn of the White House. At 7:25, they
were joined by the President and Mrs. Ford, Susan, and Janet Ford
and Army One took off for Andrews. Army One landed at Andrews at 7:40. At 7:42, the President made brief remarks, which
concluded at 7:47. The President and Mrs. Ford kissed Susan
good-bye and told her to have a wonderful Senior Prom. We all
boarded Air Force One, and at 7:50 Air Force One left Andrews en
route to Zavatem airport, Brussels, Belgium. The press plane followed at 8:20.

It was hardly spontaneous. The details of take-off were worked
out well in advance, as were all the other details of this trip. Between May 28th and June 3rd, the Fords will visit Belgium (to reassure NATO allies of America's reliability in the post-Vietnam era),

Spain (to negotiate a renewal of the U.S. lease on Spanish military bases), Austria (where the President will meet with Egyptian President Anwar Sadat), and Italy (to discuss Italy's economic and political problems with its leaders). And every detail for every hour of every day has not only been planned, but also diagrammed out in a pocket size small looseleaf notebook with a plastic cover that says "SCHEDULE." It tells me, as I flip the pages, that tonight at 9:18, Mrs. Ford will depart the Royal Palace in Brussels en route to the U.S. Embassy residence, that the President and Egypt's President Sadat will meet from 10:35 to 12:05 in Salzburg, Austria, on Monday, that at 10:38 on Sunday morning, after passing by the ceremonial honor guard, the President and Mrs. Ford and Chancellor and Mrs. Kreisky will pause, while two young girls present flowers to Mrs. Ford. And that when the President poses for pictures with President Leone of Italy at 1:30 next Tuesday, the President will be "seated on a sofa to the right of President Leone, who is seated on a chair." The book also includes seating charts of the NATO conference rooms, diagrams for motorcades and processions, and a step-by-step diagram of the arrival and departure routes including which elevators to use for the audience with His Holiness.

Everyone on this trip has reading material. The press is given a booklet that offers schedules, background information on the castles and regions to be visited, plus tourist tips, such as maps, currency conversion tables, and generalizations about climate. And the President and Mrs. Ford have the most detailed handout—briefing papers that tell them what will happen when and, most important of all, with whom. There are diagrams of palaces and details on princes. The personal background papers have a picture of the person in the right-hand corner. On the left side, the copy states his name, what he should be addressed as, where he stands in the political pecking order, what his history is, his interests are, and so on. Taboo subjects of conversation are also spelled out. Thus, at this very moment, as Air Force One whizzes across the Atlantic, Mrs. Ford may be discovering which areas and why the wife of a Head of State, who is an accomplished pianist, considers too sensitive to talk about.

\* \* \*

*JUNE 3, 1975*

The schedule came alive. All the actors in the play followed their stage instructions and, step by step, stop by stop, the drama unfolded. What was lacking in plot was compensated for in the cast of characters. All over Europe, the briefing papers turned into real people. While the President met with the leaders, Mrs. Ford met with their wives. And I watched. It was a study of contrasts. In Brussels, there was the established royalty—Queen Fabiola, surprisingly warm and down to earth considering her aristocratic background (and the fact that protocol dictates one must address her as "Your Royal Highness") versus Margaret Trudeau, wife of the Canadian Prime Minister there for the NATO conference, who, at only twenty-six, pregnant with her third child, seemed very young and somewhat unsure of her role. I thought it significant that in conversation both Pierre Trudeau and the Fords told her how much she would enjoy Susan Ford. Apparently they share an interest in photography and a passion for blue jeans.

In Spain, there were really two First Ladies: Mrs. Franco, wife of the Generalissimo, and Princess Sophia, wife of Prince Juan Carlos, who is expected to succeed Franco, if and when Franco permits anyone to succeed him. (A thirty-six-year term of office indicates a certain reluctance toward change.) Mrs. Franco, a mother, grandmother and great-grandmother, is a very traditional woman who never travels out of Spain. Sophia, in her thirties, is a modern woman who travels extensively, speaks impeccable English, and is quite independent. Both women appeared to be very strong and quite serious about their roles. Mrs. Ford enjoyed Princess Sophia's energy and curiosity. And I think she shared Mrs. Franco's old-fashioned feelings about the importance of home and family.

Home and family must not be underestimated as a valid international bridgegapper. Motherhood, I've decided, has incredible potential as a diplomatic tool (granted, it will remain an undeveloped one until more Heads of State are mothers). Being a mother is both an intense personal experience and a universal one. Its universality makes it an easy conversation opener. Its personal side means that quite often the conversation will zero in close to the human psyche and be quite revealing. I have the feeling that while the men talked troops, the women really communicated.

Another profound generalization from the neophyte international traveler: there are palaces and there are palaces. The fact is, in spite of the propaganda caused by all those fairy tales, there are palaces in which it would prove difficult to live happily ever after, even with Prince Charming. Case in point: Moncloa Palace where the Fords stayed in Madrid. It is beautiful from the outside, and I'm sure it was heaven way back when, but this is 1975, and Triple A would not waste a single star. Rundown is the word.

On the morning before our departure from Spain, I came into the kitchen to get a cup of coffee and I could not find a cup that was not cracked. Really cracked. With whole pieces missing. (The rumor later was that there were exactly two uncracked cups which a butler had been assigned to guard for the Fords—along with the only pint of fresh hot coffee in the palace.) The kitchen floor was filthy, the scent of dying elegance pervasive. In a decrepit dining room, adjacent to the kitchen, the White House staff fought over cups and juice. Bob Hartmann stole someone's half-finished orange juice in a moment of desperation. Meanwhile, upstairs in the Presidential Suite. . . .

The sleeping accommodations were not much better. Apparently news of the Fords' "erotic" behavior (i.e., sleeping together) had reached Spain. Greeting them in their palatial Presidential quarters was one bed, higher than the average bed, and a little wider than a single size, but not as wide as a double. Mrs. Ford took one look at it and announced that there wasn't a chance in the world that she was going to sleep in that size bed "with him." To accommodate madame, they brought in a little cot which they placed next to the other bed, but it was lower and smaller. Together the two beds were quite a sight, it looked like one for the King and one for his lackey—especially because his bed had a gilded headboard and hers had none.

Make no mistake, though, there are still some good palaces around. The Schloss Kressheim, where the Fords stayed in Salzburg, Austria, is one. And it was really put to the test, because it rained the entire time we were in Salzburg, and Mrs. Ford never left the palace. In fact, it was pouring when our plane arrived. It was so bad that when I got off Air Force One, I sought shelter under the plane's wing. Thus, as (the schedule dictated) "The President and Mrs. Ford are escorted by Chancellor and Mrs. Kreisky past the ceremonial guard," I had a beautiful view of distant umbrellas. And I missed the one "unscheduled" happening, the President tripped getting off Air Force One. (Mrs. Ford said he was too impatient and went running down the slippery steps too fast.) He immediately regained his balance, but apparently not before Peter Bregg, an AP photographer, captured the fall in a series of shots with his motorized camera. Karl Schumacher, Mrs. Ford's photographer, told me about it on our way to the palace. I hoped he was wrong.

But back to palaces. Franco's palace in Madrid is definitely palace-issimo. Exquisite. Room after room of treasures. But "His Holiness" has the fanciest abode. Throughout Europe, there was pomp. There was ceremony. There were kings and queens and princes and princesses. But the only "royalty" that really lives like royalty these days, is the Pope. When the Fords had their audience with him in Rome, I couldn't get over the throne rooms, the hand-carved extravaganzas on the walls, the magnificent paintings, and the men of the court, in uniforms adorned with gold chains and ornaments. I thought it ironic that protocol dictated that I remove my necklace and ring.

Spain produced the fanciest motorcade of the trip with horses in parade dress marching beside the cars and enormous crowds lined up along the path. When it was over, Mrs. Ford said, "I want to do that again!" She rode with Mrs. Franco, who, she said, kept apologizing for the horses that were blocking the car, but Mrs. Ford loved the pomp and ceremony of it all, the "spirited horses that had to be kept in check to proceed at a slow pace so Franco and the President could stand and wave."

I had a clearer vision of the men who walked quietly behind the horses with brooms and pans.

And the expressionless crowds. Huge in numbers, small in passion. Armed military men lined the streets between the people and the parade, but the restraints were unnecessary. This crowd needed warm-up exercises. They were not hostile. They were ambivalent. It was as though they had been ordered to appear, but no one had told them how to feel about it.

A memorable evening on the trip was Franco's State Dinner, because that was when I got a chance to see the Royale Palace and because the set-up for the dinner itself was incredible: one hundred fifty people seated around one single dinner table. There were twenty-six candelabras on the table. Or maybe thirty-two. I was so impressed that I took the time to count them, and now I can't re-member which number is correct.

I had a lot of time to count at the State Dinner, thanks to a com-munications problem. My dinner partner was a distinguished-look-ing Army general, a man in his sixties with white hair, an impres-sive carriage, and almost as many medals as Franco. He looked like a man whose life would make fascinating dinner conversation. Unfortunately, his English was as good as my Spanish. Precisely. "Why don't we practice with each other?" I asked him in Spanish.

It took several minutes to transmit the message. He thought it was a terrific idea (I think). So I talked to him in broken Spanish, and he talked to me in broken English (I think). I told him his En-glish was really quite good, and he told me my Spanish was really quite good (I think).

We had a lot of time, since we wasted little time eating. Franco, it seems, is not much of an eater. But his reputation as a dictator has not been overestimated. When he's finished eating, that is the signal to take everybody's food away. A mere flick of the fork and *poof!* My course was gone.

The Franco State Dinner was not the only communications prob-lem I had on this trip. I had many. It's just that the rest were with Americans. There seems to be a total lack of understanding among the White House people who plan these trips as to who I am and what I do.

I am not Mrs. Ford's secretary. I am her Press Secretary. Thus, I have to be with the press, with Mrs. Ford, or close to each, in order to do my job, in order to give out details, interpret a story, or clari-fy a question before it becomes a mistake blown out of proportion. On every stop, that closeness became a challenge to my ingenuity, as I was inevitably assigned to a distant motorcade car far away from both the First Lady and the press.

In Madrid, for example, Mrs. Ford was scheduled to see Mrs. Franco and some other women at the palace while the President got together with the men. Ron Nessen, of course, went where the President went. I expected to be going with the First Lady but learned not a moment too soon that when her car turned one way, toward the palace, the car I was assigned (with the President's va-let and various secretaries) would be turning in the other direction, headed for the staff office. I jumped out of that car and into another which was going to the palace.

I complained later to the head of the advance team, Red Ca-
vaney. He said to take it up with Nessen, as I was part of his staff.
Nessen said that that was ridiculous, I was by no means part of his
staff. I agreed that it was ridiculous, but perhaps he could still help
me out. He said he'd love to but since I wasn't part of his
staff. . . .

## JUNE 5, 1975

Today was Susan's graduation from Holton Arms, and the President gave the graduation address. It was typical of a high school
graduation—the proud parents (the President had tears in his eyes
as he handed Susan her diploma) and the tearful farewell to
friends. Susan and her friends the twins, Reagan and Ellison Golubin, seemed locked in an interminable farewell embrace, as though
oblivious to the fact that although they will no longer be attending
Holton Arms together, they will still be in touch.

Susan leaves in two days for Yosemite, California, where she'll
be attending an intensive ten-day photography workshop under
Ansel Adams, one of America's most famous creative photographers. Susan's been interested in photography for some time now.
She's been taking courses at nearby art galleries, and her senior
school project was to "follow Daddy around shooting." (The only
problem was that her mother would not let her shoot in blue jeans,
which irritated her. "David [Kennerly] does!" she argued. She
lost.) David tells me that Susan's work is getting better and better.
She's working hard on it, he says, and he is impressed with her eye
and her growth.

Ansel Adams met with the President in January to talk about National Parks, and when he heard about Susan's interest in photography, he invited her to take part in his workshop. Susan is very
excited.

Meanwhile, down on the range, Steven Ford plans to spend the
summer backpacking, studying grizzly bears and attending rodeo
school, plans that are not being met with parental pleasure. Mrs.
Ford says, somewhat nervously, that she hopes he "gets it out of
his system" (as quickly and as uninjuriously as possible, I suspect)
and the President says that frankly, he'd rather have his youngest
son stay around "gentle cows and old horses."

The Secret Service is equally enthusiastic.

If indeed there is a "bucking bronco" within the First Family, I suspect it is the son in residence. Jack Ford skipped his own graduation at Utah State University so he could attend Susan's. Driving cross-country he got as far as Ohio before his car broke down, and he pulled into the White House in the wee hours of this morning. He opted for bed over Holton Arms, thereby becoming the only Ford who did not attend Susan's graduation, and doubtlessly setting a family record for missing two graduations in one week. Last summer he worked as a ranger fighting forest fires in Idaho. Before that he worked as an airline baggage man, a hotel bellman, and a deck hand on a freighter. But he plans to spend this summer out of the labor market ("Trying to put it all together") and I have a funny feeling that it is going to increase my workload.

"You can bet it will," the man on his Secret Service detail assured me. "I'd put money on it. That's a rotten apple, that kid."

"Hmmmmm?"

"You should have seen the way they lived out there in Utah. You should have seen his friends. College kids with no goals. Slobs, that's what they were. There were six of them who roomed together in this red brick house across from the campus. What a mess—empty beer cans, dirty ashtrays, records stuffed into orange crates. It was a wild place. A flop house. 'The Dead Meat House'—that's what they called it."

I hoped he would not explain why they called it that.

He didn't.

"He never carries money," the agent went on, "so he's always borrowing money. Which I might add, he rarely remembers to pay back. He never smiles. Never says a friendly word to us. Sullen, that's what he is. And scornful. And wild. He does some pretty crazy things, let me tell you. And reliable? Not on your life. He'd tell us one set of plans, and then change his mind suddenly—'spontaneously'—and run off in a totally different direction. We spent most of our time running after him. And that is a *lot* of time."

I could see it only too well: there was Jack, the self-proclaimed spur-of-the-moment, free-spirited, outdoorsman and there was the Secret Service, upright, uptight patriots with a sober job to do. Perfect foils.

"I used to be able to just split for the day and get away from everything by riding in the mountains," Jack had complained in

April. "Now if I want to, I have to get horses for the Secret Service too!"

Perfect adversaries. I would be more amused, though, if the "war" had not moved into my own backyard.

I wonder if Michael Ford's Secret Service detail ever gets bored.


## JUNE 6, 1975

Don Hewitt called. He wants to put Mrs. Ford on the first "60 Minutes" show of the summer.

Too soon?


## JUNE 17, 1975

Myra MacPherson interviewed Mrs. Ford today for a story she is doing for the September issue of *McCalls*.

Sitting on the rim of the bathtub in Mrs. Ford's bathroom as she put on her makeup before the interview, I "warmed her up" by going over some of the topics I thought Myra might be interested in.

We talked about the last year.

"I think the opportunity came at a perfect time for me—just when Steven had graduated from high school and Susan was in her last year. It gave me a career that filled in that gap with children having reached an age of independence."

We talked about her bout with breast cancer.

"It knocked the wind out of me. It took a period to recover. I accepted it though. My family was so concerned—I had never seen my husband so upset—that I felt I had to lift their spirits, to prove to them it wasn't a major catastrophe. When you analyze it, what would you rather lose, a right arm or a right breast? I'm right-handed. An arm would be a greater loss. Jerry was cute. He said 'If you can't wear dresses low-cut in front, wear them low-cut in back.'

"I guess the cancer operation was a terrible jolt, but it was also the first sign I had of how powerful this position is. My experience sent the message out. I've had letters from people who found that they had cancer . . . young girls twenty-seven, twenty-eight, thirty years old. In spite of it, they are grateful. If it had not been detected, it would have spread. If you can save one life, you're glad. If you can save many, you're really happy."

We talked about White House entertaining.

"I like the kind of entertaining we're doing. I think we've changed the atmosphere. Jerry and I are very ordinary people who enjoy life and aren't overly impressed with ourselves."

We talked about abortion.

"I'm glad to see it brought out of the backwoods and put into the hospitals where it belongs."

We talked about the ERA.

"The Equal Rights Amendment is a must. I've never heard a good Phyllis Schlafly argument."

"60 Minutes," we might just be ready.

## *JUNE 20, 1975*

Yesterday was the date of the Martha Graham fund-raising gala in New York City. Mrs. Ford and I flew up together. She was terribly excited about the performance scheduled for that evening, and about Martha Graham in general.

"I spent two summers studying with Martha Graham at Bennington College in Vermont, and then when I was twenty, my mother let me move to New York City just to study with her some more," Mrs. Ford said going up on the plane yesterday. "I remember the first summer, after the first three or four days of concentrated exercise, we were going up and down stairs on our bottoms, our leg muscles were so sore. We walked around barefoot all the time. And one of the things I particularly remember Martha doing was getting us to spread our toes and see how much grass we could pick up with our toes. It was a marvelous training for our feet. It still is an excellent exercise.

"I worked as a model when I studied with her in New York. I had to support myself. Martha said my problem was that I had a job and a social life. To succeed, I needed complete concentration on the dance."

Mrs. Ford performed professionally in New York with Martha Graham in *American Document*, but it was a short career. Her mother prevailed upon her to return to Michigan.

"I began dancing when I was about eight," she told me. "Many of my friends say that I had really no childhood—just dance. Every day I practiced. After school I headed straight for the studio while they all went off in cars to listen to records or do whatever high school children do. Until I got this pinched nerve in my neck, I never dropped it. I danced after the children were born, too."

Today was the opening day of the U.N. International Women's Year conference in Mexico City, and I knew the press would want something related to that. So I asked Mrs. Ford whether she considered herself a liberated woman.

"Any woman who feels confident in herself and happy in what she is doing is a liberated woman. It's a general feeling of positiveness and really being able to live with yourself, I think. Yes, I feel liberated."

The gala presentation was the premier of Martha Graham's newest ballet, *Lucifer*, starring Rudolf Nureyev and Dame Margot Fonteyn. Halston designed the costumes worn by Nureyev and Fonteyn too, which reportedly contained diamonds and jewels worth nearly $100,000. (Nureyev's "costume" amounted to a bejeweled band aid!)

When the performance ended, Mrs. Ford ran backstage and presented flowers to Martha Graham. It was more than a presentation. One could tell by her excitement and delight how much Mrs. Ford cared. She took the dancers' hands and when they made their bows, she made hers. The audience was delighted. And she was delighted. It was a very special moment.

It was the second performance of the evening, however. The first one was put on by comedian Woody Allen—unintentionally. He is also a Martha Graham fan, and he was to escort Mrs. Ford to the gala. Well, the truth is Woody Allen *is* Woody Allen. The insecurity act is no act. He was terrified at the idea of meeting Mrs. Ford. He got out of his cab, and ran inside the building just as Mrs. Ford was about to arrive. Patti Matson said she practically had to drag him out bodily. "Don't you want to meet Mrs. Ford outside?" she asked, and in reply, Woody Allen hid behind his girl friend Diane Keaton. In the end, he did greet Mrs. Ford, but with all the social grace of an eleven-year-old forced to go to dancing school.

"He was like a little boy," Mrs. Ford told me later. "Diane Keaton and I each took a hand and kind of led him in. But he was really funny. He told me why he gave up dancing—his self-consciousness in a leotard. He wasn't at all what I expected. He's really inhibited and self-conscious. He was scared to death to go before the mike in front of the press. He couldn't understand how I could put up with all that jazz.''

The third performance was the party Halston threw at his townhouse after the gala. Both the party and the townhouse were very, very. I wore the wrong kind of dress, but in this group, had I worn nothing, no one would have even raised an eyebrow. It was that kind of party—beautiful women draping themselves all over modern furniture in an architecturally perfect townhouse on East 63rd Street. The Andy Warhol crowd. Not Mrs. Ford's normal circle, but they loved talking about the dance and so did she. Everyone was rich, and almost everyone was gay. (I later told Mrs. Ford that we were the only straight ones. She laughed.)

Halston took us on tour. The first floor, where the party was taking place, was very stark, white with recessed lighting. Through the window in the back you could see an enclosed garden which rather resembled a jungle. They used to have parrots in it, but not anymore. ("We didn't like the way they talked back to the people we had over.") As you go up from floor to floor, the potential for vertigo increases dramatically. Each floor is a huge, open space with a balcony. A balcony with very low railings. One wrong step and you've switched floors. They had an elevator, but Mrs. Ford wanted to walk and see everything. When we got to the fourth floor, no one was there but a girl, sitting all by herself in a chair, staring off into space. Immobile. It was as though she were modeling, or as though she herself were a still shot. A new art form? She never acknowledged our presence. For all I know, she's still there.

I struck up a friendship with Halston's roommate, a Latin American artist named Victor Hugo (a nice name, though not terribly original). He showed me one of his creations—a plastic see-through heel with a spoon resting on top of it (in such a way that the whole thing looked like a shoe). Under plexiglass.

"You know what I'm grooving on now?" he whispered. "Eggs."

"No kidding."

"Yeah. Do you want to see some?"

"Sure."

He took me to the bathroom where, in a storage area, he had about 100 drawings of eggs—scrambled eggs, fried eggs, poached—however you like it. A breakfast addict's delight. He gave one to me and one to Mrs. Ford. On the back of hers it says "A FRIED EGG UPSIDE DOWN Victor Hugo."

## JUNE 27, 1975

Ric Sardo left today, frustrated and bitter and angry at Donald Rumsfeld for seeing to it that his hands were tied and that he was kept at a distance from the President. He's being transferred.

He said he isn't sure what he will be doing next, but that he is looking forward to a change. He says he really needs a change.

## JUNE 28, 1975

The East Wing press office is made up of me, Patti Matson, and Fran Paris whom I hired to replace Nancy Chirdon as secretary. Three people. The only other time within recent administrations that anyone can remember the press staff being that small was in the midst of Watergate, when the Nixons were in hiding.

Three people to handle press for Mrs. Ford, the Ford children, Shan the cat and Liberty, the world's most written to golden retriever. Three people to handle all press for White House parties, social functions and State Dinners, write press releases on daily East Wing activities, answer all incoming mail and telephone queries, write articles to be published in magazines under Ford family bylines, generate and research ideas, draft speeches and advance trips.

Three perkless people, two of whom Bill Gulley won't even give special permission to carry out trays from the Mess. Believe me, perquisites can be more than status symbols. They are tremendous time and labor savers. When you have no car at your disposal, for example, it means that when Patti goes out to advance an event Mrs. Ford is taking part in, she wastes a lot of time looking for a parking space. OK. But not when cars and drivers are sitting idly in the garage. And I waste a lot of time either cajoling Gulley or doing without on those days when I simply can't bear having to go through the sexist shuffling involved in flattering him into bequeathing to me the use of a mini-bus to take Mrs. Ford's reporters to the Kennedy Center. (Walking in to ask a favor of the head of the Military Affairs Office is like walking past a group of construction workers, and then stopping and responding to their remarks.)

We have become three live-ins. As a result of the workload we all work seven days a week. Since I began working here officially, almost nine months ago, I have had only three weekends off. I rarely get home before nine, often much later, and always with "homework." Then it's back to the office by 8:00 in the morning. (Edward is more than willing to document such statistics.) But there is a more upsetting result. I do not have time to do my job, not the way I envision it. I spend so much time running just to stay in place that I have too little time to take the initiative. There are things I want to do. I want to continue to build Mrs. Ford's public image so that she does become a First Lady with easily identifiable and respected personality traits. The more she is taken seriously, the more she can do.

I told all this to Mrs. Ford today. I wonder if she understood.


## JUNE 30, 1975

The President said, "Betty, why are you talking to me about this? Don Rumsfeld is in charge of staff. Tell him. He'll work it out for you."

She did. He didn't.

"He says he's trying to cut down on White House manpower, Sheila, both for the East Wing and the West Wing."

"You have an East Wing staff of twenty-seven, which includes the caligraphers," I said. Pat Nixon had thirty-one. Lady Bird Johnson had thirty-one. That means you have four fewer people than they had to handle two more children than they had. What is left to cut?"

"Apparently he wants to reduce the entire White House staff to 450. He says if he gave you one more person, that would make it 451."

"Not if he moved a West Wing person into the East Wing." (How about that person I won from Ron in the famous swimming race?)

"How could he do that?"

"Just by doing it. There are a lot of people in the West Wing with nothing to do. I see them sitting, doing nothing. That is why the staff is being reduced. But we have the opposite problem here.''

"Don says he doesn't understand the East Wing," Mrs. Ford said.

(Oh yeah?)

"I've offered to explain it to him many times. I think perhaps he does not want to understand the East Wing.''

"Well, I don't know what I can do.''

"You are not under Rumsfeld. You are the one who has to support your staff. Mrs. Ford, *you are Mrs. Ford!*''

Two minutes later I got a phone call. It was Joyce Rumsfeld (as in "Mrs. Donald Rumsfeld''). She wanted to know if I could send her a picture of myself. It seems the dress shop where she works in Georgetown wants to put a sketch of me in their window display "as an example of the Working Woman.''

*Chapter Nine*
JULY, 1975:

# SMOKES WHAT? SMOKES WHAT!

*JULY 1, 1975*

"We've worked it all out," the Secret Service agent told me with pride. "Jack will be sitting in the front row. As soon as the Rolling Stones finish, he is to jump right up on the stage before the rest of the crowd so he has less chance of being trampled."

"*Less* chance? That is some maneuver. What kind of advice is that?"

"He's going to jump on stage anyway."

"How do you know?"

"He always does. Sheila, there are two sides to Jack Ford. He goes bananas at these rock concerts. He smokes and he listens to the music and he goes bananas. Just like all of them."

Smokes. Smokes what? Smokes what!

"Hey Sheila," said a grinning David Kennerly, "did you hear our great idea? Jack's going to take Mick Jagger and Bianca out on the *Sequoia* after the concert tonight. There'll be about four or five of us. What do you think?"

("Dad, can I have the keys to the Presidential yacht? I just want to get stoned with the Stones." What is this ridiculousness? Am I crazy or is everyone else?)

"Uh, David, really, I don't think it's so hot . . ."

"Why?" His grin fades. He is confused. He is sincere. He is *really* asking me why.

"It's too cool, David, too pat. They're taking advantage of him because he's the President's son, and he's taking advantage of being the President's son. If he wanted to do it privately, okay, but—"

"It's going to be private. Just four or five of us. We wouldn't be telling anyone."

"Who's going?"

"Me, Jack, Mick, Bianca, Tom Zito, the rock reporter for the *Post—*"

"Now wait a second! You're taking the *Post*'s rock reporter and you expect it to be *private*? You expect him to spend an evening like that and not write anything about it?"

"Sheila, he—"

"And just tell me something else. Is Jack going to—uh—a—relax?" (Why am I unable to say it out loud?)

"What do you mean, 'relax'?"

(Say it, Sheila!)

"Will he—smoke?"

(There, I said it!)

"Smoking grass? Smoking dope? Is that what you're talking about?"

"Yes."

"You mean that it wouldn't be so good to read in the papers that the President's son is smoking dope on the *Sequoia*."

"Yes! Look, David, I don't care what is done in private" (just don't tell me, please don't tell me) "but isn't it absurd to make it a public issue? I mean if he's for the legalization of marijuana this is the *last* way he should handle it. Not only won't he get it legalized, but his father won't get re-elected."

Jack walked in as we were discussing it.

"Sheila thinks this is a bad idea," David explained. "She's lukewarm about it."

"I'm not lukewarm about it," I corrected, "I'm cold about it."

"It's turning into such a big production," Jack said, "I don't know if I want to do it anyway."

"Right! What do you want to make a big production out of it for? Do something spontaneous—like just all go out for dinner afterwards."

"It'll be too late."

"Okay, then tomorrow. Do something just to have fun. I'll tell you quite frankly, Jack, I don't know you very well. But I do know that you have a lot of different interests, and all I see these days is one. I suppose it's a neat thing to do, to be the President's son and entertain Mick Jagger, but it seems a bit contrived to me."

I think I was persuasive, but I worried about it all day. On the one hand, I felt like the squarest person in the world. On the other hand, I felt like the only sane one. Smoking pot in public. The President's son. Few things would have more potential for explosion. Finally I couldn't stand it anymore. I called David Kennerly.

"Tell me something, David. . . . Do you think . . . I mean, if it's so important . . . could Jack . . . before the concert, before he leaves . . . so that then during the concert itself. . . . I know I'm neurotic, but. . . . Yes, David, please tell Jack to get stoned *before* he goes to the concert!"

David laughed. "Sheila, look, don't worry about it."

More easily said than done.

## JULY 2, 1975

I was in the West Hall waiting for Mrs. Ford to finish dressing for the ceremony (she was to receive the Golden Rose Award from the Florists' Transworld Delivery Association for her "leadership in the use of flowers in the White House") when Jack and David walked in. They wanted to let me know that Jack had consented to an interview for Andy Warhol's *Interview* magazine. Bianca Jagger and Warhol would do the interviewing.

"Does this have to be your first press exposure, Jack? *Interview* Magazine is a statement in itself. Wouldn't you rather talk to a more general publication first?"

"No. I think the *Interview* idea is good. I really don't think I should go conventional at first."

"I think you have to think about your impact. You have to be careful, Jack. If you're going to be in Washington, if you're going to be working on your father's campaign, you have to have a solid public image. I think you're being used by these people. What you should be doing is using them—using the press to your own advantage. Before you do an interview, you should think about what qualities are your best qualities and how you can play up those

qualities. You have to actively prepare for being interviewed. Now
when is this one with Bianca and Warhol going to take place?"

"Right now."

"What?" (Here I am about to watch Mrs. Ford receive fifty
long-stemmed roses while elsewhere in the White House Jack Ford
is making his public debut.) "Just wait a few minutes until I finish
doing this ceremony with your mother."

"I don't think I can."

I had never been enthusiastic about the Golden Rose Award.
Now I was extraordinarily *un*enthusiastic about it. "Gardening and
getting out, being with flowers, gives you a great sense of relaxation," Mrs. Ford told the florists as my heart beat reached record
speed. "It is therapeutic for me."

I ran upstairs as soon as it was over. Jack had said something
about the Truman Balcony. I opened the door and rushed out.
Empty. The door slammed behind me and I realized I was locked
out—locked out on the Truman Balcony with its airy charm and
splendid view. A nice place to reflect, but I was not pensive, I was
imprisoned. I became frantic; the door wouldn't open. I was pulling and twisting the knob and about to shout for help when I saw
Jack, David, Andy Warhol, and Bianca Jagger walking calmly toward me. Jack must have given the guests the grand tour first.
("This is the Yellow Oval Room, and this is my mother's Press
Secretary screaming for help.") They had trouble opening the door
from the inside, too, but finally it opened.

Bianca was decked out in a yellow floppy hat with a bow and a
yellow see-through dress that revealed the presence of little bloomer undies with lace on the bottom. I felt very conservative. The
style of my undies was irrelevant, given the thickness of my skirt.
And then there was my "straight" silk blouse, to say nothing of my
little earrings and platform heels and, most embarrassing of all, my
wedding band. I felt terribly uncomfortable. But, I assured myself
I would have felt more uncomfortable wearing the yellow floppy
hat and see-through dress. Admit it, Sheila, you're not that hip.

I sat in on the interview. No, to be fair I actively intruded in the
interview. Intentionally.

"How do you like being in the White House?" they asked Jack.

"Oh," complained Jack, "it's very difficult. It's very hard to relax. I have all these Secret Service agents around."

"I can't imagine it being any different for *you*, Bianca!" (Yes, it was my voice I heard.) "I mean you have body guards too, don't you?"

Soon Bianca was complaining about her body guards and gossiping about how much money Cher spends on her clothes and make-up.

Bianca had brought her own makeup with her (in an enormous tool case that her makeup man carried into the White House).

"Cher must have *two* of those," I said charitably. I was beginning to feel good. The heat was off Jack, and it was, well, a different kind of afternoon for me. I was even beginning to feel a little less square. The publisher of *Interview*, who had come along, greeted me with a warm "Hello, Sheila!" (There are side benefits to attending a Halston party!) I could tell David was terribly impressed and, as I replied "Oh, hi!" oh so casually, I promised myself that on pain of death, I would never admit to David how we knew each other.

It was picture-taking time. Everyone was taking pictures. David, Andy with his Polaroid camera. Dirck Halstead, a photographer friend of David. Dirck told Jack to stand near Bianca. Closer. "Put your hand there."

There?! Oh well, who reads *Interview* anyway?

Feeling good, I went up to see Mrs. Ford who was feeling angry. Her picture was not in the paper. Nor was any mention of the awards she presented at Catholic University yesterday to ten handicapped citizens who had designed Christmas angels.

"Nothing," she complained. "No picture, nothing. I really don't understand why."

"I understand it. There was just nothing to it." (Shades of the Golden Rose Award?)

"Well, I just don't understand the press."

"Yes you do. You know the kind of stories you read and the kind of stories you like to watch on television. Put yourself in the place of readers and you'll know what the editor wants."

I was pleased. I admit it. I was pleased with her growing thirst for publicity. I was pleased with her irritability, too, and I was pleased that she felt relaxed enough with me to let it show.

"I bet you didn't know about this side of me that can get mad," she said.

"What do you take me for, a fool?"

\* \* \*

## JULY 3, 1975

I've known comedienne Joan Rivers since 1968, when I was talent coordinator for her television show, and I've always liked her. She is warm and she is very bright, and she is as funny off stage as she is on. She's appearing at Shady Grove Theater in the Washington area at the moment and she wanted to show her daughter, Melissa, the White House.

They came for lunch today.

I felt like an intermediary between celebrities. The White House staff was awed by Joan Rivers ("If you have time, please stop by," requested the head of the Situation Room) and Joan Rivers was awed by the White House. She insisted that Melissa, who was dressed beautifully, put on her white gloves before meeting Mrs. Ford. It was the first time I've ever seen Joan at a loss for words. Luckily, once she was with Mrs. Ford, she regained her stage presence. They all got along quite well.


## JULY 7, 1975

Maybe it was last week's Bianca-Warhol experience. Maybe it was the stories I heard about Jack's mingling with celebrity-stars in New York City. I don't know what triggered it, but I cornered him. I told him that if he wanted to have the reputation of a do-nothing playboy, that was his prerogative. If he wanted to be the Fords' answer to the Roosevelt children, it was up to him. Just remember, I said, the reputation will live on with you after you leave the White House.

He said the whole thing was too silly to discuss.

Then I set about making his mother a television star. The "60 Minutes" show is all settled. Don Hewitt is going to come to the White House next week to work out final details, and the taping itself is scheduled for the week after that. I have purposely set up two magazine interviews for Mrs. Ford prior to the taping. (One, for a story in the November issue of *Family Circle*, will take place tomorrow.) I thought they would serve as good warm-up experiences, since in each case the interview will take place before the "60 Minutes" taping, but the story will not appear until after the show is aired.

I have not discussed "60 Minutes" with anyone but Mrs. Ford. The less said, the better.


## JULY 8, 1975

MEMORANDUM FOR: Mrs. Sheila Rabb Weidenfeld
FROM: Captain L. S. Kollmorgen

I am pleased to inform you that your membership in the White House Staff Mess has been changed from group one to group two, effective this date.


## JULY 14, 1975

"It is so typical of the unverified rhetoric these people put out!" he bellowed into the phone at me. Happily, I discovered the object of his wrath was not me, but an editorial in the *Washington Star* which attacked his father for permitting "clearcutting" of Federal forests. The editorial offended both his filial and forestal sensitivities, and for Jack Ford, those are prime areas of sensitivity. "Armchair conservationist," he sneered.

His tone changed. "I was thinking about writing a letter to the editor, telling them the facts about clearcutting, and how, actually, it is good for forests. Uh, what do you think?"

Well, well.

"Good idea. Why don't you try it?"


## JULY 15, 1975

The *National Enquirer* has submitted yet another request for a picture of Liberty posing with the newspaper's mascot, Lucky. "The Ford administration," they complained, "is the first one that has refused to let its dog pose with Lucky."


\* \* \*

## JULY 21, 1975

The truck from CBS arrived at dawn's early light. By 6:30 A.M. the crew, brought in from New York City, was setting up cameras, lighting, and audio equipment in the solarium, the chosen site.

I was excited. I'd planned this thing slowly and carefully over the months, waiting for the right timing, the right show, the right interviewer, and the right day. Today was the right day.

All the details were worked out in advance, from the timing to the topics to the dress Mrs. Ford would wear. I'd even talked to her hairdresser about cooling the hairspray a little for a more natural look.

At 10:00 A.M. Mrs. Ford's secretary, Nancy Chirdon, called.

"She's not going to do the show."

"You're kidding."

"No. She wants Jack to do it instead."

"I'll be right up."

I found Mrs. Ford in the beauty parlor. She was distraught. "I don't know what I'm going to do about Nancy," she said.

"Nancy?" (Nancy who? Nancy Howe? Nancy Chirdon? Nancy Lammerding Ruwe? There are too many Nancys around here!)

"Nancy Ruwe. Her assistant came and complained to me last weekend. She wants to quit. She says that everyone does. She says that Nancy is never around when crucial decisions have to be made, and that she gets furious if any are made without her. She says she's impossible to work with."

(What does this have to do with today? With right now? With me? Couldn't we just put Nancy on "hold" until tomorrow?)

"And now everyone is coming to complain," Mrs. Ford went on. "The maître d', the chef, the head usher." She was on the verge of tears. I couldn't believe it. "Do you know," she blurted out, "that they say Nancy has padded State Dinner lists to help further her interests? And do you know that there have been State Dinners where Nancy made decisions so late that the men were arranging centerpieces in the dining room *after* the guests had already arrived for dinner?"

"Yes, well—"

"Well I didn't. I feel so betrayed! I had no idea she was driving everyone crazy. No idea."

There was an overwhelming temptation to say "I told you so," because I had. After Nancy Howe left, I had encouraged Mrs.

The author with Press Secretary Ron Nessen, who said, "NBC's loss is the White House's gain—twice!"

*Photo Credit: Ken Schumacher*

**Les Girls: Mrs. Ford, Susan, and Sheila, May 16, 1976**

*Photo Credit: Ken Schumacher*

Talking to the President at his party. Palm Springs, April 6, 1975

*Photo Credit: Ken Schumacher*

Nancy Howe, Mrs. Ford's Personal Assistant, who left after her husband's suicide

*Photo Credit: Sheila Rabb Weidenfeld*

Dr. William Lukash, the
White House physician who
treated Mrs. Ford
*Photo Credit: Sheila Rabb Weidenfeld*

Taping "60 Minutes." Foreground, Morley Safer with Mrs. Ford. July 25, 1975
*Photo Credit: Ken Schumacher*

Producer Ed Weinberger, Mrs. Ford, Mary Tyler Moore, and Sheila. November 14, 1975

*Photo Credit: Ken Schumacher*

Mrs. Ford, Sheila, and Halston after Martha Graham Gala. June 20, 1975

*Photo Credit: Ken Schumacher*

David Steinberg, Mrs. Ford, Peter Sellers, and Sheila. August 26, 1975

Jack and Susan at the Republican Convention in Kansas City. August 18, 1976

Gayle, Michael, Steven, and Mrs. Ford at the Republican Convention. August 18, 1976

*Photo Credit: Ken Schumacher*

Mrs. Ford coaching her touch football team at Vail. August 26, 1976

*Photo Credit: Ken Schumacher*

Jack talking with his father on Air Force One. July 3, 1975

*Photo Credit: David Kennerly*

Liberty gives birth. Bill Brockett, Liberty's trainer, President Ford, Susan, Sheila, Edward, and the vet. September 14, 1975

*Photo Credit: Ken Schumacher*

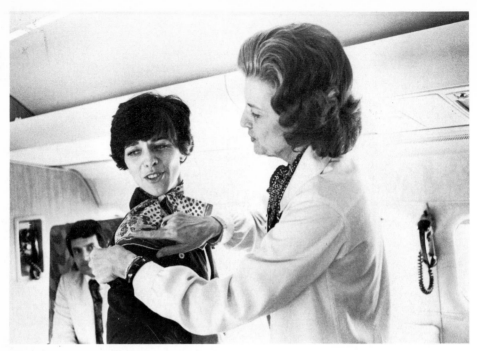

Mrs. Ford showing Sheila how to fix her scarf with Jerry Ball in the background.
March, 1976

*Photo Credit: Ken Schumacher*

A last hug. January 20, 1977

*Photo Credit: David Kennerly*

Ford to have an office downstairs in the East Wing to avoid exactly this—the sudden realization that things had been going on without her knowledge. But she had not done it. This was definitely not the time to get involved in that issue anyway. It was the time to put off the Nancy Lammerding Ruwe issue and get ready for the big event of the day.

"I'm not going to do the interview. I don't feel up to it," she said. "Jack will do it."

(So *that*'s what all this was leading up to. A case of stage fright?)

"Jack can't do it. They don't want Jack. They want you."

"I'm not going to do it."

I tried some more. She was adamant. I realized I was getting nowhere. I started to leave, but before I did, I gave it one more try.

"I think you're making a big mistake. I think this interview would make you feel good. These people like you and I'm certain you'll like them. The interview will be a distraction from all this—a happy distraction—and you can use a distraction. I think if you don't do the show, you'll work yourself into a real depression."

Pause. No takers.

"I'm sorry you're not going to do the show. I'll go take care of it."

I walked out of the beauty parlor and stood in the West Hall. How on earth would I "take care of it"? I thought of all the research, the equipment, the briefings, the phone calls, the phone calls, the phone calls. And I thought of the crew from New York. I thought that I could work *myself* into a real depression.

Mrs. Ford walked out. "Okay, you win. I'll do it."

I ran downstairs, told my secretary to please entertain Morley Safer, Don Hewitt and Don's girl friend. Mrs. Ford was "running a little late." I ran upstairs to make sure everything was all right. It was.

I ran downstairs and brought up my guests. I was right; she did like them. After lunch, we went up to the Solarium for the taping. They moved the furniture around and tried to get both Morley and Mrs. Ford comfortable on the couch. The interview began.

It seemed a little stilted—as though they were having trouble getting into it. I was just about to ask Hewitt if we could stop the tape and start over again when he yelled out "STOP THE TAPE!"

"I don't see that special sparkle in your eyes," he teased Mrs. Ford. "I want to see it!" He went over some points with Morley and I went over some with Mrs. Ford. I told her how much I loved her definition of a liberated woman, which, in case she'd forgotten, I repeated verbatim. (Press Secretary turns stage mother.)

They started rolling again. I put on earphones and watched on the television monitor. Much, much better. The sparkle was back. ("Well, I would say that my definition of a liberated woman is . . .") She was obviously relaxed and her words were nicely paced. An enthusiastic, excellent camera presence.

The substance was good, too. She was open but not outspoken. Honest. She sounded just plain intelligent. The words seemed as legitimate as the smile. Questions were answered thoughtfully, not politically. Abortion, the ups and downs of being a political wife, getting along in marriage, premarital sex. He asked, she answered with a candor rare in a human being, unheard of in a First Lady.

I was delighted. So were they. So was she.

## JULY 23, 1975

George Hoover from CBS called today to tell me that they will be announcing Mrs. Ford's appearance on "60 Minutes" tomorrow, which means it will be in Friday's newspapers. He read me the press release. "This is an unusual interview with an unusual woman. She is open, honest, and completely frank as she discusses her attitudes about her role as First Lady, wife, mother, and as an independent person."

## JULY 24, 1975

"I'm involved in the campaign now," Jack Ford explained to Scripps-Howard reporter Ted Knap in my office this morning. "I'm in the process of familiarizing myself with delegate selection, but I'd really like to work at the grassroots level. I'd rather do the nuts and bolts of it. I don't feel I'm enough of a celebrity to handle the national campaigning. I'm really not an arm-twister."

Knap had wanted to talk to "a Ford" for a story he was doing, and I suggested Jack. I listened carefully to the "loner" Ford son, as he sat there in dirty moccasins, dungarees and a lumberjacket, discoursing about his father, his life and, of course, forests, and I couldn't help feeling that there was tremendous political potential here.

*Chapter Ten*
AUGUST, 1975:

# IF THERE ARE ANY QUESTIONS YOU FORGOT TO ASK—I'M GRATEFUL

*AUGUST 4, 1975*

I just got back from my second European trip in two months. Join the White House and see the world. And go first class, at that.

Traveling with the President means never having to lift a suitcase. City to city, country to country, White House baggage men make sure the baggage is wherever you are going to be before you get there. ("This must be my hotel room. That is my suitcase.")

Traveling with the President means never having to deal with traveling. No ticket stubs, no language problems, no customs waits, no red tape, no late planes, no overbooked hotels.

Traveling with the President means being part of the world's largest tour group. Whither the President goes, so goeth the whole White House community. The family doctor, the family nurse, a beautician, a valet, the kitchen staff—and even part of the kitchen. Large refrigerated boxes hold fruits, teas, coffee, cheeses, and other foods brought from home for "residential lunches and dinners" along the way, and also to provide a certain amount of security regarding what the President eats. (And a certain amount of convenience: there are times when the President and the First Lady only nibble the fare at a State Dinner, preferring to eat back at their suite.)

The family phone system is brought along, too. Indeed, at least thirty people in the President's party on these trips are members of the White House Communications Agency (WHCA) whose responsibility it is to keep the President constantly in touch with the Washington White House and with the rest of the world, and with advisors who are traveling with him. They come in their own transport plane along with enough communication gear to support an army. That means at each and every stop, WHCA sets up a signal board, a completely portable telephone switchboard system that maintains that constant contact. There were always two phones in the rooms I stayed in. One was the standard housephone, the other a White House signal phone. The signal phone connected to the trip communications center, which connected to Satellites, which in turn connected to the White House. The trip communications center also activated my beeper, provided walkie-talkie service, and high security teletype communications.

The people most responsible for the ease and comfort of Presidential travel are invisible. They are the pre-advance teams, who check out the stops about ten days ahead of time, and the advance teams who follow and set up the specific details: the transportation plans, press room set-ups, security escorts, as well as the most detailed of details. There is always one doctor on the advance team, for example, whose job it is to check out facilities at all hospitals along the itinerary.

When you travel with the President, the plane lands when it is supposed to land and you never have to hail a taxi. Vehicles are always waiting for you at the airport.

Not always the vehicle of your choice, however. I guess my problem is that I am more drone, than passenger. I have work to do on these trips, and whereas I appreciate the luxuries, many of them get in my way. The planners don't seem to realize that I have work to do. My job is the press. Thus when the press bus turns left, en route to one destination, and my vehicle turns right, en route to my hotel, I become frustrated. Likewise, I find it difficult to inform when I am uninformed. How do I tell reporters what Mrs. Ford did when I was three miles in the motorcade back from where she was doing it? I complained after the last trip, and was patted on the head. I got the message. This time I just jumped into whichever vehicle seemed strategically appropriate. It worked. What's more, it gave me a feeling of power—the only kink in the links of the most beautifully planned motorcades in the world.

The main event of this trip was a summit meeting in Helsinki where the President joined the leaders of thirty-five Eastern and Western European countries in signing the agreements drawn up by the Conference on Security and Cooperation in Europe. Like the NATO conference in Brussels, the Helsinki signing gave the President opportunities for behind-the-scenes conferences with other Heads of State. On the way to Helsinki, we stopped first in Germany (for economic talks with Chancellor Schmidt) and then Warsaw. After Helsinki, we went to Rumania and Yugoslavia.

While the President's staff dealt with arms and trade and military security, I was pre-occupied with Mrs. Ford's health. She was fine in Germany, exhausted in Poland, high in Helsinki, but low in Rumania. "You can have me for the train ride or the State Dinner," she told the President, "take your choice." When she was up, she was very up, dancing all night at an elaborate boat party on the Rhine, for example. When she was down, though, she was very down. In Rumania, she was so pale and weak she looked as though she were on the verge of either passing out or falling asleep.

I could not figure out the cause (lack of stamina? depression? jet lag? neck pains?). Nor could I figure out the roller coaster effect, the consistent up and down and up and down mood swings.

But whatever it was, I was sure it was *not* cancer. The press was sure it was. They are a single-disease-obsessed group. I tried to explain what I didn't understand as rationally as possible. I said she was doing too much, that the ups and downs were directly related to the heaviness of her schedule. But by the time we got to Yugoslavia, my credibility was zilch. (At one point, Helen Thomas screamed "WHO DO YOU THINK YOU ARE TELLING ME SHE'S ALL RIGHT?" with such a convincing tone of condemnation that she almost convinced *me* I was lying.) On the plane trip home, I decided to let the evidence speak for itself. Once again, Mrs. Ford had gone from exhausted to fine in twenty-four hours. I knew it was Helen's birthday, and I suggested Mrs. Ford walk back on Air Force One to the press pool to wish Helen a happy birthday. She did, and Helen saw for herself that Mrs. Ford was fine. What more can a Press Secretary do?

Mrs. Ford's health took a lot of my time, but her need for rest gave me some extra time. In Poland, when she canceled her plans, I suggested to Jack that we go to Auschwitz, the former concentration camp. I thought it would be interesting and I thought he needed something with substance. He was getting a little restless in this, his first taste of the formalities of international protocol. Henry Kissinger's son, David, came with us. He's only fourteen years old, but so mature intellectually and emotionally that he seems much older. He's an awfully nice kid, too. The three of us had a private tour of the camp, and Jack and David asked innumerable questions, prompted by the mixture of fascination and horror you feel when you are shown a crematorium, a gas chamber, cloth made from human hair, and unheated barracks that once housed eight people in an area the size of a twin bed. We only saw part of the movie they show, but part was enough. It was powerful. We left in silence, and got back just in time to board Air Force One for our next stop.

New entries in my book of State Dinner comparisons: Franco still remains top in the "longest table" category, but Germany's was definitely the most lavish dinner party yet. It was a splendid evening cruise down the Rhine River on an enormous boat with what seemed like thousands of people and beautiful music and much, much after-dinner dancing.

The Communists win for choreography at the State Dinner in Rumania. In an exquisite setting, twenty-two uniformed waiters came out, in perfect unison formed a long line down the room, and then in some-what synchronized step spread out to serve the crowd. It looked like part of an old Busby Berkeley movie. Would that the toasts had been so organized! President Ceaucescu gave a forty-minute oration, first in Rumanian, then in English, then in Rumanian, then in English, in a monotone outdone only by the translator's.

It was in Rumania that Jack decided to jog along the palace lake. He said that every thirty feet he saw another soldier. When he got to the end, a guard stopped him. He had no credentials on him, and he had asked his Secret Service men to stay behind. He was passed from guard to guard and finally taken to the guard shack, where it took some time to clear him. On his way back, he told me, the guard who escorted him looked nervously both ways, saw no one was looking, and then stuck out his hand to shake Jack's.

In Air Force One's family quarters coming back, Henry Kissinger told me it was quite possible that even my room had been bugged in all three countries. It seems bugging is a thriving industry in Eastern Europe, one that employs first of all, the buggers, who install the bugs, then the bugging transcribers, who listen to the tapes, and finally, the transcript readers. A bugging bureaucracy. It all made international espionage seem less than exotic. Henry says he uses something known as a babbler when he travels. (A tip from the top!) It's a tape cassette that makes it sound as though there are at least 100 people in your room, and when you talk, no one can tell what you're saying.

## AUGUST 5, 1975

The problem is Nancy Lammerding Ruwe. And the problem is Mrs. Ford. The handwriting has been on the wall for a long time. Mrs. Ford has just refused to read it. The West Wing has joined the list of complainers, insisting that Nancy comes on too strong, antagonizes people in the process of getting her job done, and keeps using her position to further her status, not the President's. The social secretary, after all, has a lot to say about who participates in which White House activities.

But the real problem is that Mrs. Ford does not like firing anyone. So, like Nancy Howe, Nancy Ruwe has been lingering. She was supposed to be fired on the European trip (A Rumsfeld decision which struck me as a little peculiar; why do it on foreign shores?) but no one got around to it. Instead, she antagonized a few more people. And Mrs. Ford internalized the stress, creating the emotional pressure that may have caused some of her physical problems.

It's bad management. If Mrs. Ford had spoken to Nancy earlier, perhaps the firing could have been avoided. The fact is, Nancy has a flair for the job; she throws a good party.

But now it's too late for remedies. It's getting too late for firing, too. People are impatient—the chef, the ushers' office, Gulley, Rumsfeld, the maître d'—someone is going to complain out loud soon.

Mrs. Ford says that Dick Cheney, Don Rumsfeld's assistant, will talk to Nancy tomorrow and then Mrs. Ford will meet with her the next day to plan a graceful exit.

I made Mrs. Ford promise that if I ever get the ax, it will be administered quickly.

## AUGUST 6, 1975

I read the edited "60 Minutes" transcript today. It's going to be a good show. But when I read a transcript, I feel very much like a television producer. It leaves out so much—the facial expressions, the sounds, the tones, the speech patterns, all the ingredients I think are necessary for the total impression.

There were some words in the transcript I hadn't remembered. At one point, Mrs. Ford says that for a marriage to work, each person must go overboard. "You don't go into marriage as a 50–50 thing. You go into it, both of you, as a 70–30 proposition." I like that.

There were words that had been taken out. One statement I particularly remember occurred in a discussion about premarital sex among the young. In the original interview, Mrs. Ford had said that perhaps "affairs" might lower the divorce rate. But she then completely altered any impression of sophistication by going on to say, "I read that Cher got married and nine days later got divorced. Perhaps she'd been better off if she'd just waited and had an affair herself." I remember cringing. Somehow, the speculation that Cher had opted for marriage instead of trying premarital sex was *so* naïve that I found it embarrassing. I guess CBS did, too. They knocked it out.

I checked for controversy. There's a pro-abortion stand; she's said that before. She says she wouldn't be surprised if her children had tried marijuana. She's said that before, too. As a matter of fact, she tells Morley Safer that the last time she said it, she got "the devil" from one child who insisted he had never tried it and resented her assumption that he had.

Her statements are frank, but not brash. Those words, though— "divorce," "abortion," "marijuana." Definitely shock words. But I suppose these are shock times. (Would anyone have dared ask Mamie Eisenhower about subjects like that?)

\*  \*  \*

# AUGUST 7, 1975

Jack is going out with Jacques Cousteau on the *Calypso* to help on a project Cousteau is doing for NASA, and I'm delighted. It was my father who came up with the idea (he knows someone connected with the project) and it seemed perfect. Jack is an enthusiastic scuba diver, an admirer of Cousteau, enamored of adventure, and in need of an identity that extends beyond Bianca Jagger. I talked to him about it the other day, and he wanted to think about it. He gave me the answer today, an enthusiastic "yes."

Meanwhile, the big question that kept telephone lines open all day between Topeka, Kansas (where Susan is working as a newspaper photographer for six weeks), and Washington, D.C., was, "Should Susan drive to a friend's wedding in San Diego?" Her mother said, "No, too much publicity," which stimulated a call to Daddy ("No, too much publicity") which stimulated a call to me, just to talk. Susan is currently "in love" with Brian McCartney, a ski instructor she met in Vail over Christmas, disappointed about San Diego, but pleased about an alternate plan of hers which received parental approval, she is going on a two-day raft trip with twenty-seven other people down the Colorado River.

It was in between Susan and Jack that a UPI story broke announcing that Nancy Lammerding Ruwe had been fired.

It appears to be difficult to make a graceful exit from the White House.

It was a leak, and it was a well-informed leak because the reasons for firing Nancy were well documented in the story. It was not an East Wing leak, I calmly told an hysterical Donald Rumsfeld when he called me at home tonight. He said I was a liar. I remained firm. And calm. I repeated, "No one here leaked it." (One of the advantages of having virtually no staff is that you can make a statement like that with relative certainty.)

I am certain. I am certain because the leak was counterproductive for us (Nancy had talked to Dick Cheney yesterday and worked out graceful exit lines with Mrs. Ford today, per the "schedule"). It had to be someone who did not realize Nancy was on her way out and who wanted to make sure she left.

I read Rumsfeld the statement I had prepared to release to reporters tomorrow. He moaned and groaned and said he did not like it. When I asked for suggestions, for guidance, he said he had none.

## AUGUST 8, 1975

"Lady Bird Johnson was a thoroughly political creature, like her husband," Morley Safer is quoted as saying in an article in yesterday's *Christian Science Monitor.* "Jacqueline Kennedy, I found to be a pampered dilettante. . . . Pat Nixon always seemed one dimensional. . . . With Betty Ford, you feel there is a great person there, a person of great strength whose first interest . . . represents the strongest element in a country like the U.S.—her family." He says that the "60 Minutes" interview with Mrs. Ford was a "terrifically pleasant surprise because he hadn't expected to find a woman so strong and straight and frank."

"Perhaps a few people will be affronted by her frankness," he says, "but I believe for the most part the American people will be pleased to know that a woman like Betty Ford is in the White House, not just a pallid shadow of her husband, with a set look on her face smiling numbly at photographers."

I sent the article upstairs to Mrs. Ford to read. She called me right away to tell me she loved it—every word of it.

"Now don't get carried away by it," I warned. "Remember, you go into some pretty controversial areas on this interview, and as he says some 'people may be affronted by your frankness.' "

She grunted—but amiably.

"I'm thinking of sending a copy of the *Christian Science Monitor* story to Ron Nessen," I told her.

"Do. Send one to Don Rumsfeld, too."

I did.

## AUGUST 9, 1975

Dear Nancy,

It is with deep regret that I accept your letter of resignation as my social secretary. You have done an excellent job and will be greatly missed. I have enjoyed working with you professionally and deeply appreciate your hard work and dedication. Our personal association has been most meaningful to me.

I an well aware of the amount of time that must be put into the job of social secretary and can fully understand your reasons for wanting to leave.

I wish you and Nick the very best and look forward to a continuing friendship.

Fondly, Betty Ford.


## AUGUST 10, 1975

On Air Force One, I handed out copies of the "60 Minutes" transcript to the President, Mrs. Ford, a few staff members and the traveling press. I wanted everyone to know about it. This was the big day. I was terribly excited.

When we arrived in Vail, I went right to my hotel room. I invited Susan's boyfriend, Brian McCartney to watch the show with me. I wanted to watch with someone, and Edward was flying out on the press plane and would not get to Vail for a few hours.

Then it went on. It looked good—still. The sparkle was there, the spontaneity. I tried to be professional about it, systematically checking for possible flaws. But I could find none. As a matter of fact, after all that preparation and monitor-watching and transcript-studying, I was too familiar with it to evaluate it. I watched Brian for his reaction. He chortled out loud when Morley Safer asked Mrs. Ford what she would do if Susan came to her and said, "Mother, I'm having an affair," but other than that, he remained poker-faced.

"It's good!" I thought to myself. "Is it good?" After waiting for weeks for this moment, I suddenly wanted it to pass, so I could find out how it went.

It passed. Brian said he thought it was good (would he have dared say he thought it was bad?) and before he left, I told him that after the affair question, people would be watching the two of them. "When Susan gets here next week, even holding hands in public could cause a stir." He promised to be proper.

When Brian left, I called the White House for a report on reaction. They had already received twenty-five phone calls, fourteen pro Mrs. Ford, six con. Not bad. Good, as a matter of fact. (What on earth makes a person pick up a phone and call the White House?)

I called Mrs. Ford and announced early returns. "How did the President like the show?"

"Well, first he said 'You just lost me ten million votes,' and then he said, 'No, you just lost me twenty million votes!' But Don Rumsfeld, who watched with us, retorted, 'Nonsense, she won you thirty million votes!' Actually, the President was very supportive. He didn't kick me out of the house, but at one point in the middle of the interview, he did throw a pillow at me!" She was laughing, thoroughly enjoying this domestic controversy.

Edward arrived, and we went down to the press room together, where I happily handed out more transcripts and told the weary travelers that they had all missed a great show. Ed and I went out for a bite to eat, and then took a walk in downtown Vail, which is about one block long, and reminisced about how terribly cold it was the last time we walked here.

Tomorrow is our anniversary. I have a feeling this is going to be a wonderful vacation.

## AUGUST 11, 1975

I can't remember what I was dreaming, but first the phone rang in my dream and then it rang in my blurry reality. I looked at the clock: 6:30 A.M. Who is calling me at this hour of the morning in Vail?

I picked up the phone and someone began hurling many words at me very quickly. I listened. I was still not sure who was calling me at this hour of the morning in Vail. The words began sorting themselves into subjects, verbs, objects, sentences, thoughts, sense. A reporter from the East Coast wanted to know Mrs. Ford's reaction to the article on page 16 of today's *New York Times*.

Translation: there's bad news on page 16.

Reply: calmly tell the reporter what she already knows. It is only 6:30 A.M. here in Vail and Mrs. Ford has not even seen the *New York Times*. And hang up quickly.

Edward gave me That Look—the one reserved for broken promises. Happy anniversary.

He went out to get newspapers. I called my office in Washington to get a count of the phone calls, letters and telegrams with samples of each, pro and con. The public response to the show was generally good. The story on page 16 was not.

"Betty Ford said today that she wouldn't be surprised if her daughter Susan, eighteen years old, decided to have an affair," began the *Times* article. "Mrs. Ford suggested that in general premarital relations with the right partner might lower the divorce rate."

Now, wait a minute!

There were similar headlines elsewhere:"SUSAN'S A BIG GIRL. AFFAIR WON'T JOLT MRS. FORD" (*Los Angeles Times*); "AFFAIR BY DAUGHTER WOULDN'T FAZE BETTY"(*Indianapolis Star*).

I re-read the transcript.

Q: What if Susan Ford came to you and said "Mother, I'm having an affair."

A: Well, I wouldn't be surprised. I think she's a perfectly normal human being like all young girls, if she wanted to continue, I would certainly counsel and advise her on the subject and I'd want to know pretty much about the young man that she was planning to have the affair with, whether it was a worthwhile encounter or whether it was going to be one of those . . .

She's pretty young to start affairs.

Q: But nevertheless, old enough. . . .

A: Oh, yes, she's a big girl.

Same words, different interpretation. What I heard her saying was: "I would try to keep all lines of communication open. I would try to be loving and understanding."

At least one other person shared my view.

"Have you *seen* the papers?" Mrs. Ford said. "That's not my emphasis! My life is basically so square. I was trying to be open minded. They all just picked out the bedside stories, the misleading sensationalism. I tried to be honest, and in return, I get this. What would people have me do, kick my daughter out of the house? Susan called me last night from Kansas to tell me she watched the program, and that she was very proud of me. You know what else she said? 'Mother, what is an affair?' "

That was nothing to what Michael said. The serious son, apparently had *not* been proud of his mother's on-air performance. He knew what an affair was, and did not think she should have tossed off premarital sex so lightly. I don't really know Michael. He is rarely around, and when he is, he seldom opens up to outsiders. He's not unfriendly—quite the contrary, he is very nice. But he is a private person. In most family matters, he is an off-stage presence but one who wields considerable influence with his parents and with his siblings. Maybe it's because he's the oldest and therefore a sort of substitute father figure. Maybe it's because he has dedicated himself to religion. Whatever the cause, Michael's opinion is valued highly by all Fords. When Michael disapproves of his mother's appearance, his mother is upset.

"Don't worry, I'll straighten it out," I told Mrs. Ford. "I assume total responsibility. I talked you into doing it in the first place and, believe me, in the long run, it will work out to your advantage. It was a beautiful interview."

Paraphrasing the old tune, "You Made Me Love You," she sang to me, "You made me do it; I didn't want to do it, I didn't want to do it." She told me she hadn't finished writing the concluding lyrics yet.

I laughed (with tremendous insincerity) and assured her that not only would she be happy that she'd done the show, but the President would be happy, too.

Everyone was clamoring for an interview with Mrs. Ford, but an interview would only lead to more misunderstanding. I had to clarify things myself. Edward and I talked it over and I outlined my check list for reporters' queries: 1) She was given a hypothetical. She was not asked, "What would you prefer?" It was, "What if." Thus, Mrs. Ford did not advocate having an affair. 2) In fact, Mrs. Ford is a very traditional woman who believes very strongly in marriage and family; but 3) because of her belief in family, she feels all lines of communication between parents and children should be left open. She hopes that she will always be able to talk to and understand her children. "You don't kick a daughter out of the house."

I also supplemented my statement with quotes from the pro and con telegrams and phone calls the White House had received. Like the ERA mail, I felt publicizing adverse reaction might stimulate supportive letters.

Eight reporters later, Ron Nessen called. "The President is very upset. Lay low. Talk to no one."

"I don't think that's possible, Ron. The story needs to be corrected."

Time and again—"hypothetical," "misunderstood," "communications." Those were my three key words. All day and into the evening hours. Vacation, eh?

Ron called, furious. "I just saw the wire stories. I thought I told you not to talk to reporters!"

I read the wires. The clarification helped. I thought it helped. I was so tired, I was sure of nothing.

I walked over to the table and looked at the piece of paper I had placed there the night before, and I smiled. It was a statement I had *planned* on releasing today. It said that Liberty, who had been mated with Oregon Golden Retriever Misty Sun Gold Ladd last month, might be pregnant, and because of that, her diet had been changed from Purina to "canine lactation," a special diet for pregnant dogs.

Funny, no one had asked.

Happy Anniversary.

## AUGUST 16, 1975

On the national scene, we're up to reaction to the reaction to the reaction. Public response to the television program was more good than bad. Public response to the newspaper articles on the television program was more bad than good. And public response to the public response to the newspaper articles on the television program is both good and bad.

My room and I have become a single entity. I rarely see the weather. I talk only to reporters (to clarify) and Mrs. Ford (to bolster) and Ron Nessen (to be yelled at).

Vacation, eh?

I often ask Edward for clever captions for the autographed pictures Mrs. Ford sends out, and last night, when I hung up the phone after an especially lengthy explanation for one reporter, Edward turned to me and said, "I've got it! MORLEY, IF THERE ARE

ANY QUESTIONS YOU FORGOT TO ASK . . . I'M GRATEFUL. Sincerely, Betty Ford.''


## AUGUST 19, 1975

Just as things had begun to calm down, the Myra MacPherson article on Mrs. Ford in *McCalls* hit the newsstands. I had forgotten that the September issue comes out in mid-August. I read it and got nervous. I called Mrs. Ford and told her the article was out.

"Oh no.''

(Have we both become paranoid?)

I went over to discuss it with her. "Maybe I'm being silly, but you refer to the Shah of Iran as a 'swinger.' I think that has the connotation of playboy—someone who plays around. Is that what you meant?''

"Oh dear. Until you said that, I would have described my husband that way! He likes to look at pretty girls, and go to parties and enjoy himself, that's all I meant. I guess I'm just not up on the current vernacular, but to me, a swinger is just that—a person who knows how to enjoy himself at a party. And the Shah is a swinger.''

"Myra also quotes you as saying about (Presidential advisor) Bob Hartmann: 'Bob and I don't always jibe. I'm willing to admit that I think perhaps my resentment comes from his trying to run my husband's life . . . perhaps I feel he oversteps his boundaries.' ''

"Oh dear.''

"If I'm asked, is there anything you want me to say about that?''

She thought, cleared her throat, and said in monotone; "The article misinterpreted my feelings about Bob Hartmann. I like Bob very much and consider him a good friend.''

I said nothing. But I knew I would *never* give that out to reporters. It was the first out-and-out lie I had ever heard Mrs. Ford utter.

As I got up to go, she showed me a letter her correspondence section had drafted to send to the people who had written to her criticizing her stands. It was dreadful. But it gave me a terrific idea.

"Could I work on it a little?'' I asked her.

"Sure.''

I brought it back to the room, convinced the letter would be a wonderful mechanism for answering the critics. If we could draft a really good letter, and then send it out to everyone who has written in, it could be an extremely effective way of clarifying her feelings. More than likely, the letter would eventually be published. But *eventually.* We would not release it from the White House. We would let someone who received it do the releasing. Once again, I thought, the message would be most effective if it came back *from* the hinterlands.

I asked Bob Orben for help in writing this "Perfect Letter."

"I have to tell you, Sheila, I was very upset by what she said on '60 Minutes.' I think she hurt the President badly. I think she did him a real disservice."

Thud. It wasn't depression I felt so much as fatigue. The thought of having to go through the whole clarification speech again made me terribly tired. But I did.

Bob kept shaking his head, unconvinced. That gave me extra adrenaline.

"Bob, in a few months, you'll be congratulating me. Really. Things are going to turn around. But I need your help."

Still shaking his head solemnly he began work on the first draft.

## AUGUST 22, 1975

Up and down and mostly down. A good editorial precedes a bad editorial. Everytime I begin to feel that it is playing itself out to our advantage, a Baptist Minister howls. Or my beeper goes off and it is Ron Nessen telling me that my last release was "the last straw, really the last straw as far as the President is concerned. He's furious." It is very confusing. Every time I ask Ron what specifically the President is upset about, he refuses to discuss it.

I am an outcast. No one from the White House staff speaks to me. Only reporters call. I haven't seen Mrs. Ford in days. Knowing how angry the President is, I'm reluctant to call and she hasn't called me.

No one, I admit, has actively rejected me. It's a passive rejection. No one has tried to find me. Only the press. Always the press.

Edward says I'm being silly. But Edward also admits that he heard that the White House opinion poll shows that the President's popularity has dropped since August 10th, and I can imagine who is getting most of the credit.

I wish someone would call me and scream (someone other than Ron). Really scream, saying, "YOU HAVE ERRED AND HERE ARE YOUR GRIEVOUS ERRORS!" Cold shoulders can kill. Shades of Nancy Ruwe? Will my next phone call come from Dick Cheney?

We had dinner tonight with Fran Lewine and Helen Thomas and some other wire service people. THE SUBJECT came up and Fran said she thought I chose "60 Minutes" for Mrs. Ford's debut because it was "glamorous" and I knew it would make a big splash. I told her she was completely wrong. I chose it because I thought it was the best interview show on television, and the only one where Mrs. Ford could come across as she was—an open, three-dimensional human being.

I told Fran I think she came across exactly that way. The greatest number of positive responses are from those who saw her on the show. Letters to the editor columns almost always contain at least one letter that says something like, "Having seen Mrs. Ford on televison Sunday night, I was a bit jarred to read your headline Monday morning." Very few people were shocked by the interview. Most people felt they really got to know her in it. And they liked what they got to know.

"It's the print media you don't understand," said Helen. She is 100 percent right. The print media took my three-dimensional human being and made her a one-dimensional sensation. They took the words right out of her mouth (and out of her meaning) and they made them into headlines. In truth, it was the questions that were radical, not the answers. The only thing about the answers that was unusual was the fact that she thoughtfully tried to answer the questions as a mother who loved her children and simply wanted to understand the not-so-simple times in which they were growing up.

The conversation with Fran and Helen underlined both my securities and my areas of insecurity. True, "60 Minutes" was a great production. But did she *want* to be produced? Did I push her into it? It's one thing to have a man on the moon and a woman in the Cabinet. Is the nation ready for a human being in the White House? Can a President's wife be honest without becoming the Ex-President's wife?

Should she have insisted "Susan would never," fainted at the mere mention of the word "abortion" and replied "Marijuana who?" Or, more to the point, knowing that Mrs. Ford is forthright, should I have resisted the irresistible temptation to make her a star—to have someone ask her such questions? Or, more to the point, shall I stop analyzing and get on with the business of rectifying?

Bob Orben, then Edward, then I have worked on the Superletter for Mrs. Ford to send out. I must discuss it with her, because it must go out soon, if it is to be effective. I am afraid to venture over there, however. Maybe tomorrow.

Tonight, we tried some diversion. The Fords' friends, Pepi and Sheika Gramshammer (an Austrian couple; he's a former ski champion, she's a former show girl) own a ski lodge in Vail and this summer they opened a night club. We joined everyone else there to hear the oldie-but-goodie Inkspots (a Presidential favorite) and an extra unexpected attraction, At one point in the evening, Ron Nessen's wife, Cindy—formerly an entertainer in Korea—grabbed the microphone and belted out a couple of tunes with a flamboyant flair. The President appeared to be thoroughly delighted. He really loved it. After all, like the Shah of Iran, he's a "swinger."

## AUGUST 23, 1975

I was greeted by Mrs. Ford, Susan, and some of their friends.

"I feel a little timid being here," I said. "I didn't know if you wanted to talk to me."

"Sheila," said Mrs. Ford (friendly?) "I wondered what happened to you!"

"Well, it's been a little tough."

"Yes, I can imagine." (Friendly. Definitely friendly.)

"I've been getting it from everybody."

"*You* have," laughed Mrs. Ford. "What about *me*?"

We compared notes and laughed and talked about the letter and it felt just like . . . well . . . August ninth. Susan and the others left, and Mrs. Ford said she wanted to talk but she wanted to rest, so I sat on her bed and she talked about her prime concern. ("60 Minutes"? Nonsense. Susan and Brian.)

"She's at an age when she thinks she has to be in love with someone," Mrs. Ford observed. "I remember I got engaged a couple of times when I was young, but as soon as the guy said 'we've got to have a talk,' I broke the engagement. I didn't want to lose my freedom."

The President came in and my heart sank. Here goes.

"I've got to talk to you for a second. I know you're mad at me."

He laughed (genuine?). "I'm not mad at you." He sounded surprised. (Surprised?)

"*Yes*, you are. I know you are mad at me. But I just want to tell you this: I would not do anything to hurt you. This thing will work out fine in the end. We just have to get it around to sounding more traditional. But we've thought it through. Just have some confidence in me."

"Sheila, I'm not mad at you at all," he said, and put his arm around me (sincere?).

Mrs. Ford explained that the President would be leaving Vail in two days, but that she and Susan planned to stay on longer. The President said he thought I should stay with her, since there will be some press around and that I should move into the Fords' house for the extra days. "Edward could move in here, too, if he wants to stay." (Why do they keep changing the subject?)

"It's going to work out fine," I told the President. "I mean that. In the end, you'll be happy about her performance. During the campaign she will be the one person who will have credibility when she talks about you."

"I really don't think it's all that bad." (Again, surprise.)

"Well, if you don't think it's all that bad, *think* about how good it's going to be a little bit later!"

The President laughed and kissed me on the cheek.

Ecstatic, I returned to Edward, and we decided to go out and celebrate the end of my self-imposed imprisonment. I told Helen and Fran that Mrs. Ford was busy drafting a letter to answer all the telegrams and telephone calls and letters she had received on "60 Minutes," but that the contents of the letter itself would not be made public.

And we went out for a wonderful time, clouded only slightly by the fact that my beeper went off two times within what must have been a two-hour period. Both times it was Ron Nessen, furious. Screaming how angry everyone, especially the President, was at the way I was handling the situation.

## AUGUST 27, 1975

The crowds disappeared. The chaos ended. The noise ceased. Farewell to the Chief. The President left Vail Sunday and took it all with him—the staff, the Secret Service, and the excitement. Even the White House phone was cut. He left behind Mrs. Ford, Susan, and me. And tranquility and picnics and quiet dinners and backgammon and an almost-completed "perfect letter."

We pored over it, together, separately. Finally we had a draft that both of us agreed sounded personal enough, sincere enough— the Perfect Letter! It was at this point that Billy ("God's Got a Better Idea") Zeoli arrived. I walked into the house and asked where Mrs. Ford was and was told that she was in the bedroom talking with Billy Zeoli. (An emissary of the Lord? Or Michael Ford?)

"Sheila, dear, how are you?" Billy said as they emerged from the bedroom. "We were just talking about the letter."

("Just my luck," I thought to myself.)

"Betty was very, very concerned about it, you know, because nowhere in it did it mention the fact that she does not believe in adultery."

(Where on "60 Minutes" is adultery even mentioned, I thought to myself.)

"So we've been talking about it," he smiled warmly, proudly at Mrs. Ford who was walking out of the bedroom behind him, "and we've thought of a way to say it."

(Hallelujah, I thought to myself.)

"I'm so grateful to Billy for helping me with that point," Mrs. Ford said, smiling at him gratefully. "It was really important to me to put that in."

"If it's that important to you, it should be in the letter," I said (out loud). "After all, it's your letter."

"It's that important."

Now it is en route to Washington, where it will be typed and mailed out, this Orben/Weidenfeld/Weidenfeld/Ford/Zeoli masterpiece.

Last week, during the chaos, I got a call from David Steinberg, Peter Sellers' agent. He said that Sellers, who is an excellent photographer, would like to shoot some pictures of Susan. Sellers will be going to Switzerland soon, for the European premier of *The Re-*

*turn of the Pink Panther* and then will be on location, making Neil Simon's *Murder by Death*. Could he come to Vail first?

Why not? He and Steinberg arrived yesterday, and we all had a marvelous time, first at lunch, and then throughout an afternoon of clowning, laughing, mugging for pictures, and, generally, acting very silly. Sellers was delightful, and Mrs. Ford was delighted. Everyone ended up taking pictures of everyone else. I took several of Mrs. Ford, hamming it up in a Coors Beer hat with Sellers by her side. Doubtlessly, another First Lady first.

## AUGUST 29, 1975

We sent out the autographed picture today. "Dear Morley," the inscription reads. "If there are any questions you forgot to ask—I'm grateful. Sincerely, Betty Ford."

*Chapter Eleven*
SEPTEMBER, 1975:

# BLESS YOU, LORENA CHEVALIER!

*SEPTEMBER 2, 1975*

The White House was packed this weekend with the President and Mrs. Ford, Michael and Gayle, Jack, Steven, Susan, and innumerable visiting friends (including, for example, Steve's ranch foreman and family). It was a nice, full family Labor Day reunion before the school year. A pleasure. An unexpected pleasure, considering one family member had not planned on being present.

Jack called me Saturday from Fort Lauderdale after three days of the Cousteau trip.

"There's a layover for a couple of days. I'm coming home."

"Home? Is something wrong? Why come home?"

"Nothing's wrong. I'm coming home."

I asked his Secret Service agent if there had been a problem. The agent assured me that no, quite the contrary, it had been very exciting and Jack seemed to be enjoying it. (Then, why come home?) I was afraid, frankly, that if he came home, he would never return to the expedition.

And I was right.

I saw him this morning up in the Family Quarters talking to Michael.

"Are you going to return?"

"No."

"Why? You have to! You know the best thing you can do for yourself, Jack, is to follow through on this, show that you *can* follow through on a commitment."(No response, new tack.) "I guess I've been pushing you." He smiled.

In the "other news" department, Labor Day finds us en route to labor. Summer's suspicions have turned into autumnal reality. Liberty is "with puppies." Due date: mid-September. Mrs. Ford is delighted. Susan is ecstatic. I am . . . hesitant. (The puppies will undoubtedly arrive before my extra staff person.) The fact is, Liberty already attracts a good amount of personal mail. A small proportion of the letters are addressed to Liberty directly ("How does it feel to be the Number One canine in the nation?"). Most are addressed to family members ("First let me tell you how pleased I am that your breast cancer surgery turned out so well"). A surprisingly small number are from children. Many are from free-lance writers (who will write stories that will stimulate more mail) and most are from dog havers, dog lovers, and those anxious to become dog sharers ("Is there already a man in Liberty's life?"). Liberty answers all her mail with her paw print.

Televised talk of premarital affairs is one thing. Am I strong enough to handle puppies? I guess I don't take Liberty seriously enough.

Edward says I'd better start.

## SEPTEMBER 5, 1975

He is a tall, dark-haired man, meticulously groomed with a carefully contoured moustache and a stern look about him. A lean man. Lean, and perhaps a little mean. Strict, in any case. He believes in law and order. Absolute order. In his book, there are rules of behavior, rules of dress, and rules of respect, and this is a man who goes by the book.

He works for the Secret Service. He has for a long time. His favorite assignment to date was guarding Vice President Spiro Agnew.

"A great guy, Spiro Agnew," he says reverently, "a man of tremendous integrity. An important man, but still a regular guy who enjoyed sitting down with the men on his detail every so often and having a drink, talking man to man. We really respected him and I think it was mutual. Vice President Agnew had guts," he reminisced. "The guts to say what he thought, to tell *them* all off when they deserved it."

Those were, of course, the good days. Now the agent's career has gone downhill—almost as far as Agnew's. He presently is guarding Jack Ford—undoubtedly a "them" to Spiro Agnew. He hates it with a vindictive vengeance that is almost frightening.

## SEPTEMBER 6, 1975

The big news always comes out in requests for reaction.

"What did Mrs. Ford say when she heard about the assassination attempt?" the reporter wanted to know.

The story was just coming over the wire. A woman had pointed a pistol at the President from two feet away while he was shaking hands with a crowd in Sacramento. A Secret Service agent saw the gun and leaped to grab it and the woman holding it.

I read the wire and went upstairs. Mrs. Ford was fine, but, she told me, she hadn't been so fine ten minutes before. She was talking on the telephone when the White House operator cut in and told her she had an emergency call from Dick Keiser, the head of the President's Secret Service detail. He told her "not to worry. The President is all right." Since she had no idea what he was talking about, she was very concerned that something had really happened to the President. Fortunately, David Kennerly got on the phone and told her the details.

That was yesterday.

The after-shock seems to be worse than the initial reaction. "I felt fine when he got back," she told me, "but today, I'm really upset. It's something I have to live with, I suppose. I've got to get myself squared away."

In some ways, it's more difficult for the relatives of potential assassination targets. When the Fords went to Ford's Theater back in April, and the President became the "First President to attend a performance in the theater since Lincoln was shot," Mrs. Ford said, "I don't think he even thought about it. I did. All evening."

She would like him to travel less. "I'm going to try to get him to cool it for a while. But I know him. He feels it's the right of the President to see the people. I'm going to tell him the people need him. I need him."

I would like him to travel less, for political as well as personal reasons. I think he is being overexposed, that his candidacy would be strengthened by his staying home and tending to the business of the Presidency. A solid White House image is a stronger image than handshaker. The *Christian Science Monitor* had a cartoon yesterday of Ford looking in his closet at suits with different labels: "President of the USA," "Convention nomination," "Candidate," and "Head of the Republican Party."

The caption reads: "Hey Betty, you didn't lay out a suit for the speech tonight!"

## SEPTEMBER 9, 1975

Sunday was my birthday. Mrs. Ford sent me a funny card with the inscription: "To my bouncing Press Secretary who is forever getting me in and out of trouble. May it last forever."

September 7th is not only my birthday, it is also the birthday of the twins, Reagan and Ellison Golubin. Since I, too, am a twin (albeit non-identical) we had long joked about how we should celebrate together. And we did yesterday at lunch. Susan treated and Patti Matson (also a Virgo) and Barbara Manfuso joined us.

My birthday was followed by "gift day" at the White House. The public constantly sends presents to the President and the First Family. As the gifts come in, they go directly to the Gift Unit, a special office which has been run by a woman named Marge Wecklein since the Eisenhower Administration. There, the gifts are logged, filed, and thank-you notes are drafted for the signature of the appropriate family member. (It must be nice to open a present with the comforting knowledge that you already sent out a thank-you note!) The gifts then go to the family residence. Mrs. Ford puts them in what used to be Tricia Nixon's bedroom on the second floor. When they accumulate to the point where the room is too crowded, the Fords open their presents. Today was gift day.

People send the First Family everything. Mention a skiing vacation, and dozens of hand-knitted scarves, mittens, sweaters show up. They send ties with pictures of the President reproduced on them, sweatshirts on which people have drawn his face, trinkets, records, hats.

Food is the one forbidden item. For security reasons, the First Family can only eat food prepared for them in the White House. (Apples once sent to the Fords by a good friend in Michigan were destroyed by the Secret Service.)

Today's loot dramatized the fact that the bicentennial is weighing heavy on America's creative energies. Everything was red, white, and blue with messages such as "HAPPY BIRTHDAY, AMERICA!" embroidered, knitted or scrawled in. There are always some misspellings. One of today's offerings was a big pillow across which someone had embroidered in red, white, and blue: TO JERRY FORD, THE PRESIDENT OFF THE USA."

Liberty swells. The excitement mounts. Susan went around collecting money for the White House Liberty pool today. Everyone had to guess the number of puppies and the time of birth. I guessed today at 5:00 P.M.

I lost.

## SEPTEMBER 11, 1975

Bless you, Lorena Chevalier of Dallas, Texas!

Mrs. Chevalier was "bewildered" by Mrs. Ford's comments on "60 Minutes," so she wrote the First Lady a letter including clippings from local newspapers that were critical of the statement. Mrs. Chevalier "felt you should know what was being said."

Well, two days ago, Lorena received a *wonderful* letter from Mrs. Ford which explained everything. The letter was so good, that she took it to the Associated Press to print. They did.

"I want other people to read the letter if it will help straighten things out," the Associated Press quotes Mrs. Chevalier as saying, "One mother always wants to help another."

Bless you, Lorena Chevalier!

\* \* \*

## SEPTEMBER 12, 1975

The *New York Times* today printed Mrs. Chevalier's letter from Mrs. Ford in its entirety:

> Thank you for writing about my appearance on the "60 Minutes" interview. The concern which inspired you to share your views is appreciated.
>
> I wish it were possible for us to sit down together and talk, one to another. I consider myself a responsible parent. I know I am a loving one. We have raised our four children in a home that believes in and practices the enduring values of morality and personal integrity.
>
> As every mother and father knows, these are not easy times to be a parent. Our convictions are continually being questioned and tested by the fads and fancies of the moment. I believe our values to be eternal and I hope I have instilled them in our children.
>
> We have come to this sharing of outlook through communication, not coercion. I want my children to know that their concerns—their doubts and their difficulties—whatever they may be, can be discussed with the two people in this world who care the most—their mother and father.
>
> On "60 Minutes," the emotion of my words spoke to the need of this communication, rather than the specific issues we discussed.
>
> My husband and I have lived twenty-six years of faithfulness in marriage. I do not believe in premarital relations, but I realize that many in today's generation do not share my views. However, this must never cause us to withdraw the love, the counseling and the understanding that they may need now, more than ever before.
>
> This is the essence of responsible parenthood. It is difficult to adequately express one's personal convictions in a fifteen-minute interview. I hope our lives will say more than words about our dedication to honor, to integrity, to humanity, and to God.
>
> You and I, they and I, have no quarrels.
>
> Sincerely, Betty Ford

Other papers today printed excerpts. Still others have been calling for copies (which I explained were not being made available by the White House). Reaction to the letter appears good.

I think it's working.

I hope it clarifies things. But I think it is more than a clarification. It is constructive parental advice. And these are days when constructive parental advice can be most useful.

Our mail could use a few favorable reactions. Thus far the count runs 28,000 letters, only about 8,000 "pro." Many make interesting reading such as the one from the priest who wrote to tell Mrs. Ford that he agrees with the stand she took on "60 Minutes," in spite of the fact that he preached a sermon against her stand from his pulpit last Sunday.

## *SEPTEMBER 14, 1975*

It was a home delivery. But what a home.

Everything done in the White House is done right. Liberty gave birth in a bedroom transformed into a delivery room on the second floor, where an enormous box for giving birth—a whelping box—had been built and expert medical assistance was right at hand.

Several puppies had already been born when Edward and I arrived. Mrs. Ford was taking a nap, after having been up half the night patting and soothing and talking to Liberty. She left her in good hands; the "medical team" consisted of Bill Brockett, her trainer, and her veterinarian as well. Spectators included Susan, Edward, me, and—later—the President, who walked in wearing casual Sunday attire and puffing on a pipe.

One or two were born while we watched. I'd never witnessed a birth of any sort before, and I was fascinated by the process. Nature provides. The body works. It was biology at its finest.

It all looked like a Norman Rockwell painting: The President of the United States, pipe in mouth, patting his fine dog, Liberty, as she brings forth a new generation.

## *SEPTEMBER 16, 1975*

I have no idea how many shopping days are left, but let the record show that we are planning ahead. People from the Abby Aldrich Rockefeller Folk Art Collection in Williamsburg, Virginia, came to the White House today to show Mrs. Ford examples of homemade ornaments that will decorate this year's tree.

We are behind in finding a social secretary, though. Mrs. Ford has gotten many applications, but it is difficult to separate the talented from the non-talented. I suggested a few weeks ago that Mrs.

Ford have the applicants she was seriously considering put together a State Dinner package, including guest list, table settings, theme, entertainment, and so on. She has given the assignment out to a few applicants. We shall see.

Everybody wants a Liberty puppy. And, starting with a letter going out today, everyone is being told that the puppies will go to family and friends and the Leader School for the Blind. Tomorrow, a whole new batch of "everybodys" will write and call.

At least Liberty's puppies have cut down on the number of requests for pictures by Susan we have been getting.

## SEPTEMBER 18, 1975

Jack just returned from a camping trip. A much-needed camping trip. Not necessarily for the camping, just for the pleasure of spending nine days *not* being Jack Ford.

"Man, I'll tell you it was such a relief. I was really going crazy around here. I couldn't sleep. I couldn't do anything. I felt imprisoned. Getting out of Washington was wonderful. I dropped my Secret Service detail, too."

"Dropped your detail? What do you mean 'dropped'?"

"I told them not to come. I refused to let them come. It's my choice, you know."

"Jack, that's irresponsible—irresponsible and dangerous. This is not a game. They are there to protect you."

"Do you know what it is like to have them shadowing me all the time? Participating in every aspect of my life? I have no privacy. I have no freedom. And even if I forget they are there, no one else does. Everyone I'm with feels this obligation to invite them in, to feed them, to talk to them."

"You could try a different tactic. You could try talking to them, too."

"I've tried. Some of them I can talk to, but the others speak a different language."

I immediately thought of the Spiro Agnew fan. "You know, Jack, you could request a new detail, or at least substitutions for the agents on your detail you don't get along with. I think the Secret Service tries to work it out so there is as little conflict as possible. I'm sure they would rather reassign people than have you drop the detail."

He is really having a hard time. Susan has learned how to use the spotlight effectively when she wishes and how to shun publicity effectively when she wishes. Steve and Michael have come to grips with the situation by keeping their distance, as Jack did before he graduated, and by submerging themselves in other preoccupations. Michael is absolutely determined that his father's being President is not going to change his life, Gayle's life, their relationship, or their devotion to religion. And Steve—though he's four years younger than Jack, seems to have a greater sense of who he is and what he wants to be.

I think it is Jack's ambivalence about the White House that makes him so vulnerable. Michael and Steve want no part of it. Jack is not so sure. An avid political observer, he is frankly fascinated by what he sees in the White House. If only he could see without being seen.

But he is very visible. And he is very free. He has no school, no job, no arbitrary source of structure. It's hard to find yourself while everyone watches you look. How on earth do you assert yourself and establish your autonomy in the shadow of the most powerful man in the world? If he were a few years younger or older it would be easier.

Someone else with Jack's interests and background would seek a government job in some area related to ecology, or forestry or environment, and work there while pondering the abstractions of career. That option—interesting salaried autonomy—is not open to the son of the President, so he looks elsewhere: to a foreman's job on an Indian reservation, to an instructor's job at a ski resort, to graduate school. Those were the alternatives we talked about today in my office. I think we rejected all.

Mrs. Ford in the meantime is having as hard a time finding a social secretary as Jack is finding a career alternative. She called me to tell me the results of one applicant's answers to the State Dinner hypothetical.

"I told her to plan the big event for next July when Queen Elizabeth is scheduled to visit us," Mrs. Ford said. "And she thought, 'wouldn't it be neat to have bronco busting and bronco riding on the front lawn of the White House?'"

(Not neat. Messy if anything.) I laughed and waited for the "No, to be serious." It was not forthcoming.

"Well, you know the Queen loves horses," Mrs. Ford offered.

(Only well-behaved ones.) I kept trying to think of something to say. No luck.

"Well, I know it wouldn't work, really, but it *is* imaginative."

"Yes," I said truthfully, "It *is* imaginative."

"Another idea she had," Mrs. Ford said, "was to use saddles at the State Dinner as centerpieces."

(That just might rid the Queen of her love for horses.) "It . . . *is* imaginative."

"Yes," she said, "but it wouldn't work."

"No."


## SEPTEMBER 19, 1975

Nancy Reagan told the Women's Republican Club of Grosse Pointe, Michigan, that she was opposed to the "new morality" among the young people including premarital sexual relations, and criticized the easy access the young have to abortion.

"The difference in opinion between the President's wife and the wife of Mr. Ford's potential rival for the Republican Presidential nomination was not lost on the Grosse Pointe audience," the *Los Angeles Times* reports.


## SEPTEMBER 22, 1975

Four days of handshaking in Oklahoma and California. I was not enthusiastic about this trip, especially since it came right after a handshaking Presidential tour of New Hampshire, Missouri, Kansas, and Texas last week. The President, I keep muttering to people in the West Wing, would get more support by being above all this obvious campaigning right now, by being President.

It falls on deaf ears, which is just as well. If they heard me, they would get angry.

I became even less enthusiastic as we went along, these past few days. This is Mrs. Ford's first time accompanying him this year, and she came as "wife," in the most traditional political sense; a sweet smiler, who beams with pride at the magnificence of the oratorical power of her man.

So this is campaigning.

I was appalled. It is one thing to mishandle the President. His image, I admit, is someone else's business. But don't ruin *her* image! Don't take the woman Americans have come to respect as an honest, forthright, intelligent lady who speaks her mind and make her into a podium princess!

There will be some changes made.

The President went into San Francisco this morning and Mrs. Ford and I stayed behind. It was a "free day," the last day of the trip, and she decided to forgo San Francisco and meet him on Air Force One this afternoon at departure time. As we drove to the airport she had second thoughts. "I love San Francisco. Maybe we should have spent the day there instead. It's such a beautiful city."

We got to Air Force One and met the Presidential party totally unaware of the fact that less than an hour before, just as the President was leaving the St. Francis Hotel, a woman named Sara Moore had tried to assassinate him.

"Did you have a good time, dear?" Mrs. Ford asked the President very sweetly as she kissed him hello. He calmly led her into the Family Quarters, as Helen Thomas told me the details as they knew them.

Rumsfeld, who had been very close to it all, drew diagrams for the press pool, showing where the gunwoman had been standing, where the President was, and so on. He was very excited with the surplus of nervous energy that comes after such an experience.

I felt numbed. I still do. Twice in one month. Two peculiar women. How can anyone ever adequately protect the President of the United States?

"Thank God she was a poor shot," said Mrs. Ford.

## SEPTEMBER 25, 1975

In a Harris Poll taken between August 30th and September 6th, 50 percent of the people polled felt that Betty Ford was doing a good job as First Lady. Forty-one percent gave the President a favorable rating.

* * *

## SEPTEMBER 30, 1975

It was Don Hewitt. "Now, Sheila, before you say 'no' let me finish."

"Do I ever say 'no' before you finish?"

"Well, we're going to do two special '60 Minutes' shows in November, and I think it would be a perfect opportunity for Mrs. Ford to have a forum to spell out the ideas she had before."

I didn't say no, but I did say, "Well . . ." and pointed out that there were other shows who wanted Mrs. Ford. I promised I would ask her.

"You'll never guess who I got a call from," I told her later today. I gave her the message. She just smiled.

Today's other urgent request came in the form of a telegram: "WOULD LIKE TO REQUEST SUSAN FORD PHOTO ASSIGNMENT FOR NATIONAL ENQUIRER. TO PHOTOGRAPH LIBERTY AND PUPS AND LUCKY OUR MASCOT. ASSIGNMENT WILL PAY WELL."

*Chapter Twelve*
OCTOBER, 1975:

# THE WHITE HOUSE CAN'T SHIELD YOU

*OCTOBER 2, 1975*

Mrs. Ford has made her decision. The White House has a new social secretary.

"I'm going to hire Maria Downs."

(Downs . . . Downs . . . which applicant was Downs?)

"She worked in Ann Armstrong's office during the Nixon Administration."

(Still no recognition. Downs . . . Downs . . . )

"She's the one Don Rumsfeld recommended."

(A Nixon holdover recommended by Rumsfeld. Terrific. I am displeased. I am also still unsure of which one.)

"You remember, Sheila; she's the one who had that very imaginative State Dinner plan for the Queen's visit?" (The haze lifts, replaced by a vivid image of a rodeo on the front lawn of the White House.)

"Maria Downs. Oh, yes, *now* I remember."

Oh dear.

\* \* \*

## OCTOBER 6, 1975

Eleven different State's Chairmen were scheduled to attend the Republican Western Region Conference in Portland, Oregon, last week. They requested a Ford family member. The White House sent Jack with everyone's blessing. He is the Ford most closely attuned to the West, a Ford capable of giving a youthful viewpoint of what is happening in the administration and the Ford who is about to become actively involved in his father's campaign. He and George Gorton (a young man Jack worked for during the '72 campaign whom Jack considers a political genius) put together a program for enlisting volunteers in New Hampshire and submitted it to Stu Spencer at the President Ford Committee. Stu said fine. They plan to start next month.

This, we all agree, was a perfect place for Jack to begin actively campaigning for his father's re-election, the perfect place for Jack to declare himself.

But the declaration was a surprise.

"I've smoked marijuana before and I don't think that's so exceptional for people growing up in the nineteen sixties," he told the *Oregonian*, the state's largest newspaper. He went on to say that he had not tried hard drugs, but some of his friends had, and "I don't think that will exclude them as my friends."

Wonderful.

It was not an off-the-cuff remark. It had been carefully orchestrated by Jack and David Kennerly, who grew up in Oregon and had set up the interview for Jack with the *Oregonian*.

"We thought the issue should come out in the open especially if I'm going to get into the campaign. There are all sorts of rumors floating around about me and marijuana and we thought that by saying this out loud, we could clear the air and prevent the gossip. Oregon is a very liberal state, and so the place just seemed right."

Good intent. Bad timing. Oregon may be a liberal state, but President is a national office. This was not the best way to secure Republican votes in, oh, say, New Hampshire.

Staying ahead of the story was not such a bad idea. It could have been handled better. And I could have been told. To be honest, I was hurt. I felt Jack had begun to trust me, and confide in me and I was jolted by his doing something like this without telling me.

"What did your father say?"

"I went in to talk to him about it. He was reading the newspaper.

He folded it over and I could see the picture of me, upside down. I felt very uncomfortable. He looked up at me and said, 'I've been reading about you.' "

"I started to apologize and Dad cut me off. 'Don't apologize. At the most I'll be here six years. You're going to live with yourself all of your life.' "

The maternal reaction was pure maternal: she was relieved to hear he had never tried hard drugs. Although she was disappointed at his admission, she hastened to say that she was sure he did not use marijuana habitually, because she would have noticed it. She did not sound like a First Lady. She sounded like a veteran of a war waged by many a mother in the late nineteen sixties.

"My kids went through the worst of the drug scene. It was at its height when they were in school. That's where you get my reaction. I once asked them how long it would take them to get marijuana, and they said 'ten minutes.' Don't think I didn't worry, and don't think I didn't attend meetings at the high school about it, and don't think I couldn't smell it when I did. Drugs were very heavy. And, frankly, I feel I more or less got them through the worst of it without a scene."

## OCTOBER 7, 1975

Jack's role in the campaign was short lived. The marijuana statement infuriated Stu Spencer, who told Jack he could forget New Hampshire, and for that matter he could forget any role in the Presidential campaign.

## OCTOBER 8, 1978

Madame Huang Chen came for tea this afternoon.

It was hardly spontaneous. Madame Huang Chen is the wife of the Chief of the People's Republic of China Liaison Office in Washington, and her visit to the First Lady was designed to lay the groundwork for a possible Presidential trip to Peking later this year. Inviting her to tea was an expression of hospitality, and a very carefully contrived act. Mrs. Ford was briefed ("It is possible Mme Huang will bring a Chinese handicraft project. A small reciprocal gift in return would be appropriate.") briefed ("Mme Huang plays an active political role within the embassies in which she has served. You should assume that any of your comments will be reported back.'') and briefed (''A round jolly lady who loves gardens, has seven children, and speaks Hungarian.'').

Mrs. Ford had received a biographical sketch of her guest as well as a long list of suggested talking points. (''If you show Mme Huang around the residence,'' the briefing paper read, ''you might show her the Lincoln Sitting Room, and mention that this was where President Nixon and Secretary Kissinger prepared for Dr. Kissinger's first secret trip to Peking, or the Rose Garden, where the People's Republic of China ping pong team was received in April, 1972.)

Then, just in case Mrs. Ford found herself at a loss for words, the briefing paper had several catchy little suggestions such as ''I remember with many fond memories my own visit to your country in 1972,'' and ''The President is looking forward very much to visiting China this year.''

Briefed and impressed with the international significance of this social courtesy, we waited for Mme Huang Chen and her interpreter to arrive in the Diplomatic Room this afternoon at the appointed hour.

We waited.

And waited.

And waited.

Where were our most illustrious guests?

A call to security ended the mystery. Yes, the guard admitted, he had been holding two Chinese ladies down at the White House entrance. What did we expect him to do? They lacked appropriate identification!


## OCTOBER 9, 1975

*People* Magazine has heard that Jack and his father are not seeing eye to eye these days, and that Jack is into hard drugs. The *Los Angeles Times* has heard that Jack's Secret Service detail had to protect a party he gave from a local plainclothes drug raid. And *Time* Magazine has heard that two of Jack's Secret Service agents are quitting because they find themselves in the awkward legal position of protecting him when he smokes grass.

Nothing like bringing an issue out in the open to dispel rumors.

"Nonsense!" I told *People* Magazine (and meant it). "Nonsense!" I told the *Los Angeles Times* (and meant it).

*Time* Magazine created a more difficult problem because I was less than sure. (It was possible Jack had requested new agents. It was *very* possible some of his present agents had talked to reporters.) To make matters worse, the inquiry came from Bonnie Angelo, someone I value as a friend and respect as a journalist.

Consciously avoiding Jack's agents, I called Jack Warner, the assistant to the director of public affairs for the Secret Service. He said he'd check and call me right back. He did.

"Not true," he reported. "Nobody on Jack's detail has asked to leave."

Voilà: the official line. I called Bonnie and diligently gave her the report.

"I don't believe anything that comes from an official Secret Service spokesman," she told me.

"Bonnie, he meant it. It was a definitive answer."

"I'm sure."

"How are you going to write the story?"

"I'll say, 'Jack's agents say they are leaving, because of this and that and the Secret Service officially denies it.' "

"What kind of a thing is that? You're going to set up a rumor and then deny it. What facts do you have?"

"I hear he took a bunch of models out on the town when he was in Helsinki and the President was furious."

"He might have. I don't know. But I do know that he had a very busy schedule in Helsinki and he did everything he was supposed to do."

"He didn't miss anything?"

"He did sleep through a tennis match one morning, but that was the only thing he missed. And that was recreational and not protocol."

"I've also heard that he doesn't want his father to run."

"I'm sure he has mixed feelings. Look, Bonnie, the White House is a difficult place for Jack. Personally, I think he would be happier if his father weren't President. But he is President, and he is running for re-election, and, given that fact, Jack certainly wants him to win."

"Sheila, there are too many people saying too many things."

"I can only tell you what I know."

"It's impossible for you to know everything."

"I know that I went out with Jack and David Kennerly in Helsinki and, frankly it was one of the more boring evenings I've spent."

The *National Enquirer* called to say that 65,000 people have filled out a special coupon the paper ran begging President Ford to prevent further cruelty to dogs and that they would like to photograph Mrs. Ford receiving the 65,000 coupons.

The nice thing about the *National Enquirer* is that you can always give them a definitive, unqualified "NO!"


## *OCTOBER 10, 1975*

It was a "Michigan State Republican Salute to the President" and we traveled all the way to Detroit for it. There was a press conference, carried on regional television. There were speeches. The only thing lacking was substance. The President boarded Air Force One with the First Lady. Immediately upon landing, however, they became transformed into an overtraveled politician and his smiling, flower-receiving wife.

When will someone realize that there is a difference between quantity and quality? A voice does not get votes because it is familiar, but because of the words it utters. A political trip, if not disguised, should at least be camouflaged, so it does not appear that the President of the United States is spending half his Presidency trying to become the President.

"The man is being mismanaged," I told Jim Connor, Ford's Secretary of the Cabinet who had been assigned to the same minibus during the Detroit motorcade.

"What do you mean?"

I was startled by the reply. A question! I looked up. He was actually waiting for an answer. A West Wing person who really wanted to know what I thought! I told him I thought Ford was being overexposed, underprepared, and handed rotten scripts. He said that he, too, has been concerned about it, that Ford as he knows him seems a political natural, someone for whom public popularity should come easily. He can't understand why his image is so bad. It baffles him.

It was comforting to have a give-and-take conversation with

someone, to share ideas. More academic than political, he had none of the ego vulnerabilities I've sensed in other West Wing men. He was interested in solving a problem. He did not particularly care whether it was *his* idea that won. He's easygoing, with a patience and a respect for ideas, even women's ideas. Unlike many of his co-workers, Jim Connor is married to a career woman (his wife Judith, is Assistant Secretary of Transportation for Consumer Affairs) and I think that makes a difference in his attitude.

He's a prodigy of what they call Rumsfeld's "Junior Varsity" (a select group that includes Rumsfeld's assistant, Dick Cheney, and a few others) but it's hard to believe.

We talked about how different the job of Secretary to the Cabinet is from what it was in my father's time. He told me that he handles administration matters (as in "extra staff people?" I wonder) and that he controls all perks. I told him that Gulley controls all perks.

"Gulley, technically, can only implement what we tell him to implement." he said.

"Technically."

"Technically."

We both laughed.

## OCTOBER 13, 1975

"Betty Ford has won the support of New Yorkers for publicly expressing her views on premarital sex, pot smoking, and abortion," according to a *Daily News* public opinion poll released today. A majority of those polled felt the First Lady should have spoken out, and that her statement on such subjects on "60 Minutes" in no way hurt the President's chances for re-election. Men gave her stronger support than women, and her strongest support (81 percent) came from college graduates.

## OCTOBER 14, 1975

It was Dick Cohen from the Metro section of the *Washington Post*. He said the *Post*'s police reporter had phoned in a double murder-suicide in Northwest Washington. A man named Nicholas

Golubin, fifty-two, an employee of the Environmental Protection Agency, had shot and killed his estranged wife, Patricia Golubin and his mother-in-law, Agnes Forgeron and then put a bullet through his own head. Was he any relative, Dick wanted to know, to the twin "Golubins" who were such good friends of Susan?

"I hope not. No, couldn't be. Well, I'll check."

He gave me the address. I called the White House operator and asked for the twins' address. It was the same.

I did not react. I did not feel stunned, I suppose, because I still felt certain that there was some mistake. I knew Reagan and Ellison Golubin well enough, certainly, to know that they are not products of a family in which double murder-suicides take place. These are special girls, emotionally solid girls, girls who have been reared carefully and with warmth and affection. You can be sure of that. It shows.

I called the police. It was no mistake. Breon, Reagan and Ellison's fourteen-year-old sister, had discovered the bodies when she came home from school this afternoon. The children had been notified.

I tried to track down Susan. I found out that she was still in class. I got through to the head of her Secret Service detail, who said he had heard and planned to tell Susan in the car coming home.

I called Mrs. Ford. She, too, had just found out. She had been in touch with the children. "The twins are flying home from Atlanta tonight," she told me, "and I will meet them at the plane at National Airport with Susan."

She has offered the Solarium to the Golubin children as a place to stay. She thought it would be very difficult for them to go home under the circumstances. There are six children, she explained: Gregory, twenty-six (the oldest, and only boy); Jannen, twenty-four; the twins; Danele, and Breon. At a time like this, Mrs. Ford said, they will need to be together, and to be together in privacy. She was very upset, but she was completely in control of the situation. Mrs. Ford is incredible in an emergency. And this was indeed an emergency, an unbelievable tragedy.

The Golubins and the Fords had more than a casual friendship. Susan and Reagan and Ellison had shared everything from sandbox toys to teenage secrets. Their parents, as a result, had spent fifteen years sharing PTA meetings, car pools, and daughters. Susan often spent the night at the Golubins'. Reagan and Ellison were frequent White House boarders.

Mrs. Ford talked about the little things you talk about at moments such as this. Patricia Golubin, who had a thriving real estate business, had sold the Ford Alexandria home for them. She had looked well the last time Mrs. Ford had seen her. The twins had been excited last month about going off to Emory College in Atlanta.

As she talked, I thought about all the conversations I had had with Reagan and Ellison, conversations which ranged from boyfriends to "life"—conversations with teenagers, true, but with teenagers who seemed to be unusually sensitive and mature. I had tried to convince them to go to separate colleges, the way my twin sister, Emily and I had, but they would not hear of it. They were not only identical twins, they said, they were best friends as well. They wanted to go together. And so they had—with such big plans, happy hopes.

Deep down, I was still convinced the whole thing had not happened.

Susan's Secret Service agent called to tell me that Susan had handled the news very maturely, that her only desire was to get in touch with the twins as soon as possible.

Mrs. Ford and Susan met Reagan and Ellison at the plane from Atlanta tonight, and the four other Golubin children were scooped up and protectively sheltered from the public eye in the Family Quarters of the White House, comforted by Mrs. Ford and Susan.

I sit here, staring at a blow-up I have on my wall of Susan and the twins at graduation. It captures the moment, and the "moment" lasted for a split second. The three girls are running toward each other, their arms extended for the embrace, their faces bearing tears and smiles, the visible signs of the high emotions that accompany graduation for three very, very close girls—friends who find themselves making the step from past to future.

I can't stop looking at it.


## OCTOBER 17, 1975

I know what I read in the papers. And for three days now, I've been reading the papers. They tell me that when Patricia and Nich-

olas Golubin separated, he stayed in the family's Virginia home
and she moved into a townhouse in Washington with her mother
and the children. That's where the murder/suicide took place. The
papers tell me the Golubins were married for twenty-six years, divorced for one, that Mrs. Golubin was a "real go-getter" that Mr.
Golubin, a high-level career federal employee, had not looked well
lately.

The papers answer none of my questions.

The White House continues to provide a sanctuary for the Golubin children. The huge mansion seems suddenly personal. Real
people live here with real friends unprotected from real tragedies.

Mrs. Ford says the girls are taking it very hard, but that their older brother Gregory is holding everyone up. "He's a remarkable
young man," she said.

Yes, he is. At the very small, very private funeral today in
Georgetown, Gregory stood up and delivered the eulogy for his
mother, his father, and his grandmother. He read an essay his
youngest sister had written about her mother. He spoke of his father's oft-used maxim: "Never never never never let a day go by
without telling your family that you love them." He was moving
and articulate and he did not break down. I think he was the only
one in the whole church who did not.

Patti Matson and I rode out to the cemetery in a car with Nicholas Golubin's two older sisters. They were in bad shape. They
talked about "Nick" as a child, and "Nick" as a grown man who
loved his family. They talked about "Nick" and Patricia, and how
they had met and how difficult he had found their separation. They
talked about "Nick" and his children, his wonderful children.
They could not understand what had happened. They said the doctors had said he had a brain tumor, and that that was probably what
altered his behavior.

That explained it. That solved the mystery. But it did not soothe
the pain.

Patti and I tried to comfort them. It was a moment when total
strangers become close. The sisters talked and their eyes would
sparkle every so often as they relayed anecdotes of happier days.
But each gleam faded, clouded over by sadness, bereavement, despair. The stories were just prologue, after all. Inevitably, they
found themselves faced with an ending that was unbearable and
unacceptable.

## OCTOBER 23, 1975

Another check-up, another clean bill of health. The word from Bethesda Naval Hospital today is: no recurrence of cancer. What is more, Mrs. Ford is in "excellent general health."

We may celebrate with another television appearance. Bob Orben worked with Ed Weinberger, the producer of the Mary Tyler Moore show, and Bob told me yesterday they were interested in a cameo appearance by Susan. I suggested Mrs. Ford instead, and talked to Weinberger myself today. He explained the gist of the script: Mary Tyler Moore and her editor, Lou Grant, go to Washington, D.C. Grant boasts about knowing all the important people. Mary does not believe him. The phone rings. "Hello Mary, I'm Betty Ford," Mrs. Ford says. Mary Tyler Moore makes a face. "Hello Betty," she says sarcastically, "I'm Mary, Queen of Scots!"

I told Weinberger to send me the script. I said I loved the idea and I thought Mrs. Ford would, too.

Then I set about convincing Mrs. Ford that she loved the idea.

No, I assured her, it is not "too frivolous." It is not a frivolous show. It is a funny show and there's an important difference. It is a clever, nationally acclaimed series respected for its wit and populated by a very likeable cast of characters. If anything, a cameo appearance on the Mary Tyler Moore show would mean that a large, prime-time audience would associate you with their favorite television program. At best, you would come off as a good sport with a sense of humor and you would have some fun doing it, too. The best part of all is that there is no "at worst," alternative. It will be carefully scripted. No spontaneity, for once!

She said she would do it.

Then she went over her plans for the *Good Housekeeping* article with me.

They had wanted to do a big fashion spread: *Good Houskeeping* would dress her and she would model the clothes. Other First Ladies had done it.

I said no, because it was very commercial, and because, with all the fittings, I knew it would waste a lot of time. And for what? For an enormous story on the First Lady as mannequin? (Now *that* is frivolous.) The fact is, Mrs. Ford is very talented as a fashion coordinator, her own wardrobe is very artfully put together, and I felt

she had more to offer as a coordinator than as just a model. I told
*Good Housekeeping* that Mrs. Ford had a wonderful sense of how
to mix and match clothes and stretch a wardrobe, and I suggested,
as an alternative, that Mrs. Ford model her own clothes for the story, demonstrating how, with a little imagination, a few different
outfits could be translated into many, many different looks. (The
mannequin is transformed into an intelligent, creative, economy-
minded fashion designer.)

They loved the idea. Mrs. Ford loved the idea. She put a lot of
thought into it and today she went over it all with me, explaining
which clothes would go with which accessories and how different
the looks could be. She had laid everything out meticulously on
clothes racks and the demonstration was very impressive—so impressive that I was furious I had no camera crew there to shoot as
she did it.

## OCTOBER 24, 1975

"This is not generally known," the reporter whispered into the
telephone, "but I thought you might be interested: Ronald Reagan's daughter is living with the drummer of a Rock 'n Roll group
known as the 'Eagles.' "

(Let *her* Press Secretary worry!)

## OCTOBER 25, 1975

I've been turning down ERA requests for months. But the issue
was "where," not "whether."

I was looking for the right place (not radical, not conservative)
the right audience, (housewives, not feminists) and the right timing
(to insure national coverage).

Then along came the Greater Cleveland International Women's
Year Congress, a three-day conference with solid community support put together by local housewives, feminists, and garment
workers. The conference was to have booths, exhibits, speeches,
and a large model day care center for the children of women attending the convention. Amidst the national glut of IWY programs,
this one seemed especially well planned.

The timing could not have been better—for all the wrong reasons. The latest Roper poll shows that the public favors the Equal Rights Amendment 3 to 1. But state legislators who are nervously tabling the measure right and left appear preoccupied with ERA opponents' dire predictions of doom, gloom and sexually integrated boy scouts. The hysteria is snowballing. Only one state approved it this year. Nebraska and Tennessee voted, instead, to rescind their earlier approval, and Phyllis Schlafly is chirping, "We've got the momentum!"

It was time for a responsible, calm voice in the spotlight, to dispel the distortions and Cleveland was the perfect format. It would be a sympathetic audience but not necessarily one that was already converted. It would be an audience of women with backgrounds similar to Mrs. Ford's, women who cared about their families, and about their options as well.

It had to be a good speech, a speech that could serve in the future as an official outline of precisely what Mrs. Ford's views were on this issue. It has to state that the ERA would have no adverse impact on the family, that opening up new options to women in no way lessens the importance of being a wife and mother. That the emotionalism surrounding the ERA was caused by the changes that had *already* taken place in the United States, not changes that would be caused by the Equal Rights Amendment. That the ERA will open up new doors, but that women will have to value their own talents more before they can walk through those doors. It had to be a simple and dramatic speech, one that Mrs. Ford could deliver comfortably.

All of which is a long way of saying that Mrs. Ford told a large group of women in Cleveland, Ohio, that "Being ladylike does not require silence. I spoke out on this issue because of my deep personal conviction. Why should my husband's job or yours prevent us from being ourselves?" She went on to clarify the myths surrounding the impact of the Equal Rights Amendment, and stress that women must work on increasing their own self-esteem. "We must take the 'just' out of 'just a housewife,'" she said, "and show our pride in having made the home and family our life's work. Downgrading this work has been part of the pattern in our society that downgrades individual women's talents in all areas."

She was terrific. They loved her. She was delighted. It got nice coverage.

I guess it was just a case of the right speech at the right time in the right place.

## OCTOBER 27, 1975

"I need more staff people," I told Jim Connor today, trying to make it sound like a new idea, and one that required immediate action. "We have been understaffed for a year. We have compensated by overworking. Now, with the traveling that is coming up, we will be incapable of compensating. Patti Matson will be advancing Mrs. Ford's trips, which means she will be on the road almost constantly. I need someone to do her office work. Mrs. Ford will be making many speeches. I need someone to write them."

He said his instructions were to decrease White House Staff.

"That's easy," I told him. "There *are* too many people in the White House. I can show you how to streamline the White House. Especially the West Wing."

"How about the East Wing?"

"The East Wing, too, can be streamlined."

"Okay," he said, "I'll make you a deal. If you can figure out a way for me to cut the East Wing Staff by five, I'll get you two extra people."

Racing Ron Nessen was less complicated.

But Jim Connor sounds as though he means it.

*Chapter Thirteen*
NOVEMBER, 1975:

# RUMORS

*NOVEMBER 2, 1975*

I felt it as soon as I got to Air Force One. Something had happened. No, something was happening. The press pool was buzzing with rumors of an administration shake-up that had been leaked to *Newsweek* before it was completed. Was it true? Was Henry Kissinger being demoted? Were White House Staff being reshuffled?

They looked up at me expectantly. I told them I knew nothing. They sniffed and scrutinized and gave me a hasty once-over, their journalistic skills developed over the years to detect liars in moments such as this.

They agreed: I knew nothing. As far as they were concerned, I was useless. To the men at the other end of the plane, however, I was priceless. And for the very same reason.

"Sheila!" boomed Ron Nessen with a tone of pleasure he had never before associated with my name, "I want you to do me a favor today. *You* handle all the press questions."

He laughed. His companions, Don Rumsfeld's Assistant, Dick Cheney, and Brent Scowcroft, Kissinger's Deputy at the National Security Council, guffawed. Jolly good fun. The joke was on me.

But what was the joke?

"If you do a good job, Sheila," said Nessen, Big Shot, "I'll make you an assistant in the press office."

More guffaws.

"In that case, Ron, I'll botch it up."

Laughter. They were happy enough to laugh at anyone's jokes. Regardless of what had happened, it was obvious Nessen, Cheney, and Scowcroft were still employed.

And I was to play the part of the fool. I was to be the uninformed Press Secretary sent to the hungry press pool without a morsel. I was the perfect shield. I knew nothing. They knew I knew nothing. I could therefore be honest without having to reveal anything. Obviously, there had been some staff changes made. What they were, I had no idea. But obviously, again, they had been leaked. The administration was caught off guard, and this was the strategy for handling it. Strategy? Was this a game for grown-ups? Especially grown-ups in charge of informing the public of Presidential policies?

We were not taking an excursion for fun aboard Air Force One. We were en route to Jacksonville, Florida, where the President was meeting with Egyptian President Anwar Sadat. Yet when the press pool sought background information on the summit meeting, the men up front laughed again.

"I don't know what you are doing," I told Ron. "I hope you do."

He assured me he did. More guffaws. We landed.

We were taken to the home of Jacksonville Pontiac dealer Luther Coggin (where the Fords would be staying for the day).

It was a day of many levels. Mrs. Ford and I behaved like "ladies." We visited the next-door neighbors, admired their daughter's art work and chatted lightly over lunch with Nancy Chirdon, not even mentioning the word "rumor" and yet I am sure she knew the whole story. And I'm sure she knew that I knew that she knew.

After lunch I ventured over to the press room where chaos reigned. *Had* Kissinger been removed from the National Security Council? Had Schlesinger been kicked out of the Pentagon post? Confirmations were not forthcoming. Ill will was escalating. A helicopter crash, visible from the press room window, only temporarily distracted reporters from deploring the way "this thing" had been handled.

And not only reporters. Most of the White House Staff were uninformed. Bill Greener, Nessen's affable deputy, had no idea what was happening. *Newsweek* reporter Tom De Frank called Bill late last night and gave him until 5:00 A.M. this morning to confirm the rumors. De Frank told Bill he had called Nessen and Nessen had not called him back. He had called Rumsfeld, and Rumsfeld had not called him back. He had called Cheney, and Cheney had not called him back.

Bill Greener then called Rumsfeld, who is a good friend of his. "Is Kissinger losing the National Security Council Post?" he asked. Rumsfeld said he would check it out.

When Rumsfeld did not call back, Greener called Cheney. Cheney said "I can't waste the President's time with a question like that."

"What do you mean 'waste the President's time,'" roared Greener. "If I came to you and said, 'The head of the Office of Management and the Budget is leaving,' wouldn't you think it is important enough to check it out?"

Bill Greener was angry and frustrated. "I've known Rumsfeld and Cheney for so long now that I know when they are trying to put one past me," he said. Then he settled back and joined the reporters watching the Dallas-Redskin game on television.

Meanwhile, back at the Coggins', spirits were still soaring and the Redskins-Dallas Cowboys game was on the television set in the living room. At game's end, the President and Mrs. Ford went to the San Jose country club for a dinner given by Florida Governor Askew for the two visiting Presidents. There is always a holding room set up on such occasions, where the President and the staff can relax before and during the festivities. I walked in during the dinner to get some coffee, and I heard Brent Scowcroft, usually a calm, mild mannered man, yelling into the telephone: "Colby is out! Colby is out!"

Colby? As in CIA Director Colby?

There was chit-chat in the Family Quarters on the trip home, Mrs. Ford and I once again playing "ladies."

Dinner had been quite pleasant, she said, and the Fords and the Sadats discussed their mutual acquaintance, NBC's Barbara Walters. (What else would Heads of State talk about?)

Mrs. Ford and I talked about the trip to China that is scheduled for the end of the month. "When we went in 1972, I didn't get to the Ming Tombs," Mrs. Ford said. "I went to the wall though. Frankly, I'd rather not go to the wall again, unless, of course, not going would be taken as an insult."

In the next chamber, you could not tell the winners from the losers without a scorecard—and no one had one. Kissinger was chortling, along with the other merry men. It looked as though the coup had been perpetrated against the press, and they were all winners.

From the back of the plane, the "losers" composed an angry "press pool report" for their fellow reporters:

> At planeside, just before takeoff, Nessen was asked for confirmation of reports about resignations, transfers, etc., of Kissinger, Rumsfeld, Schlesinger, Scowcroft, Bush, and Cheney. Nessen listened to several attempts to elicit an answer but would only say "I'm sorry, I can't." He was asked if he would have anything to say on the plane. "No." He was asked if there would be an announcement on landing. "No." A note was dispatched to Nessen to come back to talk to us. He sent Sheila Weidenfeld back to say that he would not come.

> Shortly after takeoff, a note was sent to Kissinger, asking for an explanation of the reported events, telling him of the widespread newsplay and telling him of speculation that might be expected lacking any information from the White House. Kissinger jokingly answered: "It's a coup—a military coup. Don't be surprised if we land at an Air Force base." Earlier at planeside, when he was asked about the "rumors" he said, "What rumors? I don't know what you are talking about."

I brought the report to Nessen and Cheney and they laughed and laughed and laughed.


## NOVEMBER 3, 1975

It is official. Defense Secretary James R. Schlesinger and CIA Director William P. Colby have been fired. Henry Kissinger is still Secretary of State, but no longer head of the National Security Council. Donald Rumsfeld is going to become Secretary of Defense. George Bush will become Director of the CIA. Richard Cheney will succeed his boss Rumsfeld. And Nelson Rockefeller will not be the President's running mate.

The plans, apparently, were made weeks ago, but leaked prematurely. (Schlesinger was called by *Newsweek* before he was called in by the President.) I was right! Mrs. Ford knew. So did Jack. As a matter of fact, he told me that they greeted each other yesterday whispering nervously, "I didn't tell—did you?" "No, I didn't tell!" The "leak" still remains a mystery.

The suspense is over. The bad taste remains. A firing-hiring reshuffle is not unusual. It happens in private industry and government all the time. In this particular case, it was to be expected. Ford inherited a Presidency staffed by another man. After one year, it was only natural that he would bring in more of his own people. Is it so important that the changes were leaked before they were completed? Was it necessary to punish the press for finding out? By hiding from reporters, didn't they make the event seem more like a coup d'état than a mere changing of the guard? What would have happened if the administration had appealed to the press on a professional level, if they had just said, "You are partially right. We are in the process of making some changes. Give us a day or two?" We'll never know.


## NOVEMBER 4, 1975

Last week, President Ford delivered a speech at the National Press Club in Washington, D.C. The topic: the growing financial troubles that have brought New York City to the brink of bankruptcy. The question: will the Federal government help out? Ford's answer: no. The general warmth of the speech was captured by the headline the *New York Daily News* ran the next day:

### FORD TO CITY: DROP DEAD!

I have no problem with the basic position that the city and its inhabitants must bail themselves out. I am appalled at the way it was handled. Granted, there is no good way to say, "I will not give you money." But why go out of your way to spank seven and a half million New Yorkers one year before a national election?

I went over to talk to Jim Falk today. He is the New York specialist among the President's domestic staff. Mrs. Ford is going to New York City this week to address the annual American Cancer

Society dinner, and I wanted background and suggestions on how she could soften the President's words without undercutting his policy. Obviously she'll be getting a lot of questions about the President's position. We decided we should play it straight, by talking openly about her feelings for New York, that regardless of its present financial woes, it is one of the richest cities in the world, the cultural center, the financial center, and that she has a special feeling for New Yorkers, having been one herself for several years when she worked there and studied under Martha Graham.

En route back to my office, I stopped off to take a look at the West Wing correspondence section. Jim Connor's offer to give me two extra staff people if I show him how to decrease the East Wing staff by five is very much on my mind. I've figured out that nine of the twenty-seven people on Mrs. Ford's East Wing staff are in the correspondence section. A large number of them are strictly clerical. The President's correspondence section is far more efficient. Could they handle the clerical end of the East Wing correspondence?

The answer I got today was "perhaps." I have to get a more accurate count on our volume first. I've already discussed my idea in general with Mrs. Ford and she is receptive. I explained that if we could get a good writer on board (in the two for five deal) it would improve the content of her letters as well as the speeches. The letters, I've always felt, are terribly important. Each one should be good enough to be framed. After all, many of them will be.


## NOVEMBER 8, 1975

"I feel absolutely marvelous," Mrs. Ford told the American Cancer Society in New York City. "Thanks to that check-up last September, good doctors, a loving supportive husband and understanding children, I can really say this year has been the richest in my life."

The speech was important and we felt it would be strong if it were personal. It was both. "It isn't vanity to worry about disfigurement," she told the audience of nearly 2,000. "It is an honest concern. I started wearing low-cut dresses as soon as the scar healed and my worries about my appearance are now just the normal ones of staying slim and keeping my hair and makeup in order."

The whole overnight trip to New York—expressly to dramatize the importance of routine examinations for early detection of breast cancer—was both forceful and personal. At the American Cancer Society meeting, and in the streets of the city, Mrs. Ford was welcomed by crowds of well-wishers. I had expected some heated questions regarding the President's statements. There were none. I don't know how they feel about the Chief Executive, but New Yorkers seem crazy about Mrs. Ford.

## NOVEMBER 9, 1975

"Did you see it?"

"See what?"

"What do you mean, 'see what?'" Jack raged on the phone. "Don't you read the newspapers? Isn't that part of your job?"

The "what" turned out to be an item in a Washington gossip column, "Ear," saying that Jack was seen in a gay district in Washington a few nights ago.

"Were you—"

"Absolutely *not!*" he yelled into the receiver. "I was at *your* house that night as a matter of fact. Remember?"

"Yes, you're right, you were—"

"And if they need more proof, they can ask my Secret Service detail. They were with me. Wow, I mean this is *really* it."

"Look, Jack, I'll correct the story if I get any calls."

"*Correct* it! Is that all?"

"What do you want me to do?"

"Make them admit it's a *lie!*"

"Jack, just think for a minute. Think about what that would mean. Do you want a follow-up story in the column that says, "Mrs. Ford's Press Secretary called to say Jack wasn't gay?"

"I'm *not* gay!"

"You are not gay, right. But gayness is one of the all-time touchy issues. Getting excited and denying it would make it explode. I think if I personally deny the column and publicly ignore it, the whole thing will fade away."

"It better."
"It will."


## NOVEMBER 10, 1975

This was the day I *knew* would come—except during those dreadful moments when I knew it would never come.

Thank you, Louis Harris, pollster.

Thank you cross-section of adults surveyed nationwide.

This was the day that Mrs. Ford's appearance on "60 Minutes" was officially transformed from a political liability into an asset, the day a Harris Poll found that public opinion for Mrs. Ford's statements is decisive and final.

"Whatever President Ford's problems with the public," Harris writes in his syndicated column, "Betty Ford has now become one of the most popular wives of a President to occupy the White House."

In each of the statements listed by pollsters, a majority of those polled supported Mrs. Ford. The size of the majority ranged from 60 percent ("She would not be surprised if her daughter had an affair.") to 70 percent ("She favors the Equal Rights Amendment.").

Harris' conclusion: "Mrs. Ford's outspoken statements have won support from those younger and more independent elements in the electorate who are indispensable to her husband in a contest for the White House next fall. In short, Betty Ford has a wide and deep following in the mainstream of American life, and surely must be judged a solid asset to her husband in the White House."


## NOVEMBER 13, 1975

Mrs. Ford and I had talked often about the idea of appointing a woman to the Supreme Court. When Justice Douglas resigned yesterday, she called me to assure me that the lobbying effort on the home front ("pillow talk" she calls it) would begin as soon as possible.

"The first thing I did was dash in to ask him about it when he walked in last night," she told me this morning. "He looked at me

and said, 'Now just hold your water!' I said, 'Well, if you aren't
going to let me have my say, then why don't we just make a deal?'
'Deal?' he said, 'what deal?' I told him that if he put a woman on
the Supreme Court, I'd put in a good word for him with my friends
in New York.''

He assured her that he had already asked his staff to compile a
list of qualified women candidates.


## NOVEMBER 17, 1975

Another opening! Another show!
And another case of stage fright.
Today was the day Mary Tyler Moore came to the White House,
and Mrs. Ford tried to sneak out the back way.
Well, almost.
Nancy Chirdon called me this morning to tell me that Mrs. Ford
wondered whether the taping could be postponed. In the back-
ground, I heard Mrs. Ford putting the request a bit less delicately.
"She *can't* make me do something I don't want to do!" she was
yelling. "She can't ruin my life!"
First I calmed myself down. Later I worked on Mrs. Ford. By
the time the cameras were ready to roll, the star was ready to star.
It was another case of mutual admiration: Hollywood worship-
ping the "center of power" and vice versa. Mary Tyler Moore, her
husband, Grant Tinker, and producer Ed Weinberger toured the
White House and tested the chairs in the Cabinet room. "You're
the *real* Mary Tyler Moore," she told me as we compared notes on
jobs in television.
Perhaps. But when it came to access to top staff at the White
House, she won hands down. Everyone wanted to meet Mary Tyler Moore. Don Rumsfeld interrupted a meeting with Defense Department officials just to pose for pictures.
We did the filming at the Hay Adams Hotel across the street.
They had wanted to do it in the White House, but I said no. It is
one thing to have the First Lady come off a good sport but I didn't
feel the White House should take part in a situation comedy.
I changed one line of the script, too. In the original, editor Lou
Grant is bragging to his assistant, Mary, about all the famous people he entertained at a party in his hotel room the night before. The

phone rings and it is Mrs. Ford calling to see if the President left his pipe behind. In the original script the line was, "He is always leaving it somewhere." I asked Weinberger to take it out and he did. He thought I was being silly. Maybe I was. But at a time when national polls indicate a majority of Americans think the President is a "nice guy" but doubt his capabilities, creating an image of Ford as a forgetful bumbler—however subtle the message—would be counterproductive.

The final version had Mrs. Ford saying about six lines, and she did it beautifully. It only took four takes. More important, Mrs. Ford had a wonderful time doing it. She admitted to me later that in spite of her pretaping jitters, she had had a lot of fun.

"Next time," she told me when we got back to the White House, "we'll go to Hollywood!"

## NOVEMBER 20, 1975

The Harris Poll has its spin-offs. The poll itself is syndicated all over the country. The syndication is followed by short stories, little blurbs with headlines such as "Betty Ford Ranks High" . . . "First Lady Outspoken, but Listened to" . . . "Betty Big Plus" . . . "A Solid Asset."

A Harris Poll that reports national popularity increases national popularity, if only by the power of suggestion. It has to.

It's done wonders for mine, that's for sure. All over the White House blank stares have been replaced by smiles of recognition. People speak to me who never did so before. I would not go so far as to say I am "one of the guys." Even "warmth" would be an overstatement. But there is a definite thaw.

Today, Donald Rumsfeld was sworn in as Secretary of Defense and I was there. What's more, I was invited. What's more, I was the only person from the East Side who was invited, a fact I only realized when I looked around at the people in attendance in the middle of the ceremony. As the cannons went off to salute the new Secretary of Defense, I told myself that the invitation was the result of a change in Rumsfeld's attitude toward me, that in one year he has come to respect my ability (*BOOM!*) and he has also come to understand that an articulate First Lady is a Presidential asset (*BOOM! BOOM!*). It felt like a crescendo ending to a movie, the guns punctuating my march into the sunset as the ultimate Press Secretary to the First Lady.

The only problem was that the cannon salute was really for Donald Rumsfeld, and I had this nagging feeling that the invitation may have been his way of thanking me for introducing him to Mary Tyler Moore.

I almost did not make the swearing in ceremony. I spent all morning with Jack at the Park Service Department. He is doing three thirty-second safety spots for the Park Service for use next spring, and I made him do them over and over and over again.

> "Hi, this is Jack Ford. I've spent a lot of time visiting national parks and working in them as a ranger. I know that only experienced and well-equipped persons should participate in high country climbing. Climbers should always register with the park rangers. Hikers should stay on well-established trails. Keep risk within reason, and above all, use common sense."

I wanted it to be good: relaxed, friendly, informative. I know it is only a public service statement, but any public view should be complimentary. Public is public, after all. So he did it, and he did it, and he did it. Especially the beginning. I told Jack that the hardest thing for anyone to do is to say his own name right. By the end of our session, he was in full agreement (and we were both a little punchy). "Hi, I'm Jack Ford." "Howdy, I'm Jack Ford." "Hello, I'm Jack Ford." I don't even want to speculate on how many times we did it. Everytime I close my eyes, I hear it. But in the end, we had three very good thirty-second promos.

And a Park Service studio producer who thought I was out of my mind.

## NOVEMBER 25, 1975

"First the President went, then the Senate leaders, then the House leaders. So when we went with Hale and Lindy Boggs in the summer of 1972, we were just the third group of Americans to tour China. Many places we went, from the Peking Zoo to more isolated parts of northeastern China, people gathered around us, staring. Some of them had not seen Caucasians since World War Two. The young ones never had."

We were going through scrapbooks in the family quarters; Mrs. Ford was reminiscing and I was scribbling it all down to give to the reporters who wanted to preview the upcoming trip to China (we leave in four days) with recollections of the last trip the Fords made to China.

As we glided over banquet pictures, Mrs. Ford said, "The food is delicious. The President loved it, too. It is not too spicy. The only problem is that they give too much. One of the first words you learn is 'Gola' which means 'That's enough.' I remember saying it all the time, 'Gola! Gola! Gola!' "

"This schedule is empty compared to the one we had back in 1972," she told me. "Then we felt we had to see everything. And we did, acupuncture operations, school sessions, libraries, a rice commune, a jeep factory. We traveled at an unbelievable pace. But I loved it. I really loved it. I remember when we took the train from Peking to Hong Kong, I felt I left part of myself in China because I loved it so. "

We put the albums away and talked about other things: the book she was reading on China, the clothes she planned to take, and the "mood ring" her good friend Barbara MacGregor had just given her. Mood rings are the in thing. I've read about them in the papers. Apparently you wear them on your index finger, and the stone of the ring changes colors as your mood changes. When the ring is sapphire, for example, the wearer is enjoying "a blissful feeling of inner peace"; aquamarine means you're "approaching the threshold of relaxation." Green indicates "controlled emotional warmth." And so on, all the way through brown ("emotional flux, insecurity") to black ("you are in a state of high anxiety, tense and inhibited").

Mrs. Ford's was green. "Try it, Sheila. See what it does." I tried it on and was relieved to see that there was no immediate change in color. The idea of wearing my emotions on my index finger does not appeal to me much.

We talked about Jack for a long time. He's got to find a job. Edward has a client in the travel business who has been looking for someone to help him create and market leisure travel projects for young people, especially students. Jack seemed perfect for the job, because he is an avid traveler and camper with a good business sense and excellent rapport with young people. We got Jack and

Edward's client together and they hit it off. Jack is scheduled to be-gin working sometime next month.

Mrs. Ford and I agreed that it was not a moment too soon. The President had given Jack a deadline of October 1st to find a job, and when the deadline passed, both father and son became quite upset (separately). Jack began frantically considering a variety of offers which included a job in the tuna industry in California, another in a bank, and another working on the Alaskan pipeline. I tried to discourage him. The only thing I thought he would find more depressing than no job was a job he didn't like. He needed something he could enjoy, and something he could be good at. His self-confidence was at an all-time low.

Meanwhile, the President, according to Mrs. Ford, was every bit as upset as Jack. He was so concerned about Jack's life and his fu-ture, she said, that he had been unable to sleep at night, and that, she said, was very unusual for the President. (I rather liked that. How many Americans could cite the one burning issue that could give the President of the United States insomnia?)

In the middle of our conversation, the President walked in. He is always warm and relaxed when I bump into him this way, but it al-ways unnerves me. He can forget he is President. I can't. He thanked me for "taking care of Jack."

"I could not do it. A father can't get away with telling his son what to do. It sounds like interesting work, and something Jack would be good at."

"Yes. I think the project is right, and the people are right. The salary is not going to be much more than the average—about a thousand dollars a month—that's probably good, too."

"Fine," the President said. "He and I are getting together to talk about it tonight." He went on to tease me about what I'd done for the "rest of the family."

"Frankly," he said, "I think we're going to have to run Betty for President."

We all laughed, but the remark made me nervous. I have a feel-ing the West Wing is anxious to seize the Harris Poll and run with it; to take Mrs. Ford's new national popularity and propel her into active campaigning, which would, I'm convinced, lead to the same kind of watered down overexposure the President is suffering. In order to work, public appearances must be selective and meaningful, otherwise we will transform a First Lady who is not afraid to speak her mind into a wife who talks Republican.

I just smiled. The President said, "You know, they want her to stop off in Hawaii on the way home from China for a fundraiser. I don't see anything wrong with that. What do you think?"

What do I think? I think that first of all the timing is dreadful. She will be exhausted from the long trip to China and in no mood to be charming and smiley. But even more important, I think that one sure way to negate the sense of "Presidential Presence" that a diplomatic venture to China conveys is to stop for a fundraiser in Hawaii on the way home! The trip to China is a terrific campaigning tool. Why stop behaving like a President as soon as you hit American shores and revert to the role of candidate?

"I don't know," I sighed. "I'm not sure it is such a good idea."

"Well," he said, "you work it out. See what you think."

I know what I think. Why couldn't I convey what I think? As I stepped into the elevator, I looked down at Mrs. Ford's mood ring, still on my index finger. It had turned black.


## NOVEMBER 26, 1975

No, Jack did not purchase cocaine from a drug dealer in Salt Lake City, Utah, last year. In fact, he was not even in Salt Lake City at the time of the alleged transaction.

A rumor that he had made the cocaine deal was circulating several weeks ago, and when he was informed, President Ford told the Federal Narcotics agents to proceed as they would in any other investigation. They did, and have now officially announced that the rumors have been proven false.

Other rumors appear to be harder to squelch.

The letter from the National Gay Task Force was addressed to Jack in care of me. I called Jack and read it to him.

*"Whether or not you are gay, we staunchly believe in your right to privacy. If you are gay, you should have the freedom to come out at your own pace."*

He groaned.

*"If you are not gay, you should just as certainly be left in peace. In either case, we here wish to offer such aid as may be in our power."*

I finished.

"Man, I am really bummed out—"

"Oh, come on now, Jack," I said cheerfully, "it's just wishful thinking on the part of the gay community!"

He did not laugh.

"I thought you told me this would all die out," he said soberly.

"It will."

It will—followed, undoubtedly, by a different inaccuracy.


## NOVEMBER 27, 1975

We had a little excitement here last night. A man identified as Gerald Bryan Gainous, Jr., twenty-four years of age, lurked around the White House environs for about two hours and then climbed over the fence. He was within about five feet of Susan, who was outside taking a walk, when he was apprehended by the Secret Service. He said that he wanted to talk to President Ford, in hopes of securing a pardon for his father, an Air Force sergeant convicted of smuggling drugs. They're checking it all out now.

The Secret Service was quite upset—after all, he got very close to a Ford "principal." But Susan was not upset—at least not when it happened. She said she was totally unaware of anyone there. (It was pitch black. She couldn't see anything.) All she knew was that the Secret Service agent told her calmly, "Susan, could you please go upstairs? You can come down in about ten minutes. Okay?"


## NOVEMBER 28, 1975

"Well, we wanted an equal opportunity, not special treatment, and he assured me that he gave women an equal chance to compete. But in the end, he just felt that this man would be better qualified than the female alternatives," Mrs. Ford told me. She was referring to President Ford's decision to appoint John Paul

Stevens to the Supreme Court seat left vacant by the resignation of Justice Douglas. She said she knew his decision before the announcement.

"It was after the Judiciary Dinner the other night. We got up to dance, and while we were dancing he whispered in my ear, 'The top man on the list is here tonight.' "

"Man?" I said, " 'MAN'?"

*Chapter Fourteen*
DECEMBER, 1975:

# COME-AS-YOU-ARE
# WHEN MAO IS READY

*FRIDAY, DECEMBER 5, 1975*

There was a one-night stop-over in Alaska, where we all donned heavy outer gear and watched the President examine the Alaska Pipeline. Then we were off to the People's Republic of China (PRC).

I used the long flight on Air Force One to study the briefing papers. As always, the amount of background information (supplied, in this case, largely by the U.S. Liaison office in Peking) was impressive. There were personal background details on our hosts, sightseeing pointers, notes on Chinese history, weather reports, shopping tips, and, of course, a thorough list of the do's and don'ts of PRC etiquette. ("DO be precise about the use of titles when known since the Chinese do not freely substitute their equivalent of 'Mr.' for the titles of even low-ranking officials. DON'T touch or put your arm around the Chinese, some of whom may be offended by this friendly American gesture. DON'T beckon to the Chinese with hand or arm, as this is used for children and inferiors and would be insulting to an adult. DON'T stand with hands on hips or arms folded, traditional Chinese postures which denote defiance, anger, and arrogance.'')

I had been reading up on China for a long time. I had gotten firsthand descriptions from reporters who had been there with Nixon in 1972 and from Patti Matson, who spent a week in the PRC completing pre-advance plans for this trip. But none of it helped. The country seemed unreal to me still. I guess that is to be expected. I grew up in an era when the People's Republic of China was closer than outer space, but less accessible. A time when there was no hard news on China, but a lot of soft news: rumors of brainwashing and atrocities in a country composed of millions and millions of hard-working robots. Then came the "thaw" and with it, tales from China travelers of beautiful people, happy people, formerly starving Chinese masses now content and well fed.

Neither description made the People's Republic of China seem like a real place.

Cultural generalizations of the briefing paper made it all seem even stranger. I felt I was traveling to another world.

Landing heightened the sensation. Four long green lines—hedges? No, people. It turned out to be an honor guard of hundreds of Chinese, standing at attention in the olive-green soldier's uniform. Four perfectly parallel, seemingly endless lines of immobile human beings. As we promenaded in front of them, following the President, and I looked from face to face, the words of the briefing papers kept running through my mind: "The Chinese take great pride in their food." "The Chinese will encourage you to dress warmly." "The Chinese are always on time." "The Chinese do not usually give their names." "The Chinese enjoy assisting Americans to learn simple Chinese phrases. The gesture of asking how you say 'thank you,' 'good morning,' and 'good night' in Chinese is appreciated."

I looked at all the unblinking faces staring straight ahead and decided I'd ask later.

At the end of the honor guard stood the PRC officials. The olive-green faded into grays and blacks. This was my first sight of what turned out to be the color scheme of China—a rainbow of olive-green, gray, blue, white, and black. All adults wear very drab clothes. In contrast, the children's clothes are bright and colorful. (Is there a cut-off, I began to wonder after a few days of observation, a set age where one denounces color and pledges himself to a life-time of black and white?)

I stayed in Villa number 5 in the compound set aside for White House staff. The room was immaculate. And stark. Blond furniture. Bland walls. No floral print sheets here. No pastels. No frills. With one amazing exception. On top of my dresser there was the most elaborate collection of makeup I had ever seen, including three colors of lipstick, moisturizer, three different shades of fingernail polish, astringent, cologne, hairspray, powder, and so on. I couldn't get over it. I had read that the Chinese women wore no makeup. Were these gifts the government had deemed appropriate for the "painted women of America"?

A mystery not covered by my information sheets!

The rest of the first day went exactly according to schedule, however. No more mysteries. In fact, the banquet that night followed the preplanned program so closely that I had a feeling of déjà vu.

It was held in the Great Hall of the People, an enormous official building that serves as the meeting place for major political events, such as a convening of the Party Congress. Soft drinks were served downstairs first. (There are two big national beverages: orange soda and Mao-t'ai, an alcoholic drink that is used for toasting and which, we were warned in the briefing papers, is very, very, very, very powerful stuff. The orange soda tastes like orange soda, never a favorite of mine. And I have no idea what the Mao-t'ai tastes like, because when I finally got up enough courage to try some on our last day, I could not reach an objective opinion, my palate had been so dulled by fear.)

Just before our group was seated for dinner, we were arranged on bleachers in front of a large painting with an excerpt from the Mao poem "Snow," and photographed with Vice Premier Teng. (Pictures like this were taken throughout our trip, and at the end, each of us was given an individual kit, including all of the photographs taken of us during our stay in China.) After the bleacher shot, we were marched out, taken to the dining room, and seated. It was a brilliant maneuver on the part of our hosts, for this was an enormous crowd to move along so speedily. Everyone in the entire American party had been invited to this banquet, from top White House staff to airplane crews.

I am sure that the dinner began at 7:56 P.M. because that is what the schedule had specified.

At the appointed time (I think it was after the ten appetizer dishes and the Consommé of Silver Agarc, but before the Shark's fin en casserole) Vice Premier Teng Hsiao-ping climbed to the stage and gave a toast and the clinking began. ("Don't clink glasses with American members of your party," the information sheet specified.) Teng moved around to each of the first five tables individually clinking glasses with the Americans seated there. A few courses later (I believe it was after the Chinese cabbage with chestnuts but before the steamed Wuchang fish) it was President Ford's turn to toast and clink. Everything went smoothly, despite my anxieties. There was an excess of cross-cultural clinking going on at my table between an American military aide and a Chinese official. You can only drink the Mao t'ai if you toast someone, and when you *do* drink it, the glass is immediately refilled. And so, the two toasted each other, bottoms-upped, toasted each other, and bottoms-upped. All night. It was a case of Chinese-American diplomacy carried out at a college fraternity drinking level. The military aide was feeling no pain, and I had visions of his saying something outrageous when the President came by to toast the Chinese at our table, but he did not. The drinking contest ended happily in an inebriated draw.

The next day, we took a planned excursion to the Great Wall and an unplanned detour. It was Susan's day for press coverage. We had purposely planned it that way, figuring that Mrs. Ford would enjoy the chance to relax, and Susan would enjoy the chance for good pictures. The Great Wall was built over 1,500 miles of China some twenty-two centuries ago (the section we visited is one of the portions that has been more recently restored) and, in addition to being an historical and engineering landmark, it is obviously a visual sensation.

The press bus had already gotten to the Great Wall when Susan, her interpreter, and I arrived in our limousine. Many reporters had come; it looked like a Great Wall take-over by American tourists. Everyone had cameras, either for professional or private reasons (I had even brought mine). The press photographed Susan who photographed the press. Then the press photographed Susan photographing the view. It was a steep climb up, and at the top we celebrated in a great crescendo of clicks—a photographic grand finale.

Finally, we returned to the bottom. The press boarded their bus. We boarded our car. Destination: the Ming tombs, burial place for the thirteen emperors of the Ming Dynasty, and—today—our lunch stop.

We were almost there when an automobile coming in the opposite direction swerved in front of us and stopped so abruptly that we came to a screeching halt, narrowly missing a head-on collision. About six Chinese jumped out of the car and beckoned to our interpreter Miss Wong. She got out. The seven of them huddled for a few minutes, and she returned to our car.

"Miss Ford must return to the residence immediately."

"Why?"

"I cannot say. It is extremely important that she return."

We asked why again. She would not answer. I could tell Susan was getting very nervous about her parents. So was I. What else could it be?

I told Miss Wong that I was concerned about the press. They had not come to see the Ming tombs; they had come to cover Susan. They would need an explanation. I had to tell them something.

Miss Wong jumped out of the car, conferred again with the men, and returned. "The press is not important," she said with conviction.

And we were off. At very high speed. "Cars must drive slowly in our country," Miss Wong had sweetly informed us on the way to the Great Wall, "in order not to hit the pedestrians and bicyclists who govern the road." I prayed they were all safely home eating lunch. We had to be traveling at a rate of eighty miles per hour. Susan's agent tried repeatedly to make radio contact with the base, but he could not. It was all a nightmare.

We finally reached the residence and were greatly relieved to find the Fords safe, talking with Henry Kissinger. "It sounds like Mao is getting ready to invite the official party to see him," said Kissinger, when we told him what had happened. He explained that the same thing had happened last time. His wife, Nancy, had been out shopping, he said, when suddenly she was told she had to rush back. It was a summons from Mao.

It said nothing in the briefing papers about a Chinese fondness for "come-as-you-are-when-Mao-is-ready parties."

What is more, Kissinger said, being hastily summoned back to the residence did not necessarily mean that Mao wanted the pleasure right away. It could be hours before the official request for an audience came. They just wanted the official party close by, ready. He suggested that Susan and the Fords do what they wanted, as long as it was close by, instead of waiting around.

"Don't worry, the Chinese will let you know when you have to return."

They did. Susan and I went shopping, and were enjoying our spree when our interpreter announced solemnly, "Your shopping tour is over." At the Temple of Heaven, where the Fords had gone, following their planned schedule, the President got the word and whispered to his wife, "We are leaving now." Back at the residence, the three Fords were given fifteen minutes to get ready, and, at the last moment, the official party was reshuffled and weeded out. Ron Nessen, Dick Cheney and David Kennerly were not permitted to go. Several Secret Service agents were also omitted. Dick Hardwick, head of Mrs. Ford's detail, got into one car and was told to get out. He got into a follow-up car and was told by the Chinese, "Either you stay and we go, or you go and we stay."

He stayed.

Apparently, the last-minute hysteria is an old Chinese custom—three years old, at least. (The same thing happened to Nixon in 1972.) And there was a lot of speculation as to motivation. Power games? An attempt to throw the U.S. party off balance? The explanation that made the most sense came from NBC's John Chancellor. He said that now that Mao is so sick, his aides never know when he is going to be in condition to have visitors. If they notice in the morning that their leader is in pretty good shape, that he appears lucid and may be all right after his tea, all the principals that are to be invited are put into a holding pattern until his aides feel he is in good enough shape to have company.

The press returned from the Ming Tombs fed but furious, unaware of my futile attempts to contact them. They marched on Ron Nessen chanting "Where is Sheila, where is Sheila." Instead of paging me on my beeper, Ron, ever my defender, grumbled "I don't know; she is never here when you want her. If I were you, I would complain, and complain loudly." By the time Susan and I returned from the Friendship Store, Helen Thomas was complaining loudly. I listened and tried to explain. I found myself envying Miss Wong her ability to be so sure that "the press is not important."

Of all the planned events, the one I looked forward to most was our visit to the Chinese dance school. It had taken several phone calls from China to set up. Pat Nixon had visited ballet dancers when the Nixons were in China in 1972, and I wanted Mrs. Ford's visit to be different. I had told Patti Matson, before she left to advance the trip, that I wanted one of the Chinese dancers to teach Mrs. Ford a few steps. Patti had called from China to report. "The dance school is perfect—very picturesque—but my suggestion was greeted with nervous giggles. They said that the wife of a President could *never* do that."

"No matter what," I told Patti, "I want Mrs. Ford to learn the dance steps."

Several phone calls later she had good news: hesitant, reluctant, they had nonetheless consented.

I told reporters ahead of time that this would be the best part of the trip, that they should not miss it, and as a result, we had an excellent press turnout at the dance school. But bad communication.

We got to the room where Mrs. Ford was supposed to learn the dance steps, and nothing happened. All of a sudden, her Chinese hosts began leading Mrs. Ford into another room. I told Patti to get the press set up in the next room, and ran from official to official. I finally found those in charge. "Mrs. Ford was disappointed that the dancing did not take place in the last room," I said with an air of authority that hinted at dire consequences. "*We will do it now in this room.*"

Apparently, it worked. Moments later, just as the press rushed in, Mrs. Ford kicked off her shoes and began following the Chinese dance instructor. The cameras ran, the flash bulbs flashed. The "spontaneous gesture" was recorded and carried by newspapers all over the world. Photographically at least, it was the best thing that came out of China.

Which brings me to the Associated Press photo set-up, which impressed me almost as much as the other sights of China. Toby Massey, AP's news photo editor in Washington, had arrived in China about a week before us with one staff person to set up things for photo transmission. They were later joined by two additional AP photographers. It was all done out of Toby's suite, which consisted of a living room, bedroom, one closet (which was light tight) and a bathroom. The negatives and prints were made up in the bathroom. In the bedroom, the negatives were then dried on a clothesline and the prints were dried by hairdryer. Captions for the photos were written at a desk in the living room. AP had a direct satellite circuit from New York to Peking, and the pictures and captions were sent through a transmitter on the window sill. A photo-electric cell scanned the pictures, and eight minutes later, the sequence of light and dark tones was completed at the AP photo desk in New York City and 1,100 other locations. Toby said they rarely got to bed before 3:00 or 4:00 A.M. I was given a "tour" of the set-up. It was an incredible sight.

But there was one even more incredible press occurrence. As we were leaving the dance school, Barbara Walters had a few questions she wanted to ask Mrs. Ford. "Will I be able to ask her later, or is this the last time?" Barbara wanted to know. I told her now or never, as the schedule was very tight. Suddenly, on the crowded sidewalk, in between people and cars and other vehicles, Barbara amassed a camera crew and a microphone and Mrs. Ford. The reels turned, the interview went on, in the midst of total chaos. There was only one problem. The camera crew was not the NBC camera crew. It was the CBS camera crew. And Barbara works for NBC. But it is difficult not to respond to a Barbara Walters order, and, seeing that the NBC crew was nowhere to be found, and sensing that this was her last chance for a while, she *ordered* the crew to shoot, and, sweetly submissive, shoot they did. When it was over, both the sweetness and the submission faded. They refused to turn over the film to Barbara. "CBS doesn't photograph for NBC," they said, an argument, that, one must admit, is traditionally sound. There ensued, I am told, an enormous fight that went all the way to the top executive offices in New York City. In the end, Barbara won. I was not surprised.

Now I am Jakarta-bound on Air Force One, exhausted but hyper. My eyes want to sleep but my mind is still on the run. Every time I close my eyes I see a different part of the last four days. I see gymnasts jumping. I see women working at a rug factory, clustered together patiently, artfully hand weaving a masterpiece at the rate of one inch per day. I see the color scheme of the highways. Olive-green for soldiers, trucks, jeeps, and other vehicles. Black-and-blue-suits for the civilians, male and female. Male or female? So often it was hard to tell. I see American chaos at the Friendship Store where large glass cases line the aisles with bargains, everything from cloisonné vases (copper topped with lacquered enamel) to one-hundred-year-old jade objects, cashmere sweaters, suede jackets, leather pants and White House Staff reporters hysterically buying bargains, as, on the sidelines, somewhat baffled, Chinese customers stare and then quietly purchase the necessities that brought them in in the first place: soap, toothpaste, and so on. I see the little men who arrived at our villa and, item by item, hand wrapped each of our purchases for the trip home.

So many pictures, but still no overall impression, no general understanding. I told the Peking correspondent for Reuters that I felt four days was not long enough. He told me that he has been stationed there for a year now, and the longer he stays, the more confused he gets. There is, he said, a "no man's land" between the Chinese people and "outsiders"—an area that cannot be crossed. "No one," he told me, "ever gets close."

One minute the Chinese life seems a simple life—the next it is a mysterious existence shrouded in secrecy. Everyone is equal but leaders seem to live luxurious lives (by comparison) completely hidden from the common folk. Happy people? Repressed people? Brain-washed millions? None of the earlier stereotypical generalizations has been clarified for me. But my appetite has been stimulated. I loved seeing China, even if what I saw was restricted to what was to be shown. It was fascinating. I wish we could have stayed longer.

## DECEMBER 8, 1975

I slept through Indonesia (one of the built-in hazards of traveling at the rate of one nation per day) and woke up in Manila, the Philippines, where we were greeted by the most lavish parade ever. Both sides of the highway from the airport to the palace were crowded with throngs of people dancing for us, singing, performing in wondrous ways. ("It just happened," President Marcos later told reporters. "You can't organize happiness.") Perhaps. But other sources indicated Mrs. Marcos had played an important role in encouraging the spontaneity.

From the People's Republic of China to the Philippines—from abstinence to decadence. Welcome. Culture shock? A little. But frankly, I was in the mood for unnecessary extravagance. And I got it.

Early the next morning we all boarded the Marcos' yacht, *Ang Pangulo*, for a breakfast trip to the island of Corregidor, a scene of battle during World War Two. The food aboard was excellent. The setting was lavishly lovely. And so was the First Lady of the Philippines, who changed her clothes five times in the course of the trip. Ever the center of attention, she chatted with reporters, guests, danced, sang, surrounded always by her "blue girls"—the group of young, attractive women who serve as ladies in waiting to Mrs. Marcos—and she exchanged barbs with the U.S. Secretary of State.

"I like it here," said Kissinger.

"I'm glad, Mr. Secretary. It's about time you recognized our existence."

She continued to tease him about being West-oriented in his diplomacy. He complimented her on the charm of her country.

"That's our soft sell," she shot back. "See, unlike you, we can't afford a hard sell!"

It was the first time I've ever danced at breakfast. It was also the first time I ever saw a President and First Lady entertain guests by singing a romantic duet, but apparently it was not the first time President and Mrs. Marcos had done so.

We collapsed aboard Air Force One en route home via Hawaii. On the voyage over, spirits and energy levels had been high. I had been talking with Mrs. Ford when suddenly David Kennerly appeared wearing a crown and carrying a sceptre he had made out of aluminum foil, and squirted water in our eyes. It was, he explained, an initiation into the "Equator Club"—a ceremony commemorating the fact that Air Force One had just crossed the equator. Mrs. Ford grabbed the crown, sceptre and water bottle and, grinning, went into the private Air Force One office to initiate the President.

Coming home, we crossed quietly. There was no such frivolity. Just snores and darkness and complaints from many of us that it was impossible to sleep. And we wanted to sleep. Oh, how very much I wanted sleep. Air Force One is a luxurious way to travel, but it's a rotten motel. Way up at the front of the plane a light burned throughout the trip—at least as long as my insomnia lasted—as Mrs. Ford and Henry Kissinger talked and talked and talked.

When I got to my hotel here in Hawaii today, I smelled a peculiar odor. I opened the suspected suitcase. It was the bottle of Mao'tai that I had brought home with me, which had broken and spilled over everything.

It was the bottle I planned to taste in the quiet of my home, where the resulting intoxication would not cause international embarrassment.

## DECEMBER 11, 1975

We returned from China just in time for a media blitz. Cover stories on Mrs. Ford or the Ford family will appear this month in *Parade* Magazine, *Newsweek,* and *People* Magazine. Those are just the ones we accepted. Many were turned away, including an impassioned plea from the *National Enquirer* for a story with Jack Ford's byline entitled "MY MOM THE FIRST LADY." (It was more the *Enquirer*'s style than Jack's.)

The *Parade* Magazine piece, a family feature which will come out the Sunday before Christmas, was done last month. But the others involve scattered interviews with family members that are still going on.

When Jane Whitemore interviewed Mrs. Ford in Hawaii for the *Newsweek* piece, they were talking about Mrs. Ford's neck problem and tension and Mrs. Ford said she takes Valium for relief— that, in fact, it was her psychiatrist who first prescribed the drug. Jane asked how often she takes Valium. Mrs. Ford replied "Once a day," and I almost fell off the sofa I was perched on. Later I told Jane she misunderstood, that I was sure Mrs. Ford meant once a day when her osteoarthritis was acting up. And I *was* sure. I kept telling myself today.

## DECEMBER 12, 1975

It was Steve Ford's turn today to come down to my office and answer questions on how it feels to be the son of. . . .

I stared at the handsome, tall, very blond nineteen-year-old, attired in his habitual "uniform" of jeans, boots, and flannel shirt. I kept hearing his mother say, amidst sighs, "If I could just get Steve off a horse, I'd be real happy."

I doubt that it will happen anytime soon.

"I never rode a horse until about a year ago," Steve was telling the reporter, "but I guess I've always had a fantasy about being a cowboy. I like using my body both physically and mentally. I wasn't made to sit behind a desk. I guess that's why ranching appeals to me. I worked on a ranch last year. And now I'm majoring at Utah, at least tentatively, in animal science. It's a major that would fit well for a future foreman of a ranch. Sure, there's a lot of money in ranching these days, but expenses run so high that the average person can no longer afford to buy a ranch. You almost have to inherit a ranch. And then you have to pay an inheritance tax.

"I was raised in a political family. If that was what I wanted, I certainly got good background training. But politics is not for me. I'm not the kind of person who can play those types of games, and so much of politics is making the right deals. I think my mother and I were the most against his taking the Vice Presidency and the Presidency, too. I walked in here the first day and found myself wondering what a 'First Family' does. My idea of the White House was tuxedos and fancy State Dinners. I remember sitting down in the White House and saying 'what are we doing here?' I think other people wondered, too. Like the Secret Service. I got stopped a number of times when I came in from Montana last year dressed like this and they wanted to know who I was, did I live here. Other First Families seemed more sophisticated. They learned to be. They were political children, groomed for this position. We are just down to earth . . . the way we've always been.

"It's opened doors for me, but it is difficult, too. At school, people look at you as though you are a freak. You can't let it get to you. The foreman at the ranch I worked on last year told me he thought I would be different. Anywhere I go it takes two weeks to get people to get that idea out of their heads. 'He's the President's son. That's why he has that job.' I have to work twice as hard. I feel I constantly have to prove myself.

"I don't want my father to run, because it is so hard to lead a normal life, but I spent a month home last August and I talked with him about it a lot. He loves being President. He seems to thrive on the pressures of it. He thinks he can do a good job and he wants to run. And so I want to help. I want to campaign for him, in a low key, personal kind of way. As a family member, not an issue spokesman.

*DECEMBER 13, 1975*

According to the latest Gallup Poll, national approval of the President's performance as President has dropped from 47 percent to 41 percent, and there has been a 31 percent shift in popularity from Ford to Reagan. In October, the poll shows, Republicans favored Ford over Reagan 48 percent to 25 percent. In November, Republicans polled favored Reagan *over* Ford by a margin of 40 percent to 32 percent.

"We are suffering from a perception problem," I told Jim Connor over coffee yesterday. "However something is perceived, it then becomes reality, whether or not it is true. Perception *is* reality. That is the President's problem. The press reports impressions and summaries of what they have been given. Their perceptions then become the public's reality. It's up to us to improve the quality of what the press is given."

He sipped.

"Look, here's an example of what the administration is doing to itself. Here's a *Washington Star* story headlined: FORD TO VETO BILL ON PICKETS' RIGHTS. The sources of the story are White House officials . . . *White House officials!* And what is the primary reason these White House officials give for the veto? Look, it says right here, 'Ford can gain nothing politically from signing the bill.' The tone is set by *our boys.* White House officials have served the press one more portrayal of Ford-as-politician, as opposed to Ford-as-President. Now there must have been many good, substantive reasons for the President's change of mind."

He agreed.

"The administration has to set the stage. Instead of back-to-back events every Presidential message should be special or relate to selling a concrete issue or program. He needs *good* speeches. He needs thought-out appearances. Television has been used as casually and as poorly as his public appearances. Television really *is* a public appearance."

He wanted examples.

"Okay. Take the tax, energy and common situs bills. They give us an opportunity for real direction. The President should announce all three bills in one speech, tying them together, explaining his actions in terms of a consistent direction."

"Good," said Jim Connor, finishing his coffee. "Write it all up in a memo."

Today I did. Just as I finished, the phone rang. It was Bill Nicholson, the President's appointments secretary.

"I just wanted you to know that the President has agreed to go on '60 Minutes' and Mrs. Ford will appear on it with him."

"*What?*"

"You heard me. ['60 Minutes' reporter] Mike Wallace went to Phil Buchen to get the President for the show, Phil went to the President. The President said 'Okay.' After all, you know Reagan's going to be on the show the week before."

Unbelievable. Preposterous. My experience proved that if you hold off, choose the right show for the right person at the right time, work overtime at rectification, and have a little good luck to boot, it could work out in your favor. They were missing the point and remembering only the show's name.

I called Mrs. Ford. She agreed with me entirely. Bolstered, I called Jim Conner and exploded.

"Jim, has anyone questioned what the President will *get* out of '60 Minutes'? The national impression that he's a nice guy? The polls show that most Americans think he's a decent man already. It's his *Presidential* abilities they wonder about. Has anyone thought through Reagan's appearance the week before? There are primaries where we have to follow Reagan appearances. Why bring the contest to television? Especially when the Reagan family's TV expertise gives them an advantage?"

"You're right," said Jim Conner. "Put it in a memo."

Today was the first day in my life I ever wrote two memos.


## DECEMBER 14, 1975

If the polls don't get you down, the family will. After dinner tonight at the White House, Steve confessed to his parents that he skipped classes during the last four weeks of the semester. He remained at school, but he did not attend his courses. As a result, he will probably not get any credit. And, he told them, he does not like school. And, he told them, he does not like the White House. And, he told them, he does not know what he does like. Except ranching.

Then Jack joined in. He talked about the pressures he feels, his confusion. He is now not sure he should take the job with the travel agency—the one Edward set up for him which, one month ago he felt was perfect, "the answer." He's not sure he could handle it. Frankly, ever since he moved into the White House he doesn't seem able to handle anything. Not even his own unhappiness.

"If this is what the White House is going to do to my family," the President exploded [according to each of my two sources: Mrs. Ford and Jack], "then I will get out of the White House. I just won't run."

They felt guilty. They tried to assure him otherwise.

He's a funny man, Gerald Ford. Public criticism seems to just heighten his resolve. If anything could make him change his mind about running, it would be his family.


## DECEMBER 15, 1975

"I think the problem is a communications failure," Jack told the *Newsweek* reporter. "Programs, ideas, issues, the message isn't getting across, the Presidential message. One of the things about coming back to Washington is that I've had an opportunity to experience the White House. Now maybe I can get some messages across. I can't make policy, but I think I can translate policy in a way people could understand. I don't claim to be Frank Zarb [the energy administrator] but I can explain the Ford Administration's energy programs.

"I have very negative feelings about his running in terms of myself. I don't think it's beneficial for any family to have a father who is President of the United States. But I don't think it would be fair to tell him not to run.

"I was much happier before any of this took place. The hardest part of it is the identification and notoriety of it. I find myself craving anonymity. Like, it's hard for me to believe that people want my autograph. I haven't accomplished anything. I'm purely a product of luck.

"Even though I may not be totally happy here, I'm glad I spent the last six months here. I experienced the experience. I touched the stars and I found I don't have much in common with people on that lofty plane of life. Frankly, I had trouble communicating. I have a much better relationship with my old friends. I found out at age twenty-three that the life of the star is not the kind of life I'd like to live.

"You live here in Washington, and you set yourself up for people to take cheap shots at you. You wonder who is sincere, who isn't. It was exciting at first. But sooner than most people would suspect, it becomes burdensome. I've had six months in the White House. Now it's time to move on . . . to a different job, to a different location. I'm a free spirit. I'm the sort of person who will try anything—once."

## DECEMBER 16, 1975

Today the *Newsweek* spotlight was focused on the Ford offspring who has adjusted to White House life best, and enjoyed it most. Susan Ford is slimmer, sleeker, and better at fielding questions than she was in the dreadful AP interview one year ago. She still hates politics. She still loves boys. Her interest and ever increasing capabilities in photography have given her a sense of direction. Her life is settling in. But aside from that, the changes are mostly external, I think. The inner truth, the "real" Susan Ford lies somewhere between this year's polished, self-presentation and last year's unfairly simplistic portrait.

"It would be wrong to say being the President's daughter hasn't changed me," she told the reporter. "I think I'm more mature, more of a lady than I've ever had to be. I've had to grow up quickly. The first months were rough on all of us. We were all very scared of losing our family relationships. But as far as the family is concerned, if anything, I think just the opposite has happened. I think we're closer. We've got to stick together.

"I'll be fifty years old, and I'll still always be Daddy's girl. I'll always sit on his lap. He keeps a very close eye on me. He'll come up to see if I'm home. I will have to check in when I come in, wake him up and tell him I'm here. I also see him every night at dinner, before I go upstairs and do my homework. We love to tease him. He'll start talking politics and we'll make him stop.

"I thought '60 Minutes' was interesting. My mother said 'Don't watch it. I don't think you'll like it—it's all politics!' I enjoyed it. I was proud of the way she answered the questions so honestly.

"She's a real ham, you know. My mother keeps me in stitches. I'll come home from school in the worst mood, and she'll cheer me up. She'll tell me something amusing, or she'll do a little tap dance or sing a song—she can't carry a tune!—anything to break my mood. We do a lot of clowning. She's a nut. I don't know what I'd do without her.

"I'll make campaign appearances, but I'm not much for making speeches. I get too nervous in a crowd. I really give my mother a lot of credit. She definitely has more guts than I do. She's really gotten good at speech-making. How do I feel about five more years? I want to make it through this year first. I hate to think it will be five more years before we go back to Alexandria, Virginia, where we used to live. I really miss being there, and I really miss the neighborhood."

## DECEMBER 17, 1975

Pine garlands hang from the lantern in the North Portico. There's a gingerbread house in the State Dining Room, a cranberry tree in the Red Room, holly and bowls of pomegranates in the Green Room. And evergreen arrangements adorn the mantels of the East Room.

Ah, those little tell-tale signs of the season.

This year, we are on top of Christmas. At least compared with last year. Like last year, handmade ornaments adorn the tree, and like last year, there is a White House do-it-yourself brochure which explains the artistic intricacies of putting together a "soap snowflake" or a "clothespin cardinal." But unlike last year, it was not a do-it-myself procedure. The brochure was drawn up by artists and printed—well in advance—to be foldable, and ready for mailing.

We live and learn.

## DECEMBER 23, 1975

I don't know when it started. (The too-short baggy pants in Japan? Tripping on the plane steps in Austria? The "Bozo the Clown" piece in the *New York* Magazine last year?) I just know that no one has stopped it. The momentum has become devastating. The President as stumbler, as bumbler, as the butt of every old ethnic joke. From joke we get rumors, some serious (alcoholism?), some amusing (a recent *National Enquirer* headline: "3 PSYCHIA-TRISTS AGREE: PRESIDENT FORD IS ACCIDENT PRONE BECAUSE HE FEELS GUILTY ABOUT HIS JOB"). From the rumors, more jokes. It is a vicious cycle, and a self-perpetuating one. The news facts, the origins are blurred and irrelevant. The stand-up comedi-ans have taken over, and Johnny Carson can be a powerful nation-al mood creator. Reporters filing stories against a backdrop of anti-Presidential giggles have to look for a "certain angle," con-sciously or unconsciously.

Today a *New York Daily News* poll reported that New Yorkers think Ford should work more and make fewer trips. The *New York Times* described President Ford as "less Presidential than his rivals in both major parties," and a White House UPI news story began, "In an unusual attempt to characterize President Ford as a hard-working leader, the White House said today. . . ."

And we left for a Vail Christmas vacation.

How do you stop it? It may stop itself. For a year now, President Ford has been the only candidate, thus the only target. (Welcome to the race, Ronald Reagan!)

Perhaps you stop it where it started, with the fact-finders, and transmitters, those open-minded, intelligent members of the fourth estate. Edward and I decided tonight to try a little quiet lobbying while we're out here. Vail is a holiday for everyone, including the working press. There's much more of a festive relaxed atmosphere than in Washington. And closer contact. We all live together, party together, share the press room. There is more time for talk, for per-suasion. Besides, it is a perfect place to point out that the President is no stumbler.

He is a good athlete, and he is a really good skier. Most of the re-porters, on the other hand, are rotten skiers, and those who are good know how good the President is.

I wish I knew a couple of Ronald Reagan jokes.


## DECEMBER 24, 1975

It is silly. And impossible.

Rumor has it that Secret Service agent Gary Sorrell went to one of the White House nurses who came out here with the Fords and said he had a burning sensation in his crotch and would she take a look at it.

Rumor has it that he dropped his pants, revealing a lit candle.

Rumor has it that the nurse thought it was not a funny joke. She went to Dr. Lukash, who, rumor has it, went to Dick Keiser, the head of the Secret Service, who, in turn, yanked Sorrell out of . Vail.

It can't be true. It is too preposterous.

But why are there signs up all over Vail right now that say "FREE GARY SORRELL!!!!"

And why are all the Secret Service agents walking around mumbling that nurses have no sense of humor?


## *DECEMBER 25, 1975*

The Fords' tradition has become mine. For the second year in a row, I spent my early morning hours on the telephone madly scribbling the priceless give-and-take details of another First Family Christmas. Practice does not make perfect. This year it seemed to take me even longer to get my who filled whose stocking with what lists tallied up on both the filler and the fillee sides. (Would *Parade* Magazine be interested in how *I* spend *my* Christmas?)

Lists done and fed to the reporters, Edward and I went out for Christmas dinner with *Newsweek* reporter Tom DeFrank and his wife. I must admit that one of my all-consuming passions since November 2nd has been to find out who leaked the Schlesinger/Kissinger staff changes to the press—or, more specifically, to *Newsweek*—or more specifically, to *Newsweek* reporter Tom DeFrank. During our Christmas meal together, I confess, I was less than subtle.

When I asked a question Tom didn't want to answer, he shook his head. I then changed the question. Gradually a pattern emerged. I would name a name and then give a lengthy explanation of who thinks he is the leak and why. As soon as Tom gave me a definitive "NO," I went on to the next possibility. We covered:

"Kissinger?" ("NO.")

"Rumsfeld?" ("NO.")

"Scowcroft?" ("NO.")

"Sonnenfeldt?"—Kissinger's assistant—("NO.")

"Cheney?" ("NO.")

"*Someone* at the State Department?" ("NO.")

"Someone at the White House?" ("    ")

CLICK!

"Someone at the White House?" ("    ") . . . again!

Suddenly I got an idea. "Maybe it was someone like a secretary in the White House, someone who overheard something . . . who typed a memo, maybe, that was revealing . . .

I did not get a definitive ("NO.") as a matter of fact. I was getting a definitive feeling that what I was getting was a definitive NON-"NO." I could feel Tom's lie detector start twitching. Well, I could at *least* feel my pulse rate jumping.

A secretary?

A typist?

A memo.

A memo!

Maybe.

I did not get the big answer I was seeking. But I did get at least a small confirmation of the validity of my memo-writing paranoia.

## *DECEMBER 26, 1975*

Progress report on lobbying maneuver: Progress!

The main strategic component is the ability to listen. Deep down, reporters really prefer answering questions to asking them. Especially when the questions call for shrewd political analysis. ("Help me. What do you think. . . .") So I've been spending a lot of time asking questions, listening to answers, and occasionally trying to sprinkle some hard data of my own.

I think it is working. I think *something* is working. It may just be backlash time. Often when the press goes overboard in one direction they begin the self-doubting process themselves. But there is a change—subtle, but discernible. Example: the President fell on the slopes today. That's not unusual. As he joked himself: "More skiers fall down than stand up."

But when one reporter sneered about the fall, several others said, "That's not unusual. As he joked himself 'More skiers fall down than stand up.' "

Now *that*'s unusual!

*DECEMBER 29, 1975*

Scratch the progress report.

Ron Nessen blew his cool. After a routine news conference yesterday, some reporters showed him a cartoon from the *Denver Post* which showed the President skiing downhill backwards with the caption: "I understand his ski instructor is also his campaign manager."

Ron did nǒt laugh.

He angrily denounced the press for its "Most unconscionable representation of a President," and delivered a lecture on the subject. It was actually rather similar to what reporters have been mumbling to each other lately—but self-criticism is one thing, Ron Nessen's criticism another. Besides, Ron's lecture contained an ingredient that is intolerable to the press: Rage.

The result: Retaliation. They brought out all the old pictures and stories and jokes today. Ron Nessen had turned an old story into a new story.

"NESSEN FLIPS OVER CLUMSY CARTOON" proclaimed the *New York Daily News*, its story accompanied by four pictures: The *Denver Post* cartoon, and the President 1) bumping his head last year; 2) falling in Austria; and 3) falling on the slopes.

The *Washington Star* ran the Salzburg and ski shots across the top of its front page, headlining the spread with the Nessen quote "HE KNOWS HE'S COORDINATED."

And now, Heeeeeeeeeeere's Johnny!

*Chapter Fifteen*
JANUARY, 1976:

# Love Serving Love

*JANUARY 7, 1976*

Happy Bicentennial.

I sit here surrounded by the souvenirs of 1975. Here is the *Time* Magazine cover that features Mrs. Ford as one of the eleven women chosen to be *Time*'s "Man of the Year." Here is the *Good Housekeeping* poll that ranks Mrs. Ford number one among the most admired women. Here is the *People* Magazine cover carrying Mrs. Ford as one of America's "Three Most Intriguing People." Here is the campaign pin someone gave me today that reads: "Betty Ford's Husband for President!"

Those are last year's trophies.

What was the toll? Edward is tired of being "Mr. Sheila Weidenfeld," of riding in back-up planes on trips with White House wives and crying children, of having me leave home early in the morning (weekdays and weekends) and come home late at night, able to think and talk about nothing but work. He is tired of meeting me at my office at the appointed hour, only to find that he has to wait for one more phone call, one more letter, one more event. He is a combination of frustrated and angry the weeks before and after I leave

246

on a trip, depressed while I am gone. "We used to have a rich, full life together," he says, "and now you have no life, just an obsession."

When I got back from China, he asked me to choose between the job and him. I pleaded with him to just let me finish, just one more year.

"On January 20, 1976," I said, "it will all be over and we can go back to what we had, which was very special."

At this point at least, he consented.

Others are not so lucky. All over the White House, the marriages come tumbling down. Many are old marriages, solid marriages. In Vail last year, we went out for dinner with a couple who had been college sweethearts, and marital partners for twenty years. She has since called Edward for legal advice. She can't take it. She wants a divorce.

The Secret Service has the highest rate of marital failure, and a correspondingly high rate of promiscuity. That isn't true among the men on the White House staff, however. There the cause of divorce is less likely to be "sleeping with other women" than it is "sleeping with a beeper under the pillow." Work is the aphrodisiac. Endless absence is the result.

The only marriages that do well are the bad ones. If, for example, you have never gotten along well, the White House affords the opportunity for a glamorous means of "separation." If you have spent decades in the little leagues of Washington politics, your husband's promotion to the "Big Time" can be a delicious sensation, coming as it does with a whole array of new social entrees that can be cashed in while he works.

Of the marriages that have "made it," thus far, many have been helped by socializing (commiseration?) among the wives, who keep each other company while their husbands are elsewhere. Others are the marriages where the wives have careers of their own which keep them busy and their egos intact. But these, like mine, can only be described as "marriage on ice," a good solid relationship, hopefully capable of being preserved for a future time when it will be able to flourish once again. When you work in the White House, everything becomes subsidiary to your job. You are working for the United States and the President. When other things become more important than the job, you probably owe it to the President to resign.

One more year. Will there be more trophies? Will Edward wait?

Instead of feeling "accomplished" about the year that was, I feel terribly anxious about the year that is. On all fronts.

The New Hampshire primary is forty-eight days away. (Who's counting?) Today's Gallup Poll states that more respondents (46 percent) disapprove of the way President Ford is handling the Presidency than approve (39 percent). That's a 7 percent drop from his approval standing one month ago.

In New Hampshire, Ronald Reagan insists that it's time to "eyeball the Russians" and that "détente has become a one-way street."

*Boom!* And they're off and running. Just as I have begun to feel somewhat in control, to feel like a Press Secretary who is on top of her job, a new dimension is going to be added. A campaign. It is an unknown entity. But that is not the only reason it bothers me. There is an ominous feeling I cannot really define that I get from the look in Mrs. Ford's eyes when she says, "I think it takes a special woman to be a political wife."

That feeling is intensified when I think over the political wives I have met, the women who submerge their egos and personalities into a kind of supportive anonymity. Those smiles. Those joyless smiles.

They make me wonder. Was 1975 the first year Mrs. Ford was freed from being a political wife? Because the Presidency came so suddenly, and because of the many other traumas of the year, and because of the demands imposed upon her as First Lady, she had a role of her own to worry about. She had no time, or at least little time, to share the podium. Was that a once-in-a-lifetime luxury?

## JANUARY 9, 1976

We're in the midst of our peak starling season here at the White House. It begins in November and continues until the end of March. Last year I thought I was imagining things, but one of the White House groundskeepers, Dale Haney, has assured me that—much to his regret—I am not.

A starling is a field bird with a compressed sharp bill, long pointed wings and a short tail. To the non-knowing, its overall appearance is: bird. Every night at exactly 5:15, thousands of starlings (yes, really thousands) swoop into the South Lawn and fill the trees. It is such a regular occurrence that I can tell time by them.

They commute in reverse, Haney explains. They spend their days in suburbia, and then at night, they come to the city because it is warmer. They love night lights and greenery (because it protects them from the wind) and the magnolia trees near the well-lit White House apparently add up to a starling's dream come true.

Not Dale Haney's, however. Starlings, it turns out, have a foul odor, a high degree of acidity in their droppings, and a tendency to hurt the trees which serve as their motel.

So there has been a starling-Haney war going on for quite a few years now, a war in which some rather elaborate weaponry has been employed, such as an eight track tape recorder that blares sounds of birds in distress—sounds guaranteed to upset any starling, but sounds which (alas) the starlings seem to have gotten used to.

And so every night at 5:15, I look outside my window and see them come home to the White House. And later every evening, when I go home, I do so in a car completely covered with starling droppings—tangible evidence that poor Dale Haney is still losing the battle.

## JANUARY 12, 1976

"It's not a campaign debut. This is just my club, and I'm coming here for lunch," Mrs. Ford was telling reporters as she arrived at the Mayflower Hotel today to attend a luncheon sponsored by the D.C. League of Republican Women. "It's a reunion, in a way. After all, I've been a member of the League for so many years."

The reporters clustered around her. Another question. Another answer. Both muffled from where I was standing. This has become a problem for me. It is impossible to hear what Mrs. Ford says in a noisy crowd of reporters. Yet it is essential that I hear it, because I will be asked for specifics later by those too far away to hear for themselves.

I have found a solution; a tape recorder that is tiny enough to fit—unnoticed—where I can't.

So, as the reporters gathered at the Mayflower, I whipped out my little machine and plunged it into the crowd to catch the First Lady's spontaneous remarks.

Suddenly, Jack started shouting, and shouting his name, of all things. "Howdy, I'm Jack Ford!" "Hi there, I'm Jack Ford!" "Hello, this is Jack Ford." It startled all of us, because we couldn't see him but the voice was unmistakeably his. Where was he? It sounded as if he were doing an imitation of his Park Service announcement.

His Park Service announcement! I pulled out my tape recorder and looked. I had pushed "play back" instead of "record."

## JANUARY 13, 1976

Charlie Brotman, the public relations man for the Virginia Slims women's tennis tournament called me today. The tournament is in town, and one of its stars, tennis champion Chris Evert, would like to meet Jack Ford.

Really? The sincerity of her desire was somewhat questionable, given the obvious publicity potential. Tennis champ, President's son, flash bulbs click, stories splash. I pictured the rendezvous. Suddenly I liked what I saw—*because* of the obvious publicity potential: nice, young, clean, athletic, wholesome Chris Evert—a positive way to wipe out the old Bianca Jagger image.

Jack was enthusiastic about meeting Chris, but less than enthusiastic about having two press agents play matchmakers. I called Charlie Brotman back.

"Jack thinks it would be better if the two of them talk directly." I told him.

"Have him call her."

"Have her call *him*! It was *her* idea!"

"I'll tell her, but I don't know if she'll do it. She's very timid."

Timid? Isn't this the up-front generation? How can a tennis star be timid anyway? Timid. I like that, too. Nice, young, clean athletic, wholesome, timid Chris Evert.

I hope she calls.

## JANUARY 16, 1976

Steve has begun his second college semester at his second college! California State Polytechnic University in Pomona. He will be a part-time student, part-time worker, but a fulltime cowboy, since his job is on a ranch nearby and his academic courses include four credits in "farrier science" (horseshoeing) and two credits in "basic equitation" (horsemanship).

He's happy.

But the "graduate" is not. And the parents of the graduate are despondent. While the nation awaits his forthcoming State of the Union message, the chief executive is preoccupied with the state of the second son.

I think Jack would love to throw himself into his father's campaign. But ever since the President Ford Campaign Committee declared him "out" (because of his marijuana confessions in October) that area of involvement has been off limits. The ice does appear to be thawing a little, partly because Jack spends a lot of time over there (in spite of a lack of invitation). And partly because I think Stuart Spencer, the Deputy Campaign Manager, has come to realize that Jack has access to the Presidential ear. When he talks, his father listens.

But a thaw does not a swimming pool make. So for the moment, Jack must find something else. All attention is focused on the great abstract entity known as "Jack's Job." After all, each of the other Ford children has, if not an occupation, at least a pre-occupation. Michael studies religion, Susan photography, and Steve horses. Jack's strong suit appears to be hesitation.

His initial enthusiasm about the job with the travel agency, has been tempered by doubts, resulting in apathy and procrastination. Although I think it is only a matter of time, tension is high in the Family Quarters where both parents have "promised not to mention a job for the next ten days." Apparently the President forgot to mention this pledge to an old family friend who came for dinner last night, and, according to Mrs. Ford, spoke the unspeakable.

"And so," the friend said, turning conversationally to Jack, "what are you going to be doing?"

"All of a sudden, you could feel the tension in the air," Mrs. Ford told me. "I could have killed Jerry for forgetting to tell him not to say anything. So I said cheerfully, 'Well, Jack recorded three public service announcements for the Park Service recently.' That didn't help. In fact, I think it made things worse. Jack got all huffed up and said 'Yeah. That took exactly half an hour. A half hour out of six months of doing nothing!' and he walked out of the room."

## JANUARY 20, 1976

It's simple. See, the East Wing Correspondence Section was both oversized and underorganized. Ineffective. By streamlining it, and transferring part of it into the West Wing Correspondence Section, we made the whole set-up more efficient. We also decreased the East Wing staff by five. (Perhaps I should go into administration.) That magic number, five!

And unlike Ron "the racer" Nessen's idle poolside promises, the vows of Jim Connor are kept.

Which is a long way of announcing that there are, as of today, two new people in the East Wing press office: Kaye Pullen, a speech writer I stole from the West Wing, and Sally Quenneville, an excellent secretarial assistant.

My two for five deal has been successfully completed.


## JANUARY 21, 1976

The big date was last night. The President's son took the tennis star out for dinner after the match. Jack told me that as Chris Evert jumped into the car with her little suitcase and all the flashbulbs went off, he suddenly had the feeling he had just gotten married.

It took almost as much preparation. Indeed, I've developed a new respect for Cupid. A few days after our first contact, Charlie Brotman called back. I asked why Jack hadn't heard from Chris.

"I told you. She's just too timid. But she really wants to talk to him and invite him to the match. Could he call her at 11 A.M. today? She'll be waiting."

Jack called (in a manner of speaking; he came to my office at the appointed hour; I dialed the number, and handed him the phone). He was nervous, but playful. It was a nice telephone conversation (at least the part I could not help but hear) but it was also inconclusive. No one invited anyone anywhere.

A few days later, Charlie Brotman called again.

"Nothing doing," I told him. "Jack has already called her once. It's her turn." (Am I playing public relations, or am I playing adolescence?)

She called. They talked again—on my phone. (Has privacy lost its appeal? Is Charlie Brotman listening in at the other end?) This time they made plans. They would have lunch. And he would watch practice. And they would have dinner.

Could they use my car? ("I can't take her out in my jeep.")

"Chris Evert?" I responded when reporters jumped on me today with questions about the possibility of a budding romance. "They enjoy each other's company," I said truthfully, hoping they would interpret it as an understatement.

But the newspaper photos were better than any words. Pictures of two nice, young, clean, athletic, wholesome people on a date.

In my Volvo.

I worked late and did not remember until it was time for me to leave that I was carless. Explaining I'd lent mine to Jack, I tried to order through Gulley a car to take me home. "No."

At best the man is irritating. At worst he can be maddening. I was furious and I decided I had had it. The time had come to make an issue out of it. Since Bill Gulley is "accountable to the Secretary of the Cabinet," I went to Jim Connor and told him what had happened. "Jim," I said, "I've had enough. I have to get home right now and I need a car."

I waited for him to lift the phone and make the command that would move the mountain. Instead, he smiled sweetly, showing me both of his dimples and his timidity. He grabbed his coat. "C'mon, uh, I'll drive you home."

That is Gulley's superior talking.


## JANUARY 27, 1976

"He will be Director of Youth Marketing," I told the reporters (with delight). "He'll be responsible for developing programs and coordinating the production of a student guidebook. He will be based in Washington."

I didn't tell them his "base" for the moment is Edward's office, that Jack is sharing space in Edward's law firm. I would have told them if they had asked, of course.

I would not have gone on to tell them some of the other details, though. Like Edward's stories.

Jack and the Secret Service have signed a truce of sorts. He does not drop security anymore. In return, they have made some personnel changes. The Service appears to be elastic enough to bend to blend. During the Nixon Administration, they all wore ties and jackets and conservative dress. Now they wear casual clothes, and personalities that somehow complement those of their subjects. Susan's agents, for example, tend to be clean-cut big brother types. Mrs. Ford's are all gentlemen.

Jack's, Edward says, are all the misfits. Edward refers to them as the "Baa Baa Black Sheep," and, since they, too, are now spending a lot of time in Edward's office, he has stories to document it.

Thus, either Edward is home, waiting impatiently for me to return from work, or he is at work, hearing detailed accounts of the sexploits of the Secret Service.

"You gotta be saying to yourself, 'What does this guy have?'" says the agent who describes himself to Edward as a "huge ugly Irishman." "You gotta wonder why I'm gettin' it three times a day!" Then he explains: "See, say we travel. First I meet a stewardess on the plane and I arrange to see her first thing in the morning. . . . . " concluding with: "well, three sometimes. . . . But at least *twice*. I get headaches if I don't get it twice a day."

The sidekick of the enormous Irish agent is a little Italian whose idea of fun, Edward says, is to shake your hand and break three fingers in the process, smiling all the time.

Jack is delighted. Because they amuse each other, which, I suppose, takes the heat off him, and because the head of the detail (who is a more conservative "by-the-book" type) is so busy worrying about his agents that he has no time to criticize Jack. "I keep seeing my whole career flash before my eyes," he moaned to Edward recently.

*Chapter Sixteen*
FEBRUARY, 1976:

# THE FIRST HURRAH

*FEBRUARY 9, 1976*

Air Force One flew North today, to New Hampshire—America's own Brigadoon—the state that wakes up to a hotel boom and a media blitz every fourth February, and then goes back to sleep until it is again time to fight over a new administration. Since 1952, every man elected President has first won the New Hampshire primary. As long as that winning streak holds out, every Presidential hopeful will make the fourth February pilgrimage to kiss babies through frost-bitten lips in the land of ice and snow.

It was like riding on the team bus to the first football game of the season, such was the level of eager anticipation aboard Air Force One. Oh-boy-oh-boy-oh-boy, here we go! There is a whole new cast of characters now. The White House Staff has stepped aside slightly to make room for the President Ford Campaign Committee, hyperthyroid types who dance frenetically to the sound of the latest polls and really couldn't care less about governing the country. (It is winning the chance to govern that matters.)

Ron Nessen did not brief the press this morning, for example. Peter Kaye did—Peter Kaye "spokesman for the President Ford

Committee.'' The big decision maker on this trip is not Dick
Cheney, Chief of Staff. It is Stu Spencer, of the PFC, an energetic
short man with shiny eyes and the appearance of a chipmunk on
speed. Stu is the ultimate campaign "junkie": A fast-thinking,
fast-talking, quick, shrewd, knowledgeable man who carries with
him the aura of "I've-done-it-before-and-I-know-what-I'm-
doing." It is justified. He has and he does. He has a distinguished
political campaign résumé. But the fact that one of the prime credits on it is the successful management of Ronald Reagan's campaign for governor only heightens, for me, the feeling that this is all
one big game. Kids' stuff, played by grown men. Like football.
*Just* like football. (I don't understand football.)

The President loves it, just like football. No one on board Air
Force One is more enthusiastic about pressing the flesh in New
Hampshire snow than President Ford. Many were just as excited,
though. Mrs. Ford wanted to join in the kick-off, in spite of the fact
that the PFC was worried about the reception she would get in conservative New Hampshire. (They benched Jack. The President
Ford Committee is still reeling from his marijuana admission last
October and was terrified he would say or do something harmful to
the campaign in New Hampshire.) Susan, who hates politics but
loves Daddy, was brought along to demonstrate the latter.

The spectators were licking their lips, ready to cheer and boo.
The press have said their farewells and opened new expense accounts in anticipation of the national tour that begins in New
Hampshire. The game is being put on for them, after all, campaigning is a media event. One picture is worth a thousand handshakes
(especially if it is carried by wire service or network) and so, eager-
ly looking forward to an exciting game (and perhaps some interesting injuries along the way) the journalists buzz with anecdotes that
will be tomorrow's news. The season of high journalistic employ-
ment and recognition is on!

I felt like such a killjoy. New Hampshire in February? Frankly,
I'd prefer the Virgin Islands.

Or the White House.

We are greeted at Manchester, New Hampshire, by not enough
people. A cold reception at a cold airport. The polls are right, I
thought to myself. Ronald Reagan is winning.

Then the official party split up. Susan was off to the ski slopes.

(Campaign events must stress the positive, and at the moment, Susan's most marketable political asset is her ability to ski.) Mrs. Ford was off to watch the handicapped work, see senior citizens dance, and make a few "spontaneous" phone calls. She did beautifully, especially considering the limitations of today's script. She added a verse all her own, a sparkle from within. Still, I thought, as I watched her swing with the geriatrics, if this is the way a man gets to be President, we're all in trouble.

The best event turned out to be the last event: the family regrouped to attend a rally tonight at the University of New Hampshire where Mrs. Ford's introduction was followed by an enormous standing ovation—cheers, whistles, and applause. The noise was unbelievable. Later, in response to a question on abortion, the President began by saying, "As you know, my dear wife took another position on that," and the audience erupted into sustained cheers and applause again.

The President was at his best. Direct confrontation turns him on, and the kids at the University of New Hampshire had come to challenge him. It was a lively exchange and it put everyone in a good mood for the return trip tonight. The President enjoyed his performance. Mrs. Ford loved her ovations. I felt respectful glances coming my way from the President Ford Committee campaigners on board (due to Mrs. Ford's ovations). The press was on a campaign high. The press pool noted "with pleasure and some astonishment that now that President Ford is actively seeking to keep his job, the cuisine in the rear of Air Force One has taken a quantum leap upwards!"

Again, I felt like the killjoy. The grouch. "Who is running the country while we all play football?" I asked one of my traveling companions, only half in jest.

"Hey," he replied, "don't worry about it. If we win New Hampshire, we'll be home free. We won't have to do any more campaigning until the general election."

That made me feel better. Temporarily. In the back of my mind there was this nagging feeling that it was the President's premature campaigning last year that got us into this mess in the first place.

\* \* \*

## FEBRUARY 11, 1976

They loved her in New Hampshire! At least the newspapers say
so: "Gerald Ford may have problems winning the New Hampshire
primary, but Betty Ford is not one of them." "The New Hampshire reaction pointed up yet again that the Fords' much-publicized
differences can work to Mr. Ford's advantage." "Betty Ford is the
clear favorite in New Hampshire. Her husband is running neck and
neck with Ronald Reagan in the Republican primary, but she's out
front with both parties, with young and old, with liberated and un-
liberated alike."

And so on! I read the reviews and daydreamed about the possibility of declaring the 1976 Presidential campaign over.

Then I got the ultimate accolade, which promptly erased the
hope. Apparently the President Ford Committee has been reading
the papers too. "We believe it is top priority that Mrs. Ford return
to New Hampshire with the President on his second trip. As you
know, her first visit was extremely well received, and she is highly
thought of by the people in the state," the memo from the President Ford Campaign Committee said. "Our people very much
want her, and consider her one of the most valuable assets for
building momentum in the campaign."

Oh, my! This is not a signal of success. This is a precursor of
trouble. They want her because they have finally discovered (much
to their surprise) that her popularity is an asset. What they do not
understand is that she is popular because she appears to be *non-
political*. People see her as honest, open, someone who thinks and
says what she thinks. Excessive exposure will undermine that image—especially exposure that involves going through the mun-
dane, hackneyed rituals of campaigning. In impact, more will mean
less. One well-placed gesture or event is worth a million podium
waves.

Then there is Susan. Things did not go so well at the slopes, according to Patti. Susan is simply not comfortable campaigning and
the discomfort shows. When she is shy and nervous, she tosses her
hair back, and holds her head erect, and comes off haughty.

Verbally, her fear is translated into petulance. "What are your
feelings about abortion?" she was asked.

"I don't want to get into politics," she said.

"What do you think about people who say your father doesn't deserve to be President?" she was asked.

"If he doesn't deserve it he doesn't deserve it," she answered.

"You didn't mean that," I told her today. "You *meant* that if people don't want him, he won't get elected, but you certainly think he *deserves* to be President."

"Yes."

"Susan," I said, "your answers don't have to be political. You aren't his advisor. You are his daughter. Talk about him in personal terms. You know how hard he works—how dedicated he is. Talk about that."

"Okay."

"Think of the whole thing as fun, as a lark, an adventure. If you do, you'll start enjoying yourself more."

"If the people don't want him, he should not be in office," she told reporter Nick Thimmesch on the phone later. "That's what I *should* have said. He's a very, very dedicated person. You should see him work. He certainly deserves to be in office." She hung up the phone and handed me back the piece of paper on which I had scribbled "See him work . . . dedicated."

Jack arrived after Susan left. "I'm quitting," he said. "I'm quitting the campaign before I even enter it. I spent a week over at the President Ford Campaign Committee. Watching. Just watching. They have no idea how to run a campaign. No concept of local work organization. They want to make me a star—another Ed Nixon!" Behind the disgust, there was real disappointment. "Well, they're not going to make me a star. Any campaigning I do will be on my own."

Having thus expressed his feelings, he left. Leaving me to contemplate the ironies. Susan is already overexposed. Mrs. Ford is about to be overexposed. And what I suspect may be the Ford Family's biggest political gem is being left untapped.


## FEBRUARY 13, 1976

Richard Nixon has accepted an invitation to visit the People's Republic of China. He's scheduled to leave just a few days before the New Hampshire primary. I just can't believe he has the nerve to go and resent his timing.

Mrs. Ford is ignoring it. Icily. Our conversations tell me she does not like Richard Nixon, but she is a lady about it. Her resentment comes out in what she does not say, not in words. She talks about Pat Nixon frequently, remembers her birthdays, sends her notes. But the former President is neither the subject of such thoughtfulness nor even a participant in a fond memory. He is always excluded. Talk of Nixon makes Mrs. Ford behave most like the traditional political wife—polite, suppressed, afraid of being either honest or dishonest, and therefore silent. Carl Bernstein and Bob Woodward, the two *Washington Post* reporters who broke the Watergate story, have written a second Watergate book, this one chronicling Nixon's last days in office. While he was researching it last year, Carl asked me if Mrs. Ford would be willing to talk to him. He said the information would be on background—unattributed to her—and that he was just trying to get information on how things were. I told her about it. She smiled. I explained to her that it would be off the record. She nodded and smiled. I asked her, finally, if she would do it. She said "No." And smiled. But it was the type of "no" that was definitive. She didn't like talking about Nixon.

Today I ranted and raved about Nixon's plans, and she agreed—but went no further than simple agreement.

"I told them I'd go back to New Hampshire," Mrs. Ford said, changing the subject. "And after that, I'd love to go to Florida."

"Stop worrying," Brent Scowcroft, the Head of the National Security Council told me at an East Wing party. "He's going to China as a private citizen. Only a private citizen. This trip is just a private venture between Nixon and the leaders of China."

I can't stop thinking about the voters of New Hampshire though. As they get ready to go to the polls on February 24th, they will undoubtedly see splattered across their newspapers pictures from China of the former President who was "too ill" to come to Washington to account for his conduct. Will the pictures make them angry? Will the pictures make them think twice before voting for "Pardoner Ford," the man who made it possible for Richard Nixon to avoid jail and see the world? At best the gesture is callous. It is also inexcusable. And confusing. Why bite the hand that pardoned you?

"My temperature rises every time I think about it," I said to no one, to everyone, at the party. "A crook behaving like an ambassador."

"And living like a king," interjected a Secret service agent nearby.

"And living like a king," I repeated. I looked at the agent and caught him exchanging looks with someone from the Military Affairs Office. It was a "gotcha" look, a look that said "click." Some morsel of information had been exchanged. And I had missed it.

I waited and watched. The agent looked as though he felt important and I hoped he might feel important enough to want to share it. Whatever "it" was. Perhaps a little prodding would help.

"Well, until now he's been living like more of a hermit than a king," I ventured.

"A hermit with all kinds of Presidential trappings," the agent said.

"Like what?"

"Like White House wine whenever he wishes." The agent and the Military Aide again exchanged knowing looks and snickered.

"From where?" I asked.

"From the White House, of course!" They laughed together. As in joke.

"How does he get it?"

"Think. Who has the power to get Nixon wine?" the agent asked me.

"The usher? The chef?"

"Wrong," he said. "You're concentrating on the 'wine' and not on the rest of the sentence. Who has the power to *get* Nixon wine?"

"You mean deliver it?"

"Yup."

"Like on an airplane?" I asked.

"Yup."

My eyes wandered over to a distant corner of the room where Billy Gulley was laughing heartily with a group of friends. The agent saw where I was looking.

"Yup," he said.

And I wondered what other unauthorized perquisites Gulley was providing at our expense.

## FEBRUARY 14, 1976

"The guy's a creep," Jack said. "I can't believe he'd do it to my father. Doesn't he have any sense of responsibility? Well, if he doesn't, he should. And I'm willing to tell anyone who is willing to listen: The guy is a creep!"

The President may have pardoned Nixon, but Jack Ford has not. He let his father convince him that it was best for the country to bury the hatchet and go on. For the country, yes. For Jack, no chance.

Jack takes Watergate personally because in 1972 he worked very hard to get Richard Nixon re-elected. He dedicated his whole summer to the chore, organizing rallies on college campuses, traveling all over, losing sleep, laboring endlessly. So did many other people, of course. But Jack was young and excited and naïve. It was his first personal involvement in politics, and he loved it—and just as he felt somewhat responsible for the victory, he felt betrayed by the misconduct of the victor.

I decided not to mention the wine.

## FEBRUARY 20, 1976

"I have a question to address to Mrs. Ford," said a voice in the crowd. A New Hampshire accent. A hostile tone? I squinted. I could see a woman. Forties. Blond hair. There were hundreds of people squirming excitedly trying to get the President's attention so they could ask their questions. Colors and faces were blurred.

Mrs. Ford stepped forward, smiling. "Yes?"

"I want to know what you have done as First Lady, other than have all your clothes designed by one designer and invited show business people to the White House."

Yes, a hostile tone. An outrageous question. The crowd grunted its disapproval.

"Well," answered Mrs. Ford timidly, shakily, "I've always worked for retarded children and I was active in the PTA as a wife and mother when my children were younger. And I've taught Sunday school."

What kind of an answer is that? I was embarrassed.

I was the only one. The crowd, who had been told by the media in advance that they would love Mrs. Ford, reacted according to plan. They seemed more annoyed by the question than the answer. Later, several reporters commented sympathetically that "she must have been really taken aback by the question."

As we boarded Air Force One on the way from Keene to Portsmouth, New Hampshire, several staff people patted her on the back and told her she'd really handled a difficult situation well.

"What is this craziness?" I asked Dr. Lukash aboard the plane. "She was terrible. That was an inexcusable answer to a question that was so outrageous it should have been easy to answer well."

"Tell her that," he said.

"I have this feeling we've come full circle," I said. "Now she can do no wrong. Everyone looks at her and thinks of the latest popularity poll ratings. Even she is beginning to believe her own press releases. And it's all so ephemeral. Two or three more answers like that and everything will begin shifting in the other direction. She can't coast. Not now. She's campaigning, Dr. Lukash. It's the real thing."

"You've got to tell her that," Dr. Lukash said with the type of conviction reserved for conclusive medical diagnoses. "You've got to tell her while it is still fresh in both your minds."

I made up a list of "talking points" for Mrs. Ford's future use and went into her cabin.

She was smiling happily. Her other aides—the good fairies—had made her feel good. "Now," I thought, "a word from the wicked witch."

I smiled. "You know how you always say that you are the President's most severe critic?" I began. "You say that even when everyone else says he is fine, you tell him what you really think? Well," (here goes) "I'm *your* worst critic. I really thought you could have done a better job today on that question."

She smiled. After all, she believes in constructive criticism.

"First of all," I said, "the woman asked you about clothes. You could have answered her specifically and truthfully. You could have told her you don't have just one designer, that, in fact, you have several and all are American because you are trying to stimulate the economy and show the public that American designers are excellent."

"*Mmmmmmmm.*" So far so good.

"The thing about show business people was ridiculous. Your State

Dinners are meeting places for all kinds of people from different fields—the arts, science, medicine, education."

"*Mmmmmmmm.*"

"And if you're going to talk about retarded children or handicapped children, for heaven's sake say that you taught dance to the handicapped and elaborate on how rhythm improves motor skills. Be specific. That makes the statement interesting. As to what you've accomplished, you could have—"

"You're going to say 'ERA.' " she interrupted. "I purposefully didn't want to talk about ERA again. I want the people to think of me as more than a spokesperson for ERA."

(Well, a person can take just so much constructive criticism.)

"I agree," I said. "But you don't have to say ERA. You can talk around it, about your beliefs in people's rights, about lives that include *all* the options—homemaker, worker, whatever. You could talk about cancer, too. Say that it was something you couldn't control, but something that you were candid about."

"I'm *sick* of the cancer thing," she snapped. "I'm tired of reading about it all the time. I hate the thought that every time people look at me they clutch their bosoms. I've just had enough!"

"Well, all I know," I told her, "is that I am always meeting women who tell me that you saved their lives; that if you had not publicized your breast cancer and urged examinations, they would not be alive today. That is something pretty important."

(First ERA, then cancer, I thought to myself; she's rejecting her two major contributions for fear of rocking the boat.)

I left her looking at my "talking points"—hoping she'd understand but fearing I had done irreparable damage.(To her?To us? To the campaign?) Once we landed, she refused to see anybody, including me. To comfort herself, she called Susan in Portsmouth and missed one of the campaign events as a result. But by the time we got back to Washington, she seemed less withdrawn and willing to be my friend again.

I wish I could figure out why some things seem to get to her.


## FEBRUARY 23, 1976

"Patti said you were fantastic!"

He grinned, concurring. On his own, Jack traveled up to Massachusetts last week and spent the day working out of the President Ford Phone Bank Center there. Patti Matson, who advanced the trip for him, told me that he had been sensational—charming, lively, a real natural.

"That was just the beginning," he told me. "I'm going to go out on my own. George Gorton, the guy I worked for in '72, is going to do my advance. We have decided to pick a state and blitz it—spend four or five days there, making many, many short appearances each day, just really do the state. George knows the kinds of things I can do and can't do. I trust him. I really don't trust anyone at the Campaign Committee. They don't know their asses from their elbows over there."

"That's a heavy pace," I said. "Five days of short appearances. Do you plan to keep blitzing from now to November?"

"I don't know. I just can't stand the possibility of my Dad losing to Ronald Reagan. It would do me in. More so, even, than losing eventually to some Democrat."

"Which is the lucky state?"

"I think Illinois. The primary is mid-March. We're thinking of blitzing the first week in March. We'll go primarily to high schools and colleges."

"Why high schools?"

"High school students make terrific volunteers. They work very hard."

"Do you have someone to follow up and recruit them?"

"Yup."

"Press coverage is important," I told him. "Otherwise you'll be doing all this in a vacuum. People have to know you're there. But I think you should have only local press at first. You have to get used to campaigning—work out the kinks. Can I talk to this George Gorton?"

"I'll have him call you."

"Your speeches should be short. In fact, all you have to say is that you're campaigning for your father, and that you'd rather hear from them, find out what's on their minds, open the floor for questions."

"I like that. It makes sense. I don't feel comfortable making speeches anyway."

"And you're terrific at answering questions."

"Yeah," he grinned.

## FEBRUARY 24, 1976

We left Washington this morning for a five-day excursion to Florida, a non-campaign, campaign trip. In truth, the trip is one enormous package of compromises. There is something in it for everyone. For the President Ford Committee, there is the presence of the First Lady in Florida two weeks before primary time, where she will solo for five days and then recouple with the President on the 29th for some campaign-campaigning. For Mrs. Ford, there will be time after her initial appearances to enjoy the sunshine, visit friends, and go condominium shopping in Naples. For me we have set up some less-obviously political stops: a school here, a cultural center there, stops that underline Mrs. Ford's interests rather than her husband's race. We have tailored the schedule to her liking; no big receptions, no long speeches, and she, in turn, has perfected her talking points for short remarks, if asked. ("The ERA? Well, I'm against every form of bigotry because it weakens a society and I believe everyone should have options open to them as to what they want their lives to be. . . .")

We boarded Air Force One today, Florida-bound, Florida-prepared.

But New Hampshire-preoccupied.

Today is the big day, the day the people of New Hampshire go to the polls. (With the happy knowledge that in only twenty-four hours their state will be clear of all political hopefuls!)

The last word from the political experts was—a blank stare. Too close to call. That, actually, is a bit of a victory, since at the beginning of February, Ford trailed Reagan badly in the polls, even the President's private polls, which showed Ford with just a little more than one third of the Republican vote, and all the rest either committed to Reagan or undecided. But then there were the trips to New Hampshire, followed by newer polls, which made things look better.

Better. But good enough? The President seemed relaxed. Jack, on the other hand, was very nervous. I arranged before we left this morning to keep in touch with Dick Cheney, so we would have the verdict as soon as possible.

On the plane we talked about Florida and we thought about New Hampshire. I went over the plans for Mrs. Ford's appearance at a bicentennial "Stand up for America" rally tonight. (Patti Matson said a crowd of about 8,000 was expected and a crowd of 8,000, we agreed, was, indeed, a crowd.) After we talked a while, Mrs. Ford said, "I have good vibes about New Hampshire. Really."

It was that way all day. We landed. We were greeted. We talked to reporters, waved at people, went through all the actions, but all thoughts were up North.

It was hardest for me to concentrate at the big rally. The people who briefed Patti must have been talking about capacity not ticket sales. It is possible that this place could hold 8,000 people, I thought to myself as I stared at the enormous pockets of empty spaces. It certainly had the power to make the crowd of about 2,000 look skimpy.

As the balloons and flags outnumbered human beings three to one, we all pretended to be in a crowd and "Stood up for America" against a backdrop of unbelievable quantities of red, white, and blue.

(And wondered what in the world we were doing here while wondering what was happening in New Hampshire.)

I called the White House several times during the rally for reports. The earliest returns from New Hampshire had been bad. But now things were a little better.

At last we were liberated from the rally to Mrs. Ford's hotel room, where Mrs. Ford, Nancy Chirdon, Patti Matson and Pete Sorum (Mrs. Ford's advance man) and I had a drink and watched the returns. They were good as opposed to bad, but not good enough. I called the White House periodically. Nothing conclusive. Finally, at about midnight, we broke up. I told the reporters that there was nothing decisive yet, and Mrs. Ford would have no statement until the morning.

I went to my room and got ready for bed. Who could sleep?

My television set and I talked to each other all night, until finally, in the early morning, it told me the good news: we won! 51–49 percent, but at least *we won!*

"President Ford has been proven electable," the commentator was saying. "With this victory, his first outside Grand Rapids, he has shown the American people that he is indeed a national candidate."

I thought of calling Mrs. Ford. I thought of calling Edward. I was sure they were both up. But not sure enough. Instead I took the paper with the statement I had written for Mrs. Ford "just in case" (the one that began, "Naturally, I wish he had won, but there are always ups and downs in politics. August is many months and many primaries away, and the President's leadership and accomplishments are just beginning to be understood") and filed it away. We won't need it tomorrow!

When will we need it?

*Chapter Seventeen*
MARCH, 1976:

# CRUISING

*MARCH 6, 1976*

There are news clippings strewn all over my desk. The headlines bear messages such as "YOUNG FORD DISPLAYS CANDOR" "JACK IS NIMBLE" "RAIN FAILS TO DAMPEN JACK FORD'S SPIRITS" "FORD'S SON BIG HIT."

Five days ago, Jack cut his hair, stored his corduroys, lumber jacket and moccasins; donned a conservative gray suit, tie and the title "Son of President" and hit the campaign trail in Illinois.

He and Gorton made twenty-five stops in four days. Time and again, according to the news accounts, he underlined the reasons for supporting his father, his belief in his father, and the fact that his father "would be here himself, but the responsibilities of being President of the United States prevent him from day-in day-out campaigning." (!)

Time after time (subscribing to the political-differences-broaden-family-support theory) Jack did not hesitate to admit the areas where he and his father disagree.

"When the students quizzed Jack on court-ordered busing," the *Chicago Tribune* reports, "he revealed that he learned to be comfortable with blacks thanks to such a program in Alexandria, Virginia, when he was in the seventh grade.''

A woman suggested his mother would make a good Vice President. "I don't think she and the President could reconcile their differences," he deadpanned.

"I don't think it's unusual for a father and son to disagree," he told a college crowd. "It's unrealistic to expect to find a candidate you agree with 100 percent. I think it's about time this country had a First Family that could think and talk for themselves."

The general journalistic conclusion, summed up by a Lake Forest, Illinois paper: "President Gerald Ford couldn't have picked a better substitute to kick off his Illinois campaign than his son, Jack."

The personal post mortem was equally positive. "The first stop was okay. The second stop was a little better. The third, better still," George Gorton said. "By the end, he was great—smooth and relaxed."

They returned on cloud nine, exhausted but exhilarated, filled with tales of crowds and the big surprise of the trip—the girls. "The college girls assaulted him verbally," Gorton said. "They'd ask, 'Do you believe in equal status?' Jack would say 'yes.' Then they'd invariably say, 'What are you doing tonight?'

"But the high school girls. They were something else. They wanted to touch him, to rip his clothes off. At one school, a gigantic crowd of kids came toward us as we were walking in the corridor and the principal got so concerned he pulled Jack into his office and gave him a high school letterman's jacket, so they'd tear at that and not his shirt."

The two politicos reminisced about campaign headquarters and student unions and historic sights and civic centers and, inevitably, about the girls. They talked about how they shouted "I LOVE YOU I LOVE YOU" and shoved notes in their hands, and how the Secret Service reaped the benefits.

"They're very edgy about campaign service," Jack said. "They won't use their radios for anything political. But on the subject of sex, they're only too happy to dive into the wake of screaming girls—to protect me, of course. The girls love them. They ask questions like, 'Do you *really* carry a gun?' and the men say 'Sure!' and just whip out their revolvers."

We all laughed at the imitation. "I thought Secret Service agents weren't supposed to reveal their weapons," George said.

## MARCH 11, 1976

Mrs. Ford wanted to go to the American Film Institute dinner for writer-director-producer William Wyler in Los Angeles.

Okay.

Then a beautifully written letter came in about a bicentennial project to reproduce a century-old adobe schoolhouse in Mesa, Arizona. "Why not make a bicentennial stop in Mesa en route?" asked Susan Porter, Mrs. Ford's appointments secretary.

Okay.

"She's going to be in Los Angeles?" the President Ford Committee said. "Great. She can attend a luncheon for grassroots volunteers."

Okay.

"While she's in the area," Ford family friend Leon Parma suggested, "could she please open the Ford campaign headquarters in San Diego?"

Okay.

Then someone discovered a senior citizens center in San Diego right across the street. While she was there, she might as well drop in and shake a few elderly hands.

Okay.

Could she come back via Illinois? That way she could join the President for a little campaigning.

Okay.

She needed something to do while she was in Illinois. I found something called The Lambs, a farm in Libertyville, Illinois, for mentally retarded citizens, started by parents of retarded children, as a way of helping their offspring live self-sufficiently, in dignity. I knew it was Mrs. Ford's kind of thing. It was a worthwhile cause, and a photogenic subject.

Okay.

Put it all together and you have a campaign trip—a trip planned by no one in particular. A trip with no plan in particular. Events in a vacuum. It turned out to be a nice schoolhouse but an awful performance in Mesa. A glittery evening filled with the face-lifted famous in Hollywood. Wonderful pictures and good coverage in Libertyville. The welcome at the Beverly Wilshire Hotel in Los Angeles was real Hollywood: a mariachi band at curbside, cheers, applause, a red carpet (literally). The scissors used to cut the ribbon at the campaign headquarters was about three feet long. A bit much. The senior citizens wanted to dance with Mrs. Ford, and they whirled and twirled her from octogenarian to octogenarian with such enthusiasm (and violent force) that finally the woman in charge stopped the music and urged the jolly geriatrics not to "wear the poor girl out." In Los Angeles, Shirley Fonda told me that she and her husband, Henry Fonda, don't go out that much ("He likes being home; he's into needlepointing") and Fred Astaire excitedly explained a dance routine to me, and Ed Asner (Lou Grant of the Mary Tyler Moore Show) whispered in my dear, "I don't like Jerry very much, but I'm *crazy* about Betty!"

And sometime, somewhere in the midst of it all, President Ford won the Florida primary 53 percent to 47 percent. (Ronald Reagan said he was "delighted about having come so close." We all enjoyed that.)

It was a sometimes enjoyable trip with an extremely complicated plot, but what was the theme? The point? The goal?

I'm concerned. I'm concerned because we're cruising and we're careening. Mrs. Ford hasn't done anything that means anything in so long. There is no time. Every time I get an idea, we can't complete it. I spoke to several people about the idea of Mrs. Ford's recording a taped tour of the White House for use by the blind, for example. One of my staff even wrote a script. Maybe she will do it. At the moment, however, her schedule is filled with other recordings. ("Hello, this is Betty Ford. I just wanted to remind you to vote for my husband in the Illinois primary next week.")

We are cruising, resting on last year's laurels, reaping the seeds of last year's popularity. There are so many worthwhile things to *do*. Must you stop being a First Lady in order to be re-elected First Lady?

So this is campaigning?

## MARCH 12, 1976

It happened almost a week ago, and I can't get it out of my head. I keep seeing it. We're at the adobe schoolhouse in Mesa. I'm standing with the press, and there, off in the distance, is Mrs. Ford giving her speech. A simple speech. Bicentennial stuff. But there is, right from the beginning of the speech, a contrast between the exciting words and the dead delivery. She starts out sounding tired.

She gets worse. Words become slurred, mispronounced. "Translating our ideas into relality," she says. "Symbols of our sociciety." She stumbles over "Declaration of Independence," and speaks of "inamdnemable" rights. In Philadelphia, she says, "The first setty . . . citizens . . . " At first no one really listens, but as the mistakes increase, everyone in the press area becomes silent and attentive. So do I.

"What's the matter with her?" the reporter next to me whispers.

"I don't know," I tell her. It is the truth. She sounds drunk. No, not drunk . . . spacey. Out of it. She had a drink on the plane, I think to myself, her usual, vodka and tonic. But one drink? Ridiculous. This is not the result of one drink. She took a pill on the plane too. Could that be it? But then again, I reassure myself, as I look at the fixed smile in the distance, she hates making speeches and the sun is in her eyes and she's tired.

"She hates making speeches and the sun is in her eyes and she's tired," I tell the reporters. Then I shrug.

She was fine at the next stop. No more slurring. But that somehow makes it all stand out even more. I've been thinking about the Jane Whitmore interview last December, when Mrs. Ford said she took a Valium every day and I was so sure it was a mistake. Whatever she was taking then, she is taking more of now. There are times when she calls me at home and speaks so slowly that I think she is drugged. She has even fallen asleep on me in the middle of a phone conversation. It is hard to tell whether this is the result of medication for other illnesses (when she has had bouts of osteoarthritis, the doctors keep her heavily sedated) or whether it is self-medication. Dr. Lukash is a stone wall when I try to pry.

In either case, I'm convinced that the cause is the same: pressure. This is an emotional and physically frail woman, a woman who, when "produced" correctly and comfortably, can shine like the true gem she is, but who, when insensitively handled, begins to crumble.

And she's crumbling.

Campaigning is the worst possible activity for Mrs. Ford, because it calls for speech-making before large crowds—never her forte. And because it is a throwback, I'm convinced, to her old life, the political wife syndrome that drove her to a psychiatrist in the first place. She is no longer Betty Ford, doing her own thing. She's back again being Mrs. Gerald Ford, pushing his thing in his style.

She spent a lifetime being supportive, applauding her spotlighted husband. She raised his four children while he raised political issues, and she brought them up to be good kids, solid kids, kids who love their mother, and with their mother, hero-worship their father.

But I think there was always something inside—maybe the "dancer" in her—that wanted to be something, too. Nothing that would conflict with her family's well-being, to be sure; they come first. But something. She was scared at first at the White House, hesitant. But gradually, over the last year, she began to realize that she was special, not because she was Mrs. Gerald Ford, but because she was Betty Ford, a woman with some special personality traits. People liked her honesty, her sparkle, her frankness. What's more, as First Lady, she had some national influence. She could push causes and areas that she believed in. For the first time in her life, she was in the spotlight because of her *own* characteristics.

Now she's back as podium princess, with all of his issues, his crazy campaign schedule, his Presidency.

Will there be more Mesas?

## MARCH 15, 1976

"You're not kidding he needs coaching," the man says as he paces around my office. "Coaching and cleansing—all that political rhetoric—awful!" He shakes his head excitedly. He seems to do everything excitedly. The words follow each other, *bam bam bam*, punctuated by hand gestures, lapses into various accents, and jokes, old jokes, new jokes, one-liners. He's like a stand-up comedian.

Better yet, he *is* a stand-up comedian. For $150 a day consultant fee, he is the White House's very *own* stand-up comic—Don Penny, fortyish, shortish, funnyish, very hyper.

His specialty is situation comedy. His television credits include "The Wackiest Ship in the Army." He obviously bears the appropriate credentials for the White House. Add to that the fact that he has experience writing television commercials, and you have the ultimate White House consultant for the 1976 Presidential campaign.

He is, I'm told, all David Kennerly's idea. The more I think about it, the more it fits. David believes in Presidential distraction, in merriment on high, and he is singularly irreverent of the "powers that be" in the White House. He feels the President does not come across as the President really is, and if ever there were a character that embodied "a new approach to the problem" it is Don Penny.

A court jester at $150 a day. Not bad.

He is a name dropper, but he has his own names for people. For example, Bob Hartmann, whom he openly dislikes ("incompetent") is called "Snow Toad" because he has gray hair and warts on his face. (Nice guy.) The President is "Big Red." No one knows why, but it is obviously complimentary because he really likes the President.

"Big Red," he says, "is gonna be great and I'm gonna help."

The muscles never relax. The routines never stop coming. ("I just flew in from Illinois and boy are my arms tired.") It is tiring to watch. It must be exhausting to be. But as he bounces around my office, telling me that he thinks he can teach the President how to project himself better, how to pace his speeches, so that his presentation is less wooden, more relaxed, I can't help nodding my head.

And hoping.

## MARCH 16, 1976

Ford's Gallup rating has jumped eleven points in two months. The Dow Jones is up and so is the delegate count. President Ford won the Illinois primary today on Jack Ford's twenty-fourth birthday.

The momentum is building.

## MARCH 18, 1976

"Hey Sheila," Ron Nessen began in an unusually warm tone. "I've been asked to appear on 'Saturday Night Live.' What do you think?"

I thought of the often funny somewhat racey late night television program, and wondered what on earth Ron Nessen and "Saturday Night Live" could have in common.

"Why do it?" I asked.

"Just to be a good sport—to show that the President and his staff have a sense of humor."

What is this, White House Comedy Month? I wondered why he had not tried to demonstrate his humor in the White House press room first.

"I think it's a bad idea, Ron."

"I don't."

"You haven't paved the way for it," I told him. "You can't just jump in to something like that. You have to build up to it gradually, especially with a show like 'Saturday Night Live,' which is volatile, uneven, and often off-color. Really, Ron, you can go in a good sport and come off a buffoon."

He was moving away from me. The more I thought about it, the more I thought it was a terrible idea. The more I talked, the more I realized he didn't really want my opinion. He wasn't really asking. He was telling.

## MARCH 22, 1976

I hadn't seen him for a long time, but that wasn't because I hadn't been looking for him. I had. I guess he's been on a different shift. I wasn't subtle.

"Tell me more about the wine for Nixon."

He laughed. "Look, Sheila, it's no big deal. It's common knowledge. The plane always goes to San Clemente loaded with wine. It always has."

"When does a plane go to San Clemente?"

"Often. To deliver papers. Documents. On business. Or whenever Gulley wants one to."

"Isn't that illegal?"

The Secret Service agent laughed again. "In what way? Gulley is 'liaison with former Presidents,' right? He also has absolute control of the Air Force and he manifests planes arbitrarily. It so happens that Nixon's Military Aide, Jack Brennan, is an old pal of Gulley's. And Bill Gulley takes care of his friends. And they, in return, keep him in office."

"Like who? Who are some of his friends?"

"Rumsfeld is a friend. Rumsfeld got to know him when he

served in the Nixon Cabinet. Gulley curried Rumsfeld's favor from day one. When Rumsfeld was called back to become Ford's Chief of Staff—coincidentally—the whole Rumsfeld family was flown back from the NATO installation in an Air Force plane that Gulley controlled. And—coincidentally—Rumsfeld asked Gulley not to resign, but to stay on when Rumsfeld became Chief of Staff. And—coincidentally—I've heard of several occasions when there were no airplanes available for the Secret Service. But the Chief of Staff always had an airplane when he snapped his fingers."

"How long has Gulley been doing this?"

"Well, I know he used to fly Ehrlichman's family all over the place. Haldeman's, too. Once a few of us had to take a commercial flight—at taxpayers' expense, you know—because the plane charged to the Secret Service was being used by one of Gulley's chosen few. I wasn't around during the Johnson days, but they say Marvin Watson was Gulley's first patron in the White House. Gulley started out as the sergeant in charge of the bomb shelter, you know."

"Yes, I know."

The agent shook his head and laughed again. "Well, he's done real well for himself, hasn't he? For himself and his friends."

## MARCH 23, 1976

The Gridiron Club, a fraternity of Washington journalists, holds a big bash every year. It is an evening of political songs and skits that gets a great deal of fanfare. (How could a journalists' organization *not* get fanfare?) Today I got a call from Lucien Warren, the Washington Bureau Chief of the *Buffalo Evening News.* He said that the Gridiron was planning a skit for this year's show in which they would love to involve Mrs. Ford. They had already written lyrics to "Once in Love with Amy." (Their version: "Once in Love with Betty.") He said a man would sing the song, and then begin to dance and they wanted Mrs. Ford to do a little soft shoe number. He went over the lyrics.

Politicians slay me
Always depress, dismay me
Over and over; disillusioned by them
We can't justify them—no way!

Ron and Rock and Terry
Don't ever make us merry—
Bore us with pledges, promises and hedges
Set our teeth on edges—all day

> (But) There's one who won't equivocate and waver
> Who always shoots straight,
> Who's candider and cheerfuller and braver—
> Our candidate!

(So) Start the draft for Betty
We'll all go daft for Betty;
Go tell the party we all want the dancer
She's the perfect answer—and how!
Let Betty have her equal rights right now!

> (Chorus)
> (Oh) Once in love with Betty,
> Always in love with Betty;
> Go tell the party, we all want the dancer
> She's the perfect answer—you'll see,
> And Betty can have equal rights with me.

At last, I thought, a chance to be "Betty Ford" again, and via an event that would entail a minimal effort and would guarantee a maximal effect.

I called Mrs. Ford and told her.

She laughed. I waited expectantly for her answer when she stopped, but she just started giggling again. (Was this her answer?)

"I think you should do it," I said.

"You do?"

"Yes. It is a sensational idea. In public relations terms this is a very important group you'd be performing for, showing what a good sport you are. But more important than that, this is the type of thing you *love* to do. You'll have a lot of fun."

"I'm not sure. . . . "

"Admit it. You're a ham. You'll love doing it."

"Send me the lyrics," she said.

I sent the lyrics upstairs and waited—not very long. The phone rang. She was laughing again. "I'll do it!"

*　*　*

## MARCH 24, 1976

"Well, you win some, you lose some," Mrs. Ford sighed over her tea this morning as the newspapers brought in the details of a Reagan win in yesterday's North Carolina primary. "I feel bad that I didn't campaign down there. But they really didn't want me. They said that since North Carolina's a sort of Bible belt state, they might consider Jack and me a little too wild." She chuckled, rather enjoying the idea. Then she got sad again. "If we had won, it might be all over—the primary fight. I didn't expect to lose, really. It's a big disappointment. But it isn't crucial. If we had to lose, I'm glad it was this one. I'm glad we got a string of victories under our belts first."

## MARCH 31, 1976

Today was the big rehearsal. I think we made history. Has any other First Lady ever rehearsed a soft shoe number in the hall between the East End and the West End of the second floor of the White House? The Gridiron group, which included Lucien Warren, Ernie Sult, the man who was to sing the solo "Once in Love with Betty" and dance with Mrs. Ford, and a professional dance coach from Washington named Vic Daumit, all came to the White House this morning. With a cellist, a drummer, and a pianist.

Mrs. Ford walked out wearing a pants jumpsuit. Vic took Mrs. Ford's hand. The band started to play and they just took off. What fun! They rehearsed the soft shoe, teaching her some new steps, and then, holding hands with Vic and Ernie, she lightly danced all around the hall.

After the rehearsal, Mrs. Ford brought out the dress she planned to wear, which everyone admired, and then, as she was walking away to put the dress back, she hesitated, took Vic by the hand and said, "Could you please show me how to hustle?"

Five minutes later, we all watched as Vic Daumit and Mrs. Ford did the hustle for us, up and down the West Hall of the White House.

*Chapter Eighteen*
APRIL, 1976:

# TRUCKIN' WITH FIRST MAMA

*APRIL 1, 1976*

"I have this client, Hy-Gain, who makes equipment for citizens band radios," Edward said sometime, someplace recently.

"Really!" I said, giving him my rapt-attention look. (But all the time thinking about some of the phone calls I had to return.)

"Do you know what a citizens band radio is?" he asked (calling my bluff).

"Nope, actually I don't." (The more I thought about it, the more convinced I was that I could wait until tomorrow to return the phone calls.)

"Citizens band radios are portable two-way communications units," Edward was explaining. "They have a range of about 10–15 miles, and they're the fastest-selling consumer item in electronics."

(I'm always good about returning calls. I'm entitled to a night off.)

"Truckers have been using them since the fifties," Edward continued, "alerting each other about police radar traps and road conditions. The truckers' strike a couple of years ago spurred a lot of interest in CB's."

"Mmmm."

"I thought it might be fun for us to get one. There's a whole CB language. For example, police are called 'Smokies' or 'bears.' A warning about police patrolling a radar trap is a 'bear story.' So a trucker might say to another trucker up ahead, 'Tell me a bear story about the eastbound side, good buddy.' They've got marvelous expressions for everything. A Volkswagen is a 'pregnant roller skate,' for instance. Coffee is a 'cup of mud.' Beer is 'cold coffee.' An ambulance is a 'bone box.'"

I smiled politely to humor him, still preoccupied. But even in my preoccupation, I knew that communicating in code with truckers about speed traps was an activity far removed from my present list of "wish I were theres."

Well, APRIL FOOLS!

Politics provides strange preoccupations. I got a call today from Peter Secchia, a Michigan friend of the Fords who has set up a caravan of Ford supporters from Michigan to campaign in Wisconsin. He calls the effort the "scatter blitz." The key element in their strategy is the CB radio. Pete explained that every car in the caravan is equipped with a CB and when he yells out "scatter blitz" over the airwaves, everyone will jump out of their car, scatter and blitz the area with Ford pamphlets and other paraphernalia.

He wants Mrs. Ford to do something with them—a rousing send-off for the blitzers—when we go to Wisconsin to campaign next week. Her schedule, I told him, is tight. So we compromised: Mrs. Ford will speak over Pete Secchia's citizen band radio to all the Ford volunteers. More easily said than done. In order to do this, she needs a temporary license and a speech.

So, lo and behold, Mrs. Ford found herself filling out an FCC application today for a temporary CB radio license and I found myself calling upon Edward's knowledge of "marvelous CB expressions" for Mrs. Ford's statement. In "Good Buddy" talk, "10–20" means place of residence, as in, "We appreciate your help in keeping the Fords' 10–20 at 1600 Pennsylvania Avenue!"

*APRIL 3, 1976*

The large chorus of costumed newsmen finished belting out their rousing rendition of "Once in Love with Betty" and stepped back on the stage to make way. The conductor of the U.S. Marine Band lifted his baton and waited: a dramatic pause. Then the orchestra picked up the melody and out onto the platform danced Mrs. Ford, her long flowing evening gown swirling softly behind her, her steps graceful and light, her facial expression one of sheer pleasure. It brought down the house. The President grinned from his seat on the dais. The Chief Justice of the Supreme Court beamed, as did the other Justices, the Senators and the rest of the Washington officialdom on the Gridiron celebrity list. When Mrs. Ford finished, she was presented with a bouquet of roses and the spectators jumped to their feet in applause. The First Lady had not only done a soft shoe number (a Washington "first"). She had pulled it off with a style all her own with both humor and class.

The President proved a pretty good entertainer, too. (It was quite a night for the First Family wit.) He did a comedy routine. Teasing Hubert Humphrey for his reputation as a long-winded speaker, the President pretended to get a phone call from Humphrey on the podium, and then proceeded to put down the receiver, take out his pipe, and light it, while, all the time, Humphrey was supposedly babbling on the wire. Ford's timing was good, as was his deadpan delivery. (I smell a Don Penny presentation.)

I watched from the Associated Press table. My dinner partner was Bob Johnson, the managing editor of Associated Press. His career included filing the first bulletin of the assassination of President Kennedy and directing the coverage of the assassination and the murder of Lee Harvey Oswald, the massacre of the Israeli athletes at Munich and the last days of the Nixon Administration. He painted a fascinating picture of a news organization that is literally on top of all the news. So when he referred to a specific date by saying, "There was nothing happening in the world that day," I was awed. Here was a man who could utter such a statement with the assurance that it was a literally accurate appraisal.

As interesting as the conversation was, I left early. (Tomorrow may be Sunday, but it is the Sunday Mrs. Ford and I head for Wisconsin.) Waiting at the elevator, I bumped into former Governor Jimmy Carter and his wife, Rosalynn. I introduced myself and we exchanged pleasantries. I scrutinized him curiously, searching for those special, secret, supernatural ingredients that make an unknown man into a primary winner. I could not detect the cause, only the effect. Both Carters grinned through acute fatigue. She especially looked drawn and exhausted.

*APRIL 4, 1976*

Gridiron is always held on a Saturday evening. Traditionally the next afternoon, the skits are performed for the spouses of the Gridiron members. I told Lucien Warren Mrs. Ford would be unable to make today's performance, since we had to go to Wisconsin, but suggested instead that someone could sing a "singing telegram" from Mrs. Ford, also to the tune of "Once in Love with Amy."

> Gee, I like your party
> But there's another party
> On to Wisconsin
> I must now be winging
> There's no time for singing, for me
> Today I'm dancing for the G.O.P.

I sang Mrs. Ford the lyrics on the plane this morning and she laughed—either at the lyrics or my singing or both.

Today's performance did not really call for a dance, but then I couldn't get "citizen's band radio" to fit the "Once in Love with Amy" meter.

It *was* a performance, though. And one I shall not easily forget.

The plan worked out with Pete Secchia was that he would greet Mrs. Ford when she arrived at the airport and, before boarding the motorcade, she would go with him to his car and talk to all the CB people from Michigan over his citizen's band radio. And so she did. I think. At first she had trouble understanding "push to talk" so she had to start over. But she did finally deliver the short message in CB lingo Edward had researched.

I never heard the broadcast. The visual image, however, was extraordinary. As the motorcade waited patiently, the President's wife stood outside Secchia's car, her hand clutching a CB mike, her upper torso thrust through the opened car window and her backside out at a dramatic angle.

I'm sure the CBers would have a colorful way of describing it.


*APRIL 6, 1976*

We struck oil! And quite by accident. Mrs. Ford's maiden voyage into CB land stirred up a lot of excitement. Newspapers and wire services want more and more details on Mrs. Ford's becoming a citizen's band radio enthusiast. WJVA radio in South Bend, Indiana, had a radio call-in contest for suggestions for Mrs. Ford's "handle" (official CB name). The winners were "White House Knight," "Model T Mama," and "Flip Flop Ford."

I told Mrs. Ford. She just smiled.

Then I started thinking that it might be a good idea for her to continue her "enthusiasm." Obviously, she hit a nerve. CB radio has always been a truckers' thing, a blue-collar phenomenon, an underground hobby, but now it seems as if CB is all over. Mrs. Ford has accidentally managed to tap into it. She got a CB radio to talk to a bunch of "blitzers" from Michigan and ended up addressing a large and delighted new audience. They passed the news on to the country and western music stations all over the country who are now happily declaring that this woman is one of theirs. Who are we to disappoint them, Good Buddy? Especially in a campaign year. For once, I've found a campaign technique that clicks—a perfect gesture. Through the CB radio, we may be able to get a big reaction from a small action. It is important to conserve Mrs. Ford's energy.

Her birthday is the day after tomorrow. I decided that a CB radio would be the perfect gift, and Jack the perfect donor. I convinced Edward to donate the radio, but had less luck with Jack.

"No way."

"Why not? It's a terrific way to campaign and to talk to *real people* while she travels around different states."

"I agree," Jack said. "Ask Edward if he could get one for me, too. But only on the condition that you tell no one I have it. I want it for fun, not for publicity. And I'm not going to help exploit this thing with my mother."

Determined not to give up, I called Susan.

"Susan, guess what!" I conned. "I have the *perfect* birthday present for you to give your mother and it *won't cost you anything*." (It is essential to appeal on the level of greatest vulnerability.)

"Huh?"

"It's a citizen's band radio. Edward already has a set for you to give her. If anyone asks you what your present to your mother is, just say it's a citizen's band radio because she got such a kick out of using one in Wisconsin."

"Okay."

*APRIL 8, 1976*

Happy and Nelson Rockefeller threw a surprise birthday party for Mrs. Ford tonight and Edward and I had a wonderful time.

The scene: splendor high above New York City's Fifth Avenue in an apartment that felt more like an exclusive club than a family residence, where magnificent art (a Modigliani here, a Klee mural there, a Léger fireplace, a Giacometti sculpture) formed a backdrop for a small and exclusive guest list (Mayor Beame and his wife; Pearl Bailey and her escort, E.B. Smith; Barbara Walters and John Diebold, one of New York City's most eligible bachelors; Polly Bergen and writer Peter Maas; the chairman of the board of Time Inc. Andrew Heiskell and his wife, Marion; Walter Cronkite and his wife, Betsy).

And of course, the Weidenfelds.

There was delicious food served on the most magnificent china. Abe Beame and Pearl Bailey brought in the birthday cake as Barbara Walters and Polly Bergen came to the conclusion that there were no sexy men in Washington, with the possible exception of Senator Edward Brooke. Vice President Rockefeller, even more exuberant than usual, put his hand on Edward's shoulder and said, "Isn't this fantastic, Ed? Can you imagine, only eighteen months ago the country was in the depths of despair over Watergate and now we're a happy nation, a country that's prospering again. Can you believe that in one room you have Pearl Bailey and Abe Beame singing happy birthday to the wife of the man who made it all possible? It's only in America, Ed, only in America!"


*APRIL 13, 1976*

It turned out to be quite complicated. I thought by casually telling reporters that Susan had given her mother a CB radio for her birthday ("because Mrs. Ford got such a kick out of using one in Wisconsin") we could effortlessly cash in on the CB boom. At first it seemed that way. There were published quotes from the cult. "CB people trust one another," one man explained to a reporter in the midwest, "and we figure that if Betty's got a CB, Jerry can't be that bad."

Perfect.

Grumbles from the Ronald Reagan camp indicated that obviously we were hitting a nerve.

Perfect.

The enthusiasm keeps snowballing and snowballing. The problem is I underestimated CB enthusiasm. *Boom!* The White House has been inundated with CB paraphernalia: hats, posters, bumper stickers, scarves, cards, and directories of CB "Slanguage" pour in. Citizen's band clubs all over the United States urge the First Lady to do peculiar things such as "keep your shiney side up and your dirty side down as you cruise the highway of life."

The "handle" decision has moved from country music stations into the residential quarters of the Executive Mansion. Mrs. Ford says she would like to be "Steady Betty." The President took time out from his busy schedule to recommend that she consider "Tippy Toes." I'm pushing "First Mama," an expression comedian Flip Wilson coined when he performed at the White House last year. The Secret Service is practicing up on CB radio use for our campaign trip to Texas next week (I figure if there is any place that's CB country, it's Texas) and Mrs. Ford is taking the CB equivalent of a Berlitz crash course to try to learn how to talk right. As the nation howls, "Keep on truckin', cotton picker!" poor Mrs. Ford is anxiously trying to find out how to begin.

"What's your 20?" means "Where are you?" the information sheet I gave her today states. "You're wall to wall" means "Your signal is excellent."

"Keep your britches out of ditches" means "Drive safely."

You sign off by saying something like "Threes and other good numbers," or "Nice modulating with you!"

(So *this* is what it's like to be married to the President.)

In the midst of all this happy hysteria, there is controversy as well. Earl Stevens of the *National CB Truckers News* called me today in a state of unadulterated fury. In the first place, he said, Mrs. Ford "walked all over CBers on the channels in Wisconsin."

It turned out that that meant that she had *not* begun her statement with "Breaker breaker" which is the way you're supposed to begin in CB etiquette. I explained that she had, but that since she had forgotten to press the button down, her first words had not been transmitted.

*Whew!*

Stevens accused Mrs. Ford of getting a "quickee FCC temporary license because she is married to the man who appoints FCC members." I told him that it was my understanding that such "quickee" licenses had been awarded by the FCC for years, and that the fact that Mrs. Ford's call number is 9,532 indicates that 9,531 other CBers have previously received the same sort of license.

*Whew!*

I don't know whether it was my inner sense of guilt or his inner sense of righteousness, but I was exhausted when the phone call finally ended.

## APRIL 19, 1976

Ron Nessen made his "good sport debut" on "Saturday Night Live" two nights ago, and the word is the President was not pleased. Chevy Chase, the star of "Saturday Night Live," did his usual impersonation of President Ford as a stumbler-bumbler (in the course of which, as President Ford, Chase stapled his ear to his head, tried to hit a golf ball with a tennis racquet, and attempted to stick a flower in his lapel without removing the flower from the vase first) as Ron Nessen played Ron Nessen, the real Press Secretary, thereby making it seem that there was truth to Chevy's burlesque.

To make matters worse, Ron convinced the President to appear too, which he did in scattered film clips. By willingly appearing, he seemed to be giving the show an endorsement which was not such a terrific political idea, as the show itself included several off-color jokes—low-level off-color jokes. One whole skit took place at a urinal. In another segment, a woman kept repeatedly confusing the "Presidential election" with a "Presidential erection."

To make matters even worse, when White House reporters teased him today and nagged him with reports that the President was upset, Ron-the-sense-of-humor-man got quite angry.

## APRIL 20, 1976

It was a booming beginning to four days of Texas campaigning. The San Antonio Fiesta Parade. Mrs. Ford rode on a gold-and-yellow float down the San Antonio River as thousands of people waved and cheered from the river banks on either side. She loved it. "I've never been in Texas before," she told the enthusiastic crowd at the end.

But she didn't say "I've," she said "Ahh've" and she went on to say, "Ah've met a lot of Texans in mah day, an' Ahh nevuh met a one Ahh didn't lahk."

I did a double take.

"Isn't she speaking with a Texas drawl?" I whispered to Jerry Ball, the head of Mrs. Ford's Secret Service detail, who is also a native Texan.

"It isn't a drawl," he corrected me, laughing, "it is called a 'twang' and she sure is!"

"No I am *not!*" Mrs. Ford insisted later. I called upon Jerry Ball's testimony to back me up. "Well, I really wasn't aware of it," she said. "But to tell the truth, I'm not surprised. I have a tendency to pick up accents. Always have. My mother used to be able to tell who I was hanging around with by the way I talked. She said I was like a sponge, absorbing both the accent and the lingo."

"Texas has won a place in mah haht," she told a group at her hotel this morning. Jerry and I cringed and one reporter asked whether she was "talking funny," but the Texans didn't notice a thing.


*APRIL 23, 1976*

"If it could always be like the last four days, I'd campaign forever," Mrs. Ford said when we got back to Washington tonight.

Texas was fun. Everything in that state is larger than life spectacular: the enormous ranches, the receptions, the excitement, the never-ending fanfare, and the warmth. Mrs. Ford traveled with Lou Tower, wife of Senator John Tower, a good friend and old friend and Mrs. Tower turned out to be both a political asset and a wonderful traveling companion. In Austin, Lady Bird Johnson met Mrs. Ford and took her around the LBJ Library. Appearing with Mrs. Johnson in Johnson country obviously did not hurt politically, but, again, it was a pleasure, too. Mrs. Ford really likes Mrs. Johnson. It's a friendship, she says, that goes way back.

"I give her a lot of credit for being able to live with Lyndon," Mrs. Ford said. "I was very fond of that man, but he must have been impossible to live with!"

The LBJ Library is an enormous granite structure that houses an enormous amount of memorabilia with buttons you can press to hear LBJ and other politicians talk about each exhibit. On the top floor is a replica of Johnson's Oval Office, for example. Push a button and Lyndon Johnson's voice tells you how he worked and the meaning of each piece of furniture in the room.

There are souvenirs too. Earrings, tie clasps, cufflinks, all in the shape of Lyndon's stetson hat. LBJ scarves and LBJ pencils and color prints of the LBJ ranch. For $10.00, you can buy a 1965 Inauguration program. Five dollars gets you a tape of LBJ delivering his '64 State of the Union message or a tape of LBJ's bombing-halt speech or a tape of LBJ's humor. There are busts and statuettes of several Presidents. LBJ's is $15.00. (A bargain, JFK's and FDR's cost $26.50.) For only $6.00 you can purchase a brown bottle decorated with a picture of Lyndon Baines Johnson wearing his cowboy hat.

Very Texas.

The smoothness with which we eased our way from Texas event to Texas event was due to the frenetic efforts of Patti Matson our silent, little-noticed advance person who landed in Texas one week before Mrs. Ford with a total of one scheduled event and every local politician insisting that a visit by the First Lady was a "must." Patti toured the state, searching for "events"—events with impact, with photographic interest for the press, with good political fallout. She mapped out logistics, coordinating things like driving time, airplane schedules, local press credentials and so on. She called me every day and we went over details. She slept little. These days Patti is never in Washington. As soon as one trip is completed, she is out advancing another. She has no time for any personal life, not even time to complete the little personal details of her own life. No time to wash the clothes, cut her hair, pay her bills. I don't know how she does it, but I am very grateful that she does it.

Meanwhile, back at the White House, my resourceful secretary, Fran Paris, somehow keeps the office together but at the expense of her personal life. Across the hall, Mrs. Ford's appointment secretary, Susan Porter, valiantly struggles with Mrs. Ford's calendar.

Throughout the trip, Mrs. Ford tested the handle "First Mama" and came through "wall to wall" (loud and clear). "I've got Smokies on my front porch!" she told a CBer known as Peg Leg Charlie on Channel 19 in San Antonio during one car ride. Peg Leg Charlie interpreted that as "There are police in my motorcade." (I *think* that's what she meant.)

The Secret Service wired up her CB to work out of a suitcase. Jerry Ball set it all up. Since he always rides in Mrs. Ford's car (I usually travel with the press) I put him in charge of both the mechanics and the translations. He acts as both engineer and coach and, believe me, it is a formidable task. He manages to pull it off very well, though, thanks to both his understanding of how the machine works and—most important—a sense of humor.

The press reports make Mrs. Ford's CBing sound smooth and casual. "After exchanging CB lingo and pleasantries," one account stated, "Mrs. Ford cheerfully signed off, 'Ten four, good buddy, catch you on the flip!' " (return trip).

In truth, there is much fumbling.

"How did it go?" I'd ask Jerry in a whisper as he and Mrs. Ford got out of the car at each stop. More often than not, the man would begin to say something, and then, as though finding it beyond verbal description, he would just shake his head and laugh. Heartily.

## APRIL 24, 1976

Flip Wilson's manager called. He wants me to let him know as soon as Mrs. Ford decides whether or not to make "First Mama" her official handle, and he asked me to send him some of the literature we have on CB's. Flip wants to get one.

## APRIL 27, 1976

Sunday, *Parade* Magazine did a cover story on "SHEILA WEIDENFELD, THE FIRST LADY'S PRESS SECRETARY." Tonight I discovered the rewards of fame. It was about 10 P.M. Edward and I were in bed reading, when the door bell rang. Edward asked who it was, over the intercom, and a man's voice announced we had a package. Edward asked him to just leave it outside the door, we would pick it up shortly. Later, when Edward went downstairs and opened the door, he found two policemen standing outside.

"Does Sheila Weidenfeld live here?" one asked.

"Yes," Edward answered.

"Well, then, there's no problem," the policeman said, handing Edward an envelope with my name on it.

Edward invited the policemen in. "What's going on?"

It seems they were patrolling the neighborhood and saw a man with a moustache, blue jeans, and long black coat prowling around the house. After they saw him leave the envelope on our doorstep, they stopped him and asked him his name.

His name is "Gerald Bryan Gainous, Jr," they told me, and paused significantly.

Gerald Bryan Gainous. Nope. It rang no bells.

"We checked him out," the policeman said. "Apparently he has been arrested in the past for jumping the White House fence."

Click. *"Gerald Bryan Gainous, Jr!"* The man late last fall, the one Susan didn't even see, although he landed so close to her when he scaled the fence that he really shook up the Secret Service. And now? I looked at the envelope. A bomb? No. It was only a few papers—how could it possibly explode? Even the District of Columbia policemen were losing interest. They left, suggesting casually that it might be a good idea for me to call the Secret Service.

First I read the contents, the sheets of lined paper covered with a pencil-written saga. A personal background sketch told us Gerald Bryan Gainous, Jr., had family problems. A political treatise ("The Declaration of World Democracy") told us he had mental problems.

It seemed his father, a master sergeant, was convicted in 1972 of conspiring to illegally import heroin into the United States. The conviction resulted in jail for the father, a loss of his military pension for his dependents, social disgrace, and psychological scars. His father *was* guilty. But his military record was spotless in all other respects, and Gerald Ford had, after all, forgiven Nixon. (Gainous referred to this legalistically as "the Nixon pardon precedent.") He had jumped the gate to personally explain to President Ford the obvious logic of his plea, and now, failing that, he wanted me to plead his case. I didn't have to jump the gate; I knew them all. It said so in *Parade.* (Along with my address.)

Oh—and while I was at it, could I put in a good word for his treatise on World Democracy and his candidacy as World President? He has discovered, you see, that "with the urge to aid my family, I have the desire to initiate a revolutionary political breakthrough

. . . your support . . . may one day be the insight and the political movement that prevented World War III.''

It was sad. And a little scarey.

I called the Secret Service. They told me to bring them the material tomorrow. It looks as though his messages *will* be delivered to the White House, after all.

*Chapter Nineteen*
MAY, 1976:

# TOOT TOOT!

*MAY 2, 1972*

We lost Texas. We *really* lost Texas. In yesterday's primary Ronald Reagan won all ninety-six of the Texas Republican delegates by a victory margin of about two–one.

It is a very conservative state. There were many former Wallace supporters, Democrats, who crossed over to vote for Reagan. We were prepared for a possible loss.

But not two–one.

What's more, I take it personally. Betty Ford never campaigned in North Carolina, the other Ford loss in these first nine primaries. But we campaigned in Texas. And we loved them, and they loved us. Mrs. Ford was sensational—on the podium, on the river boat, on the CB radio. It all went so *well*. Jack was described campaigning in Houston as "President Ford's hidden asset in the pivotal Texas Republican primary." ("Jack Ford has become," the *New York Times* article stated, "the most fervent and perhaps most articulate of the surrogates who ply the primary, advocating four more years in the White House for President Ford.")

Texas memories. A sour taste.

## MAY 8, 1976

Another week spent riding the primary roller coaster. The big down was the result of Tuesday's primaries: losses in Georgia, Alabama, and Indiana.

Georgia and Alabama were expected. Indiana was a surprise, and a terrible blow, because it showed that Texas was no fluke, and because it showed that Reagan is capable of winning outside the conservative South.

It also put Reagan ahead of the President in the national delegate count.

We were on our own roller coaster when the verdicts came in, and Mrs. Ford was almost too busy acting to react. This week took her from Columbus, Ohio, to Eugene, Oregon, to Sioux Falls, South Dakota, to Independence, Missouri. Up and down and all around. Ohio craftsmen presented her with handmade leather leashes for Liberty. South Dakota Shriners demonstrated their clown routines. She waded through a student crowd at the University of Oregon. She traveled in a logging truck at a sawmill. In Los Angeles, she received an even more elaborate celebration upon her arrival. This time at the Beverly Wilshire Hotel we were greeted by the melodious strains of "I Could Have Danced All Night" emanating from a pianist and two violinists playing at curbside. Mrs. Ford, only too happy to answer Hollywood by acting like Hollywood, danced her way into the hotel on the red carpet that had been laid from the curb to the hotel foyer.

There was an Ohio banquet honoring an outstanding football player, a San Francisco visit to a senior citizens center and a star-studded Hollywood fundraiser with Cary Grant as escort. I close my eyes and I see it all whirling around and around in a visual blender. We landed and took off and landed and took off and landed.

Emotions seemed to follow the up-and-down pattern of the landing gear. Exhaustion reigned. There were peaks. There were pits. Often they occurred in irrational sequences. I don't know how or why. On the plane to Sioux Falls, a pale and drawn Mrs. Ford collapsed into her seat and fumed about being overscheduled. "I can't breathe!" she moaned. "They have just jammed me with events. It never stops."

I looked at her hands. They were literally swollen from all the handshaking. I worried about her health. I worried about more specific things. Like landing. What on earth would this exhausted woman be like in Sioux Falls?

One hour later, a peppy, radiant First Lady stepped briskly into the President Ford Campaign Committee reception in Sioux Falls with a slightly mischievous look in her eyes. "Do you mind if I turn around and say hello to my husband first?" she asked the people lined up to greet her. Much to the crowd's surprise, she then glee-fully planted a loving kiss on the big poster of the President on the wall behind her.

I never know.

## MAY 10, 1976

One more marital fatality dots the campaign trail.

"She couldn't take it anymore," he told me over breakfast this morning. "So we have separated. Just separated." A nervous laugh. "Who has time to get a divorce, anyway?"

It was bad enough before the campaign, he explained. Last year, he was coming home at about 10:00 P.M. and returning to work ear-ly the next morning. But once the primaries started, he was literally never home. So now he has no home. It isn't really that big a differ-ence. Another nervous laugh.

It was all familiar. Too familiar. Edward is a combination of an-gry and frustrated the week before I leave on a trip, and then again for the week after I come back. Since I'm traveling practically ev-ery other week, our life together is made up of either discord or absence.

And my life alone? Campaigning is a way of life removed from living. Little sleep. Grab-a-bite fast-food. We are all nomads ob-sessed with a cause. There is little personal involvement among the workers. Very little, because fatigue causes friction, because we are all so one dimensional that when we talk it is usually about the last stop.

There are many one-night stands, however. Stewardesses and local political groupies provide an eager outlet for men who want to forget the campaign for a minute without having to remember the relationship that is rapidly evaporating at home, or for men who want some ego gratification after long days of burying themselves in another man's ego. Jack's Secret Service detail tallies conquests out loud at the breakfast table each morning, but most tryst quietly, and the next day move on to the next stop. No one looks. No one cares. Indeed, the only man I know who has been teased for his exploits is one who, in his self-consciousness, introduced each new girl as his "cousin." When we arrived at a Holiday Inn recently, the marquee read "WELCOME MR. X AND YOUR COUSIN, BARBARA!"

Divorce is an occupational hazard. Separation a regular move from a physical fact to a legal one. I felt sorry for this newly separated man, sipping his coffee across the table from me. I felt sorry for his wife.

But more than anything else, I felt scared.

## MAY 14, 1976

Tuesday brought our fifth primary defeat in eleven days. "We are at peace," Ford stressed in speeches in Nebraska last week. "The economy is on the upturn and the country is emerging from a decade of scandal and war that cast a shadow over the Presidency itself." The President asked for a "new mandate" to pursue the policies of the last two years. But faced with a choice of "more of the same" or "better, better, better" the voters in Nebraska went for "better." Reagan won Nebraska 51 percent to 49 percent. We won West Virginia, but the Nebraska results put one more notch in Reagan's belt and intensified the panic. All eyes are now fixed on the state of Michigan. The primary there is next week, and the feeling here is that if the President can't carry his home state, it is all over.

The Fords go to Flint tomorrow for a whistlestop train trip. Jack left for Detroit today and I went with him. We walked through the Detroit airport anonymously. No press, no autograph hunters. It was quite different from traveling with his mother.

Our first stop: a television station where he was scheduled to appear on a talk show. "Rosalynn Carter went on right after me," he told me later. "When we were introduced in the studio, I tried to be friendly, you know, make small talk. She didn't. That's one cold lady."

From the station, we went downtown where Jack had been

scheduled to "hand out leaflets in a crowded square." But when we arrived, the crowd had left, leaving only the square and a few winos. Jack approached one and asked him whether he was voting for his father.

He nodded.

He asked him if he'd like some literature.

He nodded.

When we left the square, the man was sitting there in a stupor, with an empty pint of booze in one hand and "FORD FOR PRESIDENT" literature in the other—still nodding.

We moved on to a cafeteria.

"I'm Jack Ford and I'm working to re-elect my father. Can we count on your support?" The white teeth, the beige three-piece suit, the smile—a winning combination. And he knows it. And he hates it. ("What I do," he explained to me on the plane, "is I just pause, take a deep breath, and plunge in.")

The real con is reserved for pretty girls. They get a wistful look from the depths of his blue eyes and a "wish-I-had-time" sigh. "Your hand feels cold," he says as he fills it with Ford campaign literature. Over and over and over again.

It works. Ladies argue in whispers whether he looks like "his mom" or "his dad." Men seem impressed by the solid handshake. Girls melt. He pulls it off with charm, confidence, and amazing stamina. The grin seems real, the words a new idea each time.

In truth though, "I'm Jack Ford" has very little in common with Jack Ford. As soon as he gets out of public view he shrivels up. The taut face relaxes, grins become grimaces. The handsome athletic body slouches a little. The self-confidence seems to disappear. He becomes "Why-am-I-doing-this-crazy-thing-that-freaks-me-out" all over again. A little shy. A little scared. Slow to warm up to a reporter.

"It isn't my personality to be campaigning like this," he told Cameron Crowe of *Rolling Stone* as he nervously fiddled with his cheeseburger this afternoon. "But Susan thinks politics are boring. All Mike wants to do is graduate from divinity school and preach the gospel. Steven spends most of his time ranching and going to school. So that leaves me."

I envy him. Jack at least has found the answer. He knows what has to be done and he does it. Once it has been accomplished, he retreats back to himself.

The rest of us on this campaign are not so sure. As far as I am concerned, I am participating in someone else's show. I am no longer the producer. I don't like the production, and I am dying to play with the script a little. But it is too close to air time to begin experimenting. And I am the first to admit I am no political expert.

That's why I expect everyone else to be. But I'm confused. There is no theme to this campaign and there is just one goal: winning. I don't understand how you convince people to vote for you by running all over the country telling people you'll be a good President, especially when you already *are* President.

And where does Mrs. Ford fit in? She wonders, too. It is a difficult time for her. She's always had absolute confidence in the President. Still, she sees the polls. She sees the primary results. She reads the editorials. She does not want to lose. She knows her husband has been a good President, worthy of election. She has become accustomed to White House living, delighted and surprised by the influence a First Lady can have. But she still has mixed feelings about winning, I think. She talks longingly about "moving back to Alexandria" every so often. She never will. Win or lose, she has outgrown Alexandria. But I know what she means. Alexandria represents a way of life she misses.


## MAY 15, 1976

A jazz band plays up and down the aisles as pretty young girls march around with satin banners across their chests reading "FORD!" Michigan politicos romp, eating, drinking, dancing in the aisles. The guests have fun. The press has fun. I have fun, too. One big fraternity party.

Maybe a whistlestop tour is the way to win an election.

TOOT TOOT!

All aboard! Flint, Marshall, Jackson, Concord, Ann Arbor, Grand Rapids . . .

*How do you feel about the campaign, Mrs. Ford?*

"Very positive. There's no question we're going all the way to Kansas City and then all the way to win in November. I do not feel the least bit let down."

*Are you happy to be back in Michigan?*

"I'm very proud of Michigan. I brag about it every chance I get. I'm always telling people and foreign visitors about Michigan."

*How do you manage to look so chic in today's damp weather?*

"I used an awful lot of hairspray."

TOOT TOOT!

The train's loudspeaker system is plugged into the press room to enable the reporters to hear the President's remarks at each stop. But we can't turn it off. So everything that goes on on the Presidential platform is boomed in. "Hello there!" "Hi." "Howdy." "How are you?" over and over again. Just like Jack's Park Service retakes.

In Grand Rapids, Susan and Jack join their folks. Susan climbs on board and the President says "Hello. How are you?" shaking Susan's hand with charm and enthusiasm. Then, the realization. This is his daughter. "Oh, it's *you*, Susan," he says with an embarrassed laugh.

TOOT TOOT!


## MAY 24, 1976

This week's ride on the primary roller coaster is up up up! We won two solid votes of confidence from the states of Michigan and Maryland and we have thus "stemmed the tide" as they say in the campaign business. (How *many* times will they say it?)

The manic nature of the primary results has created some rumblings around the White House. The general consensus is that it is not "our" fault, it is "their" fault, but who "they" are depends on who "we" are.

There are undoubtedly many different factions, but the most obvious "they" and "we" teams are divided by age. On one side are the Ford Oldies—the President's cronies from his congressional days, the Grand Rapids gang, and the traditional Republican Party biggies at the President Ford Committee.

The young ones are sometimes called "Cheney's gang" after their leader, Dick Cheney, Rumsfeld's protégé and replacement as the President's Staff Director. A low-key, hard-working man in his mid-thirties, Dick Cheney lacks Rumsfeld's ego and drive for personal power. He shuns publicity, preferring the image of "worker" to "celebrity." As a result, he is more likeable than Rumsfeld, but also less awesome, less frightening to criticize. His "Gang" includes Jim Connor; two lawyers, Dave Gergen and Mike Duval; and Harvard business school graduate Jerry Jones. All are in their mid-thirties.

The. oldies think the young ones are politically naive. ("Jerry didn't have this trouble in the old days.") The young ones think it is time to get rid of deadwood and smalltime politicking ("Jerry didn't run for President in the old days.").

Whither stands the President? That's anybody's guess.

All I want to know is who is writing those awful speeches and putting together his calendar. When Jerry Jones, one of Cheney's deputies and the President's chief scheduler, came in the Mess today, I asked him point blank.

"Why, Jerry?" I persisted. "Why doesn't anyone give him anything substantive to say? Why is it that his schedule makes no sense?"

"This really isn't the place to talk about it, Sheila," Jerry said. "But every morning at 9:30 we meet in the Roosevelt Room and go over ideas. Why don't you come tomorrow?"

An invitation to the prom!


*MAY 25, 1976*

I was shocked by how large the group was. About twelve people sat at the long conference table in the center of the Roosevelt Room, and another ten or so sat on the sofas on the side. I recognized faces from the Domestic Council, the Council on Economic Policy, the National Security Council, the speechwriters staff, the President's scheduling office, Dick Cheney's office, and so on. There were many faces I did not recognize. Who was on which side?

Dave Gergen and Jerry Jones were co-chairing the meeting. Jerry introduced me and I sat down in an empty chair at the conference table, intimidated, somewhat, by this brush with the big shots.

They began talking about scheduling problems. There was a conflict: it was important that the President attend the graduation ceremonies at Annapolis, but King Juan Carlos of Spain was due to arrive the same morning. What should they do?

The great men pondered. There were creative suggestions. ("Ask the King to arrive later.") And a lot of nodding.

I wondered what made the Annapolis graduation important enough to interfere with the first visit of a new king. I waited for someone else to ask. Nobody did. Maybe everyone knew. I felt the awkwardness of someone coming in in the middle of a conversation. Obviously, I had missed something.

I turned to Bill Nicholson, the Director of Scheduling, who was sitting next to me.

"Why is it so important that the President go to Annapolis?" I whispered.

"I don't know," he answered.

Don't know? Intimidation be damned.

"Dave, why is it so important that the President go to Annapolis for graduation?" I asked out loud.

Everyone looked at me. I wondered why I have such trouble keeping my mouth shut, and I knew they wondered, too.

"Annapolis is the perfect place for a major Presidential address," he said.

Everyone nodded. Of course. I nodded too. But then I felt my mouth opening again.

"About what?" I asked.

"About . . . er . . . defense, probably," he said. "The speech hasn't been written yet."

"Does the President have anything specific on his mind he wants to say about defense?" I asked. Fury overcomes fear. One more empty speech—this one actually usurping an important state visit. One more empty speech! "If he's going to speak at Annapolis, I'd want to hear him say something that's relevant. Don't you think it makes sense to know what he has to say before you alter his schedule?"

Everyone nodded.

After the meeting, Dave Gergen—to my surprise—thanked me for raising the question.

I wondered why they hadn't.

But for once, I kept my mouth shut.

* * *

## MAY 27, 1976

The "Peace, prosperity, and trust-in-the-Presidency" theme did well for us this week. President Ford emerged victorious from primaries in Kentucky, Tennessee, and Oregon. The results, the papers are all saying, "re-establish him as the favorite to win the Republican nomination at the convention in Kansas City in August."

Jack was so delighted he let the CBS sound and camera crew follow him around all day in California. "They gave me a wireless mike to wear and I forgot I had it on," he told me. "I'm standing there in the men's room and I look down and see this microphone. Really freaked me."

They have decided to skip the Annapolis graduation address. It seems the speech "wasn't that great."

And Edward got a little care package of CB paraphernalia from the White House: a CB badge, a CB scarf, a CB visor, and a CB dictionary—gifts "First Mama" thought her Good Buddy the "Legal Eagle" might like.

*Chapter Twenty*
   JUNE, 1976:

# A DEATH IN THE WORKHOUSE

*JUNE 1, 1976*

The *National Enquirer* has managed to conduct the only no-win political poll of the 1976 campaign. In a display consistent with the paper's brand of political savvy, it asked its readers the question the whole world is asking: "Who would make a better President, Gerald Ford or his wife Betty?"

Hmmm (you can imagine the millions of readers thinking). Another *Enquirer* toughy!

They feared "the race might have a close, down-to-the-wire finish" but, lo, "the amazing result" emerged: "a clear victory for his wife, 54 percent–46 percent."

*JUNE 4, 1976*

It began badly. We took off right after the King and Queen of Spain left, thereby beginning a new campaign swing (six stops in five days) before Mrs. Ford had a chance to breathe after all the state social functions.

It got worse. At a reception at the Claremont Hotel in Oakland tonight she looked exhausted and sounded as though she were having trouble concentrating. She made a few faux pas, but seemed to recover pretty well. She referred to herself as "President" at one point, but then laughed the mistake off by saying, "Actually, you know, I was President of the Senate wives when my husband was only Vice President. I used to kid him about that all the time!"

She also talked about fate a lot. And God. "Fate brings about many unusual happenings," she said at one point. "It's all in God's hands," she said at another.

Exhaustion?

"You saw her, what did you think?" I asked Jerry Ball later as we each sipped an enormous margarita at a Mexican restaurant. Jerry is one of the few people with whom I feel comfortable discussing Mrs. Ford. I know he is crazy about her. I know he has a tremendous respect for her and that he gets a big kick out of some of her antics, too. But in addition, unlike some of his cohorts in the Secret Service, he is very reserved. Discreet. A gentleman.

"I think she's being overscheduled," he said. "You can only push a human being so far, especially a delicate lady like Mrs. Ford. They're overpushing."

The conversation made me a little nervous. "You know, I forgot to bring my radio," I told him. (When we travel without the President, the beepers don't work and so I usually carry a two-way radio with me.)

"Don't worry," Jerry said. "If Mrs. Ford wants you, they'll be able to find you through me."

Over a huge Mexican dinner, we commiserated about the rigors of travel on the drones (us) as well as the celebrities. We talked about how his wife and my husband were both quite upset these days, and about how they were probably right.

"The Fords never sit still. They are always moving," Jerry said. "You know, Nixon at least knew how to stay put. Especially at the end, when he was hiding from everyone. We spent many weeks in San Clemente that were pure vacation—for the press, for the Secret Service, for the staff. The reporters couldn't get close to the man, so they gave up and played tennis and went swimming. Even Nixon's photographers couldn't get near him. We all had a wonderful time."

"But, in the meantime, the country was falling apart," I reminded him.

"Well, yes, I suppose so." We laughed at the thought of such "good old days."

We were finishing our meal when he got a signal saying he had a call. He excused himself, but returned shortly.

"It was Mrs. Ford. She wants you to call her."

I wanted privacy but the only available phone was a public one. I had to make an extra effort to hear Mrs. Ford over the noise in the restaurant. She was crying.

"How could I *do* that? I just can't get over it. All those stupid mistakes!" she sobbed. "I'll never talk like that again. I will never open my mouth without a complete text of prepared remarks in front of me. I keep thinking of all the things I said wrong. I'm so embarrassed!"

She was hysterical. I tried to sound calm.

"Hey, look. You know me well enough to know that I would be the *first* person to tell you if I thought you had messed up. You were fine. They were little errors and you covered them beautifully . . . with both grace and a sense of humor."

We went back and forth and back and forth for a good thirty minutes. She moaned and groaned. I recited examples of times in the past I had been critical of her performances, and repeated that this was not one. And I meant it.

It was a very noisy restaurant.

"Listen, I'm going to come back to the hotel—"

"No," she insisted. "You stay there and enjoy yourself. I really feel better now."

"She told me not to come back," I told Jerry.

"I think I should take you back," he said. We left.

And I'm glad we did.

When we got back to the hotel, she was sobbing all over again. I tried every tactic. I soothed. I teased. I gave "shape up" lectures. I made her a bet that none of tomorrow's news stories will even mention the slips she is so upset about. Something seemed to work. She calmed down.

The fact is, I was not just trying to make her feel good. She had not done anything worthy of such hysterics.

Then *why* the hysterics? It is the mystery of it all that scares me.

Is it something else? A physical problem or an emotional problem I know nothing about? Do I want to know? Where do you draw the line between concerned friend and Press Secretary.

What can I do? What should I do? I shudder to think what tomorrow will be like.


JUNE 5, 1976

When I walked into the suite, she was in the bedroom crying.

"I didn't get a newspaper," she said. "What are you trying to keep from me?"

"Nothing," I assured her. "They haven't come yet."

I went out and brought back a copy. I was right. There was absolutely no mention of what had concerned her. Relief. But short lived. Within a few minutes, she was sobbing again, this time in the bathroom. I was completely baffled.

"You know something," I told her, "yesterday's remarks can't be the real cause of this. It has to be something else."

"Yes," she sobbed, "it *is* something else."

"What is it?"

"Don't ask," she moaned. "Don't ask." She spoke so fervently that I didn't ask.

I spent the rest of the day asking myself, though. And worrying.

From the bedroom hysterics she went to a press conference which she handled with pep and style. Another high after a low.

"Why isn't the President campaigning?" a reporter asked.

"He's busy running the country," she said smiling sweetly. "Reagan, you see, doesn't have a job."

Two other events, also taken in stride, and we returned to the plane. And Mrs. Ford came crashing down. She sank into her seat and closed her eyes. We were on our way to a big fish-fry and an expected crowd of 15,000. After that, a reception.

"I can't do the fish-fry," she murmured. "I can't do it." I tried to talk to her. She wouldn't look at me. She slept for the rest of the plane trip and then for an additional hour.

At the reception she rambled incoherently. I worried more. I couldn't wait to get her to the hotel.

We stayed at the Beverly Wilshire, and they greeted Mrs. Ford with yet another *rousing* First Lady Welcome (of all times). As children, dressed in costumes from the early California period, danced to the music of a large mariachi band and thousands of rose petals fell from above, a pale and fragile-looking Mrs. Ford walked slowly, tensely up the red carpet and into the hotel lobby.

I was relieved when she made it.

## JUNE 6, 1976

As a talk show producer, I was always pursued by psychics. I had whole files filled with names and addresses of those who had volunteered to come on the show, who had been recommended to appear on the show, or who had just offered unsolicited advice based on the stars, cards, handwriting, telepathy, whatever. Whenever my name was in the newspaper, I seemed to receive unasked-for advice.

I had mixed feelings. I am both rational and superstitious. I am cynical and curious. I read each piece of unsolicited psychic advice with skeptical amusement, but I read each piece of unsolicited psychic advice thoroughly.

A California friend of mine, when she heard about this trip, told me that while I was in Los Angeles, I just *had* to meet a friend of hers, a tarot card reader (a psychic who uses cards). My friend set up the appointment for this morning at ten o'clock. When I protested that I couldn't get out, she told me not to worry, the woman would make a "housecall."

Oh well, when in California, I figured, do the California thing.

"This isn't a good set-up," said Patti McLaine, the pretty red-haired tarot reader as she perused my hotel room at 10:00 A.M. sharp, "but it will have to do." She selected the bed as the place to lay out the cards. I sat at the foot of the bed. She sat across from me.

Tarot cards are like ordinary playing cards, but with different symbols and to those who understand the "inner meaning" of the symbols, the cards reveal a prophecy.

She told me to shuffle the cards in three different piles and then put them together.

Those simple instructions were interrupted by three phone calls. ("No," I told the reporters in each case, "Mrs. Ford will not be available for questions before the dedication, but you will probably be able to talk to her after the ceremony.'') Patti McLaine began to realize that this environment was a little different from the tranquil setting she was used to. (I did not even want to think about what the reaction would have been had the reporters known they were interrupting a reading.) I was suddenly overwhelmed by anxiety. I mean why was I *doing* this, I wondered as I obediently shuffled the cards. I felt nervous and fidgety and afraid and confused as to why I felt nervous and fidgety and afraid.

She told me I was the slowest shuffler she had even seen.

She laid the cards out one by one and went over their meaning. "Within a year a friend of yours will have a baby. A very dear friend. A friend who is like a sister. She is either pregnant now or will be soon. It will be a boy. A healthy boy.''

Good news for my friend, whoever she is.

One hour and a dozen phone interruptions later she had told me that Edward and I had a "Karmic marriage," and uncovered all kinds of details about me, my friends, my family—some of which seemed to be right on target, which cynic-me told believer-me was just luck.

Believer-me listened with rapt attention. "Career changes. . . . You will be leaving. There will be a new start in your life in February. No, earlier . . . January, maybe even December.''

Well, I had been planning on leaving no matter what the outcome of the election. Still . . . . "Will Ford lose the election?'' I asked her.

"I have no idea,'' she said. "But there is more. I see a death . . . a death in the workhouse.''

Workhouse? Meaning what? Place of work? Work-related? Office? What? What! My hands turned to ice. I heard Mrs. Ford sobbing "Yes, there *is* something else!'' Chills. I kept my mouth shut. Tight shut. No questions. No embellishment—PLEASE!

The believer was terrified. The cynic was determined not to give credence to such a ridiculous statement by seeking elaboration.

As Patti McLaine left, she told me that she would never come again to my hotel room for a reading. The phone breaks her train of thought.

Suppressing my train of thought, I watched Mrs. Ford slur some words in her speech as she dedicated the Cedar Sinai Hospital this afternoon. I wondered when the press would begin to notice. No one has said anything about it to me.

Tonight, thanks to a surrealistic evening as only movieland can provide, I forgot everything. So did Mrs. Ford.

Though I appreciate his talent, I have worked hard at avoiding Sammy Davis, Jr. and at insisting that the Fords avoid him, too. He took advantage of the Nixon Administration and they took advantage of him. You can argue about who took the *most* advantage, but you can't argue about the fact that, one way or another, Sammy Davis, Jr. became identified with Nixon. Since I think the Nixon pardon has hurt Ford and continues to hurt Ford each time it comes up, I have avoided all symbols that consciously or unconsciously reinforce a Nixon-Ford relationship in people's minds. Sammy Davis, I've felt, is such a symbol. His public relations man has been trying to get him to play the White House, and I have been trying to keep him out. Tonight he wanted to throw a dinner party for Mrs. Ford, and, because she was so enthusiastic I gave in. My final acceptance was more an indication of concern about her emotional state than a reversal in attitude. I took pains to make sure there was no publicity surrounding the event.

It was, as Sammy Davis would put it, "Just some dear, wonderful, old friends, Liza and Jack, Lee and Farrah, Angie, Johnny, Marlo."

If you're one of the gang, you just nod. If you're from the East Coast, you quickly add last names: "Minelli and Haley, Majors and Fawcett-Majors, Dickinson, Carson, Thomas."

The regional differences showed all night. To the celebrities, Mrs. Ford was the star: Sammy and his wife Altovise met her at her car with an enormous bouquet of roses, and ushered her past a large wooden sign at the door (WELCOME FIRST MAMA! WITH LOVE, ALTOVISE AND SAMMY) into the lavish home. At a sunken bar in the living room, Mrs. Ford relaxed and talked with Liza Minelli and Marlo Thomas who seemed enchanted by her every word. All of the guests were like that, responsive and fascinated by everything she said. This was her night, it was a meal fit for a king (a choice of entrée: Maine lobster or Greek chicken) but definitely made for a queen.

The queen brought her guards, however, and they knew who the *real* stars were. And there was only one fair Hollywood maiden worthy of the White House glass slipper. By the end of the evening she was worthy of a "Good Sport Award," too, for Farrah Fawcett-Majors had cheerfully submitted to individual photographs with each member of the Secret Service and White House advance team. The pose was their choice. Some mugged. Some hugged. Some of the men looked as though they couldn't shake the knowledge that their wives would see the picture.

There was a lot of gossip, but it was more materialistic than scandalous (*alas*). A lot of it was about wealth and real estate (perhaps because the Davis home epitomized both). Who has money. . . . Who doesn't. Who lives where and what kind of neighborhood "where" is. There were more interesting offshoots: who is successful. Who is having the most trouble dealing with his/her success. But they talked "West Coast" and I spent most of the evening trying to translate . . . mentally searching the correct last name to go with the first one that had been dropped.

"Peter is having a lot of trouble," they would say, and as the conversation moved into more interesting specifics, I was left translating. (Falk? Fonda? Sellers? Ustinov? Graves? O'Toole?)

"Not *James*!" (Gardner? Mason? Arness?)

"Well, George *would*!" (Raft? Burns? Maharis? Harrison? Carlin? Hamilton?)

The biggest first name dropper was our host, but then Sammy Davis does everything in a big way. His energy level must set some sort of record. He never stops. Up. Down. Jump. Laugh. A hug. A kiss. A quick jitterbug with Mrs. Ford. Jive talk with the waiter. The movement is constant.

He gave us a tour of the house, demonstrating, for example, how you can lie down in bed and, through remote control, switch around each of the three television sets that are built in, just below the ceiling, with the tilt that makes in-bed watching easy. It is an unbelievable home styled in if-you've-got-it, flaunt-it decor. Pictures of celebrities splatter the walls (everyone who is anyone seems to have paused for at least a moment in his busy career to put his arms around Sammy Davis) as do mod posters and modern paintings. A sunken horseshoe-shaped sofa in the living room sits in front of an elaborate mural, which folds to reveal a full screen for movie watching.

A round shower enveloped in plexiglass shares a gigantic bathroom with a sunken bathtub. Large rooms hold the collections. The gun collection, for example, includes all the guns he ever used in movies. The tape collection includes reels of every movie and television show he ever did. But the biggest and best of all is the

clothes collection. Davis' closet bears a close resemblance to a du-
plex boutique for men, sports jackets arranged according to color
take up one long rack. There are whole shelves of hats, bins of
sweaters, and plexiglass display cases filled with pairs of sun-
glasses.

It was a larger-than-life place, but a surprisingly warm and comfortable evening, much laughter, much kissing (they're very affec-
tionate in Hollywood). After a day of pressing the flesh, it was nice
to hug the flesh a little.

It wasn't until I got back to my hotel room that I remembered the
tarot cards. A cloud passed by, but the more recent vision of a
sparkling Mrs. Ford at the party made it pass quickly. Ridiculous.

I called Edward (Brooke? Kennedy?) and told him we had a
"Karmic marriage." We laughed.


*JUNE 7, 1976*

Mrs. Ford slurred again at the question-and-answer session just
before she was to attend graduation exercises at Grand Rapids
Central High School, her alma mater. The slurring bothered me.
Then I heard her refer to her husband's opposition as "President
Reagan" and I almost died. I wondered what I would say when the
press asked me "why?" I was shocked when they did not say a
word about it. Are they being polite? Is cancer fair game, a legitimate news scoop, whereas other problems are considered in poor
taste? Have they created a Betty Ford image they like too much to
tarnish? I was relieved by their reticence, but I was very confused
by it.

I knew I couldn't be polite with Mrs. Ford.

"You know you called Reagan 'President Reagan,' " I told her.

"I did not."

"Yes," I said smiling, "you did. But no one seemed to notice."

"No, Sheila, this time you're wrong. I wouldn't do something
like that," Mrs. Ford insisted. "I'll tell you what I *did* do, though,"
she said, revving up for a laugh. "There were two last names that
were exactly the same at the graduation ceremonies. And so when
the two kids came up to receive the diplomas, I said, trying to make
conversation, 'Oh, are you two related?' " Mrs. Ford burst into
giggles. "Then I looked at them again and realized one was white

and one was black. You should have seen the looks they gave me!''

She tossed her head back and laughed again. Another swing. She was up again. She seemed to be feeling good. Unusually good.

"There were some other names that were the same," she was saying, "but I said to myself, 'No, I won't do *that* again.' ''

I decided to forget the Reagan faux pas. This mood called for a celebration.

"Pete," I asked the advance man, "is there someplace around here we could all go?''

"The Back Door," he suggested. "The bar downstairs in the basement of the hotel.''

"Oh, that's a good spot!'' Mrs. Ford said. We were staying at the Pantlind Hotel, the place Gerald Ford—Congressman Gerald Ford—always stayed when he was in town. It was a little dilapidated but Mrs. Ford would not hear of staying any place else. "It's an old-fashioned bar with singing," she said. "That would be fun.''

So we all went—Mrs. Ford, Pete Sorum, Patti Matson, Carolyn Porembka, Mrs. Ford's secretary—to the Back Door where everyone wears funny hats and sings along with the piano.

*Oh I met my little bright-eyed doll, way down, down by the river side . . .''*

We drank beer, ate peanuts, and sang our heads off. It was so loud and noisy that we couldn't tell who was singing off key and who wasn't, but it was a night for singing off key anyhow, a night to just let loose. Sing therapy. And the alumna of Grand Rapids Central High School, class of '36, had a ball.

*Heart of my heart, brings back those memories . . .*


### JUNE 8, 1976

"Dr. Lukash, is Mrs. Ford all right?''

I had seen him go into Bill Gulley's office for one of his regular chats and had purposely waited around for him to come out.

"What do you mean?'' Dr. Lukash asked.

"We had a terrible trip to California. She was in very bad shape. I've never seen her so depressed. I think it's the pressure. She just can't take it.''

"Well, she's all right now," he began calmly.

"I know, she snapped out of it," I said, "but I'm worried. Did you talk to the nurse who went along? Did you hear what happened?" I asked him.

"Of course. Really, Sheila, there is nothing to worry about."

"How can you say that? Her schedule has to be eased up," I said. "It's too much pressure on her, unnecessary pressure."

"We'll see," he mumbled. It was a dismissal. Obviously he could not have understood how bad the last few days had been.

"It wasn't a good trip, Dr. Lukash," I said, my eyes looking directly into his to insure transmission of message. "The pills she is taking are having a very bad effect on her."

"The pills are for her pinched nerve and arthritis," he said.

"Just for that?" I pushed.

"Just for that," he said.

I am right back where I started. I had hoped to make an ally of Dr. Lukash. I had hoped that perhaps he would either get her off medication or, better yet, get her to give up the campaign schedule that creates the pressure that stiffens the neck which, in turn, makes her turn to medication. It is a vicious circle.

And the medication is a very vicious cure.

He knows. He knows I know. Why doesn't he level with me? Is it a doctor-patient confidence that he doesn't want to break? Or does he think that if I have the "official medical word" (Valium? Daily Valium?) I will have to tell it to the press.

I'm getting more and more sympathetic with the press on the medical issue. I keep thinking about all the rumors about Nixon. White House reporters insisted he was heavily drugged ("medicated") at the end, and that that explained some of his erratic behavior. But they couldn't prove it. And no one helped them. How do you ever know? A doctor-patient confidence is one thing. Should pills dispensed from the White House medicine cabinet be public knowledge?


*JUNE 10, 1976*

I was home, on the phone, talking to my friend Cathy Sulzberger. My close friend. My dear friend. Like a sister to me.

"Cathy," I suddenly asked, "are you pregnant?"

"No."

"Well, you will be soon."

"Huh?"

"You are going to have a baby within the year. And it will be a boy. And it will be healthy."


## JUNE 12, 1976

The good news is that the primaries are over. The bad news is that the delegate fight isn't. Ford leads Reagan, but neither has enough to guarantee a first ballot victory. Eleven states haven't chosen delegates yet. These are the states that choose delegates at state conventions rather than primaries.

The primaries are over, but the bad taste lingers. No one expected the President to have to fight so hard. No one expected Reagan to do so well. No one expected Missouri (the first of the states to hold its delegate selection convention) to give Reagan eighteen delegate votes to Ford's one. That is what Missouri did today, and, as a result, the fighting has become internal. It is finger-pointing time at the White House.

"The decision-making process is solid," Jim Connor told Edward and me over lunch. "The President has a very strong group of advisors and the quality of analysis and advice on each policy proposal is very good. What stinks is the public translation of that policy."

"Yeah, but my father won't get rid of Bob Hartmann," Jack says. "Frankly, I think they bungled the firings last November so badly that he's afraid to try to get rid of anyone now. But Bob has been with my Dad for twenty-five years. He was a good operator on the Hill. He was indispensable when Dad became Minority Leader and suddenly needed an incredible number of speeches. Bob can write very quickly. They've been through a lot together, and my father is a very loyal man. Loyal and stubborn."

"If you ask me, his big problem isn't his speaking; it's his loyalty," Mrs. Ford said. "He's digging his own grave. They're giving him lousy speeches. Hartmann is head of his speech department. He should kick Bob upstairs and bring in a real professional, a guy who can produce good speeches. And overscheduling," she went on. "He does too much. I can't get him to take a break. And I had no *idea* how much Ron Nessen is hated by the press," she said. "I mean, how can the press possibly like the person if they don't like his Press Secretary?''

It sounded as though she had composed a list. She had. She was on her way to Camp David, she said, and she planned on discussing her thoughts with the President.

"I'm just worried about how to do it," she said. "He's losing confidence in himself. I'd like to build him up, not undermine his confidence."

I told her I thought the best thing the President could do was to choose one issue that was important to him, something that he could accomplish in the remaining six months of this term, and direct all his energies toward accomplishing it. With that kind of drive, he would not only get something important done, but in the process, he would also win back some of the popularity he had lost. He would become "Presidential." The best politics is good government. I am convinced that is the best way to campaign.

She liked that idea. She added it to her Camp David agenda.


## JUNE 13, 1976

"The opportunity to talk never came up," Mrs. Ford told me tonight when she returned from Camp David. She sounded hurt.


## JUNE 18, 1976

It was fried chicken and cole slaw served on long picnic tables covered with colored paper. The people sat on folding chairs. The overall ambience: tacky. In the parlance of Presidential politics, this is the pits—the part few who campaign Presidentially ever have to see. I mean, who campaigns for the White House via the State Senate?

This year, the two top Republican contenders do. This is delegate-hunting season, and the hunt has spread to the grassroots.

It feels like Iowa. It *is* Iowa. The Republican biggies have come here to duel for the hand of thirty-six delegates over a fried chicken dinner. On the left, at the round table with the colored table cloth and the folding chairs, sits Ronald Reagan and his wife Nancy. On the right, at an identical table sits Mrs. Betty Ford. The President would have been here himself. Indeed, only a crisis in the massive evacuation of Americans from Beirut kept him away.

"I read the newpaper," Mrs. Ford told me this morning in New York City, where we stayed last night after a big Republican fund-raiser, "and when I saw how bad things were in Lebanon, I called my husband and said, 'Is there anything I can do?' He said, 'You can stand in for me in Iowa.' And I said, 'Okay.' And so, Sheila, we're going to Iowa."

(I think I might have preferred Lebanon.)

So here we are in convention hall, Des Moines, face to face, fist to fist, drumstick to drumstick—running for President.


## JUNE 22, 1976

It was a very big affair: 3,200 people attending a Jewish National Fund of America, $150-a-plate dinner at the New York Hilton. The dinner was the first step in a campaign to raise $6 million for an American Bicentennial Park to be built in Israel twenty-five miles outside of Jerusalem. Mrs. Ford was there because of the bicentennial theme, and also because of personal ties to some of the officials. Milton Hoffman, a shortish man in his sixties with a mustache, a fortune made in the frozen kosher food business, and an active involvement in many Jewish organizations, is a friend of the Fords. He has been for some eighteen years. I don't know how the friendship started, but Milton Hoffman credits the President with giving him the will to live in 1972 when he was in a plane crash that killed his wife and the other people aboard, and left him in critical condition. He was lying in the hospital, having undergone several operations, he says, when Gerald Ford called him and somehow the phone call changed his outlook and gave him new strength. He has been close to the Fords ever since.

Through Hoffman, the Fords have met several Jewish leaders, including Dr. Maurice Sage, the director of the Jewish National Fund of America.

There were 300 clergy and laymen of all faiths on the dais. Mrs. Ford was at the center, right next to the speakers platform; Dr. Sage presented her with a silver Bible, a symbol of good luck. She returned to her seat (she was scheduled to speak later in the program). Sage stepped back to make room for a different speaker.

At that moment, Dr. Sage clutched his chest and collapsed. A heart attack.

There was scrambling on the dais. Those close ran to help. The Secret Service agents worked to revive him. But the dimensions of the room, the crowd, and the dais itself were so great that the audience was unaware of a problem until Martin Hoffman, Milton Hoffman's son, ran to the microphone and said, "Is there a doctor? Please come forward. We need a doctor."

This told the audience something had happened, but not what. There were gasps of panic, of fear, of despair, of inadequacy. Thirty-two hundred people were observing an emergency—an anonymous emergency—and there was nothing they could do to help. Some approached the dais to see who it was. You could sense chaos coming.

On the dais, too. Those far away from Dr. Sage craned to see. Those close became terribly upset. Here was a collapsed man. Where was the ambulance? How long could he wait? Martin Hoffman, after asking for a doctor, became hysterical. All the prominent Rabbis and clergy on the dais sat still. No one moved to take over, to step in.

Mrs. Ford moved in. First she put her arms around Martin and held him and calmed him. Then she went on to the crowd.

Slowly, steadily, she approached the speakers platform. "Can we all bow our heads for a moment for Dr. Sage?" she asked. The voice that came through the public address system was choked, on the verge of tears, but only on the verge. There was a solid, soothing quality about it. A sense of control.

"He is going to the hospital and needs our prayers. Would you rise and bow your heads?"

A unified movement of bodies. The crowd stood, thankful at last for something specific to do, an instruction that could be followed.

"I'll have to say it in my own words," Mrs. Ford went on. "Dear Father in heaven, we ask Thy blessing on this magnificent man, Dr. Sage. We know You can take care of him. We know You can bring him back to us. We know You are our leader. You are our strength. You are what life is all about; love and love of fellow man is what we all need and depend on. Please, Dear God."

Tears streamed down faces, but silence reigned.

"Let's all join together in a silent prayer for Dr. Sage," Mrs. Ford suggested.

As an ambulance crew strapped the man to a stretcher and whisked him off to the hospital; some 3,000 people stood still, lost in silent prayer, their heads bowed.

"Thank you very much," Mrs. Ford told them when the prayer was finished. "I know it will mean a great deal to him. And I know it means a great deal to me."

We waited upstairs at the Hilton for word on Dr. Sage's condition, musing over the man, the sad irony of the silver "good-luck" Bible.

The word was not good. One hour later, Dr. Sage died.

On the plane back to Washington, tonight, I kept going over and over the event. I could hear Mrs. Ford's voice giving the spontaneous prayer. It was the sound of strength, inner strength, the sound of a truly remarkable woman. Few of us are ever put to that kind of test, but how many of us could rise to the occasion so splendidly?

I thought about Dr. Sage. Only fifty-nine, they said. He was a scientist who held many patents in the field of chemistry. I knew him only as a warm presence, a man with a twinkle in his eye. That was enough. Once again, I felt keenly aware that the White House is in no way a shield from human tragedy. Like death. Once again in this job, I had come across death.

A death in the workhouse?


## JUNE 24, 1976

It was hectic from the start. Mrs. Ford called me very, very early. She and the President had decided that I should go as their representative to the Sage funeral in New York this morning and bring Mrs. Sage a personal note from them.

Still in bed, Edward and I composed the message, then phoned it in for Presidential approval. I told my secretary, Fran Paris, to phone Milton Hoffman in New York and tell him to expect me and to please get me a White House car quickly. I had to make the 11:00 A.M. shuttle.

Gulley, she told me later, was his usual cooperative self ("No") and Fran had to argue, cajole, and threaten. It worked. The car was waiting for me when I arrived at the White House en route to the airport to pick up the typed letter to Mrs. Sage. I did make the shuttle (barely) and when I arrived in New York, a chauffeur was waiting to take me to the funeral.

I was still late. I handed the letter to someone who assured me he could get it to Mrs. Sage. The service was in progress and she was seated in the family section, he said. I was ushered into the synagogue and seated between Milton Hoffman and his son, Martin. There was only one problem: this was an orthodox temple and in orthodox Judaism, the men and the women sit in separate sections. I looked around me to check. Sure enough, all men.

"I can't sit here," I whispered to Milton as the Rabbi intoned.

"*Shhh.*"

"Milton, isn't this area just for men?"

"*Shh. Sit.*"

"Martin," I said trying the other side, "I can't sit here. This is an orthodox shul!"

"My father says it's all right," Martin whispered back. "Sit."

"Thanks to Milton Hoffman," the Rabbi was saying, "a messenger from the White House has brought a letter from the President and Mrs. Ford which I would like to read to you."

"Where's a pen?" Milton asked. He was furious.

"A pen?"

"You're not a *messenger*," he said. "You are Mrs. Ford's Press Secretary, the President's representative. How can he call you a messenger?"

Sitting there in the front row illegally in the men's section, I was perfectly willing to be a messenger. I was willing to be anything, as a matter of fact, providing that the adjective "inconspicuous" preceded it.

"Forget it, Milton," I said, terrified that he wouldn't.

He found a pen. I saw him write in big bold letters: "SHEILA WEIDENFELD IS NOT A MESSENGER. SHE IS MRS. FORD'S REPRESENTATIVE AT THIS FUNERAL." He passed the note to someone behind him and said, "Please give this to the Rabbi."

The funeral went on and on and on and the Rabbi's final words were an enigma to all but me. "We made a mistake," he said abruptly at the end of the final prayer. "Mrs. Weidenfeld is *not* a messenger."

*JUNE 29, 1976*

Lloyd Shearer of *Parade* Magazine thought *Parade* might like to do a cover story on Mrs. Ford and one of the kids. ("How about Michael?") A story that would come out the day before the Republican convention begins.

Terrific timing.

"I like the idea," I told Michael on the phone. "I'm sure the story would be complimentary. And the day before the convention . . . that's wonderful."

There was a pensive pause.

"I can't," he said. "We're part of the community up here. We're involved in the church and we're doing real well. We've built up trust and friendship. This would upset it all. If I were to turn into some kind of celebrity, the people I'm working with couldn't relate to me. We like things simple . . . the way they are."

There was no whine, no holier-than-thou tone in the voice. Just honesty.

This, I thought, as I got off the phone, this is a kid who has found his niche. A noble young man, a remarkably solid young man, the type (alas!) that *Parade* Magazine would have loved.

# FROM ROYALTY TO THE MISSISSIPPI MUD

*JULY 4, 1976*

Happy Birthday, America!

For the President, it was one of those progressive parties. He began blowing out candles early this morning in Valley Forge, then went on to Philadelphia, then to New York City, and finally home to the White House. Mrs. Ford and I skipped the first two stops but met him in New York, to observe the "greatest gathering of world navies in history."

In honor of the bicentennial, some fifty ships from all over the world arrived in New York harbor yesterday and today, as part of the fourth international Naval Review (the first was in 1893 to commemorate the 400th anniversary of Columbus' discovering America) and hoisted their flags and pennants and sailed down the harbor in a ceremonial column, booming special gun salutes along the way. The showpieces of the spectacle were sixteen "Tall Ships" —square-rigged sailing ships more than 200 feet in length from all over the world. An incredible sight, I thought, as the President rang the bicentennial bell thirteen times aboard the U.S.S. *Forrestal* (signifying something).

321

But the most incredible sight was not part of the ceremonial schedule. As we helicoptered from the *Forrestal* at one end of the harbor around the Statue of Liberty and Ellis Island to the U.S.S. *Nashville* at the other end, we looked down upon millions of New Yorkers, hanging out of windows, standing on rooftops, crowded along the Hudson River — everywhere. All of New York City was out and it was a magnificent sight to see from a helicopter. One terrific birthday party.

We came back to Washington and Edward and I went to a party tonight at CBS correspondent Lesley Stahl's home. There was some talk about the fact that Jimmy Carter had invited Senator Muskie down to Plains today (the possible Vice Presidential choice?) but for a journalistic gathering, the talk was remarkably apolitical. We watched Walter Cronkite's bicentennial special all night. Mrs. Cronkite (Walter's mother) was at the party and somehow the image of this lovely white-haired woman beaming with pride at her son's face on the television set seemed to fit in with the cozy mood. Some of us went up on the roof to watch the elaborate fireworks display put on at the Washington Monument. I thought of the Fords, watching it together on the Truman Balcony. I thought of the millions of Washingtonians, watching them from the mall itself, celebrating like the New Yorkers.

"Two hundred years ago, who would have thought we would have made it," boomed an inebriated voice behind me as the colors exploded in the sky.

"Two years ago, I had my doubts." someone else said.


*JULY 7, 1976*

"Did you see that picture of me in the paper?" Susan asked. She had held her 19th birthday party aboard the *Sequoia* and the *Post* ran a picture of her approaching the boat.

"Yes. It was all right. Was the party fun?"

"Sheila, it was *not* all right. That was my boyfriend in the picture."

"Your boyfriend?"

"You know—one of the guys I've been dating. He's a football player."

"Oh, that's nice." (What's the catch?) "Is he nice?"

"Sheila, he's *married*" she wailed. "He's getting a divorce, but he's still married and that picture was in the paper?"

(I suddenly have an image of his wife picketing the White House. The headlines scream "HYPOTHETICAL AFFAIR FINALLY TURNS TO TRUTH . . ." Phyllis Schlafly points out that the daughters of ERA supporters date married men. Oh *that* picture.)

"He isn't identified in the picture," I consoled, "and he doesn't stand out. He just looks like one of your agents. I wouldn't worry about the *picture*, Susan, but you'd better be careful in the future that—"

"Oh, I *will*," she assures, ever grateful for the calming words. (How will she? I wonder.)

## JULY 8, 1976

Jeannette Smythe of the *Washington Post* wanted to know which of the invited guests were requested by the Queen and Couri Hay insisted that as the *National Enquirer's* celebrity columnist she should be included, and Helen Thomas wanted to know whether the Queen does not like *raw* fish or *shell* fish, and Russ Ward, of NBC radio wanted to know why there were so many entertainers included.

And that was not half of it.

The Queen of England came for dinner last night and the White House is still reeling. Three days after celebrating the 200th anniversary of our rebellion from the crown, Americans trampled each other for a tiny glimpse of the current crown-wearer. We may be the country of the common man, but nothing turns "common man" on quite like royalty.

That goes for the common press corps, too. If all the reporters who requested credentials for last night's State Dinner had gotten them, the press would have outnumbered the guests 2–1.

For Social Secretary Maria Downs, it was a plan-come-true.

Ten months after designing an abstract "State Dinner for the Queen's visit next July," as part of her application for the job of social secretary, she got the chance to design a *real* State Dinner for the Queen's visit.

Happily, there were some alterations in her original idea. The Queen received a statue of a bucking bronco—an acknowledgement of her "love of horses"—rather than watch a bunch of real ones tear up the White House front lawn. Baskets of varicolored flowers made up the table centerpieces, a prettier (if less thematic) effect than Maria's original idea (saddles).

The rest of the details of the dinner were, for some reason, shrouded in secrecy, leaving my desk cluttered with questions without answers. Penetrating questions, too. Such as, "If the lobster is being shipped from New York City, why is it being called 'New England Maine Lobster'?"

The most urgent question came in a phone call from cooking celebrity Julia Child at about 5:00 P.M. "Where is my platter?" she asked.

"Your what?"

"My platter? The chef won't give me my platter?"

A little calm questioning revealed the fact that Julia Child was doing the "play by play" of tonight's dinner for the Public Broadcasting Service. She had, with the help of a White House media liaison, taped a tour of the kitchen and interviewed the chef. Now she needed a platter sampler of the State Dinner meal. And suddenly the White House people said "No." Her White House liaison was nowhere to be found and someone had suggested she call me.

"How can I tell viewers what it tastes like if I can't eat it?" she asked.

Well, that made sense. I called Chef Haller. He said he couldn't put the platter together.

"Why?"

"Call Rex Scouten."

I called Rex Scouten.

"The word is no food for Julia Child," announced the Head Usher.

" 'Word' " I said. "Whose word?"

"Mrs. Ford."

I called Mrs. Ford. She was dressing, but her secretary confirmed "the word."

"No food for Julia Child."

"Who says?"

"Maria Downs."

"Why?"

"Who knows?"

It had to be a joke. "No food for Julia Child" was, after all, a contradiction in terms. I was getting punchy. I tried Maria Downs. The social secretary was not around. I tried the kitchen again.

"C'mon," I teased. "What is this silliness, 'No food for Julia Child?' "

"That's what Maria Downs decided."

"Why?"

"Who knows? Who knows!"

I pictured the dramatic gestures that were accompanying the words on the other end of the phone. "Let me tell you something about this social secretary. A menu was recently prepared for her approval, and she called and asked 'What are scallops?' WHAT ARE SCALLOPS! Can you imagine? A social secretary who does not know what scallops are?"

Click.

I guess he felt that answered my question.

With the knowledge that the Maine Lobster came from New York, that the social secretary did not know what scallops were, and that somewhere in the White House, in front of kleig lights, Julia Child was gazing into an empty platter, I got dressed for the Queen.

It got worse.

As I stood with the press on the South Lawn watching the guests go through the receiving line, a PBS broadcaster stood nearby on camera, telling the audience who was who. The only problem was that the commentator did not know. She stood there uncomfortably saying "and now . . . uh . . . here is . . . uh . . ."

I felt as though I were part of a comedy routine.

The sensation grew stronger as I dealt with the press. I explained to angry photographers that there would be no pictures during dinner (the Queen won't chew on camera) and fought off hostilities from those reporters who were not part of the press pool. Lavish State Dinners seem to bring out the press' most tacky characteristics. As Britain's royalty dined in splendor with America's royalty (the President of U.S. Steel, IT&T, Barbara Walters, Ella Fitzgerald, Cary Grant, Telly Savalas) one White House reporter asked to take the place of another in the press pool because "I'm shorter than she is so I would take up less room."

After dinner, Bob Hope (the "Queen's favorite") told the glittery assemblage that, "In this country, when we see a crown we think of a margarine commercial!'' and then introduced the Captain and Tennille, a young soft rock duo who went into a vivid rendition of ''Muskrat Love,'' a song of sex between two muskrats—Sam and Susie—that leaves little to the imagination. I hoped the Queen's American was not that good.

But the real highlight of the evening was the dancing. It was, indeed, a moment to remember when the President of the United States (in white tie and tails) led her Royal Majesty the Queen of England (in tiara and medals and gown of ''citron organza'') out onto the dance floor to the melodious strains of the U.S. Marine Band's rendition of—''The Lady Is a Tramp.''

There were, apparently, some details that had not been thought through.

But it was a wonderful party. ''I've been coming to White House functions since 1947, and this party is number one,'' said ever enthusiastic Vice President Rockefeller. ''No, really, it is the greatest.''

And they danced amidst the floral arrangements that brought a sense of summer into the White House and among guests who reminded all that this was America's political season, too. Clarke Reed, the head of Mississippi's Republican delegation (as yet uncommitted) was there as was Texas Republican power broker John Connally.

The Queen and Prince Phillip left at a respectable hour. The Fords continued to cut the rug until 2:00 A.M.


## JULY 9, 1976

Dave Gergen wanted to have lunch to tell me the good news: a new day is coming. The President is about to become Presidential; his speeches spectacular. For David Gergen, Special Counsel to the President, is about to become David Gergen, Director of the White House Office of Communications.

As a result, that (up to now) sleepy office will become an aggressive, articulate translator of President Ford's achievements. All Presidential statements will be cleared by Dave. All television programming will go through him. All political commercials and films will need his clearance.

The political computer tallies: a big loss for the bold oldies, a major maneuver for Cheney's gang.

The critic is getting a chance to exercise his own alternatives. The objects of his criticism have had their wings clipped. The Office of Communications was under Nessen. But Gergen will report directly to Cheney. Hartmann used to direct all speech writing. Now Gergen will.

"The worst time of all was the State of the Union last January," Gergen told me in the type of expansive tone with which an Army sergeant can reminisce about a battle lost, once he knows he has won the war. "The Hartmann draft was a laundry list, no philosophy, no approach. I wrote an alternative which, I thought, put Ford's policies into a context that gave them a thematic direction. A vote was taken in the staff meeting on the two speeches. The outcome was 17–2. The two dissenting votes were Ford's and Hartmann's. I got a few of my paragraphs in, but, in the end, the laundry list won. And Ford was furious. I've never seen him so angry. "Goddamn it!" he said. It was as though by challenging Hartmann's speech we were challenging him. His whole twenty-five-year record."

Nothing succeeds like success. And nothing promotes critics to top slots like other people's failure. So now, as Jimmy Carter entertains daily batches of Vice Presidential hopefuls (Senators Mondale and Glenn went to Plains yesterday) amidst cheerful proclamations of Democratic brotherhood, while the prospect of Ford's getting the nomination is chancey and the prospect of their being any Republican unity left after this bloody primary battle is gloomier still, *now* David Gergen is getting his chance.

Can he pull it off?


## JULY 14, 1976


She wanted to celebrate his birthday quietly. Over a special lunch in a special restaurant. She chose Sans Souci, a Washington institution of sorts, famous for its French cuisine extraordinaire, and famous for its famous clientele: the senators, the congressmen, the columnists, the television celebrities, the "in" Washington people who dine there each day at lunch. She wanted it to be private. No kids. No friends. Together, "Just the two of us." It would be a surprise. She would just go to his office at lunchtime and say, "Happy birthday, dear. C'mon I'm treating."

And she did.

But she is married to the President of the United States so it was a little more complicated. Three tables had to be reserved, for one thing. One for the Secret Service, one for the press pool, and one for "Just the two of us."

Then there was the standing ovation as they entered the restaurant.

Then there were the flash bulbs that went off each time they clicked glasses.

And the need to communicate with the press pool. "We should do this more often," the President scribbled on a restaurant post-card (in between his appetizer and his entrée) in answer to a post-card sent to him by the representatives of UPI (Helen Thomas), AP (Fran Lewine), CBS (Bob Pierpoint) and the *Baltimore Sun* (Muriel Dobbin) who sat with me at another table watching. "Betty is putting it on her credit card, and I hope *your* bosses will do the same!"

And the crowd waiting outside as they left. Including TV cameras.

"I'm delighted to have such good company at lunch," the President told ABC.

"Well, I just wanted to surprise him somehow," Mrs. Ford explained to CBS, "so I set it up so I could just steal him away."


## JULY 16, 1976

Cathy Sulzberger called today to tell me the news: she's pregnant.

Coincidence?


## JULY 20, 1976

There are no more state conventions, but there is no resolution to the struggle. The "count" (which varies according to source) shows Ford ahead but not far enough ahead to make the winner's circle. As a result, we have a new game at the White House: "Call-a-Delegate"—"Call-a-*Mississippi* Delegate" to be precise. The Mississippi delegation votes by the unit rule and the object of the game is to sway a majority by swaying each delegate personally. The President Ford Committee has given Mrs. Ford a list of twenty-one female delegates and alternates in Mississippi and, slowly but surely, she has been making her way through the list. Each name is accompanied by a short biography ("active in volunteer work for the March of Dimes, Muscular Dystrophy, Cystic Fibrosis, and the Bicentennial Committee") and PFC suggested "Talking Points" ("Her volunteer work for the March of Dimes, Muscular Dystrophy, Cystic Fibrosis, and the Bicentennial Committee").

When she completes each call, Mrs. Ford is supposed to write down how long the conversation was, what they talked about, and whether she thinks she's found a supporter.

This has to be democracy in its most basic form. A call from the President's wife to say "How y'all votin' down there?" Grassroots, nothing. This is going down to the underlying layer of Mississippi mud! And what makes the whole thing even more preposterous is the fact that often Mrs. Ford discovers she is just one of a chain of celebrity phone calls. ("Oh, you've already talked to Dick Cheney?" "Yes, Mr. Reagan *is* very formal.")

As a result of all this, scattered around the Family Quarters this week there are many, many pieces of paper that say things like: "We talked for thirty minutes. She says she wants the President to address himself to 'what they say about how Kissinger, with all the détente, is making us a second-rate power.' She concluded by saying: 'I haven't committed myself, I sway like a reed in the wind. I listen to one and I'm for him. I listen to the other and I'm for him.' "

Mrs. Ford's assessment in this case: "Can't be counted on. Perhaps Rumsfeld should call. Someone better get with her at the last minute and stick with her until she votes."

Elsewhere in the White House, they're planning ahead. The mood has changed. There is a sense of victory, albeit victory in the future tense; a feeling that Ford will win the nomination. Jack has even begun planning Carter-Ford debates. That may be a bit premature (I have my reservations) but for others too, the goal is now beyond the nomination: to party unity for the general campaign.

"The problem with Ford," the wise men from New York were telling the group in Dave Gergen's office, "is that nobody knows him. The public has no idea who *Ford the man* is. This has to get out."

The men from New York had been brought in to help put together a film for the Republican convention, a film which would show *Ford the man.*

"We want to do several things," the men from New York were explaining. "Interview people who knew Ford as a person, not a politician. Use the family. Old album pictures, too. All the ingredients that are necessary to explain the human side."

Gergen asked for a vote. Most of the people in the room were for it.

I was skeptical. The *idea* was good. But what guarantee did we have that the *film* would be? A lousy film on *Ford the man* could make history as the biggest humiliation yet. And to pay money for it?

Still . . . a good idea. When I got back to my office, I started thinking about some of the album pictures that would work well and some of the people who could talk about the President. I thought of Milton Hoffman, who feels he owes his life to Gerald Ford. I thought of Silas McGee, the black longshoreman who came to the 30/30 Club reunion at the White House. He said that in high school, when they wouldn't allow blacks on the football team, Ford refused to play. I thought about David Sands, who went to school with Jack in both Alexandria and Utah. David's father died when David was eleven and David once told me that no matter how busy Gerald Ford was, "He always had time when I needed advice." I thought of Mildred Leonard, who had been Ford's secretary for twenty years. It was like watching my own mental picture show. The more I thought, the more I found myself personally moved by Ford the man.

It is a good idea. Can they do it?


*JULY 26, 1976*

She said, "Let's have lunch" and I said, "Sure" and here we were, at Sans Souci, fingering menus and sniffing each other out, about to bite into a chunk of Helen Thomas' expense account.

"Is this off-the-record?" I asked, unfolding my napkin.

"Of course," she answered, unfolding hers.

We chatted. About administrations past. About family. About things no one would want to put on the record. She was sweet. I was suspicious. Helen Thomas, veteran UPI reporter of some thirty years, top of the heap, journalism's own "female first" recipient of Martha Mitchell phone calls. Helen Thomas did not get to be where she is by being sweet. Helen Thomas acting sweet to a Press Secretary is, by definition, Helen Thomas acting.

My face was returning the smile. My words were describing my sister-in-law's impressive legal career. But my mind kept recalling the past: Helen Thomas last week screaming, "I *know* why you let *Women's Wear Daily* interview Mrs. Ford! They were planning to do a number on you and to *stop* them you gave them an interview!" Helen Thomas last month screaming, "I *never* had this trouble getting to talk to Pat Nixon! You're the worst. The *worst!*" Helen Thomas two months ago screaming, "I don't *believe* you!" And three months ago, and four. Always screaming. How many of the events of my working days have been punctuated by a Helen Thomas scream?

Nothing personal, of course.

She did not mean it—certainly not the way I took it. Nice guys may miss stories, after all. Tact makes for reportorial losers. And she wants to be a winner. We played with our salads and talked about Nancy Howe. Down memory lane.

They *all* want to be winners. I thought back to Clare Crawford, my *friend* Clare Crawford interviewing Jack last week for *People* Magazine. "Why do you bite your nails?" she accused.

Dumbfounded, he stuck his hands out for proof and replied, "I don't ."

"Would you say you are a twenty-five-year-old virgin?" was her follow-up question.

"That was the *worst* interview I ever got!" she howled at me later on. "Not one personal detail! He's terrible!" ("Screw her," was Jack's response.)

Is this the post-Watergate game of investigative journalism? If so, the rules are unfair. Dumb questions are allowed. Smart answers are not. Watergate's lesson—that an active press keeps government clean—has been overtaught. There are times when the press makes it difficult to concentrate on government. The trivia hunts are time consuming and moronic. Mrs. Ford and I spent part of the day counting how many broken bones Jack had had as a child for one reporter. I researched Susan's weight for another.

And the campaign. Who makes campaign events events? Who makes issues issues? Who likes to see their names in print every bit as much as the politicians? What if they declared a campaign and nobody covered?

I remember going out to a delicatessen with Fran Lewine back in December and on the way she was excitedly rubbing hands together and saying she couldn't wait until the campaign started. I thought she was kidding.

Then.

Now I've seen the excitement grow, the tension mount with each new byline. Politics is bread and butter to the press. It sells papers. It employs journalists.

Helen chose a bad day to get friendly, I thought. My hostility is running high.

Still, I would like to understand her better. I would like to relax more in her presence. We sipped our coffee and I looked at her for the first time, really looked at her. Behind the gleam in the eyes lay the perennial look of distrust. The sharp features were only slightly softened by the smile. The hands were muscular looking. How many words had they typed out—for how many deadlines? At the White House, the male UPI and AP reporters refuse to cover the social events. This means that Helen and Fran Lewine, in addition to their regular West Wing beat have to cover all the White House State Dinners and parties. They have to work double.

I suddenly felt guilty about being so critical. Helen has perhaps the most exhausting beat there is. And she not only does it, she does it well. When she is in pursuit of something—be it Betty Ford's health or what the Ford kids put in their Christmas stockings—she is distrustful and myopic. But maybe she *has* to be. Tools of the trade.

Softened a little, I decided to try candor. "It may be me," I said to her, "but I really don't react well when people scream at me, Helen. It takes the joy out of working. I try to do my best for you, but I —"

"Yes. Well. *When* am I going to get my interview with Mrs. Ford?"

"As soon as—"

"And did you mention the book idea? My writing a book with her? Her memoirs?"

"Yes, but I don't know, Helen. She's had other offers . . . "

"No. No she hasn't. I *know* she hasn't because when we discussed it before, *you told me she had not had other offers!*"

"She might want to write a book herself."

"Ridiculous."

I was getting that old Helen Thomas feeling in the pit of my stomach. Mrs. Ford *has* been approached by publishers and agents. But if I say that, that's a news story, and she certainly wouldn't want that coming out now. Helen would be the wrong collaborator anyway. But I don't want to say that, for obvious reasons. Helen, you and I are not destined for friendship. Forget candor, Sheila. Seek safety.

"Look, Helen, what can I say? I'll talk to her about it," I said as we walked out of Sans Souci into the hot July midday mugginess.

"You'll talk to her?" Her eyes brightened. The smile returned.

"Why don't you write out exactly what you want. That way I won't share your ideas with her, I'll share your letter."

"That sounds fair," she said softly, sweetly.

We crossed Pennsylvania Avenue and we split up in front of the White House, heading for separate entrances. She said "Goodbye," and kissed me on the cheek.

*JULY 27, 1976*

They were talking about a position on the White House Staff. "It's a commissioned position," Jim Connor said.

"What's that?" I asked.

"A commission is a document indicating a Presidential appointment," Jim said.

"Oh," I said. "Then I must be commissioned too. I have a document that I got when I became Press Secretary."

"Nope, that's not the document."

"I'm not commissioned?"

"Nope."

"What does it mean, exactly, to be commissioned?"

"Higher status," he said.

Well, I mean, that explains it—the lack of respect, and all. Here

I've been walking around the White House for two years without a commission and I didn't even know it.

"Can I become commissioned?" I asked Jim. (Who's proud?)

"Well, I suppose you could," he said. "You've done an excellent job."

Aw shucks.

"I'll look into it," he told me.

"Thanks," I said, picturing the Red Tape parting as I walked through. Me and my commission.

"You know," he said, "when you're commissioned, you get the title of 'honorable.' "

A bit much. White House silliness, I thought to myself as I walked away, hearing a voice intone (with awe and respect) *The Honorable Sheila Rabb Weidenfeld. . . ."* The voice was a cross between Donald Rumsfeld and Bill Gulley.


## *JULY 30, 1976*

On Monday, Reagan announced his selection of Pennsylvania Senator Richard Schweiker as his running mate. Schweiker is one of the most liberal and pro-labor Republicans in Congress. (In fact the ADA gave his voting record an 89 percent favorable rating.) It was supposed to be a gesture of Republican balance. It upset the cart instead.

On Tuesday, Governor Thomson of New Hampshire, one of Reagan's earliest supporters, withdrew his support.

On Wednesday, Clarke Reed, the Mississippi GOP Chairman, announced his "personal endorsement" of Gerald Ford.

On Thursday, three uncommitted Louisiana delegates moved into the Ford camp.

The President had been inching his way toward victory before the Schweiker announcement, but now it seemed to be around the corner.

Well, *almost* around the corner.

Because today is Friday and we are not home confidently doing laps in the White House swimming pool. We are down here in Mississippi where the weather is hot and humid with a 40 percent chance of isolated thunderstorms and where the delegates still haven't made up their li'l ole minds.

The trip has been a learning experience. I have learned there is nothing so powerful as an uncommitted delegate. Ford addressed the delegates in a closed session and then caressed the delegates at an open reception. We all did. Anything you can do for an uncommitted delegate, you do. Here were all the big guns of the White House, sweet-talking the grain farmers and chiropractors and businessmen and multiple sclerosis volunteer workers of Mississippi. Most of the delegates I talked to said they were "terribly impressed by the President" but that they still didn't want to commit themselves.

Who can blame them? Why end all the fun?

## Chapter Twenty-two
### AUGUST, 1976:

# THE GREATEST SHOW IN KANSAS CITY

*AUGUST 9, 1976*

The White House moved to Camp David for the weekend. It was to be a double header: a pre-convention tactical session for pollsters, strategists and top staff and a filming session for (next year's academy award nominee) *Ford the Man*. The media men had already interviewed people about the President. Now they wanted to film the President himself, relaxing at home with his family. I came to help out.

Edward and I drove up with Jack and David Sands, Jack's friend from childhood, high school and college (one of the major members of the "Dead Meat House" out at Utah, in fact).

We took our car, but we sat in the back. David drove. It was a pretty trip up into the mountains where the Presidential retreat is located, although the beauty of the view was somewhat dimmed for us by Jack's running commentary on which trees were dying from air pollution caused by automobile emissions. ("Look over there. See? You can tell by the discoloration of the leaves. Imagine what it's doing to us.")

The guards jumped to attention as we arrived at the gate (it was the first time our Volvo has ever been saluted) and then led the way to Linden, the little cottage where Edward and I were to stay. "Welcome aboard! I hope you enjoy your stay in Linden!" the Navy man said, clicked his heels and left. It is quite a place, Camp David—simple, rustic, hilly, green, and covered with non-discolored leaves, country paths, and a magnificent assortment of recreational facilities. There are tennis and basketball courts, swimming pools, nature trails, a sauna, trampoline, bowling alley, bicycles. You name it, it is there, manned by a large invisible staff of military personnel. Ghost servants. At the bowling alley, for example, Jack told us, there were enlisted men behind the automatic pin setters just in case something went wrong. Men who were on duty twenty-four hours a day.

"Ridiculous," I laughed.

"No, really, as soon as someone turns on the light in the alley, a light goes on in the barracks and someone reports to the alley. Nixon I understand used to drive them crazy in the middle of the night. He'd come in at 3:00 A.M. by himself just to relax."

"Ridiculous."

He took me back behind the bowling alley machines. Sure enough, there was an enlisted man sitting quietly reading a comic book. On duty.

While Edward and I were taking a sauna another time, some unseen person placed a bucket of ice water outside the door.

There is the luxury of being waited on. There is also the eeriness of knowing "big brother" is watching everything you do. We found ourselves whispering a lot.

As a result of "Big Brother's" presence, Camp David is a partial vacation for the Secret Service. They still have to cover their person because even Camp David is not 100 percent secure, but they keep at a more discreet distance and they relax a little. The release shows. After all the Secret Service is made up of very athletic men in their late twenties to mid-thirties, all of whom have college educations, most of whom are really first-class street cops who go into the Service because they like undercover work and the Service does a lot of undercover work. Then you take this active, bright person and give him the job of babysitter, where every fiber of his being has to be alert to any sudden move or suspicious act. Constant tension but no real exercise.

Then you take him to Camp David, where he can ease up, and,

well. . . . About a half-hour after we got there, Edward and I were exploring when we saw a bicycle coming down the hill at record speed. There was a cyclist but he was bent backwards, his feet in the air. At the bottom of the hill, he collided with another bicycle (coming from the opposite direction, also at top speed) which flew up in the air upon impact, spinning out from under its passenger. Both riders, on the ground, laughed uproariously and got up to do it all over again. It was just Jack's Secret Service detail letting off steam.

Our cottage was very simple, but it came with little extras: two bicycles; a platter by the television set filled with cheeses, crackers, peanuts and potato chips; umbrellas and Camp David jackets in case of rain; a box for newspapers that included the latest editions of the *Washington Post, New York Times, Washington Star, Baltimore Sun, Time, Newsweek* and the President's news summary which is prepared at the White House but telecopied to wherever in the world the President is.

The guest book at the main lodge brought back strange memories of the old days ("Mr. and Mrs. John Ehrlichman," "Bob Haldeman," "John Dean," "Bud Krogh," "Murray Chotiner") and there were other reminders: an unusually small bowling ball designed for Tricia Nixon. A jungle gym and swings installed for the Kennedy children.

We didn't attend the campaign strategy sessions, but Jack wandered in and out and later explained Bob Teeter's opinion poll results to us. Teeter had polled the country and determined that Ford was viewed as a social liberal (because of his family's statements and his selection of Nelson Rockefeller as his running mate) and an economic conservative (because of his many legislative vetos). Unfortunately, the country, Teeter said, was in the mood for a social conservative and an economic liberal and perceived Carter as just that. Ford's image had to change.

Teeter's general analysis was that the Vice Presidential candidate, no matter who he was, would not change Ford's image. Only Ford could. That, in fact, none of the possible Vice Presidential possibilities could be counted on to get extra votes. At best, the choice would not *lose* extra votes. In addition, a woman Vice President was out, Teeter said. The country is not ready for it.

Everyone was pushing his own Vice Presidential choice. There was general consensus that he should be an "attacker," that Jimmy Carter was very thin-skinned and that the Vice Presidential nominee should be someone who could get under Jimmy Carter's skin.

There was also a feeling that he should be a traditional politician. I pushed Walter Cronkite at one point, arguing that he was the only one who could bring instant respect and credibility—something the country desperately needed. (Is there someone you would trust more?)

Cronkite, however, was out of the question.

"To the President, politics is a profession," Dick Cheney said. "He thinks it is a noble calling, that it is nothing to be ashamed of. One of the points he wants to make against Jimmy Carter is that running for President as an outsider is really very bad for the country. The country needs professionals, people with experience to provide continuity."

I wish them luck. . . .

On Saturday morning, all political analysis stopped, briefly, as technicians, spotlights, and movie equipment took over the huge conference room. It was time for "*Ford the Man*"—that heart warming true-to-life portrait of the human being behind the Presidential Seal.

The first segment was to be a casual chat with the President, one in which he revealed his human side. So, with the cameras whirring and the lights shining, an anonymous voice from somewhere in the darkness shouted, "Reveal your human side, Mr. President!"

He had a little trouble.

The President and his off-camera interviewer kept going over and over the same stuff, the interviewer convincing the chief executive with each repetition that he was doing a terrible job. That, of course, made him more uncomfortable, and more impatient and more anxious (a fortune in campaign expenditures went out the window with each retake, after all) which in turn made his performance worse and worse.

*Ford the Man* was beginning to look like a documentary for Democrats. I suggested Jack just sit on the couch with his father and do the "interviewing." Jack I knew could relax the President, and they were only interested in the President's answers, so it didn't matter who asked the questions.

"I think David Sands would do better," Jack insisted at reel change. "He's loose, and my dad's relaxed with him."

David sauntered up to the "set," exuding a sense of welcomed lethargy. He is tall, lanky, with a little mustache, deep-blue eyes, and a general bearing that makes him look like the type of person for whom they coined the phrase "loose as a goose." I thought Jack would be better, but Jack insisted on David. Why fight? The President was always relaxed with him. Semi father-son.

But when David got to the lights, something very peculiar happened. He stopped being David and became a combination of youth-of-America and local-TV personality. "Tell me, Mr. President," he intoned, "the time has come when people of my generation, given increasingly large amounts of leisure time and material possessions. . . .

Oh, dear.

The wooden Presidential visage turned to steel.

"  . . . if you know what I mean, like, what do you think, Mr. President?"

Jack got the nod. At first he was a little nervous himself, but he has developed a good political instinct for combining honesty with the things that people want to hear. There were a few good moments.

Unfortunately these occurred when the cameras broke.

No matter. We went on to take two: The Perfect All-American Family Scene: Jack, Susan, Mom and Dad sitting around the table just chatting and munching.

Here too, perfection was a little flawed. Susan, who was supposed to arrive at Camp David Friday, had arrived instead early Saturday morning after a heavy date. Her parents were not pleased with the date himself, and were even less pleased with the indications of "heaviness"—her puffed eyes, late arrival, and generally "morning after" appearance.

So, there they were, just the four of them: the President, by this time impatient and irritated; Jack, unhappily aware that his father bombed in much of his earlier appearance; Mrs. Ford, both anxious and angry about her daughter's dating habits, and hung-over Susan, wincing visibly each time a spoon hit the side of a cup. There they were, chirping merrily as they passed the cream and sugar, the Perfect All-American Family of Ford the Man.

\*   \*   \*

*AUGUST 20, 1976*

It was West Virginia that put Ford over the top, that guaranteed him the nomination. There was mass hysteria, I'm sure. But political conventions are so huge that you never get an overall view of "mass hysteria." You witness no more than a few feet in front of you, your own private patch of hysteria.

Mine included Jack and Steve, George Gorton, Edward, and a few other people. We had all been sitting in the Ford family suite in the Convention Hall watching the state-by-state roll call on the television set, as Jack updated his own scorecard. There was tremendous tension. As the moment got closer, Jack and Steve moved out of the suite into the amphitheatre outside. The top row of the bleachers was right in front of the suite. Then the moment came and they exploded. Exploded is the only way to put it. They screamed and jumped and hugged and howled. A massive release. Joy. Delight. The happiness was apparent, but so too were all the emotions that had been stored, suppressed, withheld, during this long drawn-out fight. Over. Over at last. Done. Accomplished. Victory!

It was the most genuine display of emotion I had seen, and I had seen many, those last three days—planned, canned, timed, rehearsed, but always "spontaneous."

COME ONE, COME ALL, TO THE GREATEST SHOW IN KANSAS CITY: THE 1976 REPUBLICAN NATIONAL CONVENTION! We have popcorn, peanuts, and polyester leisure suits, choreographed demonstrations where thousands of uptight people scream hysterically, predictable speechs, and three-man camera crews standing by to record the random thoughts of every uncommitted delegate. You really have to attend a convention to feel what it is like behind the scenes. But if you want to know what is happening, stay home and watch television.

The emotional release caused by winning the nomination was short lived. A Presidential candidate, after all, needs a Vice Presidential candidate. The President went to pay his respects to Ronald Reagan (party unity and all that). Mrs. Ford did not accompany him because she did not *want* to accompany him, "quite frankly," but was angry when she discovered later that Nancy Reagan had not invited her. There was nervous talk that Ford might offer Reagan the Vice Presidency, but it was just nervous talk. ("Reagan," Mrs. Ford had said with conviction, "would be a drag.")

When the President returned from his house call, the decision-making process began. It would have been more fulfilling, I'm sure, to have sat around the table in the inner sanctum with the biggies and participated. But you couldn't beat the outer sanctum for suspense. That's where Edward, Jack and I kept vigil, along with Jim Lynn, Director of the Office of Management and Budget, and Ed Schmults, assistant counsel to the President, who had an assortment of huge folders with detailed background information on every possible Vice Presidential choice. Periodically Ed and a folder would be called into the inner room. Then he would return, tight-lipped. He didn't offer. We didn't ask. We talked politics instead. ("But the mood of the country is conservative. . . .")

David Kennerly wandered in and out with a photographer friend, as always light hearted, light headed, cool. Himself. David seems to adapt to each new atmosphere by completely rejecting its influence. Mrs. Ford was not there. She was exhausted and she had already made her decision; she wanted Nelson Rockefeller. As a matter of fact, I believe she had even offered him the nomination (informally, to be sure) and he thanked her but said he'd already served his two years.

By four in the morning, we shrewd political observers decided to turn in. We had exhausted all the possibilities. We had, however, barely mentioned Robert Dole. There lies the difference between the outer sanctum and the inner sanctum.

*  *  *  *

Steve and Jack and I got up two hours later. I had booked Jack on the "Today" show and Steve on "Good Morning, America." We were all dead tired. "I guess you're *used* to getting up early in the morning," David Hartman the interviewer, chortled at Steve. "I mean, you have to be with the horses."

"You don't have to talk to horses," Steve replied.

*  *  *  *

The President went to bed without giving the networks any word on the choice. Therefore, TV cameras and crews were stationed outside the hotel room of each Vice Presidential possibility for an all-night stakeout, in order to get instantaneous reaction from the candidate as soon as word on who he was came out.

"So there we were," the sound man said, "waiting all night in front of Elliot Richardson's door. Suddenly, about 6:00 A.M., the door opens. We jump to our feet, start the machines, turn on the lights, grab the mike, Boom! And what do we see? Elliott Richardson standing in the doorway with no clothes on! Poor guy, he'd just opened the door to pick up his morning newspaper!''

\* \* \* \*

In July, Jack accepted an assignment to write five personal reports (under his by-line) on the convention for the *New York Daily News*. I thought it was a mistake. Jack thought the money was good.

I realized my instincts about Jack's *Daily News* series were correct when I arrived in Kansas City. Edward flew out with Jack the day before.

"What about Jack's first article?" I asked Edward.

"It's fine."

"Did you see it?"

"I wrote it," Edward said.

That was article #1.

The next day I spied Jack sitting in on the morning session of the convention surrounded by family and hoopla, madly scribbling something on a piece of paper. "I'm having trouble with this one," said Jack.

So we did it in committee. Edward, George Gorton, Jack's friend Sandy Laughlin, Jack and I all went back to the Ford convention suite and munched hot dogs and dictated to Jack. Word by word. Every sentence was a group effort. One person would supply the noun, another the verb, another the preposition, and so on. Each time it was a challenge to put an entire sentence together, and when we did, delighted by the fact, we cheered before going on to the next. We continued trying to write the article in the car going to a reception. By that time we were in an acute stage of punchy. To our amazement, we got the thing done. *Daily News* White House correspondent Paul Healy was even more amazed. Poor Paul. The deadline was 4:30 Kansas City time and Paul could not find Jack and could not successfully hide from the phone calls coming in from his managing editor in New York, who was having a fit.

That was article #2.

The next day, Jack's schedule was packed full. (He had, by this time, decided that he wanted to *participate* in the convention, not write about it.) At 3:00 P.M., Healy came into the press room, frantic. I grabbed Jack. He said not to worry, he had written out a few lines. I looked at the piece of paper and saw nothing but a few lines and thought here we go again.

On the elevator a woman asked Jack whom he'd like to see as his father's running mate. Jack threw out a few names—Kit Bond, Pete Wilson, Dan Evans—adding that he didn't think Governor Evans would be interested.

Someone else in the car turned to Jack and introduced himself: "I'm on Governor Evans' staff."

"No kidding," I said.

"He's a good man," Jack said.

We had just begun to get rolling on the column back in Jack's suite when the Secret Service called. "Governor Evans is here to see Jack. What should we do with him?"

Jack was delighted. "Send him in."

The next thing I knew, the Governor of Washington State was saying that he just wanted to thank Jack and let him know that while he was thinking of leaving politics, if there were anything he could do for his party and his country, he would want to.

When the Governor left, a reporter arrived. I was getting nervous, but I knew that my anxiety was nothing to what Paul Healy was undoubtedly experiencing. I called Paul. He seemed relieved at just establishing contact. We decided that Jack would get together with Paul. We met, and within fifteen minutes, Paul had the story written.

That was article #3.

It was Jack's last stand. Article #4 was all Paul Healy's. ("I spent most of the day looking for Jack to get his thoughts," Paul told me. "Finally I found him and debriefed him. He wasn't exactly overflowing with tidbits, I'll tell you.")

To everyone's relief (including, perhaps, the *Daily News* readers) the "fifth in the series of five" never happened.

\*    \*    \*    \*

A lot of news stories were devoted to the "Battle of the Wives." Mrs. Ford walked into the amphitheatre one night in the middle of Nancy Reagan's ovation thus stealing the thunder somewhat. But it was really an accident. The "Battle of the Wives" was all media. There were no intentional attempts to upstage Mrs. Reagan at the convention.

Of course there was no love lost either. "She is a cold fish,"

Mrs. Ford told me. "I remember when the Reagans came to visit us in Palm Springs. Nancy Reagan could not have been colder. Then the flashbulbs went off and she smiled and kissed me—suddenly an old friend. I couldn't get over that. Off camera—ice. On camera—warmth."

\* \* \* \*

Cary Grant was there to introduce Mrs. Ford to the convention. I bumped into him in the Ford holding room at the arena, pacing back and forth. He was a wreck, sweating profusely, rubbing his hands nervously. I asked him what was wrong.

"I'm not looking forward to this," he said in that clipped Cary Grant way. "I don't talk publicly to groups. I'm not used to this sort of thing."

Aside from the whiteness of his hair, he looked and sounded like so many scenes in my favorite movies. I'd seen him act this part before. I somehow felt he was acting now.

"You're kidding," I laughed. "You can't be nervous. Not you!"

"Talking to an audience is quite different from acting," he said. "I don't talk to people. I talk to cameras!"

I told him that it was silly to worry, that there was no way he could help being terrific, and relished my few seconds "coaching" Cary Grant.

\* \* \* \*

There were times when the convention seemed to be taken over by men from outer space, the television crews with antennas sticking out of their heads were so prevalent. The job of convention floor chairman was calm compared to that of television producer. At one point, when everyone was scrambling for news of the prospective Vice President, I stuck my head in the CBS floor production booth. It was a zoo. There were eight correspondents out on the floor and each one seemed to be shouting via walkie talkie at Don Hewitt who was in charge of producing it all.

Noise from the cameramen contributed another level to the din, as did the noise of what was on the air at the moment. The loudest voice of all was Hewitt's as he screamed (to the associate producer) "Lesley's got Strom Thurmond. They are over at the South Carolina delegation!" (and then to the controlman) "She's near camera 8!" (to the cameraman) "Camera 8, can you see Lesley?" (to Lesley) "Lesley, wave at camera 8!" (to the cameraman) "She's waving, camera 8! Can you see her?"

Hysteria. Suddenly a special phone rang. Hewitt picked it up and everything stopped. For a moment, there was total calm. I could hear Hewitt saying in a subdued voice, "Yes. Yes. Yes. . . ."

Who, I wondered. The President of CBS? The President of the United States?

"Yes," he continued in the same respectful tone. Then, "Okay, I'll see you later then, Honey."

*   *   *   *

Mrs. Ford was not in good shape during the convention. When she wasn't waving at a camera, she was in her room having hot compresses applied to her back. Everyone wanted to interview her, and I spent a lot of time fending the press off. She put on a good show for the cameras, but the combination of pain and pain killers would, I knew, take its toll in a televised interview. One reporter, John Hart of NBC, did, in fact, jump the "fence" I had physically formed around her. The result was disastrous, an incoherent on-the-air interview in which Mrs. Ford never answered the questions he asked. Fortunately, it was not that obvious, coming as it did in the midst of so many frenetic on-the-floor interviews. But it was so bad that Don Hewitt, who had been requesting an interview with Mrs. Ford for Walter Cronkite, saw it and said to me, "I see what you mean. You are doing the right thing."

I didn't want to say that Mrs. Ford was ill again. To announce it would have made it a news story, and that, in turn, would have meant a new barrage of reporters and questions. Besides, she has been sick too often.

So I made myself into a human fence. Wherever Mrs.Ford went, I went, pushing the reporters away.

It got me into some trouble. One night, as we were leaving the Kemper Arena, I discovered there was no staff car. Terrified by the idea of having Mrs. Ford go on by herself, I jumped into the back of the Secret Service follow-up wagon. I explained my dilemma to one of Susan's agents, and he said, "Sure, Sheila, get inside." I'm small and I scrunched myself into a ball on the floor in the back taking up as little room as possible.

Everything was fine until we got there. As I got out, another Secret Service agent, Frank Dominico, an enormously husky man with the grace and bearing of a Marine drill instructor, grabbed me and screamed at the top of his lungs: "IF YOU EVER DO THAT AGAIN, I'LL BREAK EVERY BONE IN YOUR BODY!"

"If I ever do what again?" the little voice (mine) asked.

"Ride in a Secret Service vehicle."

"I asked if I could and I was told it would be all right."

He looked at me with such wild hatred in his eyes that I was terrified. He was seething. If ever there was a man physically and emotionally capable of breaking every bone in my body, I thought, it was Frank Dominico.

When he let go, I ran. I was not sure whether my goal was to get to Mrs. Ford or to get away from Dominico. But I ran. I heard him shout after me, "IF YOU EVER DO THAT AGAIN, YOU'LL BE VERY VERY SORRY!"

\* \* \* \*

I sent the kids in as substitutes for their mother whenever I could, and they did beautifully. All four appeared together at an "off-the-record" luncheon *Newsweek* held. Sitting around the big conference table, they made a beautiful picture: four handsome healthy, youthful specimens, each one sharing certain features with the rest, yet each one with his (or her) own look and his (or her) own personality to go with it. It was an important moment for Jack, because for the first time he was the leader. He had become the seasoned politician. He coached the others and took over the conversation at the beginning to give them a chance to warm up. Then he introduced his sister and brothers. Steve talked about rodeos, Susan photography, Michael the church. All talked affectionately about their upbringing and their parents. At the end, Katherine Graham, publisher of the *Washington Post*, which owns *Newsweek*, handed me a note she had scribbled on some scrap of paper. She asked me to give it to Mrs. Ford. It read:

Dear Betty,
Your family is finishing an editorial lunch with *Newsweek*. As a mother, I can't resist sending you a note telling you they are magnificent—dignified, individual, articulate, decent, human—devoted to you and to their country. They are truly moving, and I wanted you to know.

With admiration and affection—
Kay Graham

\* \* \* \*

The girls, oh, the girls. The cynical press speculated out loud that in addition to the delegates, prostitutes from all over the country had gathered in Kansas City ("they always do"). I cannot confirm that. But I can confirm the presence of an amazing number of political groupies, young women between about eighteen and twenty-five who seemed driven (really driven) by the overwhelming desire to sleep with a celebrity. "Braless Bimbos" was the way Jack's Secret Service detail referred to them. And they referred to them frequently, because wherever Jack went, he had to scrape them off. Some called him. Some slipped him notes. Many tried to sneak past the Secret Service guard and make their way into his room. Others bugged him to autograph their underwear. At one rally, a group of hysterical girls tried to drag him off the stage. And they would have succeeded had not the President grabbed Jack's belt and pulled his son back on the platform.

At one point, Rockefeller (for fun and for television) reached out and yanked a Reagan sign from a passing delegate and broke the sign into pieces, smashing it across his knees. The delegate, in turn, pulled the New York delegation's telephone out.

National politics is so sophisticated.

All television cameras zeroed in for a shot of a beaming Rockefeller holding a telephone receiver and disconnected cord up in the air for all to see.

"Goddamn it, Rocky," Senator John Tower scowled at the television set up in the Fords' family box. "Tell Rocky to sit down. He's making a damn fool of himself! What's the matter with the guy?"

A few minutes later, Rockefeller entered the Fords' box, practically skipping, he was so delighted with himself and his antics.

"Nice show, Rocky!" drawled Senator Tower as he shook the Vice President's hand.

\* \* \* \*

It had a happy ending: a pledge of Republican unity, a promise of Republican victory, an excellent movie on *Ford the Man* and the best political speech of Gerald Ford's career.

"You at home listening tonight," he said dramatically in a personal, human tone totally different from his usual delivery, "you are the people who pay taxes and obey the laws. You are the people who make our system work. You are the people who make America what it is. It is from your ranks that I come, and on your side that I stand. . . ."

It was a speech to unify Republicans and unify the nation. It even—temporarily—unified the staff.

"Big Red was something else, wasn't he?" gushed Don Penny who had spent many hours with the President and videotape machines working on the delivery. Bob Hartmann, who had written, rewritten, and rewritten, was also accepting congratulations. And the President, at the enormous party the Fords had after the last session, was a satisfied man indeed. The expression on his face said, "I have won the nomination. I have given a terrific speech. I will not think about anything else—not tonight."

The mood was contagious. Rockefeller announced he was retiring from politics and then moved around the crowd in a jubilant mood, relaxed, reflective. Agriculture Secretary Earl Butz seemed to have a whole new stable of farmer's daughter stories. He had worked hard to secure the nomination for Ford (Republican delegates, after all, are Butz people. For every neurologist, there are about three tractor salesmen—at least two farmers for every accountant) and he was celebrating.

So were the President's three brothers and their wives, all the Ford kids and friends, Grand Rapids friends and assorted Republicans the nation over. Unlike the previous four days, no one screamed *"whooppee!"* and threw confetti. But unlike the previous days, there was a prevalent sense of genuine happiness.

## AUGUST 31, 1976

We came to Vail right from the convention. The President made staff changes at the President Ford Committee, examined opinion polls and issues, mapped out campaign plans and strategy with his top advisors, and challenged Jimmy Carter to debate.

Everyone is terribly excited about this "Presidential Debate" idea, as though a debate were a political lie detector test, a mechanism that will instantaneously reveal to the public which one is the right guy. "I'm the one! I'm the one!" say each of the two men competing for the world's biggest job title. "Put my face under TV lights and my attributes will shine for all the world to see!"

My experience as a TV producer, however, convinces me that a very structured TV debate will tell us nothing about the men or their policies.

The silliness of the debate-mania was summed up in Kansas City when Bob Dole quipped drily, "And then *I'll* debate *Mondale!*" It was a great line, delivered with that air of sarcastic self-mockery that seems to affect Vice Presidential candidates. After all, the Vice Presidency traditionally is an office that transforms a man of talent, ambition, and independence into someone else's sidekick. Granted he is only a heartbeat away from the Presidency. That usually proves to be a very great distance indeed. The first Vice President, John Adams, said the Vice Presidency was the most insignificant office that had ever been created. And Dole's remark indicated he at least had a sense of humor about his "insignificance."

Someone apparently did not get the joke. Someone, perhaps from the League of Women Voters, sponsors of the Presidential debates. The word is they have recommended televised Vice Presidential debates, too. The idea terrifies me. Dole has a cold, sharp, sarcastic wit that the press keep pointing to as signs that Ford chose him as the "hatchet man"—the attack component of the Republican team. Hatchet men do not photograph well on television, they do not inspire votes during the family hour. I talked to Larry Speakes, Dole's Press Secretary, He seemed in total agreement with my arguments. He even said that in 1974, running for re-election in Kansas, Dole was a disaster as a debater, that, in fact, he had almost lost the election because of his debating inadequacies. He said Dole doesn't want to take part in televised debates and concluded by saying, "But we're locked into it, I'm afraid."

"I beg your pardon."

"We can't get out of it if the League announces it," Speakes said. "Neither Dole nor Mondale will be the one to pull out, the one who will look bad."

As such great political decisions were being made, Mrs. Ford was resting. She was in terrible shape when we arrived, still in great pain, pale, drawn, weak. In Vail she just collapsed. In Vail she could. There were stories about how bad she looked when she arrived, but once in Vail, she was out of the spotlight and removed from the need to perform. After two days rest, she began talking about the "big game"—the football game between her Secret Service agents (the "family detail") and the President's. The game was set for the 24th on the Vail football field. Jack was playing on the family detail team. Susan was cheering. Mrs. Ford wanted to be there, too.

I didn't think she'd make it, but as the teams took to the field the First Lady showed up wearing the "Blue Chippers" tee shirt of the family detail team and a funny hat. She was there to "coach." She yelled, screamed, waved her hands around, fought with the referee, huddled with the team, reprimanded them, and did not sit still for one moment. I was amazed at how knowledgeable she was about football. The guys loved it. The press loved it. And Mrs. Ford got really carried away, jumping up and down. *Really* carried away. At one point she beckoned to me to come. I did and she whispered that her prosthesis had slipped. She was holding it in one hand so it wouldn't fall out from under her tee shirt. I looked at the press looking (what was it?). I looked at the wide-open field. (No protection.) The two of us walked away and I shielded her with my body as she slipped the prosthesis back into her bra. As soon as she got herself together, she looked at me and the two of us burst out laughing.

We got to know Steve Ford more in Vail. I think Jack convinced him I was okay because he was more relaxed and less aloof. A tall, blond, handsome, lanky twenty-year-old, Steve looks and acts like central casting's version of the "young cowboy." His preoccupation is genuine. His knowledge about ranching and animals in general is impressive. But much of his act is act. "Partner, why don't you take your lady friend out on the dance floor and let her polish your belt buckle," he drawled to Edward one evening as we sat around Garton's, Vail's Country Music bar, as the strains of "Rose's Cantina" (Steve's favorite song) sounded in the background. "You know, you can tell the quality of a cowboy by how shiny his belt buckle is!"

He is Jack's little brother and he looks up to Jack a great deal. But he has always had a stronger sense of self than Jack. A sense of who he is and what he wants. Up until now, he has carefully avoided politics. Up until now.

"I'm going to quit school and campaign for my Dad," he told me one afternoon.

"Have you told your folks?"

"Not yet. I'm not sure how they will take it. Mom will be okay I think, but I'm not sure about Dad. But I have this great idea for campaigning. I want to take a Winnebago camper and a friend or two and travel through the rural area of the West."

I advised him to stress the idea when he told his parents, and especially the *education* he would be getting from his travels.

The parents' reaction was the opposite of what he had expected, he told me the next day. His father was pleased, flattered that his son wanted to campaign for him. But his mother was very skeptical about whether the prime motive was to campaign or to avoid school.

My biggest "event" in Vail was the fact that one year after the first cancellation, Mrs. Ford finally did an exclusive AP/UPI interview with Helen Thomas and Fran Lewine. It went very well, partly because I set it up at the Fords' house, and various family members kept wandering in and out contributing to the interview. It gave a real feeling of family, I felt.

Q: Has Susan had her affair yet?
Mrs. Ford: You ask her, she hasn't told me about it.
Susan: You're going to be the first to know, remember?
Q: Was that a "no"?
Susan: Yep, that's a negatory.
Q: And Steve, has he got any girl friends?
Susan: Me.
Male voice from elsewhere: My best girls are my horse and my dog.
Q: Do you want to be a grandmother?
Mrs. Ford: I'm dying to be a grandmother. (To *Susan*) Not by you, dear!
(*President walks in.*)
Q:You'd be surprised at the things we've learned about you, Mr. President. Would you like to add something to it?
President: No, I've been working downstairs, trying to get my desk cleared.
Mrs. Ford: You really *didn't* play golf today.
President: I told you I wouldn't.
Mrs. Ford: We didn't believe you.
Jack: He's been putting on the living room rug. . . .

At more serious moments, they discussed abortion, the ERA, amnesty for draft evaders, gun control, and the upcoming campaign. But "family" moments were my favorites. The mood was nice. It said a lot about the Fords.

And at long last, the AP/UPI interview is over. Fran and Helen will never bother me again—about that.)

## Chapter Twenty-three
## SEPTEMBER, 1976:

# SPREADING THE DIRT

*SEPTEMBER 5, 1976*

*Lobos!*
Campaigning means having to say "hello" in many languages. We started with Lithuanian.

*Lobos!* It earned a standing ovation.

Of course it was a partial crowd: About 12,000 Lithuanians who had gathered in Chicago to watch 2,000 other Lithuanians perform in the Fifth Annual Lithuanian Folk Dance Festival, a "special tribute to the bicentennial by American Lithuanians," some 250,000 of whom vote in Chicago.

But it was not a political trip. (Campaigning means always denying trips are political.) Mrs. Ford was just in the *mood* for a huge colorful Lithuanian event. Just as she was in the mood to attend Sunday Church services at the all-black Shiloh Baptist Church after attending a reception for Chicago's black ministers.

In both cases, she brought messages from the President, who "would be here himself, but is so busy working at the White House." (Translation: the pollsters and knowledgeables have *finally* convinced the President to campaign less and be President more.)

(Fact: The President played eighteen holes of golf today.)

We are off and running—for a World Series victory this time. No more pennant races. In Plains, Georgia, today, the opposition threw out the first ball: Chip, Jeff, and Jack Carter all admitted having smoked marijuana.

There are also some staff changes. The Chicago trip was Jerry Ball's last venture on the "First Family detail." It is just too much traveling and overtime, and, given his wife's ultimatum—the marriage or the First Family detail—he chose the marriage.

Mrs. Ford threw a farewell party for him in Illinois. A surprise. She called him into the bedroom of her suite and told him to put his gun, handcuffs, and badge on the tray she was holding. She then took him into the living room where we had all gathered for the party. (The tray maneuver was her way of telling Jerry that he could consider himself "off duty." Otherwise he would not have been able to have a drink.)

I'll miss Jerry. I realized that even more when I found out his replacement is to be Frank Dominico.


## SEPTEMBER 7, 1976

We had our second annual birthday celebration today: Reagan and Ellison Golubin, Susan, Barbara Manfuso, Patti Matson and I went out to lunch. It was the first time I had seen the twins since last October's tragedy. They seemed to be holding up remarkably well, under the circumstances. They had considered dropping out of school, they told me, but decided against it, and, in retrospect, they felt they had made the right decision. The people at college had been warm and supportive. It helped.

Since nineteen-year-olds were in the majority, the conversation quickly went on to other subjects. Who was at Winstons (a Georgetown bar frequented by college kids) last night. Who is dating whom. I was chagrined to hear that Susan's favorite "whom" was still the yet-to-be-divorced football player.

I listened attentively as she brought Reagan and Ellison up to date. She had met him at Winstons. He had been dating another Mt. Vernon student but now he had switched to Susan. And he was still working on the divorce. He was thirty years old. And he was gorgeous . . . just **GOR**geous. What a build.

What a résumé.

Susan always described boyfriends in muscular (as opposed to cerebral) terms, perhaps because she chooses beaux whose biceps are bigger than their head circumferences. No poets on the roster. Ever. So the pattern of this boy-crazy banter was not unusual. But this time the lightheaded teenage swooning got to me. The more she talked, the more edgy I got. This was no boy, after all. This was a thirty-year-old attached man who had been dating another young coed when Susan met him. (And football season was just *beginning!*) I decided to mention these facts and puncture Susan's balloon. I mentioned these facts. But the balloon remained intact.

"Yeah," said Susan. "But he's so gorgeous!"

Susan's balloon always remained intact. Solid, is the word. Her sense of "self" is so absurdly healthy that it seems to remove her from external pressures. That is both her best and worst characteristic. It makes her a wonderful daughter, in that she bucks the "generation gap" theories and peer pressures to rebel. She is very devoted to her parents and does not hesitate to express that devotion, fashionable or not. She is tuned in to them, perceptive enough to sense an anxiety and soothe it away, always concerned about her mother's health, her father's happiness. Friend, too. If she is not with them, she calls her mother every single day. Not out of duty, but out of desire. She likes to talk to her.

At the same time, however, she bucks other pressures too—the pressures to learn campaign issues, for example, to read the front page of the newspaper, to succeed in academia. All intellectual activities elicit yawns from Susan.

Instead, she is involved in her own world, which is the world of rock concerts and Winstons and boys and a new apartment she just moved into in Virginia with three other classmates.

Her brothers say her world is a vapid, superficial, selfish world.

She says so's politics.

Who is right?


## SEPTEMBER 8, 1976

At the front of the Little Theater in the White House, Jim Baker, the newly appointed head of the President Ford Committee, was talking about contacts, general campaign approaches, and who at the PFC was in charge of what. His audience—Michael, Gayle, Susan, Steve, and Jack—listened attentively. This was a special briefing for the Ford kids. They have all decided to take an active role in their father's campaign. For Jack it means more of the same. For Susan, it means trying harder. For Michael and Gayle it means a spiritual sacrifice. "They've talked about it. They've thought about it. They've prayed about it," Mrs. Ford told me yesterday. "Michael says he just came to the decision that he loves his father and he loves his country and it is important for both that his father be elected. I'm amazed; frankly, I didn't expect him to get involved."

For Steve, it means a whole new adventure. "My idea," he explained to Jim Baker during the meeting, "is to take two freinds, my dog Sally, and a Winnebago camper decorated with banners and stickers and just roam the West—Oregon, Washington, Idaho, Montana, Wyoming, Colorado, New Mexico, Arizona, Utah and Nevada—talking to farmers, ranchers, and working people and finding out what's on their minds. I thought I'd travel through October 20th, taking a day off here and there for a little R and R. We could cover 240 miles a day if we split up the driving.

"When people ask me why I'm doing it," Steve continued, "I'll just say 'My father's done a lot for me in the last twenty years. This gives me a chance to pay him back in a small way.' "

Jim Baker nodded. Michael, Gayle, Jack, and Susan nodded, too. Steve had summarized the feelings of all of them.


## SEPTEMBER 12, 1976

It was Susan. Susan on a Sunday morning. Something must be up.

"Did you read that story in the *Post?*"

"Huh?"

"Sheila, there is a story in the *Post* that says I was seen shopping with *him!* It's in the personality section."

"Oh no."

"But I *wasn't.* That's the whole thing. See, it was the other girl he dated at Mt. Vernon. It had to be. She's got blond hair, too."

"You said he wasn't dating her anymore."

"Yeah, well," said the suddenly hurt-sounding voice. "Well, I *thought* he wasn't dating her anymore. But he must have been. All I know is that the story is wrong. It wasn't me. I was in California and I have witnesses."

"Witnesses?"

"Yeah. Mother and I think the *Washington Post* should retract the story. It *is* a lie!"

I found the sudden interest in truth in journalism touching. "While I'm talking to the *Post*, shall I give them the correct caption for that July *Sequoia* picture?"

"Very funny."

Yes, I thought to myself, it really *is* very funny! "Well, what will I say when they say 'Is she dating him?' Don't you see, Susan, if I call the *Post* now, I'll open up a whole can of worms. In the process of talking to a *Post* reporter in the future, I'll casually mention that it was a mistake. In the future. Casually."

She apparently relayed the message.

"The President didn't think you should ask for a retraction either," Mrs. Ford reported later. "You know, that guy absolutely deceived Susan when he told her that his divorce was final. Now it looks like his wife doesn't want to give him a divorce at all. I think his wife has moved back."

(I for one am praying for a reconciliation!)


## SEPTEMBER 13, 1976

We finally got a letter off to Nancy Reagan. That had been bothering me ever since we got to Vail, when *Time* Magazine quoted Mrs. Ford as saying that Nancy Reagan had had a career of her own but that when she "met Ronnie she just fell apart at the seams" and gave it all up.

"What I meant," Mrs. Ford said when I showed her the story, "was that I couldn't understand how a woman who had had a professional life could show so little interest in working women. I didn't understand how she could be against the ERA."

"Right. Call Nancy Reagan and tell her just that."

"I guess 'falling apart at the seams' connotes something more," Mrs. Ford said.

"Right. Call her."

"M*mmmmmmmm*"

The call never happened. I suspect because it is easier to be hypocritical in written form.

"We have friends on both sides of the aisle," Mrs. Ford mused. "Always have. There shouldn't be any feeling of bitterness just because you're running against each other. But damn it all, she was tough from the beginning. She's a queen bee and expects to be treated that way!"

That said, she sealed the letter ("Jerry joins me in sending warmest wishes to you and your husband") and sent it off.


## SEPTEMBER 20, 1976

It was Rusty who discovered it.

Rusty Michaux is a petite woman in her fifties with red hair, Irish ancestry, and a marvelously upbeat personality who does volunteer work in my office. Part of her job is reading and clipping the wire stories. At about 11:40 this morning she rushed in with a piece of wire copy in her hands and a wild gleam in her eye. "I've got a hot one!" she said.

That she did.

My appetite was whetted by the title: "Carter—*Playboy.*" And then even more by AP's opening warning: "Editors: Phrasing in portions of this story may be considered objectionable."

"Jimmy Carter says his religious beliefs give him 'a sense of peace and equanimity and assurance,'" the story began. "But he acknowledges that 'Christ set some almost impossible standards for us. . . . I'm human and I'm tempted.'"

Was this for real? I read on.

Carter had made these confessions, the story said, in a *Playboy* interview due to hit the newsstands next month. "I've looked on a lot of women with lust," AP quoted *Playboy* quoting Carter as saying. "I've committed adultery in my heart many times. . . . Christ says don't consider yourself better than someone else because one guy screws a whole bunch of people while the other guy is loyal to his wife."

By this time I was shaking my head in disbelief (a joke?) and underlining every word (no joke!). One thing for sure, Carter is more fun than Reagan.

"Because of his religious beliefs, Carter said, 'I don't think I would ever take on the frame of mind that Nixon or Johnson did—lying, cheating, and distorting the truth.'"

I re-read. Yes, he said, "Johnson." Unbelievable.

I called Mrs. Ford. She gasped and chuckled throughout my reading.

"What do you think of that?" I asked when I finished.

"I wouldn't touch it with a ten-foot pole!" she drawled with obvious delight.

"Good," I told her. "If anyone asks, say just that."

I thought for a moment about Lady Bird. Mrs. Ford's old friend, Lady Bird. Lady Bird, whom we were due to see again on a trip to Texas next month. Lady Bird who has such pull in Texas. I wondered whether Mrs. Johnson could ever support a Republican.

"Can you believe what he said about Johnson?" I asked her, fishing.

"I don't think Lady Bird Johnson's going to be very happy with that," Mrs. Ford said sympathetically, with none of my devious desires in her voice. "She's not going to be happy at all."

Well, everyone at the White House was, that's for sure. There was laughter and there were lust jokes and general delight as we watched the wire service machines for the latest news spin-offs of the story.

Late in the afternoon, another AP story caught my eye. This one was titled "Ford—*Journal*" and it said that in the October issue of *Ladies' Home Journal*, President Ford told an interviewer that, unlike his wife, he would be very surprised to discover his nineteen-year-old daughter had had an affair.

"I don't think that would happen," he is quoted as saying. "Not the way Susan was brought up."

And we parachute down, down, down from cloud nine.

For the life of me I can't understand why, after so long, the President seized upon this as a conversation topic. A *year* has passed since Mrs. Ford's statement. Susan is a year older now, and not nearly so certifiably "innocent."

"If there is anyone she seems to be showing the slightest sign of being serious about," the President said, "I want to know all about him and his family."

(His mother, his father, his wife. . . . )

Oh dear.

I re-read the original Carter piece and felt better. On a day like this, I assured myself, who is going to worry about "Ford—*Journal*"?


## SEPTEMBER 21, 1976

UPI says that William Whyte, the Vice President of U.S. Steel, admits that he and U.S. Steel paid for three Ford golfing holidays in New Jersey.

I called Mrs. Ford. "He's our *friend*," she said. "We entertained him and he entertained us. We have been friends for a long time. What are you supposed to do when you make friends who are not in important positions, and then they become important? End the friendship? Stop entertaining them and being entertained by them?"


## SEPTEMBER 23, 1976

According to today's *New York Times*, former White House Counsel John Dean's book, *Blind Ambition*, says that as House Minority Leader, Gerald Ford cooperated with the Nixon White House in attempts to head off a House investigation of the financing of the 1972 Watergate break-in.

Dean's book is not due to come out until November, but an excerpt from the book was "made available to the *New York Times*." The excerpt quotes Nixon Congressional lobbyist William Timmons as saying that he had discussed the issue with Ford. The *Times* quotes Timmons—now in a private Washington consulting firm—as saying that he never discussed the issue with Gerald Ford, and that Dean's assertion is "an absolute lie. A bold-faced lie."


## SEPTEMBER 24, 1976

The President listened and studied and practiced and practiced and practiced. So, I'm sure, did Carter. Tonight, all America sat down to watch the result—the much-publicized first debate between Presidential hopefuls, the television program that would create an informed electorate and enable the experts to predict a winner a good seven weeks before the election. The answer, all agreed, would come right away, in the first of the three debates—in fact, the first twenty minutes of the first debate would probably make one candidate and break the other.

The President went to the agreed-upon scene of the duel: Philadelphia. Mrs. Ford sent a loving note and flowers ("Mums—fall mums—his favorite"). We all sat down to watch: Mrs. Ford at the White House with some friends, Edward and I at home with Jack and his friends. Such excitement. Such tension. Such furor.

Such disappointment.

Sipping beer, we stared at the television screen to find the answer. We didn't. Perhaps that was because we were looking too hard. Like the rest of America, we were so busy keeping score we couldn't pay attention. The candidates were so busy not failing that they each seemed incapable of success. The goal was not "be witty, charming, amusing, dramatic." It was "don't trip."

Carter, to our delight, seemed the stiffer of the two, very nervous at the beginning, flat throughout. If the first twenty minutes were, in fact, the important minutes, Carter lost.

If the last twenty minutes were the key, ABC lost. The network's sound track suddenly went out, causing a lengthy delay. "This is just like last summer," Jack hooted. "The night Reagan had his half-hour television program, all the power went off in the White House!"

The debate ended without any definite answer, but with a new question. Instead of "who will win?" everyone now wanted to know "who won?"

The answers were predictable. (Mrs. Ford thought, "No question. The President.") And in some cases, a bit melodramatic ("The American people won, because they got an opportunity to have the two Presidential candidates meet each other and examine the issues").

I thought the winner was Marshall McLuhan.

\* \* \*

## SEPTEMBER 26, 1976

The *New York Times* reports today that the Watergate special prosecutor's office is investigating whether funds from two maritime unions were covertly paid to Ford when he was a Congressman, by having the money laundered through two Republican political committees in Grand Rapids. The investigation which is being run by Ford's Attorney General, according to the report, centered on a period of ten years, beginning back in 1964.

First, the William Whyte thing. Then John Dean's accusation. Now this, I was getting nervous. I called Mrs. Ford. "Sheila," she sighed, "my husband is the most investigated man in history. Do you know how thoroughly he was checked out before he was approved for the Vice Presidency? For heaven's sake, it was the Democrats who put him in office. They are the ones who passed him for the job. I assure you, if there were anything to find, it would have been found."

It made sense to me. But who is spreading the dirt?

## SEPTEMBER 27, 1976

We had been talking for quite a while. I began to leave and then turned around at the door.

"Hey, Jim," I said, teasing, "whatever happened to my commission?"

Jim Connor laughed. "Don't worry," he said, "it's coming along."

"Just checking."

## SEPTEMBER 30, 1976

"Did you hear that Mike said that Carter's lust remarks in *Playboy* were 'just an honest expression of human nature'?" I asked.

At the other end of the telephone Jack Ford scowled. "Well, he's the big religious scholar, not me."

He had not called to discuss his sibling. He had called to tell me that he wanted out. He was in Akron, Ohio, scheduled to go to Illinois and Missouri and he was exhausted and depressed and disgusted with the schedule the PFC had mapped out for him. "I'm not in control of what I'm doing anymore," he said. "The schedule makes no sense. They've got me making long speeches to big crowds. That's not my style."

"So say that. And don't give a speech."

"It's not just that. I'm sick of having to hold hands with every little local political hack. I'm here to work for my father. I don't give a damn about getting all these country politicos in office."

"Well, tell the PFC that."

"No," Jack said. "I'm coming home."

We talked about it for more than an hour, I was on one extension, Edward on the other, trying to convince him to do it because he is needed so badly, but at the same time knowing that if anyone had a perfect right to be exhausted and want to call it quits, it was Jack Ford.

At the end, it sounded as though we had convinced him. But, being Jack, he refused to give me the satisfaction of knowing.

"Just tell me you're going to do it," I pleaded.

"I dunno," he muttered.

Click.

Later I got into bed feeling as though something was wrong. Something was bothering me, had been all evening. A feeling of doom? The scent of defeat? Fatigue? I was sleepy but I was not really sleeping. As I lay there, visions of Fords danced through my head. I saw Steve diligently hitching his horse to a campaign star out West. I saw Mike dutifully spreading the word of his father in New England. I heard Jack admit to the *Baltimore Sun* that having a Secret Service detail is like "sharing your life with eight to ten people," but then add good naturedly, "On the other hand, you *are* traveling with a ready-made card game!"

I heard Susan telling me about her parents' first visit to her apartment. "You should have seen mother. She looked in every nook and cranny, to see if it were clean and if the laundry were done. I put Daddy to work. I made him cook the steaks while mother and I talked in the kitchen." And then—somewhat sadly—"You know, Sheila, I think it kind of made her homesick. I think we'd all be happy to go back. We miss being us."

Tossing and turning in semi-sleep, I began to wonder which verdict would be a real victory. Without turning on the light, I grabbed a piece of paper from the table next to the bed, wrote something down, and then fell asleep.

This morning I found it. Some people write poetry in the middle of the night. I write press statements. On the back of a White House news summary, I had scribbled: "I truly think the family is relieved, and, while disappointed in the outcome, are eager to return to their former life—a normal life. There is nothing normal about living in the White House."

*Chapter Twenty-four*
OCTOBER, 1976:

# POLLS, POLS, AND PILLS

## *OCTOBER 2, 1976*

"Lobos!" again, this time in Pittsburgh, Pennsylvania, where Mrs. Ford donned a babushka, munched pirogies, kolbassi, and holubki, danced the polka, and broadened her ethnic sphere to include Italians and Polish-Americans. A door-to-door walk to "get out the vote" in one of Pittsburgh's working class neighborhoods proved to be one of our more colorful ventures. Smiling in the drizzling rain on a rather depressed-looking city block, Mrs. Ford's knock and casual greeting ("Hi, I'm Betty Ford. I just wanted to stop by to tell you how important it is to register to vote.") brought instant hysteria. Bare-chested men ran to find shirts, mothers madly grabbed brushes for their children's hair. One woman slammed the door in Mrs. Ford's face and then returned a few seconds later, smiling. She had gone to put in her false teeth. There were whispers on the corner ("Isn't she pretty?" "A smart dresser, to be sure!") and an occasional scream from one second-story

365

window to another ("Hey, Dominick! Did you see who's walkin'
down Sarah Street?").

From Pittsburgh's ethnics we went to the Indianapolis Children's Museum, and then on to Texas, where Mrs. Ford dedicated
the new addition to the M.D. Anderson Tumor Institute in Texas.
The Texas stop was non-political, much to my disappointment.
Lady Bird was also at the dedication, and I had hoped she might
endorse Ford. She had announced last week that she was "dis-
tressed, hurt and perplexed" about Jimmy Carter's negative
remarks about President Johnson in *Playboy* magazine. But when
reporters asked her today how she was voting, she lowered her
head and answered simply, "I'm a Democrat."

Unfortunately, Secretary of Agriculture Earl Butz is not. And in
this campaign, which seems to be a rambling course from faux pas
to faux pas, the faux pas of the week goes to Butz. En route home
from the Republican Convention, it seems, Butz had a discussion
with singer Pat Boone and former Nixon aide John Dean in which
the good Secretary of Agriculture said, "There are only three
things the coloreds want: loose shoes, tight pussy, and a warm
place to shit." Dean, who was covering the convention for *Rolling
Stone* Magazine, reported the remark, and, although his story is
not yet out, the stories on Dean's story are out. (The discreet *New
York Times* version says that "Butz described black people as 'coloreds' who wanted only three things. The things were listed in order in derogatory, obscene and scatological terms.")

That's Butz. My father knew him when he was Ezra Taft Benson's assistant, during the Eisenhower Administration, and he's
told me how "colorful" Butz was then, especially in contrast to
Benson, who was a conservative, moralistic Mormon. Self-censor-
ing has never been a Butz characteristic. Two years ago, he was
called into the Oval Office for a reprimand after publicly telling the
joke about how an Italian woman, asked to comment on the Pope's
stand on birth control, says, "He no playa da game, he no maka da
rules." It didn't go over big with Italian Catholics.

But the farmers love Butz. He's fun. Indeed, his jolly, vulgar
style is often endearing. Personally, I believe the man is tasteless,
but he is not a racist. Nonetheless, a remark like the one John Dean
reported is vile and inexcusable. The sooner Butz is out, the better,
so we can get back to the really important issues, the ones in this
month's *Playboy* Magazine.

## OCTOBER 4, 1976

The most recent Gallup Poll shows Carter ahead by only two points. That means that in only three months, Ford narrowed Carter's lead by more than thirty points. It is, says Gallup, "The greatest comeback in the history of public opinion polling."

Ford strategists say Carter's gaffs have helped, and so has the President's new stay-in-the-White-House strategy. Since the Republican Convention, he has done very little campaigning, and has concentrated on looking "Presidential." Ford's comeback was stimulated by his staying in the White House (I resisted the temptation to say "I told you so") but the White House has become an uncomfortable place to stay with the Butz controversy still roaring. Butz is still with us. The longer he stays, the longer the issue is an issue. Everyone is talking about him. Everyone is agreeing that it is "disgraceful" for a Cabinet official to have made such a remark. Even the farmers, frankly, must understand that the man has to go. But Gerald Ford is being loyal and waiting for his friend to leave voluntarily. The President is thinking like a Congressman, I think. Jack Ford won't comment on it. But the Ford women feel strongly. Even Susan Ford, that rare political commentator, has an opinion on this one.

"He's *got* to go," she announced when she called me from Missouri, where she is attending a photo journalism workshop. "I talked to mother the night I heard about it. We both were offended by it—as *women*, you know, offended."

"How's the workshop?"

"Well, it could be better," she said. "The project I was assigned was 'drought' and it has been raining ever since I got here."

## OCTOBER 5, 1976

Earl Butz resigned today. It was his most drawn-out punchline.

## OCTOBER 6, 1976

In the first Presidential debate, Jimmy Carter used 158 facial expressions, Ford used only forty-four. Carter smiled broadly ten times. Ford didn't smile broadly at all. Carter licked his lips eighty-six times to Ford's thirty-three. Carter frowned fourteen times, Ford frowned three. The President looked down on the lectern six times, and Carter looked at the ceiling sixteen times.

Those physical facts of Presidential debate #1 were uncovered by researchers at the University of New York at Buffalo. I don't know what this all means (the eminent researchers apparently are more interested in details than conclusions) but when I heard these facts reported on television this morning, I knew we had scraped the bottom of the analytic barrel. It was time for more input. We needed another debate.

Happily, politics provides. Debate #2 occurred tonight.

I watched it alone in my hotel room (we are in Los Angeles, about to begin a five-day campaign trip) and watching it alone heightened the sense of unreality. In the first debate, our group-stimulated reactions compensated for the lack of action. Tonight, staring at the two emotionless, unresponsive faces which seemed programmed to move in predetermined ways, I became immobile myself. Two glazed eyes staring at four glazed eyes.

There was hostility to be sure. Unlike the first debate, they really slugged it out tonight. But the fight was verbal, words only. Without heart. Like the first debate, it all seemed canned. Even the faux pas.

In the first debate, when Jimmy Carter referred to the "Great Depression of the 40's" we all yelled "FORTIES?" in delight. Tonight, when Ford announced that "there is no Soviet domination of Eastern Europe and there never will be under the Ford Administration," I gasped. I waited for him to correct himself ("What I *meant* was . . ."). Nothing. I began to wonder. Had I imagined it? Had he said it?

"I would like to see Mr. Ford convince the Polish-Americans and the Czech-Americans and the Hungarian-Americans in this country that those countries don't live under the domination and supervision of the Soviet Union," Carter stated later.

Yes, he had said it.

At the end of the debate, Edward called. He was very upset about the Ford statement. But when I went next door to Mrs. Ford's suite where she had watched the debate in bed, she was delighted. "It was like watching someone who knew how to dance and someone trying to learn to dance. The President has a firm grasp on foreign affairs and he demonstrated it,'' she said. ''Carter talked in generalities.''

I mentioned the East Europe statement, but she poo-pooed it. She said she felt the same way when she traveled in Eastern Europe, that no one could dampen the spirits of the Rumanians and the Poles. I said good-night and hoped that all the other debate watchers had come away with Mrs. Ford's interpretation. Maybe they did, but it doesn't matter. I just read the early editions of tomorrow's newspapers, and if the public was unaware of the goof last night, they will be very aware of it today, as they read the paper over their morning coffee.

## OCTOBER 7, 1976

The President flew in to Los Angeles today from San Francisco. He and Mrs. Ford will attend a Republican fundraiser and then go off campaigning separately tomorrow. I was on the phone in the ''kitchen'' (a White House ''traveling kitchen'' is always set up adjacent to the President's suite when he travels) when David Kennerly walked in with Norman Brokaw, vice president of the William Morris Agency. David introduced us and we talked about mutual friends at William Morris among other things. I had heard about Brokaw. He's supposed to be an excellent agent—a description which is both a blessing and a curse. Agents always create a gut reaction of distrust in me.

Brokaw was colorful and lively and very excited about an idea he had to get some more celebrities involved in the Ford campaign. I wanted to pick his brain. Many people have come to me about the possibility of a Betty Ford book—Helen Thomas, other reporters, Simon and Schuster, Doubleday. I have no idea how to go about negotiating a contract, and neither does Mrs. Ford. But, I decided, that can wait. She would only be interested in doing it if Ford lost the election.

As Brokaw talked about how wonderful he thought the President was, I wondered whether part of his enthusiasm was memoir-motivated. Such cynical thoughts. Justifiable thoughts. Norman Brokaw is, after all, an agent.

We talked a while. I told him I might be in touch with him in the future.

He smiled.

## OCTOBER 10, 1976

Everything seemed okay until Saturday morning.

There was a fundraising dinner in Los Angeles on Thursday, a "People for Ford" rally on the steps of the State Capitol in Seattle on Friday and a reception in Denver Friday night. All were characterized by smiles and brief remarks and waves and good press. Mrs. Ford tried to cut out handshaking, and wherever possible, steps. (Doctor's orders for her back.) But aside from that, there were no unusual physical restrictions.

Everything seemed okay until Saturday morning.

We were in Denver getting ready to leave for a reception and a football game in Boulder. I was packing when Pete Sorum appeared.

"She wants to cancel," he told me.

"The reception and the football game?" I asked.

"Mrs. Ford wants to go home. She wants to cancel the rest of the trip."

"Buffalo, too?"

"Everything," Pete said.

"Do you know why?"

"Nope, but she's upset with you for not giving her a written text to read in Seattle yesterday. She also says that she didn't know there would be a press Q and A when she arrived in Denver yesterday."

(Something strange is going on. True, Mrs. Ford used "talking points" instead of reading from a prepared text. But we had talked about her doing that for some time. When she talks about her husband, her words have to be convincing. They should come from her heart, not a piece of paper. In fact, Fran Lewine told me she had never seen Mrs. Ford make a better speech. And the press Q and A at the airport? We went over that several times on the plane coming in.)

"Is she serious about canceling?" I asked.

"She's serious, all right."

"I haven't seen her this morning. How's she feeling?"

"She's a little down."

"*Hmmmmmmm.*"

(The pressure's really getting to her, I thought to myself. And frankly, this election will neither be won nor lost by Mrs. Ford's attending a college football game or Buffalo's Pulaski Day Parade.)

"If she wants to cancel, then we should cancel," I told Pete. "We'll say it's for health reasons."

He went back to Mrs. Ford. A few minutes later, he returned. "She's going to do it. Now she wants to do the whole thing, not cancel any part of it."

In ten minutes we had gone from nothing to everything. I decided to wait until we got to Boulder to talk with her.

"I'm sorry you were disappointed with your speech in Seattle yesterday. Fran Lewine thought it was your best," I told Mrs. Ford.

She smiled.

"And the Q and A at the airport went more or less as we planned."

She nodded.

"You don't have to go to Buffalo," I said. "There would be no problem in just canceling it."

"No," she said with resolve. "I want to go. I don't think I'm going to do any traveling after today, though. This is my last trip. But I want to do it."

"Are you sure? You don't have to."

"Sheila," she sighed, "I'm really not feeling well. I have this terrible back pain. I've been uncomfortable the whole trip."

"I never would have guessed it," I said in genuine disbelief, thinking back on all the radiant smiles and the lively public appearances of the last days.

"I've lived with it for twelve years," she told me matter-of-factly. "I've learned to hide it. I can't let it show."

"Why not? If you don't feel well, why put on a show?"

"I wouldn't want to be around someone who spent all her time complaining about not feeling well."

"You know something?" I told her. "You don't have to do any more of this traveling. You have national stature. Public appear-

ances just frost the cake. They are nice, but not necessary. I hope
you understand that as far as I'm concerned, health is the most important thing in the world."

"I just don't want to end up in a hospital," she said.

"Then don't push yourself. Let's cancel Buffalo."

"No. I'm going to do it. But I want to go right to the hotel when
we get to Buffalo tonight. I'll talk to reporters tomorrow. I don't
want to talk to anyone tonight."

And she didn't. I made sure of that when we landed. She seemed
all right.

She looked all right, too. I can't get over how she does it. She
has, I guess, managed to perfect a way of pulling it off, masquerad-
ing as "fine"—indeed sometimes even radiant, sparkly—while actually enduring great pain. I was most aware of it at the Republican
Convention. Yet, no one would have been able to tell from the pictures. She says that the masquerade helps her feel better, forget
the discomfort a little. But she can smile the Perfect Smile for the
click of the camera at the worst moments. (Conditioned response?
The result of twenty-eight years of political wifing?)

She can't answer questions, however. Words always give her
away when she is in bad shape. That bothered me this morning because I knew that she was supposed to say something at the Pulaski
Day Parade which would alleviate the President's blunder on the
status of Eastern Europe. Could she do it?

Speaking with her in her hotel room before the parade, I felt better, because she felt better. We went over the points she was supposed to make. She understood. Great.

She rode in the parade and seemed to be enjoying herself. I was
not. I was nervous—a gut feeling that something was wrong. The
depressing landscape of downtown Buffalo visible from our parade
vehicle only intensified that fear. We got to the reviewing stand,
and Mrs. Ford impishly pinned a "Keep Betty in the White
House" button on Walter Mondale who was also in the box. Later,
during a lull in the activity, she stepped down behind the reviewing
stand with me for the scheduled press conference. It was very con-
gested, so many reporters huddling around in front of Mrs. Ford. I
crouched down a little, holding the microphone of my tape recorder up to catch what she said, but trying not to stand between Mrs.
Ford and the reporters asking her questions.

It was awful. I heard a question. Then I heard this slow, listless, confused and tense voice answering the question; slurring the words and the thoughts. She talked of the "indomitable spirit of those countries over there in Eastern Europe," adding, "I don't think President [President?] Carter knows what that is all about." Moments later, she again referred to Carter as "President" Carter, before finally demoting him to "Senator" Carter.

"Senator Carter's running mate, Senator Walter Mondale voted against the Free Voice . . . uh . . . the Voice of Europe," she said. She meant Radio Free Europe. I think. I crouched lower and lower with each answer. (This was not exactly the statement on Eastern Europe I had in mind.)

When the press session ended and Mrs. Ford stepped back up to her reviewing box, I ran. Away. Someplace, anyplace, just away. I needed to be alone to think this thing out. The streets were jammed with people. Nothing was open (not on Pulaski Day), except a Burger Chef. I walked in, ordered a Big Whopper but couldn't sit still. I walked out. My mind kept going. What did it? How could she be coherent one minute and so spaced out the next? Stage fright? No. I'd recognize that. The "pain" pills. It must be the "pain" pills. I'm sure they contribute to this erratic behavior. Contribute. There has to be something more. Did she have a drink at lunch before leaving for the parade? That's it. It had to be that. Alcohol and pills (I read somewhere) just don't mix.

Mesa in March. Los Angeles and Grand Rapids in June. Never any warning. She's up. She's down. She's up. How can we continue beyond today? I have no control. How can I schedule anything when I *never know*?

What about now? What do I tell the reporters when they ask what was wrong? That her arthritis is acting up and then there was the distraction of the noise of the parade, the congestion on the sidewalk? No, I'll be calm. I'll say nothing until someone says something to me.

Big Whopper in hand, I walked past the VIP box to the motorcade where I found the White House nurse. "Please, never let her have a drink before a public appearance."

She looked baffled. But I said it again. "Please make sure that she never has a drink when she takes pills!" And I walked away, still trying to sort it all out. It isn't alcoholism. She drinks, true. A vodka and tonic in the afternoon. A vodka and tonic with the President before dinner. She drinks, but not that way. I've never seen her have a drink in the morning. Rarely have I seen her have one at lunch time. And when she does drink, she is no guzzler. She sips. Slowly. I've been with many people who drink more at lunch than she does all day.

It must be those pills. Those pills "for pain" that she takes so casually. A pill and a drink—and a fuzzy head.

I waited for the press to pounce. No one did. Quietly, they filed their reports. Some mentioned Mrs. Ford called Carter "President Carter" but those who did excused it, saying that the crowd was so noisy, she perhaps got confused.

Am I the only one who saw a spaced-out First Lady? What makes them so tactful on this issue?

On the trip home I avoided contact. I have never lied to her and I will never lie to her. But tonight I did not want to be truthful either. On the airplane back to Washington, Fran Lewine and Ross Mark, who is with the *London Express* and also attended the sidewalk press conference, gave me significant looks. I did not respond. They requested a few minutes with Mrs. Ford on the plane. It was a gamble, but I had a hunch it might work. Near the end of the trip, I brought them into her cabin. She was delightful, lively, witty, charming, informal.

Up and down and up and down.

It was the perfect answer to their unasked questions.

It did not answer mine.


## OCTOBER 14, 1976

Dick Cheney called me this morning to tell me that a letter from Special Prosecutor Charles Ruff arrived late last night. The letter said that the investigation into the charge of "laundering campaign funds" was now complete and the investigation revealed *no* violations of the law. "The matter has therefore been closed."

I would have felt better had I not seen Nixon White House Counsel John Dean on the "Today" show this morning plugging his book by panning the President. Elaborating on his charge that Ford cooperated with Nixon aides to head off hearings into Watergate, Dean said that Richard Cook and William Timmons of the Nixon Congressional Liaison staff had asked Ford for help, and then reported back to Dean that Ford had said he would help.

Both men deny this.

There is something maddening about the fact that one of the more evil snakes in the garden reaps fame and fortune by pointing the finger at other people and screaming "BAD!"

There is something maddening about the fact that a pile of unproven accusations, all denied, can create an atmosphere of guilt.

There is something maddening about this new post-Watergate feeling that every man is guilty until cleared by investigation. Ruff now says that he may begin a new investigation, based on John Dean's charges. When will this one end? The day after the election?

I was ready to explode when Mrs. Ford called to tell me that the President already had. His rage was triggered by neither Dean's appearance nor the newspaper stories. His political skin is too thick for that. But when Steve Ford called him last night and said, "Dad, I'm getting all these questions about you and John Dean. What's going on?" *that* did it.

"He's mad," Mrs. Ford said. "He's about to explode. He said to me last night, 'I don't care if I win or not. One thing I've always had is a reputation for honesty. When my own son calls me from California to ask me what's going on, that does it. That's too much!'"

As a result, Mrs. Ford told me, the President has called a news conference for tonight at 7:30 to dispel the rumors.

"I just read that Cook denied the charges and accused Dean of cheap huckstering to promote his book," Mrs. Ford told me. "I always wondered how Dean got all the money for his house and his California lifestyle. I said to the President last night, 'Dear, John Dean would walk over his mother's body to make a buck.' He said, 'Well, he's not going to walk over *my* body!' He really blew his stack."

As I watched the press conference on the television set in my office tonight I decided that rage becomes President Ford. It speeds up his reflexes.

"The thing that means more to me than my desire for public office is my personal reputation for integrity," he said. "For too many days this campaign has been mired in questions that have little bearing on the future of this nation. The people of this country deserve better than that."

He handled questions with alacrity. He was strong and articulate, anger's adrenalin. If only Carter could make him as angry as John Dean, the debates would be much more interesting.

## OCTOBER 16, 1976

Michael called them yesterday on Air Force One to wish them a happy anniversary. "Twenty-eight years, four nice kids, what more can you ask?" I heard his mother tell him cheerfully. She gave the President a joke gift: a wooden nutcracker soldier she had bought in Salzburg last year with a peanut in his mouth and a note that read: "Crack that nut!"

Then it was whistlestop time again. *TOOT TOOT!* This time we were all aboard "President Ford's Honest Abe Whistlestop Train." Our itinerary was the picturesque Illinois countryside: Joliet, Bloomington, Lincoln, Springfield, Carlinville, Alton and so on.

They may all look alike, but a quick perusal of President Ford's briefing papers tells you that each little metropolis is quite different. Joliet makes chemicals. Pontiac was named after the Chief of the Ottawa Indians, was slept in by President Lincoln, and has a local high school football team named the Pontiac Indians. Bloomington was the site of the founding of the Illinois Republican Party in 1856. The briefing papers contain little personal details, too, such as "You have never visited Carlinville, Illinois, before, nor has any incumbent."

I don't think the President made it to the small details. "I want to tell you how pleased Betty and I are to spend our anniversary here in Joliet, Indiana!" he told the crowd in Joliet, *Illinois.*

"Gee, it's great to be in Pontiac—no, excuse me, *Bloomington,*" he told the crowd in Lincoln, Illinois.

Then there was the flyswatter idea, to make fun of Carter's plans for defense cuts by saying, "Whereas Theodore Roosevelt said 'walk softly and carry a big stick,' Jimmy Carter says, 'Speak loudly and carry a flyswatter!'"

Except Gerald Ford said, "and carry a sly stopper . . . a fly stop . . . a fly spotter . . . a . . . FLYSWATTER!" When he finally got it right, the entire press corps broke out in cheers and applause.

"It's freezing cold out there on the platform," Mrs. Ford told me. "I'm not dressed warmly enough; standing up there with the wind blowing at us, it is impossible to stay warm. I keep telling the President not to shout so. He's getting hoarser and hoarser. He is really losing his voice!"

(Let him shout!)

The day ended in a decrepit suite of the decaying Joliet Sheraton Hotel (a place where, I knew without even perusing the briefing papers, no incumbent had ever stayed) where I watched the Vice Presidential Debates on television with Dick Growald (UPI), Tom De Frank (*Newsweek*) and Aldo Beckman (the *Chicago Tribune*). Tom De Frank is a young, somewhat introverted, serious, very hard-working reporter. Dick Growald is an extremely talented but totally irreverent veteran journalist. Tom is always working. Dick is drawing cartoons and caricatures for the amusement of the press corps as often as he's filing stories. Though their work habits differ, their circumferences do not. You'll not find two more corpulent correspondents. These are men who love to eat. So as soon as we all climbed up the dilapidated back stairs of the hotel (the elevator was broken) Growald called room service. I was very nervous about the debate. Dick was very nervous about the food. As it turned out, he had less cause than I.

Soon a huge platter arrived filled with stacks of hot cheese on pieces of bread. Growald's tension ended. The men turned on the set, ready for the "fight" and then hooted and howled and applauded and booed as though it were an athletic match ("Atta boy, Mondale!" "All right, Bob!" "Go, Fritz!") all the time devouring enormous quantities of food.

The distraction worked, but only slightly. My early fears were confirmed. After a weak beginning, Mondale got stronger. After a friendly light beginning, Dole got sharper. The image of "hatchet man" came out, by the end, loud and clear. What was worse, I thought, Dole's stance on camera was disturbingly reminiscent of the young Richard M. Nixon. Just what we needed. I munched on my hot cheese snack and wished I were hungrier.

## *OCTOBER 23, 1976*

Tonight was the third debate. This time the setting was Williamsburg, Virginia, and we were there.

The press came in fours, His and Hers and His and Hers. The event attracted all four celebrities, both Presidential candidates and their wives, and each came with his or her very own coverage team of reporters. The Carter press office was right across the hall from ours, and I went over before the debate just to say hello to some friends. It was eerie. The Carter operation was just like the Ford operation and so many of the reporters in the Carter press room were familiar faces. The set-up was the same. The press was the same. But instead of joking with me, they were joking with the enemy. I had a ridiculous feeling of—well, jealousy!

Jim Karayn, the man in charge of getting the details organized for the debates, told me that the President and his staff always seem relaxed to him. In contrast, he said, the Carter walk-through rehearsals before each debate are filled with tension. "The behavior of the men is directly the opposite of the way the public perceives them," he told me. "Ford and his group are light and informal. Carter and his group are uptight and rigid."

During tonight's walk-through, however, Mrs. Ford may have overdone the informality. While the President perched at his lectern, waiting for the crew to adjust the lighting, she fooled around at Carter's lectern, writing out a note that said something like: "I wish you the best tonight. I'm sure the best man will win. Betty Ford."

It was a little too "informal" for Ron Nessen, who, with justification, pointed out as he hastily removed the note, that had Carter found it just as the spotlight zoomed in on him, it might have thrown him off balance a little.

Mrs. Ford smiled.

I watched the debate on three monitors in a room that had been set up for staff. The cheering gallery. "Brilliant," said the Greek chorus at the Ford statement. "Awful," the crowd hissed at the Carter response. "He's doing great!" Ron Nessen said to me halfway through the debate. "Uh . . . isn't he?"

It was the same old story. The duel of the wooden soldiers. All the advice and the coaching and the cramming had succeeded in sanding down all their personality traits. Deadpan meets deadpan. Vote "yawn" for President.

"Great!" "Terrific!" "Sensational!" were the cries of self-congratulatory self-deception at the debate's conclusion. Don Penny scored a point for reality. "Big Red got through with no mistakes," he said.

At the very end, Mrs. Ford, Susan and the Doles made a grand entrance on the stage as did members of the Carter family, for a show of all-American good sportsmanship. "I felt comfortable out there until Daddy took me over to meet the Carters," sporting Susan told me later. "I just couldn't stand to shake his hand!"

Everybody was busy reassuring each other on the plane. I reassured Susan instead. She has a political science exam tomorrow and she is worried.

## OCTOBER 31, 1976

I just got back from Ohio, Illinois, Michigan, and New Jersey. I am getting ready to leave for Pennsylvania and Michigan. That means it must be October 31st. I don't know what day it is. I do know that there are just two days left. I don't care what day it is.

The days blur. The cities blur. The states blur. The crowds all look alike after a while. Steve Ford visited eighty-nine cities and towns and logged a total of 14,000 miles in his Winnebago. He was the only Ford counting. I shudder to think of how many miles Jack has traveled in this campaign—or Mrs. Ford. The President, who, between the convention and last week only made six short trips, was finally let out of the Oval Office by his advisors. He is presently in the midst of a ten-day blitz—at least twenty-five cities in twelve states.

The mood as we approach the finish line is "be careful!" In a campaign outstanding for its blunders, in an election each candidate hopes to win, thanks to the opposition's mistakes, everyone on both sides is taking pains not to do anything wrong while hoping at the same time that the opposition stumbles again. It got so close that people were beginning to say that the election would be won by the person who made the next to the last mistake. "My biggest worry," Jack told me before he went on "Meet the Press" today, "is that I'll be the one to make the last goof of the campaign, the goof both sides can point to as 'THE ONE.' " (He didn't.)

Sometimes I think I am too close to see what is happening. Are campaigns always so issueless? I knew Ford was a conscientious

President, dedicated to the well being of the country. He did bring the country together, the economy does seem to be improving and we're at peace. It seems to me that the President's real problem is not that he's a bumbler, not that he lacks intelligence, but that he has no single overriding goal, no "main" issue that he feels passionately about. If you want people to follow you, you have to give them a more specific idea of where you want to lead them. "Beyond the goal posts" is not enough. What are we *for*? Ford is a Republican. Carter is a Democrat. That means they vote differently on many different issues. But a President is more than a legislator. He's a leader. He's *the* leader. Where does Ford want to take us? Where does Carter? Where are these candidates' political passions? Both speak of a "new spirit" in America. To Ford, it's the one he brought into office with him. To Carter, it's the one he *will* bring, if elected. In both cases, it's a hazy spirit—just like everything else in this campaign.

It is almost over. The verdict is almost in. The question, of course, is which verdict? Victory or defeat? Which is victory and which is defeat? For Mrs. Ford? I can't be sure. I know she does not want the President to lose because she loves him and because she thinks he is the best man for the job. I know the ham in her, the dancer, the performer, the star, loves being First Lady. But I also know that she would love to relax with her family. I know that the last months have subjected her to the worst of all possible worlds—a physically grueling schedule that requires constant contact with strangers and virtually no contact with her family. The President is now campaigning at a rate that even he, the great campaigner, has never before equalled. Mrs. Ford worries out loud that "He's doing too much. He's going to have a heart attack!" She feels hurt when he forgets to call her. And yet, she exhausts herself by racing all over the country trying to get him elected, and thereby sustain the condition! But does she have a choice? I watch him and I wonder whether all those old retirement plans were really bilateral. I think Mrs. Ford might prefer to give up the First Lady spotlight and become the center of her husband's world. But I wonder whether that is a viable alternative. Is it a real option? Do politicians ever stop running completely?

Two days to count down and it is too close to call! According to the Gallup Poll, Carter's lead went from two points on October 4th up to six points on October 11th (thanks to Butz and Eastern Europe) and has been holding at six points ever since. But 10 percent of those polled are still undecided.

Las Vegas oddsmaker Jimmy the Greek said the odds were 6–5 for a Carter victory last week. Now they're 6–5 for Ford. A palm reader in Minneapolis insists it's Carter's win, but adds, "I may change my mind before Tuesday." The *National Enquirer*'s "EX-CITING PRESIDENTIAL POLL RESULTS" reveal 49.93 percent for Ford, 49.24 percent for Carter. (And 100 percent for the *Natial Enquirer.*) And Taco Lipps, a dog in California who can do addition, subtraction, multiplication, division, and square roots with a 90 percent accuracy rate, says Ford will win.

*Chapter Twenty-five*
NOVEMBER, 1976:

# "THEY LOVE HIM IN CALIFORNIA"

*NOVEMBER 2, 1976*

The big campaign ended where all the little ones had—Grand Rapids. She came from Harrisburg, Pennsylvania. He came from Canton, Ohio. They met and hugged and kissed and, hand in hand, rode down the main street viewing what had to be the most moving spectacle of all: a parade of bands and banners and balloons and 50,000 human beings. Fully one quarter of the total population of the city had turned out and all were behaving like personal friends. Tacky, somewhat decaying downtown Grand Rapids had not looked so effervescent in years. Even the vacant stores had FORD-DOLE banners in their windows.

President Ford had traveled 16,000 miles in ten days and he looked it. Drained, hoarse, exhausted, he lifted his weary eyes and they promptly filled with tears. He threw away his prepared text. This may have been the "western portion of the state of Michigan, where the latest polls showed the President running neck and neck with Carter." But it was also home. And 50,000 relatives had turned out.

"As we came off the expressway, we went down College Avenue, past Central High, where Betty went to school, past South High School where I went. . . . You know better than anyone in this country I never sought this office. . . . Circumstances put me in a position where I stood in the East Room of the White House. Betty held the Bible. I put my hand on it. I took the oath of office at a tough time. . . ."

Thunderous applause and cheers followed every statement. In what seemed to be his last burst of energy, he led the crowd at first: "LET'S GO! LET'S GO!" But then the football player became reflective, more interested in looking back than in grabbing the ball and running for the touchdown.

Perhaps his legs were tired.

"It's nice to be back here. I see Bill Milliken. I see Bob Griffin. I see all the people I grew up with and Betty grew up with. You know, it's hard to express one's deep sentiments about a community that has been so good to us. . . ."

They stayed overnight at the Pantlind Hotel (where Mrs. Ford and I had stayed in June). There's no Presidential Suite in the slightly rundown hotel, but there are many congressional memories. That seemed to be what they were looking for.

Today the Fords voted, and then, just before leaving for Washington, attended the dedication of an eighteen-foot-long mural on the President's life. The painting looks like an enormous Gerald Ford photo album with scenes from his infancy, portraits of his parents, his mother holding him, his childhood friends, the young man in his military uniform, later with his bride, Betty Bloomer, and, finally puffing on his pipe, there is Gerald Ford, President of the United States. There are individual portraits of Susan, Steve, Michael, and Jack, too, as young adults. It was a beautiful and moving tribute to the only Grand Rapids boy who ever made it to the White House. And it was all too much. The crowd seemed awed. The Presidential entourage stopped studying polls and pulled out handkerchiefs. The President reminisced about his parents and at one point, wiped the tears from his eyes with the back of his wrist. Even Helen Thomas cried.

There was a calm, a sense of closeness on Air Force One as we flew back to Washington this afternoon (Ron Nessen put his arm around me as I got onto the plane and told me he considered us "friends"), a relief that the battle is over and that there is nothing more any of us can do now. Except wait for the verdict tonight.

## NOVEMBER 3, 1976

It's 3:30 in the morning and both ABC and NBC have projected that Jimmy Carter is the new President of the United States.

President Ford is going to bed, but is not conceding defeat—not officially, at least, About thirty minutes ago, he called Dick Cheney and Bob Teeter up to the residence where a group of us had been watching the returns and told the men to explain the options, or rather to explain that there were still some options. Eruditely, the expert tacticians twiddled their numbers in wondrous ways and came up with three adequately confusing electoral combinations that would spell a Ford victory. It did not create optimism. But it gave us all the out we needed, the excuse to call it a night and see what happens in the morning.

About thirty-five of us watched the election returns together: Jack, Steve, Michael, Gayle, and Susan (each with a friend or two), the President's brother, old family friends from Michigan and Vail, and adopted family members like Clara Powell, the woman who worked for the Fords for twenty years. ("She's a beautiful person," Mrs. Ford has said often. "She and I brought up the children together. She had a wonderful influence on my life and theirs.")

Joe Garagiola and Pearl Bailey were also there. Both of them were very active in the campaign and, in their involvement, each developed a warm relationship with the Fords. Pearl Bailey has been a good friend for some time, a cheerful, buoyant presence capable of lifting Mrs. Ford's spirits upon command. She's both a flamboyant personality and a thoughtful friend. She's crocheted some beautiful things for Mrs. Ford on her travels (since Pearl Bailey refuses to take airplanes, she spends a lot of time traveling).

Tonight Mrs. Ford, Pearl, and I made up the cheering section. Optimistic to the end (due more to our determination than to the returns), we sat on the floor in front of the two TV monitors in the Fords' den, and, at tense moments joined hands and chanted the names of the states that were essential to win. Ours was the informal watching area. (I had selected the monitors accordingly, turning off CBS which, early in the evening, seemed to be predicting a Ford defeat, in favor of NBC, whose large color map made the Ford returns [in blue] look good, since we were doing better in geographical area than in electoral votes.)

Several of the other guests wandered in from time to time to escape the reality of the returns in the living room.

Joe Garagiola is a more recent Ford friend. The baseball-player-turned-sportscaster-turned-TV-personality had never backed a political candidate before and his endorsement of Ford was primarily based on one man's respect for another man's decency. His gut instinct was that Ford was a good guy, and that instinct drew Garagiola into the campaign. He hosted several half-hour PFC spots with President Ford and other Ford supporters and they were good spots, largely because Garagiola, through wit, sports jargon, and a relaxed aura of informality, was an expert at loosening the President. One Garagiola remark at the beginning of a campaign spot and Gerald Ford's taut, tense countenance melted into a huge grin and hearty laugh. The technique worked tonight, too. "Big deal," Garagiola grunted as one of the big states went for Carter early in the evening. "It isn't even the second inning yet!"

The quietest spectators were the professional politicians: Congresswoman Edith Green (a Democratic convert to Ford), Vice Presidential candidate Bob Dole, New York Senator Jacob Javits, and the President himself. Ford could not have said much if he had wanted to. The last days of hysterical campaigning had taken his voice away, leaving behind a raspy whisper. But he did not want to talk much. He was intent and pre-occupied. It was his ballgame, after all (as Joe Garagiola would have put it), and while his guests watched because it was the evening's activity, he stared at the screen in search of an answer. I think he was getting one too, but it was one he didn't feel like sharing.

We got calls all night, from the "men downstairs"—the Cheney gang was working in the West Wing (probably with the intent of jumping on the Ford motorcade when it left for the victory celebration at the Sheraton Park Hotel. But the victory motorcade never came off. All night it seemed to be just a half-hour away).

Politicians phoned in, too. Early in the evening Ford reported their messages. "That was John Connally," he croaked to the crowd. "He was in a great mood. He said, 'Before the night's out, you'll have Texas!'"

Texas went to Carter around midnight, and the rest of the phone calls went unreported.

Bob Dole said little. He seemed somewhat bitter, perhaps because he too recognized the handwriting on the television set, per-

haps because he was a little hurt about how his own role in the
campaign had been interpreted as hatchet man, "Growler" to
Ford's "Good Guy." Dole is a very quick and witty man, but too
often his instinct for sarcasm does him in, simply because other
people don't understand his humor. In the Vice Presidential debate
with Mondale, many felt he was too cutting. And tonight at one of
the most emotional moments of the evening, his sarcasm surfaced.
When Ford called everyone together to listen to Teeter's pro-
nouncements, he concluded, "There's no way we'll know for sure
until tomorrow."

"Mr. President," someone broke in, "shouldn't someone go
over to the hotel then? They will be waiting for the word from
here."

"Yeah," Ford whispered. "Bob would you mind doing it?"

"Sure," Dole said. "I'll do it."

"Tell them," the President rasped, "tell the supporters that as
far as we're concerned, the election isn't over until the last vote is
counted."

"And *re*counted!" quipped Dole, without missing a beat.

Suddenly Cheney and Teeter's faces dropped. No one laughed.
No one moved. Silence.

"No, Bob, no," the President whispered with alarm. "Don't say
that. You can't say that."

He wouldn't have said it, of course. But once again, only Bob
Dole knew Bob Dole was joking.

Cronkite just joined the others in predicting a Carter victory. It
is so close, though. Every state has been so close that I don't feel it
is over. There must still be a chance.

Mrs. Ford seemed to feel that way too all night. Both of us were
positive to the end, the very end. As Edward and I left, I looked
over my shoulder and saw the President and Mrs. Ford locked in a
hug, holding on to each other tightly. The warmth was bilateral.
But their facial expressions were different. She looked as though
she felt the election were still "too close to call." He did not.


## NOVEMBER 3, 1976 (10:30 A.M.)

The whole family gathered in the Oval Office at noon. It was
over. The President, his words still voiceless, whispered the final

"chin up" pep talk, and then showed them all the telegram he had sent to Jimmy Carter congratulating him. The family decided that Mrs. Ford would read the telegram when they met with the press. And then, heads held high, they marched together to the press room.

The President told the press his voice had given out and introduced Mrs. Ford as his replacement. She stepped forward and read the statement in a strong voice, her eyes dry, her smile steady. A gutsy delivery. Once again, when there is an occasion to rise to, Mrs. Ford rises to it. Behind her the President stared into space. The children blinked to keep back the tears. Susan blinked and blinked but the tears came anyway.

After she finished, the family circulated around the press room, shaking hands. The President than retreated to the Oval Office, but Mrs. Ford kept going. A rock. She chatted with reporters as I showed her around the press room. Helen Thomas had her editor on the phone, and Mrs. Ford talked to him, stressing the fact that she felt the President had done an "excellent job for the country."

Susan couldn't pull it off. Her eyes were red, her cheeks sopping wet. She did not sob, but noiselessly her eyes kept filling and emptying, filling and emptying. She was not crying for the Azalea Festivals she would not be queen of, she was crying for the hurt she felt her father was enduring. "Poor Daddy," she whispered to me softly when I tried to cheer her up, "this is the first time he's lost something. He wanted to win so badly. It must be so hard for him."

The family regrouped in the Oval Office where David Kennerly took pictures (clicking and crying simultaneously) and other close associates came by . . . Rumsfeld, Scowcroft . . . wearing taut faces and bitten lower lips.

I sat outside the Oval Office. Then it finally got to me. The blunt reality of losing, coupled with the frustration of losing so narrowly. A few more people in a few more crowds in a few more states could have made a difference. The memories soured. I cried, too. Tears for someone else. Like Susan, Mrs. Ford, Jack, Steven, and Michael, I cried for the President. He was, after all, the one who had wanted to win.

*    *    *

## NOVEMBER 4, 1976

Life goes on.

There are long lines at the photocopying machine as résumés get duplicated.

"I told my mother that if we had won the election, we would have felt victorious for two days until the numbness wore off, and then we would have been losers for another four years," Steve Ford explained today. "But having lost the election, I think the whole family became winners for life."

"We all sat down to dinner last night and began exchanging anecdotes about the crazy things that had happened during the campaign," Michael said. "I told about the time I went to a store where an enormous crowd was expected and found the place deserted . . . things like that. We all laughed a lot and it was a wonderful family night. We got it all out. We're ready to go on now," he said. "Ready for a new experience, a new beginning."

Norman Brokaw from the William Morris Agency is ready too.

"They love him in California," declared the Super Agent. "I'm not kidding, people out here are heartsick about his losing. He's a great man. He can do anything he wants now." Pause. "If he wants to write his memoirs, for example, I can get him a million dollars for it."

"Norman," I gasped. "One million dollars?"

"One million dollars."

Life goes on.


## NOVEMBER 5, 1976

Ann Buchwald and David Obst called today. They are literary agents and they say that Mrs. Ford is one of the hottest properties around. Frankly, they said, Mrs. Ford is even more valuable than the President. They would like to handle her. They could give her more attention than, say, the William Morris Agency.

I told them I would talk to her about it.

The opportunity came only a few minutes later when Mrs. Ford appeared at my office. She had just stopped by to say hello and give the staff a little post-election thank you. I told her that the literary world was beating a path to her door. She laughed. I told her the specifics of the Ann Buchwald/David Obst conversations. She said it sounded very exciting, but her eyes did not back up her words. I told her about Norman Brokaw's interest in the President. She was more interested.

The President, I thought. She's worried about the President.

"You know, your life doesn't come to an end just because you lose an election. The President can do anything," I told her. "He has to understand that there are many, many options open to him. His future can be very exciting."

"Oh, I know that, yes," she said. "I got up at 6:30 this morning and Jerry did too and you know what I said to him? I said, 'I think we won! There's so much to look forward to. I think it will be another new adventure.'"

Again the eyes were saying something else.

"How did he react to that?" I asked.

"Well, he's still a little disappointed," she said softly, her gaze turning out the window and beyond. "There were so many things he still wanted to do. And there were things I could have done too. . . ."

"But you still can do them," I said. "So can he. Both of you have national influence. You must stay involved in the things that are important to you."

She nodded. "Yes, that's true," she said uncertainly.

"The old man isn't himself," Jack announced brusquely this afternoon. He didn't elaborate, but the statement itself and the look of concern on Jack's face answered a lot of my unasked questions.


## NOVEMBER 6, 1976

"Mrs. Ford has had offers, too," I told Norman Brokaw when he called again today. "I don't know what she wants to do, but another agent told me that her book could get more than his."

I wanted to stop his Super Agent fast talk, to show him that he shouldn't get his hopes up, that there were other agents circling overhead. He wasn't the only one.

He didn't say anything for a while, but suddenly I sensed what he was thinking and it was not what I had intended. Package deal. I could practically hear his pulse beat thud across the telephone wires. PACKAGE DEAL!

"When are you all going out to California?" he asked.

"We leave for Palm Springs tomorrow for the Fords' post-election vacation."

"I'll be there."

I am bothered by all this. I am bothered by the idea of the President of the United States becoming a hot property—a client of the William Morris Talent Agency. Following each phone call with Brokaw I entertain nightmarish images of Gerald Ford selling Alka Seltzer ("When you're President of the United States, your stomach gets upset a lot," says the smiling face on the television screen), Gerald Ford trading in the Presidential seal for the Gillette logo, Gerald Ford explaining that now that he can't travel on Air Force One anymore, he and Betty are sure to carry American Express Travelers checks with them at all times.

Granted, the President needs an ego boost. Granted he needs to know that there are many opportunities available. He needs to know that he can be rich. He needs someone who can give him an overall view of all the options. And Norman Brokaw certainly can give it to him.

But an agent? The Commander-in-Chief goes commercial, exchanging dignity for the dollar? It makes me very uncomfortable.


## NOVEMBER 8, 1976 (Palm Springs)

"Look, if the President gets himself a good lawyer, the lawyer can protect him by acting as a buffer between the President and an agent," Edward said. "I think you should take advantage of Brokaw's knowledge. Tell him about the kids' interests, Mrs. Ford's interests, etc. See what ideas he can come up with. Then put his ideas into the pot with everyone else's. You should get as many ideas from as many people as possible."

Today I gathered the raw data, while encouraging the Fords to see what Brokaw could offer.

"Yeah, photography is what I'm really interested in," Susan Ford said as we lay in the sun by the swimming pool in our bathingsuits.

"I don't know," said Jack, leaning back and thinking for a moment. "I guess I'd still like to do something in the environment area."

A movie about a rodeo rider (starring Slim Pickens and Chill Wills) blared on the television set in his room as Steve Ford told me he wanted to climb back in the saddle and pretend the campaign had never happened. "I want to be a rodeo rider, that's all," he said. "I don't want to do anything fancy. I'm not good enough to be a big deal. They ostracize you in the rodeo business if you play on name."

I fed it all into the Norman Brokaw computer. He swallowed it with delight.

## *NOVEMBER 10, 1976*

This is our fourth day in Palm Springs. The Fords have come to relax and to plan their future. They plan to retire here, because they have friends in Palm Springs and because the weather is warm and dry and good for Mrs. Ford's arthritis.

Those are the pluses.

Palm Springs is also filled with rich retired people whose lives revolve around playing golf and throwing lavish parties with tents and orchestras and exotic floral arrangements. Their golf carts say it all. I saw one today that must have cost about $15,000. It was a perfect replica of a Rolls-Royce, only golf cart size. It included an eight-track stereo set, a television, a CB radio, and a refrigerator. Now, you have to figure that a man with such a golf cart 1) plays a lot of golf, and 2) has a lot of money.

Retirement is a drastic change for anyone, but it is especially traumatic to suddenly switch from moving mountains to moving golf balls, fulltime. President Ford is an active, incredibly energetic man. If he retires in Palm Springs he will either go out of his mind or go out of Palm Springs a lot. I have visions of his duplicating the old record of "200 nights a year on the road" that he set as Minority Leader. Only this time, instead of being left home with the kids, Mrs. Ford will be left home alone.

The wealth bothers me, too. In this community the lavish $100,000 yearly retirement benefits of the Presidency will give the Fords the status of "your typical American couple living on inadequate fixed pension benefits."

I hear the President is despondent. I hear he is madly looking for vocational alternatives, some rather unimpressive. (How can you practice law representing the private sector when the public sector is paying your Presidential pension?) I hear Mrs. Ford is very worried about him. I hear this from the kids. I have not bothered the Fords because I think they are entitled to privacy for once—a luxury of losing.

I did see Norman Brokaw, however. Edward and I met him this afternoon at the Tennis and Racquet Club where he is staying. He was armed with an elaborate total-family approach, a typed proposal he is going to present to the President tonight which incorporates activity ideas for every member of the Ford family but Michael—the ultimate PACKAGE DEAL! Brokaw's stocky body looked ready to pounce, his tanned cherubic face expectant. His big night.

"Look, he wouldn't be the first President to have an agent," he told me, sensing my reluctance. I thought of the "deals" agent Swifty Lazar had pulled off for Nixon. It was not the sort of precedent I found appealing.

"LBJ had a big deal with CBS," Brokaw was explaining softly. He has a loud personality but a quiet voice. And dark sad eyes. "Johnson got paid a lot of money to do his reminiscences with Walter Cronkite. CBS owned Johnson's book, you know." He said, "This is just a phenomenon of the times."

Maybe.

But I see Steve Ford doing the "Marlboro Country" ads. I see Susan plugging Polaroid. I wonder what the President will see.


## NOVEMBER 11, 1976

Edward and I made our way through the Bentleys and the Rolls-Royces parked outside into the restaurant's equally posh interior. Brokaw was already at "Melvyn's" to greet us. I took one look at him and knew he had gone over big with the President. It was all over his face. He was ecstatic. "He's a great man," he purred over drinks. "The country loves him. The country owes him a lot." Norman paused, and I wondered whether he was totalling the country's tab.

He had had a wonderful meeting, he said, with the President. "Mrs. Ford was there too and it couldn't have been better. The President really liked the proposal. He liked my ideas for the kids.

I went over each kid, one by one. He kept telling me that the whole family had to stay together."

Package Deal.

"He really liked my idea about setting up a Betty Ford Cancer Institute for research at Cedars Sinai Hospital in Los Angeles. I told him I have a lot of connections, good friends who are doctors, enough contacts, I think, to get the whole thing rolling. We can throw a terrific party and raise the money. . . ."

It was such a funny mixture, the show biz hustle and jargon for a Cancer Research Institute. He talked Super Agent but his ideas were sound. I could understand his appeal to the Fords.

He told us about his other clients: Olympic-swimming-champion-turned-commercial-champion Mark Spitz; a pretty weather girl he had landed a job in network news; comedian Bill Cosby, for whom Brokaw had landed the lucrative Jello and Del Monte advertising spots (I suddenly saw Gerald Ford on television urging Jack to eat his yummy green beans).

He told us about himself, how he grew up in New York City, came to Los Angeles in 1943 at the age of fifteen and went to work in the William Morris Agency mailroom. He never left the agency, but instead he has spent the last thirty-three years working his way up. He talked about his tennis game and his country club and his twin sons in the public relations firm, and his favorite deals. And his clients. Always his clients.

He told us that he loved his work, that he lived his work and we believed him. I had never met a Super Salesman before but my instincts told me I was meeting one now. I was awed by his aggressiveness, his incredible energy, his determination. I was frightened by his lack of subtlety.

"If you do end up with the Fords," I told him at the end of yet another vivid anecdote about yet another client, "it would all have to be confidential."

He assured me that it would be. "He's a great man," he said over dessert. "The country loves him a lot. The country owes him a lot."

## NOVEMBER 14, 1976

Edward told Jack his father should hire a lawyer to stand between the President himself and an agent, if, indeed, he signed up with an agent. That way, Edward said, it would be the lawyer who retained the agent on behalf of the Fords, and the Fords could just say publicly that an attorney is managing their affairs, and he may have employed others — accountants, agents, whatever — to help.

The buffer, Edward felt, would give a sense of distance and with it, a sense of dignity.

Jack told his father.

When Mrs. Ford called yesterday she seemed a little low. I repeated what I had said before, that the President had the whole world at his doorstep, waiting, that he could do anything he wanted, in the future.

She told the President.

I believe it was as a result of both Weidenfeld utterances that Edward and I found ourselves eating lunch today at the dining room table in the Leonard Firestone home (the place the Fords were staying this trip) with the President and Mrs. Ford.

At Mrs. Ford's urging, Edward discussed the lawyer and I discussed opportunities unlimited. The President listened and asked questions. He was polite, but defensive.

Then I decided to ask one. The reporters know President Ford called Nixon after the election, and they have been speculating ever since on why he did. (This is a dull news week.) "Mr President, there's one question I have," I said. "It's about the phone calls to Nixon. I think you should have an explanation for the press."

*Boom!*

"An explanation? Why do I need an explanation?" he snapped. "He is a politician, an ex-President. I wanted to hear his analysis of the election. I just wanted to call him. And Goddam it, I can call anyone I want!"

"Well, I thought it should be explained. You could say you were calling about Mrs. Nixon's health, for example."

"Pat's health. Yes, that's another reason I called—to see how she's recovering from the stroke. But I'm not going to clear this with anyone," he said, still irritated. "I can call whomever I want!"

The anger was probably caused by his post-election blues. But the attitude, the naïve stubbornness and bull-headed loyalty were so typical. This issue of Nixon's pardon has never gone away. It has cropped up time and again in the last two years, and every time it does, the President just ignores it. He never explained the pardon satisfactorily. He did not plan its execution well in the first place. He has never smoothed it out of the public consciousness in the two years he's had. And he doesn't care.

Cynics, of course, say he made a deal with Nixon. Those who know the President know it's not a possibility. The fact is, Gerald Ford's excessive sense of "loyalty" extends even to Richard Nixon, who, according to Jack, infuriated Ford during the Watergate scandal by lying to him, too. Jack says his father believed Nixon when he told him—up to the end—that he was being honest. Then when the tapes came out, Ford told Jack he would never trust the man again, that that was the last straw.

Would it had been the last straw!

## NOVEMBER 15, 1976

We were nestled cozily in the back seat joking with the chauffeur of our White House limousine (when you fly home on Air Force One, you get driven to your door in style). We were discussing the underlying rationale for White House limousines, how in case of nuclear attack, the cars are supposed to transport the President and the White House Staff to one of the predetermined retreat points. The rumor is that there's a gold team and a white team and who is on which team depends upon the priority with which the official is to be dispatched and the location to which he is assigned. The more important people are rushed more quickly. Underneath one of the mountains around Camp David, myth has it, there's an underground city and a command post for the President and the executive officers of the United States who are designated to go there, stay there through the nuclear attack, and then when it is all over, continue to rule the country.

Our driver, an Army sergeant, was more expansive than usual, and the three of us laughed as we made out mental lists of who was on which team. "Well, tell me something," Edward said, "if you were to pick Sheila up in that kind of disaster, would you take me along, too?"

"You're a real nice guy, Ed, and I'm glad I'm telling you this at the end, but the answer is no. Orders are orders."

"No? You'd leave me to die in a nuclear attack?"

"Well, let's put it this way," the military man said. "If someone says to me, 'You've got fifteen minutes to live, go get Sheila Weidenfeld,' do you really think I'm going to do it? You think I'm going to spend my last fifteen minutes picking up Sheila Weidenfeld?"

We laughed.

"Well," said Edward as we unlocked the front door, "now you know what it's like to lose."


## *NOVEMBER 17, 1976*

Patti McLaine told Jack he is very critical of himself, feeling defeated at the moment, secretive, guarded, vulnerable to women, perceptive, determined, and, because he is so guarded, the most difficult person she has ever had to read tarot cards for.

Perhaps that's because he only did it at my urging. Edward pointed out, with some amusement, that while the West Wing has brought in professional head hunters and management groups to place the staff, my gift to my office and friends was a tarot card reader.

Well, Patti McLaine was in town anyway.

So was Barbara Walters—not to read tea leaves, however. Rather to survey the residence with ABC's production team. Barbara has switched networks, and the Fords have lost office, but finally, almost two years after our initial discussion, Barbara is going to take America on a tour of the Family Quarters with Mrs. Ford. She'll interview both the President and Mrs. Ford after the tour. The taping is scheduled for early December. The show will air in January.

"When we went through the kitchen, Barbara Walters opened the refrigerator door thinking it would be a cute touch to see what a normal American family keeps in the refrigerator. She found eight bottles of champagne, and laughed, asking, 'Can you make sure they're still there when we come back to film?' "

I'm sure I won't, I thought to myself; but I must remember to tell her to ask Mrs. Ford about the box which was labeled "TAPES: DON'T TOUCH."

It had been so long I'd almost forgotten. Mrs. Ford told me, when she first arrived at the White House, that she found this box labeled "TAPES: DON'T TOUCH" in one of the rooms. For the longest time, she said, she passed the box and obeyed the order. Gradually, her curiosity increased and the awe of the White House decreased. One day she opened the box.

She found a collection of Montovani tapes that had belonged to Nixon.

## NOVEMBER 21, 1976

We spent the weekend at Camp David. "We" consisted of Edward and me and Jack and a few of Jack's friends. It was a little awkward at first, maintaining the castle without the King and Queen. A young Navy steward (about Jack's age) wearing a red jacket waited on us at dinner in Aspen Lodge the first night, and then later, when we watched a movie in the living room, he brought each of us popcorn and a foot stool so we could watch with our feet up.

The weather was cold, bitter cold. (So cold, in fact, that the Secret Service forsook their bicycle acrobatics and used a golf cart to get around instead.) But we took advantage of all the facilities anyway. I went to shoot some arrows at the archery range, and the person in charge of archery told me he was delighted because no one had come to use the archery range in eight years. "I was getting rusty," he confided.

The skeet instructor gave us all ear plugs and took us one by one to show us how to shoot. I had never held a rifle before, except in amusement parks, and it showed.

The Secret Service kept us warm on the skeet range with stories about how President Johnson mistreated them. They said that the peacocks at the LBJ ranch used to electrocute themselves on the fences and Johnson for some reason believed that the Secret Service men set them up for it, and retaliated.

"He was really an impossible man," one agent said. "He used to fire Secret Service men on the spot. He'd say, suddenly, 'Get out of my car!' and then the next day he'd come down and say, 'Where's Johnny?' And someone would say, 'You fired him yesterday, Mr. President,' and LBJ would answer, 'Hell, he should have known I was only joking!' "

"I heard one of the guys whisper to the detail chief, 'Get me out of here before I kill the bastard!' "

We walked back past the jungle jim the Kennedys had built. "Amy Carter will soon be playing on those swings," Jack said.


## NOVEMBER 22, 1976

The new tenants came to view the property today. It was all very civilized. A little too civilized perhaps. Everyone in the White House was very cooperative. Everyone in the White House had strict orders from the top that the President wanted them to be very cooperative. "I swear he wants to kill the Carters with kindness," Mrs. Ford whispered to me.

She was very cooperative, too, however. She had an album put together for Mrs. Carter with color pictures of every room, floor plans and sizes included.

"She wanted to know about the household help and what to do with Amy. She wanted to know if I brought my own help. I told her 'No,' but that many other families had. We talked about the Truman Balcony, how we eat out there sometimes, about what we do when we have friends over, about State Dinners. It was quite friendly."

Mrs. Ford was very sporting about it, I thought—a different attitude from the one she had toward Mrs. Carter during the campaign. ("Saccharin sweet but always ready to stick a knife in your back.")

I spoke with Mary Hoyt, Rosalynn Carter's Press Secretary, a little. It was Mary who told me at a party just after my appointment as Mrs. Ford's Press Secretary that the White House reporters had given her the unofficial job of warning me about just how difficult it would be to work with Nancy Howe. I now had many warnings to give her in return, but no time today. Next month.

Things are different at the White House these days. Very Lame Ducky. Everything now centers on the things to come, the new administration. Returning to my office, I thought about this as I answered phone calls. The volume is still high, but the callers want to know who is going to be working where, job offers for me and my staff. Was the story in Friday's *New York Post* true, several reporters wanted to know. Is Jack Ford writing a book entitled "Drugs and Sex in the White House"?

I laughed. No, I told the reporters. (Well, not yet, I thought to myself.)

I opened my correspondence. More signs of the times. "Dear Sheila," the letter began. "It's been just a week but I want you to know that I already miss seeing you and Edward and I am looking forward to our getting together soon again. I will probably be talking to you sometime next week.

All the best always,
Norman Brokaw."

# LOOK ON YE MIGHTY

*DECEMBER 2, 1976*

Jack went to Mexico as his father's personal representative to the inauguration of President-elect José Lopéz Portillo. I went with him.

The trip featured five days in Mexico City, an inaugural address that seemed almost as long, and, since we Americans are at that awkward, in-between-administrations stage, a chance to observe Rosalynn Carter in diplomatic action. I was impressed. She seemed very sure of herself and even made brief remarks in Spanish at the Embassy, which I thought was a nice touch. (Jack spent more time with her than I did, however, and said she is less impressive when she speaks English.)

The greatest display of Mexican-American friendship occurred slightly below the diplomatic level. Jack's Secret Service detail got along splendidly with the detachment of Mexican police assigned to help them protect Jack. I don't know whether any long-term international benefits will result from the liaison, but it was extremely helpful on our short-term shopping spree. There's nothing quite like having the Mexican police force bargain for you with the merchants at a local market.

Jack and I flew from Mexico City to Los Angeles for a tête-à-tête with Norman Brokaw. Jack was leery at first, but the super sell is hard to resist. If you are the one to be sold, the target, Norman Brokaw is totally preoccupied with you. He never takes his eyes off you during the pitch, watching for any and all feedback—a hint of displeasure here, a flash of interest there—he senses it, immediately responds to it by adjusting his pitch accordingly and moving in a different direction. It is earnest . . . sincere in the sense that he really is looking for an answer that will make you happy. He makes his living finding answers that the market will bear.

I watch it all with mixed feelings: hope, terror, nervousness. I don't want to get involved, but I don't want Jack to be exploited. I do want him to get as much help with his future as he can. Can Norman help? Will Norman exploit? I sit there interpreting, trying to get the ideas moving in the right direction, hoping that Norman will understand Jack and be able to find what Jack wants, but at the same time terrified that if he does, Jack will become one of his client stories.

## *DECEMBER 4, 1976*

Barbara Walters taped her White House tour today and it went off smoothly. It could have turned into a wild modern version of Goldilocks and the Three Bears.

It seems Steve had quite a night last night, an evening that began in one Georgetown bar, proceeded to several others, and ended up with his taking his date (whom he had picked up en route) on a weaving tour of the White House.

"And this," he declared dramatically and tipsily at the end of the long corridor, "this is the Queen's Bedroom. You know, prior to this moment, five queens have slept in that bed. Tonight—a sixth!"

Everything blurs, thank goodness, until some daylit hour this morning, when Steve finds himself and his queen in the Queen's Bedroom with a terrible headache, a lot of noise in the hallway outside, and the vivid recollection that he promised his mother's Press Secretary he would officially "receive" the White House Christmas tree this morning at 10:30. To further complicate matters, he also remembered that he has to go to the airport first, to meet a blind date David Kennerly set up. He opens the bedroom door a crack, and matters become more complicated. There are lights and cameras and crews right outside the door.

My God, the White House tour!

(Imagine how surprised Barbara Walters would have been if she opened the door to the Queen's Bedroom.)

Steve decided neither to giggle nor to slash his wrists (the two most logical alternatives) but instead spun into action. He got Queen Number Six to her feet, briefed her carefully, and called a White House limousine for her. Then, as Steve walked—head high, shoulders back, smile firm—out of the Queen's Bedroom, intentionally attracting the attention of the representatives of the American Broadcasting Company, last night's queen sneaked out of the room, around the corner, and down a hidden stairway to her waiting get-away car.

I heard he was "excellent" at the White House tree ceremony.

I am grateful that that was all I heard until after Barbara Walters and Mrs. Ford completed the tour.

## DECEMBER 8, 1976

I tried to buy the Nixon chairs, the two gold wing chairs that had stood imperially on either side of Richard Nixon's desk in the Oval Office and then (as, I felt, an indication of just how far the mighty had fallen) found their way, via GSA, to my office.

Of all the objects in the room, many of which are beautiful, I covet only those two chairs. They say it all. I look at them and I think of the Shelley poem "Ozymandias" about the great king who built an empire that was to last forever and did not. All that remained in the end was the sneering head of a statue that had fallen down, and a stone that read: "My name is Ozymandias, King of Kings, Look on my works, ye mighty, and despair!"

What a souvenir!

What an impossible dream. I called GSA and found out that the only people who could take anything out of the White House were Cabinet members, who are entitled to purchase their chairs from the Cabinet room. There is a law that says that any piece of furniture that is owned by the White House must never be sold. It's just as well, I suppose. The White House can use a few reminders of the ephemeral nature of mightiness.

I purposely sat in one of the Nixon chairs when Mary Hoyt came today to talk about what it is like to be a White House Press Secretary. We must have talked for two hours.

As part of an administration that came into the White House with one day's notice, I am awed by the luxury of this transition period. Everyone, including the President and Mrs. Ford, had to learn on the job. The Carter people, on the other hand, weave in and out of the White House on a daily basis, being briefed by their predecessors.

I was thinking about how lucky Mary is to have this transition. But I wondered as I answered some of her questions whether even a transition can really prepare her for what is in store. She has been Press Secretary for three contenders: Jane Muskie, Eleanor McGovern, and Rosalynn Carter. But the White House is different from the campaign trail. Imagination is more important than stamina.

Rosalynn Carter seems to have everything necessary to become a First Lady who will make an impact. She's interested in issues. She's hard working. And she has a husband who respects her opinion. But there are other essentials. Someone must give her interests a direction and the proper context. Someone must create the atmosphere necessary to bring out her real personality, someone who understands the objectives of exposure.

In the White House you don't fight for press, you fight off press. It is quality, not quantity. Your prime concern is not getting coverage, but playing the coverage the right way. The First Lady has very little power. It is only through the press that the people know her at all. Rosalynn Carter seems to have what it takes. But "what it takes" must be shrewdly translated.

I talked to Mary about the risk of overexposure, about the importance of timing, and how perception *is* reality—what the public sees is what you get as a reputation. Every gesture the First Lady makes contributes to her public image, and the public can sniff out the difference between sincerity and insincerity.

I went over a lot of the administrative details. I recommended that she get a bigger staff than mine. I told her I had begun to make the East Wing more efficient, but never had time to finish the project. I urged her to make sure Mrs. Carter had an office downstairs in the East Wing so that, unlike Mrs. Ford, she would know what was going on. There is no other way.

I warned her about problems with the West Side. While her relationship with Jody Powell might be fantastic—now—I told her that there would probably be problems. Yes, Rosalynn Carter has her husband's ear. She is nonetheless about to find out that she is "just his wife." Yes, Mrs. Carter's staff members might be wonderfully congenial. But there will be power struggles. (Which one, I wondered, will be Mary's Nancy Howe?) In the White House, I have come to realize, jealousies and power struggles are inevitable. There are some things that don't change.

I did what I could to push for one change, however. I decided to use the occasion to see if justice could be done—finally—to Bill Gulley. I talked to Mary about the space problem (not the hall pin-ups) and suggested that the biggest favor she would do for herself was to get the military office off the floor and put Bill Gulley in the bomb shelter where he belongs.

I told her that I felt Presidential children had the most difficult time, and that she should be very careful about Amy's press, and even watch out for harmful side effects the White House spotlight could have on the Carters' other children, although they are young adults.

I continued to "tell" her things after she left. "You're only going to be here for a short time, Mary," I said to myself as I looked around my office. "Granted, there will be some days that seem to go on for years. The experience, the White House experience is a once-in-a-life-time opportunity. You have to throw yourself into it. Everything else in your life stops a little."

It's funny how the "transition" not only acquaints the newcomers with the White House, but also gives the old administration time to "look back fondly" while still in office.

I don't want to stay. But I do wish I knew this much when I started.

## DECEMBER 11, 1976

"It will be difficult for Mrs. Carter to do what she wants to do without a bigger staff than Mrs. Ford has now," Press Secretary Mary Hoyt told the Associated Press today.

## DECEMBER 16, 1976

The daily news briefing happens less frequently. Staff meetings are rare. White House hours—for the first time—are nine to five. Press inquiries are different: "What will Mrs. Ford be doing after January 20th?" they ask. "What are the children's plans?"

I've been doing those administrative chores I neglected for about two years: answering mail that did not have a specific deadline, making sure press bills for travel with the First Lady have been paid, getting pictures autographed for friends.

The mood of the White House Staff varies. Some are depressed and some are angry about losing the election, about Jimmy Carter's announcing his Cabinet appointments and, these staff people feel, "moving in" before the Fords move out. Some are worried. Ron Nessen has a wife, an ex-wife, two families, and an enormous ego to support. He is concerned about how he will be earning a living in the future. Others are resigned. Dick Cheney is behaving like the captain of the ship, calmly trying to get all his passengers into life boats (jobs) before deciding what to do with his own future. Those staff people and Cabinet members who can psychologically and financially afford to, want to take time off, rather than plunge from the White House into a new job. That's what I'm doing. I've had some offers, but I don't feel ready to move on. Not yet. No commitments until after January 20th for me.

I don't feel like a "lame duck." I feel like someone with just a finite amount of time left who wants to do everything today that I won't be able to do tomorrow. I want to remember the White House. I want to share the White House. I have, for example, been taking various members of the press on personal tours of the mansion, the grounds, and even that forbidden-to-the-press staff preserve, the White House Mess. The first reporter I took to lunch in the Mess was ABC White House correspondent, Tom Jarriel. I received a reprimand from a Mess person via telephone who told me that the Mess was off limits to press.

But *friends* in the press?

Those too.

Well, I figured, what can they do? Fire me? I now have breakfast in the Mess with reporter friends, and lunch in the Mess, and, if they served dinner in the Mess, I would probably eat that meal there too. Time is running out.

The eat-drink-and-be-merry philosophy extends to after-office hours, too. This is the Christmas season, the social season, and the parties have all had that wild "last-chance" sentiment.

Like the Fords' final State Dinner. They called it a "State Dinner for Italian Premier Giulio Andreotti," but that was just the excuse. It was really a Ford celebration. The guest list was the giveaway: a few diplomatic names camouflaging the Vail friends, Grand Rapids friends, entertainers and sports people who had worked hard for Ford and the Ford kids, each of whom had an entourage of personal friends on the guest list.

The party really began when Premier Andreotti left. I convinced the Marine Band to stop playing the kinds of songs that were good for ice-skating and start playing livelier stuff. They complied, and we were soon all doing the hustle.

Guests provided the entertainment. Cindy Nessen belted out "Around the World in Eighty Days!" Pearl Bailey sang a rousing "Battle Hymn of the Republic," Mrs. Ford boogied with Tony Orlando; Peter Graves (of "Mission Impossible") grabbed a clarinet and played "Won't You Come Home, Bill Bailey," Rod McKuen sang "Jean, Jean." Joe Garagiola hammed it up with Yogi Berra. This was a group that had gone through a lot together, and it was the perfect time to let it all out. And we did.

There was that same feeling at the White House Christmas Ball for Congress three days later, this time intensified by the fact that as the President and Mrs. Ford entertained their old cohorts and friends, President-elect Carter was across the street from the White House interviewing prospective Cabinet members at Blair House. There were, of course, many Republican Congressmen. But there were Democrats, too—Democrats who had worked to get Jimmy Carter elected. This was a bi-partisan evening, a night when Capitol Hill turned out to reminisce with a fellow legislator. The President, whose post-election depression seems to have lifted, spent more than an hour enthusiastically shaking hands and patting backs with his former colleagues. Next to Grand Rapids, Congress is "home."

Finally, there was the crescendo of parties—the press bash last night. No one eats as much, drinks as much, and enjoys as loudly as the journalistic establishment out for a good time, and last night's party was proof of that fact. It was more than the White House press corps. An enormous group of Washington journalists was invited and in between the drinking and dancing there was a lot of nostalgic anecdotes about the host and hostess. As the clock ticks, the Fords seem to be determined to keep going to the end, too. No one danced more last night than the President and the First Lady.

## JANUARY 1, 1977

It was our last trip to Vail and, for many of us, our first vacation. The President worked on the budget as the staff and the press took to the slopes. OMB Director Jim Lynn, who worked with the President, complained that he was the only one who *always* missed out on Vail fun.

Jack filled Steve's stocking. The President filled Jack's. Mrs. Ford filled Susan's. We were all pleased by the knowledge that this would be the last Christmas morning I would call to find out. I've always felt those phone calls were the ultimate family intrusion. (And, I have a feeling, so has the family.)

Jack gave Edward and me a special present—a raft trip down Idaho's Salmon River on whatever date we choose. ("Hopefully this trip will allow me to share with you both a little of what I know, in return for all that you have shared and shown me.") We were touched by the gift.

From Steve, we received two volumes of beautiful books on the Old West, with ultra-Steve inscriptions: "To Sheila and Ed, two people who have taken care of an old broken-down cowboy and even don't care if he spits tobacco. It's like what the cowboy said to the schoolteacher. She asked: 'Didn't the boys have fun riding their ponies?' The cowboy said bluntly: 'Ma'm, there weren't no ponies and there weren't no boys. Just lots of men and horses.' May your horse never stumble and your bedroll stay dry. Best of Everything, Steve." In volume two, he wished Ed "happy trails" and wrote: "May your belt buckles always be shiny and your leathers all loose."

Well, that's Steve.

This year's Vail atmosphere is a mixture of nostalgia, happiness, and depression. This is lame duck country, after all. And that goes for everyone, including the press. Those reporters who are going to continue covering the White House are off with Jimmy Carter in St. Simon's Island. Most of the reporters in Vail are getting ready to move on much the way the President is, and for many, the future is just as indefinite. Covering the White House is a little like living in it: it is classy. It is confining. So some are glad to be leaving and some are sad. But almost all have spent this year's Vail vacation skiing first, filing their stories later.

There is a real affection for the Fords among the press. Indeed, several of those now on the Carter trail, including Helen Thomas, called the Fords last night to tell the Fords that they really missed being with them, that it was "not the same." Coming from Helen Thomas, who always let it be known that she *hated* Vail because she *hated* cold weather and she *hated* sports in general, that was quite a testimonial. (I decided that there really was consistency in White House life when I watched Carter hold a news conference a few weeks ago and saw Helen Thomas screaming at the President-elect.)

For the most part, this is reminiscence week in Vail, and New Year's resolution week. "Now I can go back to a normal life," people are saying. "I can work regular hours and be with my wife and see my kids grow." Not all say it happily.

"I love my home, my wife, and my family," one party member said reverently. "One of the reasons I love them is because I've only been with them a couple of days a month. Now I'm taking a job where I'm going to be home at six o'clock every goddamn night." he said, taking a gulp of scotch. "God, is my wife boring."

*Chapter Twenty-seven*
JANUARY, 1977:

# MOVING ON

*JANUARY 12, 1977*

My father left the White House in 1958 before the end of the Eisenhower Administration. His farewell party, as a matter of fact, was a political precursor of the 1960 debates. Both Jack Kennedy and Richard Nixon showed up. Each said a few warm words about my father, and then proceeded to take a few jabs at the other. "The reception showed the power play of Washington," my father recalled for me today in the White House Mess. "Here were these two men saying nice things about me and sniping at each other at the same time."

We had been talking about leaving the White House, comparing reminiscences. Old stories I heard as a child at the dinner table take on new significance for me now. Our work responsibilities were different. The times were different. But there is something about experiencing the White House that is always the same. That goes for leaving, too. "I knew it was time for me to move on to other things," my father told me. "But once you give up your ID card, you can't enter the White House again. It's as simple as that. And I remember when the gate closed behind me, it was like shutting out a good part of my life."

We talked about White House people. My father pointed out that many of the people I've been working with will probably show up again in public life. That has certainly been true of the men he knew in the Eisenhower Administration. "What is interesting," he said, "is how little people change over the years, and how often the barely noticeable personality traits—assets or failings—become keys to success or failure later."

"I always liked Nixon and I admired his intelligence," my father said. "But from the very beginning, he showed poor judgment in his choice of friends. As Vice President, he was the Chairman of the President's Committee on Government Contracts, a committee designed to encourage minority hiring among private companies who did contract work with the government. It had been in existence since the Truman days. I was the one who suggested they make the Vice President its Chairman. At that time, the Vice President had nothing and I thought this would be a good appointment for Nixon.

"Anyway, we appointed a very prestigious honorary national committee—the publisher of the *New York Herald Tribune*, and Branch Rickey, and so on—and we needed an Executive Director at a salary of $25,000, which was a lot of money in those days. Nixon suggested his friend, Murray Chotiner. I checked around and found that Chotiner was a lobbyist with some shady business deals in his background. I told this to Nixon. I said, 'This job requires very close work with business leaders all over the country. It's a big entrée into the private sector and a temptation for all kinds of below-board activities. You would be taking on someone with less than impeccable credentials.'

"Nixon called me back. 'How about making Chotiner General Counsel then?' he asked. I said no. Then he called back again. 'What if he takes the job in title only and continues his law practice, if he takes no salary?' I told Nixon that would be a dreadful mistake. I kept Chotiner out of it. Then, you know, Chotiner in later years became infamous as Nixon's 'Political Mr. Fixit.' His questionable reputation way back then proved correct.

"I remember telling you all as children whatever happens in politics, keeping your integrity is the most important part. It doesn't pay to suffer a stain for a few perks or a few dollars. You're given an appointment to be near a President, near the making of history. It must never be tainted."

I remembered his telling us, too. I enjoyed re-remembering it with him today. He told me how proud he was that I was his daughter, and, listening to him share his White House feelings, I felt very proud to be his daughter.

When we left, we bumped into Office of Management and Budget Director Jim Lynn. He was escorting around the man who will replace him in the Carter Administration, a huge person named Bert Lance. Jim introduced me to Mr. Lance, and, feeling in the spirit of White House continuation after the conversation with my father, I said cheerfully: "I wish you luck here, Mr. Lance!"

## JANUARY 16, 1977

The President and Mrs. Ford are at Camp David. The White House is a maze of emptied rooms and packed boxes. Yesterday, among the piles in the hallway outside the kid's rooms I spotted some mail and glanced through it. One advertisement was a catalogue from an electronics firm addressed to "S. FORD (OR CURRENT RESIDENT)."

Somehow, that said it all.

I spent most of yesterday getting my things packed and shipped (thanks to Jack Ford and David Sands, my movers) to my house. Then, in the evening, Edward and Jack and I decided to go out for dinner, but first we met at the White House. I had vowed to continue the family tradition my father started eighteen years ago, the tradition of sitting in the President's chair in the Cabinet room and making a wish. (After all, my last wish came true). And last night— our last Saturday night in office—seemed right. Jack and Edward humored me. First I made Jack sit in the President's chair. Then I made Edward do it. Then I sat there myself. Then we got a little greedy (two tries each are better than one, after all) and did it again. Then Jack said, "Hell, if the President's Cabinet chair is good luck, the chair behind the President's desk in the Oval Office has to be better luck." So we all marched in there.

The sight was shocking. Everything personal had been packed. The office was bare.

We each sat in the President's chair and made a wish in the Oval Office. And then again. It was a funny feeling. The barren room kept telling us "It's all over" and we got the message, and for that very reason, stayed on.

Finally we went out to dinner, and after dinner to a bar in Georgetown, where Jack got friendly with the waitress. The only trouble was she couldn't leave until closing time, and Jack wanted to wait for her, but he did not want to wait alone. At 3:00 A.M. the place finally closed. "Hey," said Jack, "why don't we all go back to the White House?" The waitress thought that might be fun.

"Hey," Jack said to Edward and me, "why don't you two spend the night at the White House?"

The next thing I knew, Jack was giving his new friend an impromptu tour and Edward and I were trying to decide between the Lincoln Bedroom and the Queen's Bedroom. We chose the Queen's Bedroom, because Lincoln never slept in the Lincoln Bedroom and five Queens (and Steve Ford) had slept in the Queen's Bedroom. And because the Queen's Bedroom is beautiful. Absolutely beautiful. Down to the smallest detail. In the Queen's closet, there are hat stands and shoe stands and special drawers for different articles of clothing, and every hanger matches every other hanger and each is adorned with red-and-pink silk ribbons.

Down to the smallest detail. In the center of the bathroom ceiling is a small convex mirror, which captures the entire room in miniature.

And down to the *very* smallest detail. In the bathroom, the toilet seat is an elaborate wicker chair-like structure, designed that way in 1957 especially for the visit of Queen Elizabeth, because, "The Queen always sits on a throne."

We sat in the Queen's sitting room, desperately trying to stay awake. It was 5:00 A.M. but this was our first and last time to be where we were and we wanted to enjoy the feeling of the room—its history, its elegance—as long as we could.

But it *was* five in the morning.

Finally we gave in. We called the White House operators and left a wake-up call for 10:00 A.M. and then we fell asleep in each other's arms in the marvelous downy luxury of the bed of Queen Elizabeth and Queen Wilhelmina and Queen Juliana and Queen Fredericka and Queen Elizabeth II.

An hour and a half later, we were startled by the strains of the Marine Band. It wasn't reveille. It was a more familiar tune: "Hail to the Chief!"

"Hail to the Chief"—joyously, triumphantly on Pennsylvania

Avenue right outside our window at the crack of dawn on Sunday morning. But the Chief was at Camp David.

Precisely. That's why they were practicing *now*; they knew they would not disturb anyone. They were rehearsing for Thursday's inaugural parade. (It wasn't even our chief they were hailing!)

We tried to blot it out, but the Marine Band doesn't blot out easily, and after we tossed and turned (albeit luxuriously) for a few hours, the phone rang.

I picked it up to hear the melodious voice of the White House operator chirp: "It's time to wake up, Your Highness!"

## JANUARY 18, 1977

It is tour season. Mrs. Ford guided the White House switchboard operators around the Family Quarters last week. Many of them have served the White House dutifully for years—some since Truman—but few have ever seen the residence. It was a little different from Mrs. Ford's usual tour. In addition to all the historical pieces in each room, she was careful to show the women where the telephone was, so they will be able in the future to picture where the person they are talking to is sitting.

I've been running regular tours for the press. On one of our trips to Camp David, Jack showed me the "pen" near the helicopter landing pad Nixon had built to restrain the press. Reporters are not allowed to roam around Camp David, but some are sent each time the President goes just to make sure his helicopter doesn't crash. (They call it the "death watch.") The sight made me think about how the press is restrained at the White House, too. (How different is a press room from a press pen?) It is a terrible beat in that way. They see so little of what really goes on in the White House.

And whereas it seems quite glamorous each day to report to work at 1600 Pennsylvania Avenue, in reality they are reporting to a cubicle in a crowded office where they are fed news. When they growl and bark they may be tossed an extra morsel. Some who sniff around ingeniously uncover a bone. But that is rare. The fact is White House reporters miss a lot (like Watergate) and for most, the White House is a dull job, attractive largely because it guarantees them a fairly regular front page byline.

So, during lame duck season, I have taken to liberating the press,

ushering interested reporters around White House Family and
Staff environs. My first stop is usually the Situation Room, which
is directly across from the Mess. It is the intelligence command
center and was built by John F. Kennedy in 1961 after the Bay of
Pigs, because he wanted a place where defense information could
be funneled from all over and where CIA, National Security Council, State Department and Defense Department officials could hold
meetings that could not be either bugged or overheard. (The conference room walls in the Situation Room are lined with lead to
prevent bugging.) He made the conference area small because he
felt the fewer people who knew, the less likely it was that information would be leaked.

Johnson used the room more than any other President. He visited it continually during the Vietnam War, often coming down in
the middle of the night to get information on how "his boys" were
doing.

Video display terminals and modern computerized machinery
give the room a science fiction look, intensified by buttons in the
conference room that part curtains, and lower maps and screens. A
shredder stands at one end of the Situation Room, along with a super photocopying machine that transmits by telephone information
to various locations.

From the Situation Room I might progress to the Cabinet room,
and then to the Oval Office (the President usually works in his
study, off the Oval Office) then to other offices in the West Wing,
through the East Wing and, weather permitting, I like to take people outside around the White House grounds. I show them the
swimming pool, the new kennel for dogs, the tennis courts. It always amazes me how completely hidden from public view the
White House grounds are. I show them the "Children's Garden"
adjacent to the courts that the Johnsons built in 1968 for their
grandchildren. It is a little hideout for sitting with a white wrought-
iron bench, a tiny pond, and a flagstone path with Johnson's grand-
son's footprint and granddaughter's handprint pressed into the ce-
ment. Then we move back inside to the doctor's office across from
the resident elevator and then into the White House kitchen where
I introduce them to Chef Haller or Heinz Bender, the pastry chef.
Today when we went to the kitchen Heinz was making what looked
like thousands of cookies for the inauguration. I had heard that the
figure was 18,000 cookies a day, but when I asked Heinz about it—

trying to add a little color to my tour—he remained tight-lipped, refusing to admit the number. (Art Buchwald, who was with me, pointed out that there appears to be greater security in the White House kitchen than in the White House Situation Room, where my friend had answered all questions without hesitation.) We did get to taste a cookie, though. It was peanut butter. I wonder why.

## JANUARY 19, 1977

At 2:30 this afternoon, I became The Honorable Sheila Rabb Weidenfeld, Special Assistant to the President.

My commission reads: "From Gerald R. Ford, President of the United States of America to Sheila Rabb Weidenfeld: Reposing special trust and confidence in your integrity, prudence, and ability, I do appoint you Special Assistant to the President of the United States of America, authorizing you, hereby, to do and perform all such matters and things as to the said place or office do appertain, or as may be duly given you in charge hereafter, and the said office to hold and exercise during the pleasure of the President of the United States for the time being. In testimony whereof, I have caused the Seal of the United States to be hereunto affixed." It was signed by both the President and the Secretary of State.

My witnesses at the swearing in: Edward, Jack (who had been in my office talking about a future job with the publisher of *Rolling Stone* when the call came announcing my commission), the publisher of *Rolling Stone*, Joe Armstrong, and photographer Karl Schumacher, whom I grabbed en route to the impromptu "ceremony" to record the historic moment.

A husband, a photographer, a publisher and a President's son (in old corduroy and torn moccasins). What a group. What a moment. It was great fun, and now I can walk around the White House, head held high, with the lofty status that goes with my new title.

For the next twenty hours.

## JANUARY 20, 1977

The Fords' breakfast for Cabinet members and senior White House Staff started at 8:00 A.M. I went to my office first to say "good-bye." The walls were blank, the bookshelves empty, the

surfaces clear. No sign of me anywhere. I had a group picture of
Mrs. Ford, Mrs. Carter, Mary Hoyt, Madeline MacBean (Mrs.
Carter's personal assistant) and myself that had been taken when
Mrs. Carter came for the visit in November. I left it on the desk for
Mary with a personal note. It was Mary's desk now. I decided to
make one more phone call. I called Edward who told me that the
*New York Times*' quote of the day was mine: ["It's been two and a
half good years. He is sad that it is over. He is already feeling nostalgic for his friends. But he is satisfied with the job he has done
and looking forward to his new life."] I took a long look and
left . . . for good. I knew I didn't want to see the room looking
that way again.

The breakfast was like a close family gathering, a final reunion
before departure. I realized just how friendly when I heard a voice
say to me, "You did a great job, Sheila," and looked up to find the
voice was attached to Donald Rumsfeld. I thanked him. We
beamed graciously at one another, and someone interrupted to talk
to him. I should have walked off graciously at that moment. But instead, I just stood there. I thought about the article in last week's
*Star* on "outgoers advice to incomers." Rumsfeld was quoted as
saying: "When an idea is being promoted on the basis that it is 'exciting,' 'new,' 'innovative' . . . *beware!* Exciting, new, innovative ideas can also be foolish." I had wondered when I read it
whether the ideas he had been referring to were mine. I knew that
this was my only chance to find out. Why not? When his other conversation ended, I stepped back into the ring. We refixed our gracious smiles. I wanted to just say outright, "Now aren't you sorry
you fought me every inch of the way? We did it without you and
the West Wing, but it could have been so much easier if you had
supported me." but I did not come right out with it. I eased in instead.

"You know, one of my most memorable experiences," I began,
"was the day two years ago that I went to your office with a memo
on how the First Family could help the President's image. I thought
it was a wonderful memo. You didn't."

We both tittered. Down Memory Lane.

"When I read your advice to the new administration in the *Star*,
I thought that might be the explanation."

He cut me off in the middle of the sentence and snapped, "You
are misinterpreting. That's not what I meant at all."

"Well, then, what was our problem?" I asked him.

All signs of graciousness had evaporated. "I learned one thing from Haldeman," Rumsfeld retorted, "and that was never to get involved with the East Wing. Never! And," he added with pride, "I didn't."

Male chauvinism, learned at Haldeman's knee. Suddenly I realized that Rumsfeld *still* did not believe that a strong First Lady could be a Presidential asset—that to him the ideal Presidential couple was composed of one leader and one follower. A First Lady should be treated with kindness and condescension. What is she, after all, but the quintessential political wife? I looked around the room and wondered how many of the men in the room would have agreed with him. I even wondered about the President. He loves his wife. He was proud of her popularity and found it politically useful, but he never seemed to understand it. He thought of it as "cute" as opposed to public recognition of her great inner character. And I bet he thought it was all accidental.

The breakfast was followed by a private Ford Family farewell to the household staff in the State Dining room. Then the President and Mrs. Ford came to await the Carters in the Blue Room, with Dick Cheney, Dave Kennerly, Ron Nessen, and me. It was a tense emotional moment, and Mrs. Ford decided to break the tension in her own way. She looked at me and with a mischievous gleam in her eye, announced, "I've got some unfinished business to take care of!"

The next thing I knew, I was over her knee and she was spanking me. I had a feeling that this was a substitution for the never completed last verse to the song she sang to me after the "60 Minutes" airing—"You made me do it, I didn't want to do it . . . I didn't want to do it . . ." It *did* break the tension. Everyone found it very amusing, including the President. It was not exactly how I envisioned the last moments of the Ford White House, but, I suppose, it served a purpose. When she finished, we hugged each other and I felt the emotions well up again.

The Carters arrived. The White House butler, an old black man who, I assume, has witnessed many such administrations switch over, stood by the door, awestruck nonetheless, gazing at the Fords with tears in his eyes. He was moved. So moved, in fact, that he couldn't move. Mrs. Carter walked in and stood around awkwardly with her coat, unable to get the butler's attention. I filled in and took it from her.

The President and the President-elect of the United States stood off to one side, smiling and talking amiably. I had a feeling that at this important historic moment the two great men were discussing the weather.

In another area, Mrs. Ford and Mrs. Carter chatted uncomfortably. They were trying harder than the men, but they were not succeeding. They looked very ill at ease. More people arrived—the Mondales, the Rockefellers, Carter people, Congressional people—and the atmosphere relaxed. People began to mingle. I spoke with Mrs. Carter a little. I spoke with Jimmy Carter. I wished him the best and he bent over and kissed me (the friendly kiss of a man whose lust remains in his heart).

I briefed the press quickly, and we were all off to the swearing-in.

The ceremony itself did not affect me. I was very conscious of the Carter people standing near me, though—Mary Hoyt, Madeline MacBean, Tim Kraft, Carter's appointments secretary. They seemed to be in a state of suspension, half participants, half observers, a little dazed by what was happening. When Chief Justice Warren Burger administered the oath of office to Carter, I saw the three of them look at each other with tears in their eyes, and throughout Carter's speech their eyes were watery.

My time came at the end when I kissed Mrs. Ford goodbye at the chopper that was to take the Fords from Capitol Hill to Andrews Air Force Base. We talked about getting together in California next month. She teased me about bringing Edward—the "legal eagle," as she calls him—but not even banter, no matter how light hearted, seemed capable of halting the steady flow of tears down my face. Nothing.

The Fords did not go directly to Air Force One. They took a sentimental journey around Washington, D.C., first, hovering in Marine One over the monuments and the special parts of the city that held sentimental significance for them. When they finally landed at Andrews and were preparing to give their final farewell on the airplane to a few very close friends, they discovered several White House secretaries would be flying out with them. Bill Gulley, it seems, had told the secretaries that, as a special treat, they could fly out to California on Air Force One on the Fords' final flight on that aircraft. I don't know why Gulley made the promise (to impress the secretaries? to obligate them? to reward them?) but I do know that when Bob Barrett, the President's aide, called Gulley from Andrews, furious, and said, "Get these people off the plane. This is the Fords' last flight. It is an emotional time and they want their privacy!" Gulley replied, "Okay, but I'm warning you. It can be a long, cold exile."

Air Force One took off—without the secretaries.

In the meantime, I rode back to the White House with Mary and Madeline in the press van. They thanked me for the ride. I thanked them. It was now their van.

I walked into the White House and began to walk into the press room, but ten feet from the entrance, I turned around. I felt like an intruder. I decided it was time to "check out," to go through the governmental ritual of officially being "signed out" in each of about twenty different offices. I knew I would feel worse if I put it off until tomorrow. I made my rounds, meeting for the first time many of the old-line civil servants who staff the White House, the men and women who have been around for five, six administrations. I was barely noticed. They were all watching the Inaugural Parade on television.

By 2:30 I had gotten all the signatures required, returned my White House identification card, my two-way radio, my page boy, and my diplomatic passport, and vowed that as soon as possible I would scrape off my White House parking sticker.

There was nothing to do but leave. I walked out the front door and down the driveway to the Southwest Gate as the bands of the Inaugural Parade played loudly and joyously on Pennsylvania Avenue. I looked at the gate, and told myself solemnly, that, once I walked out, it was all over. And then it hit me. Relief. Exhilaration. I reached my arms up toward the sky and took a deep breath and practically danced down the driveway to the gate, where a somewhat bewildered guard waved me on.